A Brief
History of Rock,
Off the Record

A Brief History of Rock, Off the Record

Wayne Robins

Routledge
Taylor & Francis Group
New York   London

Routledge
Taylor & Francis Group
270 Madison Avenue
New York, NY 10016

Routledge
Taylor & Francis Group
2 Park Square
Milton Park, Abingdon
Oxon OX14 4RN

© 2008 by Taylor & Francis Group, LLC
Routledge is an imprint of Taylor & Francis Group, an Informa business

Printed in the United States of America on acid-free paper
10 9 8 7 6 5 4 3 2

International Standard Book Number-13: 978-0-415-97473-8 (Softcover) 978-0-415-97472-1 (Hardcover)

Library of Congress Cataloging-in-Publication Data

Robins, Wayne.
   A brief history of rock, off the record / by Wayne Robins.
     p. cm.
    ISBN 978-0-415-97472-1 -- ISBN 978-0-415-97473-8
    1. Rock music--History and criticism. I. Title.

ML3534.R574 2008
781.6609--dc22   2007015172

Visit the Taylor & Francis Web site at
http://www.taylorandfrancis.com

and the Routledge Web site at
http://www.routledge.com

Contents

the celebrity aspect of the people I spoke to; I always considered interviews a forum to query a professional about their art and work. Some of those artists include Little Richard, Mick Jagger, Keith Richards, Billy Joel, Stevie Wonder, Madonna, Jerry Leiber and Mike Stoller, Paul Simon, Ringo Starr, Cyndi Lauper, Joan Jett, Jon Bon Jovi, Gene Simmons and Paul Stanley of Kiss, Steely Dan, James Brown, Bruce Springsteen, B.B. King, Robert Plant of Led Zeppelin, Joey Ramone of the Ramones, Debbie Harry of Blondie, Patti Smith, Jerry Garcia, REM, U2, Pete Townshend of the Who and many more. I am especially indebted to Keith Richards, not only for the frequency, kindness and candor of his interviews, but for allowing me to duet with him on air guitar as we listened to playbacks of his unfinished mixes to his production of the soundtrack to *Hail! Hail! Rock and Roll*, the movie biography of Chuck Berry.

I was fortunate to have been born (in 1949) at the peak of the baby boom, so I could experience many of the connections I write about first-hand. I was in second grade when Elvis Presley became a national phenomenon, young enough to be bewildered by the hysteria caused by his records and TV appearances, old enough to detect the discomfort he elicited in adults. I was starting junior high when "The Twist," surf music, a doo-wop revival and the girl group sounds seemed to firmly distinguish our youthful musical culture from that of our parents; and was just beginning a desolate, lonely ninth grade in a new school, in a new neighborhood, when the assassination of President Kennedy made things much worse, and the near-simultaneous emergence of the Beatles restored hope.

Long before touring became an important part of the music industry, I eagerly sought rock concerts wherever I could find them. I saw the Beatles at Shea Stadium, the Rolling Stones (for the first of a dozen times) at New York's Academy of Music. New York venues like the Fillmore East, the Anderson Theater, Wollman Rink and the Bottom Line made it possible to see the Doors, Jimi Hendrix Experience, the Grateful Dead, Bob Dylan, and Janis Joplin with Big Brother and the Holding Company at a moment when the culture they would come to symbolize was still developing.

I cannot argue that rock 'n' roll is as important as it was then. It has been supplanted in the hearts of its natural teenage constituency by

Preface

"I know it's only rock 'n' roll, but I like it," the Rolling Stones sang in their 1974 hit. I like it too. But for me, it's never been "only" rock 'n' roll. Now more than 50 years old, rock 'n' roll has been around for nearly one-fourth of the history of the United States. And it is my opinion that no other popular art form has been as actively interwoven with the critical, transformative events of this nation's history.

With that in mind, I wrote this book aimed at students wishing to familiarize themselves with both the meaningful music from 1954 and the events that left the world "all shook up" ever since. It is also, of course, aimed at teachers looking for an informative, illuminating, entertaining—and opinionated—text for not just rock music courses, but for American studies and American or 20th century history curriculums at the advanced high school, community college and university levels.

In addition to the reference works and research cited throughout, much of the quoted material is from transcripts of interviews I conducted for *Newsday* (Long Island, N.Y.) and its city edition, *New York Newsday*, where I was the pop music critic and an entertainment reporter from 1975-1994. During this period, I was fortunate to have interviewed a vast number of rock's most important musicians, songwriters, producers, executives and performers. I was never interested in hip-hop, iPods, multitasking cell phones and social networks. Nevertheless, I am hoping that teachers can use this book to unlock their students' enthusiasm in late 20th century American history, and that students will be able to absorb the music of their parents (and grandparents!) with new appreciation and understanding. And I hope this is a smooth, easy read. It is not meant to be comprehensive and encyclopedic; it is a narrative that has its eccentricities. In attempting to tell a narrative history of the time and the music, even some of the artists I have interviewed numerous times received short shrift, and I hope to make it up to the likes of Mr. Townshend, Ms. Jett and others in the next edition, or the next book. And even if you're not a student, but, like me, a perpetual learner, I hope that if you wander into a bookstore and find this book on the shelf, you will pick it up and enjoy an evening with me, engrossed in my favorite subject: rock 'n' roll.

INTRODUCTION

What Is Rock 'n' Roll?

Philosophers since the dawn of humanity, or at least the 1950s, have thought long and deeply about a definition for rock and roll. But a clear and precise definition has eluded them.

"Rock 'n' roll itself can be described as music to accompany the rite of passage," said Pete Townshend, one of rock's foremost philosophers as well as guitarist and songwriter for the Who.

Link Wray, one of early rock's most influential electric guitarists, had an emotional definition: "It's about feeling and hurting and pain."

Rock 'n' roll certainly brought pain to some of the stars of show business in the 1950s. It threatened their livelihoods and offended their artistic sensibilities. Frank Sinatra, the greatest American pop singer of the twentieth century, disliked it intensely, at least at first: "Rock 'n' roll is the most brutal, ugly desperate, vicious form of expression it has been my misfortune to hear," he once said.

Even the spelling has its variants: rock and roll, rock & roll, rock 'n' roll. The *Billboard* magazine style book specifies "rock'n'roll." The Associated Press style book specifies "rock 'n' roll," which is one spelling we have chosen for this book.

An Internet search with the request "define rock and roll" offered numerous choices, none of them entirely satisfactory. "A type of popular dance music originating in the 1950s and characterized by a heavy beat and simple melodies," is the disappointingly skeletal definition provided by the *Compact Oxford English Dictionary*. You could say almost the same thing about stamp collecting.

Another description comes from the glossary of musical terms used by the Capistrano School in California: "Popular music that was born from jazz and the blues. It has a strong beat and a melody that repeats often."[1] This definition ignores country music as an essential ingredient in the rock 'n' roll stew. It relies on the truism of the bluesman Muddy Waters, who sang "the blues had a baby, and they named it rock 'n' roll."

An online study guide called America and Its People says of rock: "This form of music appealed to American youth during the 1950s. It was an original product of a heterogeneous American society in that it combined black rhythm and blues with white country music. Its acceptance and success reflected the demographic changes that had occurred since 1940."[2]

Another source, an online dictionary, defines rock as "a genre of popular music originating in the 1950s; a blend of black rhythm-and-blues with white country-and-western; 'rock is a generic term for the range of styles that evolved out of rock 'n' roll.'"[3]

All are accurate to some degree, yet miss something essential. Definition two brings us closer to the right combination of ingredients, but the recipe doesn't capture the flavor of the music. I would argue that the demographic changes resulting in and reflected by rock 'n' roll would not have been possible in 1940: The Great Depression of the 1930s was not yet over, and World War II had not yet begun for the United States. There was little in the way of leisure time and disposable income that would allow the phenomenon of rock 'n' roll to take hold as it did in the mid-1950s.

Rock 'n' roll thrived because it was inexorably linked to a demographic group that didn't really exist as a singular, self-conscious entity before the war, that is, rock could not have existed without the emergence of the teenager.

The "teenage" years as a unique transitional period of life did not really begin until after World War II, and really not until the early 1950s. The United States had moved from an agrarian/industrial society, which required young people to do farm or factory labor as soon as possible, to an urban/suburban culture, in which society for male adults was the corporation, for female adults the home, and for teenagers, the high school. Yes, teenage girls in the early 1940s swooned and screamed for young singing star Frank Sinatra. But Sinatra's musical values — the well-sung, big band swing tune or artfully crooned ballad — reflected no great distinction between the preferences of teens and their parents.

But rock 'n' roll was a generational line in the sand. It was the artistic representation of not just differentiation between teens and their parents, but opposition. In the 1960s, rock 'n' roll would be a

cornerstone of what was called the generation gap, but that fissure first appeared as a collateral result of rock's rise in the fifties.

Other cultural landmarks enabled this distinctiveness between generations. J. D. Salinger's 1951 novel *The Catcher in the Rye* had as its protagonist the teenage Holden Caulfield, whose complaints about the "phoniness" of adults was one of the first expressions of adolescent disdain and discomfort that rock 'n' roll would tap into a few years later.

"A case can be made that *The Catcher in the Rye*, created adolescence as we now know it, a condition that barely existed until Salinger defined it," wrote Jonathan Yardley, book critic of the *Washington Post*, in a (substantially negative) reappraisal in 2004.[4] Yardley continued: "He established whining rebellion as essential to adolescence and it has remained such ever since. It was a short leap indeed from *The Catcher in the Rye* to *The Blackboard Jungle* to *Rebel Without a Cause* to *Valley Girls* to the multibillion-dollar industry that adolescent angst is today."

If Salinger unknowingly anticipated it, Chuck Berry described it in the most minute, painstakingly accurate detail. Berry, the first great singer-songwriter of rock 'n' roll, was not coincidentally an astute chronicler of teenage life in the 1950s. He wrote and sang about such teenage obsessions as automobiles ("Maybelline"); rebellion ("Johnny B. Goode"); girls ("Sweet Little Sixteen") and rock 'n' roll itself as a break from the ingrained cultural impositions of the past. As Berry sang, "Roll over Beethoven, and tell Tchaikovsky the news."

Berry sang those words with a cockiness bordering on arrogance. And that brashness also made rock 'n' roll distinct from every other form of music. It is true that rock 'n' roll was musically the crossroads where blues, country, and popular music met, but that element of attitude was, if you will, the secret sauce. From Elvis Presley and Little Richard in the 1950s to the Beatles and Rolling Stones in the 1960s, from the Ramones and Aerosmith in the 1970s, right up through Green Day and Eminem, Radiohead, and 50 Cent, from Brooks & Dunn to Bruce Springsteen: all possess an attitude that gives the music its impact.

That impact is undeniable. "It is the most vital, unpredictable force in pop culture, and the exception to every rule," wrote critic Jon Pareles. Its contradictions are huge. "Rock can be amateur or

professional, innocent and slick, subtle and crass, sincere and contrived, smart and stupid."

The most compelling, original, and unforeseeable aspect of rock 'n' roll is the way the music has played out America's hopes, fears, and obsessions about race and race relations for more than fifty years. Rock came about at a time when segregation was the law of the land. It derived much of its original potency from the tension of its mixed-race ancestry. "In the fifties, pop was infiltrated by rockabilly from Memphis and blues from Chicago and rhythm & blues from New Orleans and doo-wop from city street corners, more like outbreaks of some mysterious contagion… than contrived artistic movement."[5]

"Contagion" is a perfect word because of its dual meanings. Rock spread contagiously among teens in the United States and around the world, an enthusiasm that spread in a way we in the Internet era describe as "viral," instantaneously and mostly in a good way. But it also stirred a fierce backlash because detractors feared it represented another kind of contagion: a viral epidemic, a kind of mass sickness.

Such detractors came from all sides. "Commercial rock 'n' roll music is a brutalization of the stream of contemporary Negro church music an obscene looting of a cultural expression," wrote Ralph Ellison, one of America's foremost African-American writers. Annette Funicello, who represented the all-American girl of the 1950s as an original member of Walt Disney's "Mouseketeers," noted: "Thousands of concerned citizens, police chiefs, and religious leaders called rock 'n' roll garbage and blamed it for everything." The ever-polite Annette thought this was unfair.

It is entirely appropriate, then, that Webster's *New Dictionary of Synonyms* suggests some other words in place of the verb *rock*: *shake, agitate, convulse*. Those terms resonate in much more than a lexicographical sense. Rock 'n' roll revealed a generational chasm in the 1950s that would explode into a culture war in the 1960s and whose repercussions we continue to feel in the present day. In this book, we will look at not just the music, but also the impact the music, its players, and its audience had on the social, cultural, and political events of the last half of the twentieth century.

Alan Freed, The Disc Jockey Who Called It "Rock 'n' Roll"

The man who is credited with popularizing the phrase "rock 'n' roll" was disc jockey Alan Freed. As a high school student in Ohio in the early 1940s, Freed was a trombonist for a band called the Sultans of Swing — perhaps the ones memorialized by Dire Straits in their hit record of that name. But his passion was radio, and he made the climb: Youngstown, Akron, and finally Cleveland, Ohio, where he did a R&B show on WJW radio beginning in 1951. His radio name was Moondog.

It's uncertain when Freed used the term "rock 'n' roll" for the first time. Or who first used it in song. Scholars trace its recorded usage in a 1922 blues song called "My Baby Rocks Me in One Steady Roll" by Trixie Smith. It had been a familiar phrase in R&B and jump tunes since the late 1940s: "Good Rockin' Tonight" by Wynonie Harris was a huge hit in 1948; Billy Ward & the Dominos' provocative 1950–1951 hit "Sixty Minute Man" used the phrase "I'll rock you, roll you, all night long."

By the time Freed moved to WINS in New York, he was using the word *rock 'n' roll* to describe the R&B songs that had wide appeal to teenagers of all races. The unusual integration of both performers and audiences was evident in the live shows Freed would host at the New York and Brooklyn Paramount theaters.

Freed also appeared as himself in a series of rock exploitation movies, quick cheapies with a minimal story line and appearances by a number of acts, both hits and misses. Typical was *Rock, Rock, Rock* (1956), which featured Frankie Lymon, Chuck Berry, the rockabilly Johnny Burnette Trio, and the hot teenage starlet Tuesday Weld making her film debut.

In 1957, his national TV show for ABC was cancelled when Lymon of the hit group Frankie Lymon & the Teenagers was seen dancing with a white girl. The network affiliates, especially in the South, howled until Freed was gone. In 1958, a riot ensued during a Freed concert at Boston Arena. Most reports call this a police riot, again, with the authorities perhaps infuriated by the easy mingling of black and white teens.

He found himself in considerably more trouble the following year. In 1959, the House of Representatives Oversight Committee* investigated payola — the giving of gifts or money to disc jockeys in return for playing a certain record. The perceived wisdom was that rock 'n' roll was entirely meritless; the investigation was based on the assumption

---

* http://www.history-of-rock.com/payola.htm

that rock was "evil, ugly, unintelligible and bad, and that teenagers were passive victims who never would have listened to it unless it had been forced upon them by illegal activity."[*]

Two dozen other disc jockeys went before the committee. But the committee focused on the two most popular: Freed and Dick Clark, host of TV's *American Bandstand*. Clark acknowledged having a financial interest in some records, but brought a statistician whose mathematical gymnastics perplexed and distracted the committee. Ordered by ABC to divest himself of all outside interests (including the Jamie Record label, in which he was said to have invested $125 and earned a nearly $12,000 return), Clark denied taking payola, and though skeptical, committee chairman Owen Harris called Clark "a fine young man."

Freed was arrogant and stubborn, and he refused to admit involvement. In 1960 he was tried on misdemeanor counts of commercial bribery; he paid a fine and was released, but his career was in ruins. In 1965, he died broke, bitter, and alone as a result of his heavy alcoholism. He was forty-three.[†] Freed was admitted into the Rock and Roll Hall of Fame the day it opened.[‡]

---

[*] Stuart A. Kallen, *A Cultural History of the United States Through the Decades: the 1950s* (San Diego: Lucent Books, San Diego, 1999), 85.

[†] http://www.history-of-rock.com/payola.htm

[‡] Other Freed information garnered from Alan Freed biographer John Jackson, http://www.alanfreed.com/biography.html

THE 1950s

Rock Begins

Leiber and Stoller: Songwriters and Producers

Rock 'n' roll was born in the 1950s through the give-and-take relationship between black and white culture in the segregated United States. Though Elvis Presley, a Southern white with a gift for singing black rhythm & blues, emerged in 1955 as rock's first great star, the foundation for rock's explosion was built a few years earlier by two Los Angeles teenagers, Jerry Leiber and Mike Stoller. They became rock 'n' roll's first great, and its most important, songwriting and record producing team.

They met in 1950, when they were each seventeen years old, their families having moved from the East Coast to Southern California. Stoller, an accomplished pianist, grew up in a fertile musical environment. At five, he took piano lessons from an aunt who had been trained at the Vienna Conservatory. At seven, Stoller attended an interracial summer camp, where he was impressed by older kids who fooled around playing boogie-woogie on the piano. Already having a developed ear, he was able to play what he heard, and when he came home from camp, some lessons were arranged with boogie-woogie piano master James P. Johnson. Stoller's family moved to Los Angeles in 1949. At the time, the teenager was enthralled by the bebop explosion — the jazz improvisations of Charlie "Bird" Parker, Lester Young, and Dizzy Gillespie.

Leiber, like Stoller, was born in 1933 on the East Coast. He grew up in Baltimore. His father died when he was five, and Leiber's mother started a grocery store in a black neighborhood. While making deliveries, he became infatuated with the R&B music he heard emanating from people's homes. In 1945, Leiber's family moved by bus to Los

Angeles. He brought his enthusiasm for R&B with him. While still attending Fairfax High School, he went to work in a record store.

Leiber's passion for and knowledge about R&B caught the attention of Lester Sill, a salesman for Modern Records, one of the half-dozen or so companies specializing in R&B, the popular music made by and for black people in the United States after World War II.

Sill found the effusively energetic Leiber an engaging kid, enthusiastic, quick, and knowledgeable about the records of Modern and the other R&B labels. "What do you want to be when you grow up?" Sill asked Leiber.

Without hesitation, Leiber replied, "a songwriter." Leiber sang a few lines of a blues lyric he had written, and Sill was encouraging. But if he wanted to create more than blues poems, he would have to find someone to put them to music.

A high school friend who played drums in a band gave Leiber the phone number of Mike Stoller, a pianist who was already performing in local clubs. "Jerry called me, very businesslike, and started bugging me to write songs," Stoller said. "I told him I didn't write songs. I was sure with the name Jerome Leiber he wasn't writing the kinds of songs I would like."

But Leiber was persistent, so Stoller invited him to his house. Stoller looked at some of the verses Leiber had written on loose-leaf paper.

"These aren't songs," Stoller said, meaning, they're not conventional pop songs. "These are blues, right? Ditto marks here, that means repeat, right? I like the blues, let me take a crack at them."

Through their mentor Lester Sill, they were introduced to Gene Norman, a Los Angeles R&B disc jockey. The great R&B singer Jimmy Witherspoon was the first to record a Leiber-Stoller composition: "Big Ugly Woman." Another West Coast hit was "Little" Willie Littlefield's late 1952 recording of Leiber & Stoller's "K.C. Loving," the title given to it by Federal Records A&R man Ralph Bass. It is better known as "Kansas City," and has been recorded by more 100 artists. In 1959, six versions of the song competed for sales and airplay, and four made *Billboard*'s Hot 100. The most famous version was by Wilbert Harrison, a No. 1 record in 1959. The song presents an idealized picture of Kansas City as a kind of Shangri-la of soulfulness. It was a wonderful work of imagination, since neither Leiber nor Stoller had ever been to

THE 1950S: ROCK BEGINS

Kansas City, and never did visit there until the mid-1980s, when the city (actually, two cities: the mayors of both Kansas City, Missouri, and its smaller sister, Kansas City, Kansas) declared Leiber and Stoller Day and gave the writers the keys to the cities.

Leiber and Stoller started hanging out in black L.A.'s bustling Central Avenue jazz and R&B clubs, soaking up music, atmosphere, and attitude. "It was an easy kind of coming and going," Leiber says. He notes regretfully: "You couldn't do it today. Too much hostility, too much separateness." Evidently, most people in this otherwise all-black environment found the two precocious teenagers amusing. "We were affected; we acted, but it became us," Leiber recalled. "Like the Blues Brothers." But it was the songs of Leiber & Stoller that were making the strongest impression. Word got around to Johnny Otis, a band leader, songwriter, performer, disc jockey, TV host, entrepreneur, and producer who was one of the major figures of the postwar Los Angeles R&B scene. Otis was one of the most unusual figures in American culture. Though a Greek-American (his family name was Veliotes) by birth he "loved jazz and R&B so fervently that he adopted the African-American culture as his own."[1] Otis invited Leiber and Stoller to a "garage rehearsal," where he would showcase and try out new songs and talent. There was the gifted Little Esther Phillips; an oversized gospel trio called Three Tons of Joy; and another woman of no small stature named Willie Mae "Big Mama" Thornton.

"She was very big and intimidating, with scars all over her face, like she had been in a big bar fight somewhere," Leiber said. "I think when we walked in, she was singing 'Ball & Chain,' which was later done by [Janis] Joplin. She was one of the saltiest chicks I'd ever seen, and I loved the sound of her voice, so I said to Mike, 'let's write a song for her.'"

They raced back to Stoller's house, composing a draft in the car while they drove. They finished, Leiber said, in twelve minutes, and drove back to Otis's rehearsal.

Otis asked them to play the song for Big Mama Thornton. Stoller, looking everything like the "pasty faced white boy" Thornton thought he was, reluctantly sat down at the piano, and Thornton began to sing from the lyric sheet. It was terrible, Leiber recalls.

"It was like Ethel Waters's 'Cabin in the Sky' thinking that's what the song required," Leiber told me, referring to a popular 1940s all-black Broadway, and movie musical. "I said, wait a minute, wait a minute. It don't go like that."

Thornton appeared to be coming to a boil. "Don't you go tellin' me, boy, how to sing the blues."

Otis diplomatically stepped in the middle. "Now Willie Mae, they wrote the song. They're not telling you how to sing it, but they know how it's supposed to go."

After a few more placating words from Otis, Big Mama looked scornfully at Leiber and said, "OK, white boy, get up there and show me how it go."

"In those days," Leiber continued, "I could sing the blues. I had a voice that was really window rattling. The band cracked up right away. I sang about eight bars, and Big Mama says to me, I got it!" Thornton's attitude changed. She started comically pulling at Leiber's hair, looking for tight, kinky, African-American curls. "That's store-bought hair," she said, tugging at his wavy coif, putting him on, letting him know he was accepted. The song was called "Hound Dog," a strong woman's scathing put-down of a good-for-nothing man.

Otis was to produce the recording session. But Leiber and Stoller were already developing the ability not just to write the songs, but to envision how they should sound: the arrangements, the relationship of the voice to the musicians, intuitively figuring out how the performance would best sound on a record, on a jukebox, on the radio. After the first take, Leiber and Stoller heard a problem. Big Mama's drummer didn't have the same syncopated feel for the song that Johnny Otis did when he played drums at the rehearsal. Fearlessly confident and ambitious, Leiber insisted that Otis should play the drums. Who would produce the session? Leiber and Stoller, of course. With Otis on drums, Big Mama at the mic, and Leiber & Stoller, still not twenty-one, in control at the recording console, Leiber says, "They got it in two takes. It was one of the only records we made that we thought was perfect."

Listeners who heard the Thornton recording thought so, too. Big Mama Thornton's "Hound Dog" was No. 1 on the R&B charts for seven weeks in early 1953. Three years later, Elvis Presley would hear a musical comedy group called Freddy Bell & the Bellboys sing their own humorous rendition of "Hound Dog" in a Las Vegas lounge. Presley recorded this milder, amusing version of "Hound Dog," which, paired on a 45 rpm record with Otis Blackwell's "Don't Be Cruel," was No. 1 for eleven consecutive weeks beginning in August, 1956.

Unlike so many insultingly tepid versions of R&B hits by white singers in the 1950s, Presley's "Hound Dog," despite its lyrical modifications, had a fiery intensity of its own. The tempo was nearly twice as quick; Scotty Moore's guitar solo is considered among early rock 'n' roll's greatest "for its utter drive and wild excitement, and for the way Scotty moves like a flash from the growly low-string licks into the bright, cutting upper-register stuff." And Presley's series of TV performances of "Hound Dog" would typify the challenge rock 'n' roll presented to the established show business establishment and to the straitlaced, puritanical values that that held their grip on the mainstream culture of the United States in the 1950s.

Chuck Berry: The First Singer-songwriter

"If you tried to give rock 'n' roll another name, you'd have to call it Chuck Berry," John Lennon once said. At least rock 'n' roll would be an entirely different beast if it weren't for Chuck Berry: His guitar riffs created the template for the sound and style of rock's main instrument that would last for the next fifty years. And he wrote spirited, witty lyrics of teenagers strafing under authority, establishing rock as the music of rebellion.

He was also the first rock 'n' roll singer-songwriter. Berry grew up in St. Louis in a working-class family. As a teenager in the 1940s, he served time in reform school for robbery. In the early 1950s, he had an entertaining act that did well in black nightclubs, mixing his own bluesy music with the occasional drawling country-western parody.

"Curiosity provoked me to lay a lot of our country stuff on our predominantly black audience, and some of our black audience began whispering 'who is that black hillbilly at the Cosmo?' [club in St. Louis], Berry said. "After they laughed at me a few times they began requesting the hillbilly stuff and enjoyed dancing to it.'"

He was introduced to Leonard Chess, cofounder of Chicago's influential Chess Records, by one of the label's stars, blues great Muddy Waters. "Maybelline," his first Chess release, replete with

* As detailed in Taylor Hackford's movie bio, *Chuck Berry: Hail! Hail! Rock 'n' Roll* (1987).

specific references to Cadillacs and V-8 Fords, nailed the emerging teenage obsession with cars and girls and the rock beat.

Thanks to ample airplay by disc jockey Alan Freed, it became a near-instant hit. Freed rewarded himself by claiming a cowriting credit, and therefore, substantial royalties on the song, another sterling example of the ways the white record business exploited black artists.

Yet Berry was not just another "black artist." Working with his father as a handyman in white neighborhoods in St. Louis, he heard the sounds of Frank Sinatra and Pat Boone. He thought: Why not sing with a little sweetness, and make records that everyone would buy?*

"I was trying to shoot for the whole world, not just my neighborhood," Berry explained in the 1987 movie biography *Hail! Hail! Rock 'n' Roll.*

With "Maybelline," Berry found his voice, and his audience. For the next three years, Berry's songs thrust the rock revolution into overdrive. Many dealt with the ecstatic power of rock itself: "Roll Over Beethoven," Berry sang, adding, "and tell Tchaikovsky the news."

His song "Rock & Roll Music" earned its title, a comical but timely boast about the music's superiority: it was both a definition of the thing, and the quintessential example of the thing — rock 'n' roll music — itself. And "Johnny B. Goode" presented the rock 'n' roller as mythic hero, every much as admirable and American as his pop-culture contemporary, Disney's mid-1950s frontier hero Davy Crockett.

He wrote laudatory songs about teenagers ("Sweet Little Sixteen" and "Almost Grown"), and in "School Day" empathized the notion of high school as a kind of spiritually deadening factory, no more inspiring or illuminating than an assembly line job. (One fascinating flop that was never released was Berry's attempt to write a song that would capture a transitional phase of life, called "Adulteen"; the excellent "Almost Grown" captured the essence of that topic with considerably more grace.)

"Each Berry song was a novel in miniature about American teenage life, teeming with brand-name cars, sassy high-school queens, and anarchic exhortations to forsake the classroom for just sheer driving, singing and dancing," wrote Philip Norman, author of excellent biographies of both the Beatles and the Rolling Stones.†

Berry even managed to strike the right appreciatively patriotic tone for his times with the 1959 hit "Back in the U.S.A." Yet Berry's celebra-

---

* *Chuck Berry: Hail! Hail! Rock 'n' Roll* (1987).
† Philip Norman, *Symphony for the Devil: The Rolling Stones Story* (Linden Press/ Simon & Schuster, 1984), 47.

tion of the land of hamburgers, highways, and high school turned out to be supremely ironic, since that year he was arrested for violating a federal law known as the Mann Act, which made it illegal to transport a minor across state lines for the purposes of prostitution.

The law was very selectively applied, and it was applied to Berry, who had brought a mature looking fourteen-year-old Apache girl from Texas to work in his St. Louis nightclub. After she was fired from her job checking hats, she complained to authorities. The judge at his first trial was so racist that the conviction was tossed out of court. But in a second trial, he was convicted, and spent two years in a Federal prison in Indiana.*

Out of jail in 1964, he entered a music scene taken over by British musicians who shared a singular distinction: they worshipped Chuck Berry. The Rolling Stones' first single release was Berry's "Come On." Growing up in the London suburb of Dartford, Mick Jagger was obsessed with Berry. "Berry's voice, light and sharp and strangely white-sounding, had a pitch not dissimilar to his own," wrote Philip Norman.†

Singing with his neighborhood group, Little Boy Blue and the Blue Boys, Jagger found a comfort zone with Berry tunes. "Singing along to 'Sweet Little Sixteen' and 'Reelin' and Rockin' he suddenly felt like something more than a mumbling impersonator."

When Jagger met Keith Richards, he found not just a fellow Berry enthusiast, but one who was on his way to mastering the notes and the subtlety of tone, the restraint, that made Berry's guitar playing so effective. Richards, who became Berry's most successful and gifted acolyte, was later producer and music director of the Chuck Berry film biography, *Hail! Hail Rock 'n' Roll.*

And the Beatles: they effectively played the entire Chuck Berry songbook in their formative years. Norman recalls a mutually warm and respectful early meeting between the Beatles and the Rolling Stones in London. "The Stones, on their side, recognized blood brothers in the R&B cause who had only reluctantly dropped Chuck Berry in favor of original material the public increasingly demanded."

Reintroducing Berry's songs to a new generation of rock 'n' rollers in the 1960s was of course a boon to Berry, who regularly worked the oldies circuit, doing his famous "duckwalk" across the stage with his guitar until he was well into his 60s. Ironically, Berry didn't have a No. 1 record until 1972, when a novelty tune, "My Ding-a-Ling," which lacked all the grace and wit of his classic material, turned to be a left-field hit.

---

* From Berry entry, *New Rolling Stone Encyclopedia of Rock & Roll.*
† Philip Norman, *Symphony for the Devil: The Rolling Stones Story,* 47.

Elvis Presley

When Elvis Presley died on Aug. 16, 1977, at age forty-two, he was a bloated self-parody. Though he had still been touring, his ample gut nearly bust through his trademark bejeweled white jumpsuits. His heart attack at his Memphis mansion, Graceland, was brought on by a toxic combination of prescription drugs. He was isolated by handlers, yes-men, bodyguards, his manager, and his own immeasurable fame, and his music had been irrelevant for many years.

It is easy to forget how profoundly important he was.

A Southern journalist, John Grooms, remembers. "Elvis was the spark that ignited the pop culture that we live in and take for granted every day. He was the great dividing line between the old, pre-war white cultural consensus and our present-day, ever-changing climate of clashing, interweaving, diverse cultures."[2]

Presley was born Aug. 8, 1935, in E. Tupelo, Mississippi. A twin brother, Jesse Garon, was stillborn; he would have been Elvis's only sibling. His father, Vernon, was a truck driver; his mother, Gladys, took in sewing work. In the 1940s, Vernon Presley served eight months in prison for writing bad checks. As an ex-convict, it was difficult for him to find steady work, and the Presley family lived perhaps a notch over the poverty line in a public housing project.

Elvis probably first sang in the Pentecostal First Family of God Church[3] his family attended. He got his first guitar for his eleventh birthday. In 1948, the family moved to Memphis; Elvis sometimes hung out on Beale Street, home of the blues, where locals like B. B. King and Furey Lewis performed.

After graduation, Presley became a truck driver for the Crown Electric Co. But he was taken with music, all forms of it: gospel from his church, blues from Beale Street, and country, or what was known as "hillbilly" music made by poor whites whose lives were not much different from that of the Presleys.

Memphis also had Sun Recording Studios, which opened in 1950, and the Sun Record label, both operated by Sam Phillips. A track recorded at Sun in 1952, "Rocket 88," was credited to Jackie Brenston, a member of Ike Turner's Rhythm Kings, one of the South's most popular R&B bands. Some historians call "Rocket 88" the first rock 'n' roll song, a topic that remains open for debate. Sun's first hit was with Memphis disc jockey Rufus Thomas's "Bear Cat," a comical record that took the man's point of view in answering the putdowns of that hit record enormously popular in the black community, "Hound Dog" by Big Mama Thornton.

Phillips loved all kinds of music, but blues were his bread and butter. He was also extremely progressive about racial matters, especially for a white man in that time and place. When the black musicians on a session would get hungry, Phillips would often go to the restaurant next door and bring hamburgers in; blacks were not allowed in the restaurant.

Aside from professional sessions for his label, anyone could pay to record at Sun for a few dollars. That's how Elvis arrived at Sun, to make a record for his mother's birthday present: "My Happiness." Phillips wasn't in, but his assistant liked his voice and wrote down his name and phone number. A few months later, Phillips called Elvis to sing some tunes with two of his regular musicians, bass player Bill Black and guitarist Scotty Moore. For a few hours they worked on some standard pop ballads, none of which sounded good or interesting. During a break, Elvis, on guitar, started some of the blues and R&B tunes he knew and liked. Black and Moore picked up their instruments and joined in. Intuitively, Sam Phillips started the tapes rolling.

The resulting 1954 recordings, now known as the Sun Sessions, are considered some of the first, and greatest, rock 'n' roll ever recorded. Symbolically, the two sides of Presley's first single underlined the duality of rock's hybrid roots. "That's All Right, Mama" was a blues song by Arthur "Big Boy" Crudup; the other side, "Blue Moon of Kentucky," was a country track by Bill Monroe, a founder of modern bluegrass.

* * *

Phillips is often remembered for saying, "If I could find a white man who had the Negro sound and the Negro feel, I could make a billion dollars." What Phillips meant was that the black sound and feel — of blues, and R&B — had an excitement and honesty that was lacking in the popular music of the time. Yet the big record companies, the mainstream radio stations, and the newly popular medium of television were as segregated as the rest of America, catering to what were thought to be the interests of the white audience while excluding others.

Elvis Presley had that excitement and honesty. Presley's singing emanated from someplace deep inside. The instrumentation itself, the combination of Presley and Moore's guitars and Black slapping an upright bass fiddle was quite different from the saxophones, piano, and, drums featured on typical R&B records. It is a revelation to listen to the power and energy, the rhythmic drive of the approximately two dozen songs Presley recorded at Sun in 1954 and 1955 and to realize that there are drums on just a handful of lesser tracks. This style, with heavy foot-tapping and guitar slapping, became known as rockabilly, and Sun was the place around which rockabilly revolved. Among those other rocking "hillbillies" who gravitated to Sun were Carl Perkins, Jerry Lee Lewis, and Johnny Cash.

Presley's uncommon enthusiasm for a wide variety of styles also set him apart. In addition to the Crudup and Monroe tunes, he embraced tunes by Leon Payne, a blind Texas country musician whose songs had been recorded by such stars as Hank Williams and Ernest Tubb; sentimental pop standards like Rodgers & Hart's "Blue Moon" (no relation to that moon over Kentucky) and "Harbor Lights"; southern blues like Little Junior Parker's "Mystery Train"; and sophisticated, uptown R&B like "Shake, Rattle and Roll" and "Money Honey."

Because of Sun's largely regional distribution, Presley remained a southern phenomenon through 1954. But word, and his music, spread quickly. "That's All Right, Mama" was recorded on July 5; two days later, it was being played on the radio in Memphis. "Is that a white boy or colored?" callers to radio stations would ask. It wasn't idle curiosity. "Presley had already started to undermine the taboos on black and white interaction."[4]

On July 30, Presley gave what is considered to be his first professional concert performance. He appeared at Memphis's Overton Park Bandshell, opening for yodeling country singer Slim Whitman. The posters advertising the event referred to him as "Ellis" Presley, which could not have pleased his manager, Memphis disc jockey Bob Neal.

In October, he sang his up-tempo version of "Blue Moon of Kentucky" at the Grand Ole Opry in Nashville. Later that month, a gig on the popular Louisiana Hayride radio show in Shreveport spread his following, and female members of the live program's audience began reacting with waves of hysteria, displays of hormonal ecstasy not usually expressed in public by young southern ladies.

Soon it was obvious that Presley's talent and potential were too big for Bob Neal to manage and Sam Phillips to distribute. Into the picture stepped "Colonel" Tom Parker, a savagely astute manager and media manipulator who edged Neal out of the picture. Parker managed Presley profitably, protectively, but not often wisely for the rest of his life. Similarly long-lasting was the relationship with RCA Records, to which Phillips sold Presley's recording contract in 1955 for $35,000. Phillips's quote about the white man with the Negro feel making a billion dollars was prophetic, although he would not be the one to gain from the fortune Presley generated in his lifetime.

Presley also had thoughts about what it would mean to be able to communicate with the authority and intensity of the black blues and R&B artists he admired. "I remember old Arthur Crudup … and I used to think if I could just feel what ol' Arthur felt, I'd be a music maker like nobody ever saw!"[5]

Everly Brothers

After Elvis Presley and Buddy Holly, the Everly Brothers were the most important country-rooted rock act of the fifties. Don (born in 1937) and Phil (born 1939) were raised in a show-business family, performing as children (from ages six and eight, respectively) on their parents' folk-and-country-music radio show, broadcast in the Midwest in the 1940s and early 1950s. The first rock act to be based in and record in Nashville, they achieved acclaim when they signed to the independent label Cadence Records, owned by entrepreneur Archie Bleyer. Their manager, Wesley Rose, was a partner in the Nashville powerhouse Acuff-Rose music publishing firm. Following the somewhat standard but greedy and shortsighted practice of the day, Rose insisted that the Everly Brothers record only Acuff-Rose tunes.

This was no disadvantage at first, when the group teamed up with the prolific married songwriting team of Felice and Boudleaux Bryant. Writing specifically for the Everly's, the Bryant's now-classic "Bye Bye Love" in 1957 introduced the Everlys and one of the most distinctive sounds of the 1950s: tight, high vocal harmonies redolent of bluegrass that managed to sound both sweet and rough, over firmly strummed rhythm guitars that were gentle and tough. With their pompadoured hairdos and aw-shucks smiles, they were teen idols, but they had real musical substance. Even more than with Elvis, the country lineage of their music goes all the way back to the Appalachian folk music of the early century, and yet they cut a hit version of the howling "Lucille" (in 1960) that was one of the rare Little Richard covers that paid respect to the original while presenting an original touch of its own.

They and the Bryants were also in touch with the emerging foibles of suburban and small-town teenage misbehavior, at the same time that Leiber and Stoller were establishing the gold standard for urban rock 'n' roll rebellion with the Coasters. "Wake Up Little Susie," one of the top hits of 1957, reveals the Bryant's gift for storytelling, which the Everlys executed perfectly from the point of view of distressed teenagers who've stayed out much too late making out at the drive-in. Like so much in the 1950s, the protagonists in the song were driven by a fear not of people finding out what they did, but by rumors of what they probably didn't do. "We fell asleep, our goose is cooked, our reputation is shot," they sing, the nervous harmonies and frantic strumming conveying waves of anxiety as they have to answer to their parents and the judgment of peers. Total teen torment, expressed through musical excellence.

The Everlys maintained their popular and artistic dominance in 1958: The ballad "All I Have to Do Is Dream" had little of the syrupy overstatement of most teen love songs: it was lean, pure, and perfect.

Brown v. Board of Education

Other events in 1954 would shake the foundations of the country, especially the South, just as surely as Elvis Presley could shake his hips. On May 17, 1954, the United States Supreme Court made a unanimous decision in a landmark case known as Brown vs. Board of Education of Topeka. The Court had wrapped a number of similar cases filed in Virginia and South Carolina under Brown, which argued it was unfair that black children had to travel long distances past nearby white schools to attend inferior, all-black schools. Therefore, their rights under the 14th Amendment, equal protection under the law, were being violated. Such segregation had been encoded in law since

The follow-up, "Bird Dog," was rock 'n' roll with a country accent, a stay-away-from-my-girl song with an attitude as virile as its vernacular was amusing. (Long before the Beatles introduced the notion of girlfriends as "birds," the Everlys emphatically sang to a rival: "Hey, bird dog, get away from my quail … leave my lovey-dove alone.")

Signing what was then a record-breaking contract with Warner Bros. in 1960, the Everlys had one more huge hit, Don's composition, the worldwide No. 1 "Cathy's Clown." (The story goes that Don was listening to Ferde Grofe's *Grand Canyon Suite*, borrowed a few chord changes and added his own teen-pleasing lyrics, about a girl who finally dumps a guy she's been treating like dirt anyway.)

But the Everlys were not natural songwriters. The pressures to keep having hits were enormous, and on a tour of England in in 1962, as historian Colin Escott writes, "It was in London that Don's problems with prescription drugs in non-prescription quantities surfaced. He was flown back to the United States."*

Their harmonies certainly were one more influence on the Beatles, and a major one on folk-rock's most cerebral and popular duo, Simon & Garfunkel, who reveled in playing "Bye Bye Love" in concert. But lack of hits, marital problems, and fatigue with each other drove the Everlys apart in 1973. A successful reunion at Royal Albert Hall in London ten years later erased some bitter memories. Phil and Don have since reconciled, and were among the original members selected for the Rock and Roll Hall of Fame in 1986.

---

* Escott's liner notes to *The Everly Brothers: Walk Right Back — The Everly Brothers On Warner Brothers* Colin (Warner Archives label, 1993).

the Supreme Court's 1896 ruling Plessy vs. Ferguson, which said that "separate" accommodations for blacks were acceptable as long as they were "equal."

Chief Justice Earl Warren, speaking for the unanimous court, found in favor of Brown. In part, Warren wrote:

Segregation of white and colored children in public schools has a detrimental effect upon the colored children. The impact is greater when it has the sanction of the law, for the policy of separating the races is usually interpreted as denoting the inferiority of the negro group. A sense of inferiority affects the motivation of a child to learn. Segregation with the sanction of law, therefore, has a tendency to [retard] the educational and mental development of negro children and to deprive them of some of the benefits they would receive in a racial[ly] integrated school system.[6]

Warren continued:

Whatever may have been the extent of psychological knowledge at the time of Plessy v. Ferguson, this finding is amply supported by modern authority. Any language in Plessy v. Ferguson contrary to this finding is rejected.

We conclude that, in the field of public education, the doctrine of "separate but equal" has no place. Separate educational facilities are inherently unequal. Therefore, we hold that the plaintiffs and others similarly situated for whom the actions have been brought are, by reason of the segregation complained of, deprived of the equal protection of the laws guaranteed by the Fourteenth Amendment.

To many people in the South — and sadly, in too many places in the rest of the United States — segregated schools were the first line of defense against the taboo of mixing of the races.

The court decision went down in May; six weeks later, Elvis Presley was on the radio in the South singing Arthur Crudup's sensually charged blues song "That's All Right, Mama." No wonder white people in the South were getting nervous. Between the Supreme Court and rock 'n' roll, the old ways were being forced to change.

Doo-wop

Doo-wop is the name given to the vocal group rock music of the 1950s. The name comes from the nonsense syllables sung by the harmony singers while the lead singer carried the melody. It could have easily been called "Shoo-doobie-doo," "Bomp-diddy-bomp," or "Oo-wie-oo-wah."

Doo-wop developed in American cities after World War II. At first it was mostly a ghetto phenomenon, with groups like the Ravens and Sonny Til & the Orioles giving R&B or gospel stylings to white pop standards. Though musically quite simple, the blend of voices, from low-down bass to high tenor or falsetto, could give even the most banal romantic clichés an intensity and urgency that had wide teen appeal. There was also a do-it-yourself ethos since all you needed were a few guys hanging around a street corner, a candy store, a high school lavatory, or a highway underpass to provide some extra resonance or echo. Like punk rock and hip-hop, it originally thrived on independent record labels with limited distribution, so each city or region had its own scene. For a very few, a hit record might mean a foot in the door of a singing career. But lack of knowledge about contracts, royalties, or any other aspect of the music business meant that many doo-wop artists were paid a flat studio performance fee, if anything, and rarely shared in any of the revenue they generated.

Doo-wop's popularity coincided and accelerated with the birth of rock 'n' roll: 1954 offered not only "Sh-Boom" by the Chords and "Gee" by the Crows, but also some hits that have since become considered classics of the ballad style of vocal group harmony singing, such as the Harptones' "A Sunday Kind of Love" and the Penguins' "Earth Angel."

Largely on the basis of its novelty appeal, doo-wop was firmly established as a basic rock 'n' roll subgenre between 1955 and 1959. There were basically two kinds of doo-wop records: fast and slow. Many of the most most memorable up-tempo doo-wop records were "Why Do Fools Fall in Love" by Frankie Lymon & the Teenagers, "Get a Job" by the Silhouettes, "Book of Love" by the Monotones, "At My Front Door" by the El Dorados, "I Wonder Why" by Dion & the Belmonts, "At the Hop" by Danny & the Juniors, and "Come Go with Me" by the Del-Vikings. Immortal doo-wop ballads include "In the Still of the Night" by the Five Satins, "Tonite Tonite" by the Mello Kings, "Desirie" by the Charts, "16 Candles" by the Crests, and "I Only Have Eyes for You" by the Flamingos.

An almost imperceptible time-shift between the end of this golden era of doo-wop and the "oldies but goodies" era from roughly 1961 to 1963 gave many of these records continued life on the radio. Artists from the early 1960s with a doo-wop sound included Gene Chandler ("Duke of Earl"), the Marcels ("Blue Moon"), the Tokens ("The Lion Sleeps Tonight") and the Regents ("Barbara Ann"). The girl-group era absorbed some of doo-wop's stylings (The Crystals' "Da Doo Ron Ron" is one example). And Barry Mann, who with Cynthia Weil was one of the most productive songwriting teams of the pop 1960s, recorded a tribute to doo-wop called "Who Put the Bomp (In the Bomp Bomp Bomp)" in 1961, while singer Johnny Cymbal paid tribute to an essential ingredient of every doo-wop record in "Mr. Bass Man," in 1963.

Doo-wop has undergone intermittent revivals since then: the soundtrack to the 1973 movie *American Graffiti,* an early triumph directed by *Star Wars* creator George Lucas, renewed interest in some of these songs; and a doo-wop parody group called Sha Na Na was one of the unlikely hits of the 1969 Woodstock festival. (The group took their name from the nonsense syllables sung by the bass voice in the Silhouettes' "Get a Job.")

Doo-wop worked as rebel music on two levels. First, adults, parents, teachers, and mainstream show business types thought it was complete idiocy, and that not only were the syllables nonsense, but the voices were often off-key. And they were offended that many doo-wop songs were revivals of standards from the 1930s and 1940s, often show tunes, which they remembered in a far more genteel way.

In 1934 Al Dubin and Harry Warren wrote "I Only Have Eyes for You," which was recorded by the Flamingos. Though it was still a ballad, the ethereal harmonies reciting the incantation "shoo-bop-shoo-bop … shoo-bop-shoo-bop" under the lead voices and over a haunting piano figure made it seem like a kind of voodoo. (Even the "shoo-bop-shoo-bop wasn't immediately apparent: at first, and for many years, this listener heard the Flamingos singing "twoah-chih-boh, twoah-chih-boh …")

Among the astounding remakes was another 1934 romantic ballad — or at least, originally a romantic ballad — by Richard Rodgers and Lorenz Hart called "Blue Moon." The Marcels' 1961 version upped the tempo about eight notches to a rocking frenzy, and led with the bass singer's "bomp-bi-bomp, bi-bi-bomp-bi-bomp-bi-bi-bomp-bi-bi-bomp dangdee-dang-dang, dingy dong ding Blue Moon …"

It is said that Rodgers hated the Marcels' version so much that he took out advertisements in music industry publications asking people not to buy the record. Nevertheless, it is the only version of the oft-recorded "Blue Moon" to hit No. 1 on the pop charts, and definitely the only Rodgers & Hart song to top the R&B charts.

Even mellow, melodic doo-wop ballads, like "There's a Moon Out Tonight" by the Capris, were in your face; the dress style, the camaraderie, the look of a passionate doo-wop group was not unlike that of a street gang, which may have been one of the messages teens sent to parents through doo-wop: this is our thing, it seemed to say. You don't like it, well, that's the way the cookie, not to mention the walls of a conformist society, crumbles. In that, doo-wop is the unheralded harbinger of hip-hop.

Cover Versions, Color War

In 1954, a singing group called the Chords had a hit called "Sh-Boom" that was a key record in many ways. It was one of the first beat records to use the multipart harmonies that would characterize the developing doo-wop vocal group style. Instead of the sweet, romantic crooning of popular groups like the Mills Brothers and the Ink Spots, who got pop airplay because their sound was so unthreatening, the Chords' "Sh-Boom" had a kind of galvanizing electricity and some tricky harmonies, and was undeniably rooted in swinging R&B. It was also edgy in a way that challenged the reassuring harmonies and bland lyrics of most 1950s pop. "Sh-Boom" [was the Chords'] own collective composition based upon the fear of nuclear war.[7]

The title is meant to convey the explosion of an atomic bomb — "sh-boom!" — although the irony was lost on most, who focused on the lyric hook ("life could be a dream") and thought of "sh-boom" as mere nonsense syllables. It was a strangely timely tune, since in the 1950s, the specter of an atomic attack from Russia was the source of persistent anxiety. Grade-schoolers in the mid-1950s can remember the "duck and cover" strategy for survival in case the Russians dropped an A-bomb in the school playground: duck under your desk, and cover your head if you see a blinding light outside. The likelihood was that every living being and most of the manmade things within a 100-mile radius would be incinerated immediately, but at least we knew how to duck and cover.

Those in cities were instructed to go underground, to subway stations that were to be put into use as fallout shelters. And suburbanites, from Maine to California, built fallout shelters in their backyards, underground living facilities stocked with bottled water, canned food, and generators for air and electricity that gave the more obsessively fearful the security that their families would survive the inevitable nuclear conflagration. Jerry Wexler, who was one of the record industry's most progressive executives for many decades, signed the Chords to Atlantic Records' Cat label. Wexler, like Atlantic cofounders Ahmet and Nesuhi Ertegun, was an R&B fanatic. He must have enjoyed the exquisite irony of having the Chords, who were black, do a cover version of Patti Page's corny inspirational "Cross Over the

Bridge." Initially, "Sh-Boom" was the B-side of this record before the disc jockeys flipped it over.

Another 1954 record, "Gee" by the Crows, was also an important crossover hit by a black vocal group. Perhaps its place in history is less gilded than that of "Sh-Boom" because white singers avoided covering it. Perhaps that was because its lyrics were so minimal that they were subservient to the syncopated voicings of "dit-di-di-dit-dit-di-dit" underneath the main melody, with agile bass singing and swooping falsetto creating a dynamic harmonic convergence that was difficult to duplicate.

The Chords' "Sh-Boom" had the distinction of being one of the few R&B songs at the time to get close to the top of the pop charts. But many at the time knew the song could be an even bigger smash covered by a white group, and "Sh-Boom" became one of the first most brazen instances of cultural bait-and-switch in the early rock era. While the Chords version was still on the charts, a group with the entirely apt name of the Crew Cuts, from Toronto, created a sensation with their "note for note copy" of "Sh-Boom," holding the No. 1 spot for nine weeks in the summer of 1954. (Adding insult to injury, the jazz magazine *Downbeat* named the Crew Cuts version the top R&B record of 1954.)

In early 1955, nearly half the best-sellers on the pop charts were tepid versions of R&B songs, including the McGuire Sisters' "Sincerely" (a copy of a record by the Moonglows); the Fontane Sisters' "Hearts of Stone" (The Charms), and both Perry Como and the Crew Cuts, who rode "Ko Ko Mo" down pop culture's Main Street while the original by Gene & Eunice stayed in the ghetto.

The suggestive nature of some R&B songs caused even some black-owned stations like Memphis' WDIA to keep its distance from Hank Ballard & the Midnighters "Work with Me Annie," with its delighted repetition of the phrase "roll on, roll on, roll on" over the rocking rhythm. If the connotation of "work with me" wasn't obvious enough, the widely banned follow-up, "Annie Had a Baby," made the meaning clear. This was the kind of song that led Los Angeles disc jockey Peter Potter, host of the TV show *Juke Box Jury*, to say, "All rhythm and blues records are dirty and as bad for the kids as dope."[8]

But the kids still liked these songs. The answer, for segregated radio and the major record companies, was to clean them up. Georgia

Gibbs, who recorded for Mercury, spent three weeks at the top of the hit parade after recutting "Work with Me Annie" as "Dance with Me Henry (Wallflower)"; her hit was a kind of medley that also smoothed the sexual edges off of another R&B hit, Etta James' "Wallflower."

This became Gibbs's specialty. She took the earthy hits of Atlantic's R&B star LaVern Baker and, made them, as they used to say in the laundry soap commercials, "100% whiter." LaVern Baker's "Tweedle Dee" topped out at No. 14 on the pop charts in January 14, 1955; Gibbs's version peaked at No. 2 two weeks later, and sold more than a million copies. "Listeners aren't given a chance to hear the original by LaVern Baker," Jerry Wexler complained at the time.

The same was true with Big Joe Turner, who had a huge R&B smash with the Charles Calhoun composition "Shake, Rattle and Roll." This would become one of the first rock 'n' roll hits by Bill Haley & the Comets, with the lyrics cleansed of their raciness.

Haley sings, "Wearin' those dresses, your hair done up so right; you look so warm, but your heart is cold as ice."

Turner sang, "Well you wear low dresses, the sun comes shining through; I can't believe my eyes all that mess belongs to you."

Among black artists, Baker was especially outspoken about Gibbs's success. But she also had a wicked sense of humor. Before leaving on an overseas airplane trip, Baker took out a $1 million life insurance policy — and named Gibbs the beneficiary. That way, if Baker died, the R&B singer quipped, Gibbs would still be able to support herself.

For her own part, Gibbs insists she had never heard Baker's versions of these songs. The first time she heard most of her material, Gibbs says, was when the producers presented it at a recording session — a typical procedure in those days. But Gibbs is a highly intelligent woman, and she understood the pull of the racial undertow. She said,

Nobody believes I never heard LaVern Baker's recording. For the sheer fact that we were living in a very segregated America. Not that we aren't now, but it was terrible then. I couldn't go into a [midtown Manhattan] record store to buy her record, I'd have to go to Harlem to buy it. R&B was only sold up there. So how was I going to hear it? It wasn't played on the [mainstream top-forty] radio.[9]

Gibbs acknowledges the racial disparities of the music business that fueled the distinctions between innocuously named categories;

> People don't know about the three categories we had, pop, R&B, and country and western. And how an artist from one category didn't record in another. Country stayed below the Mason-Dixon line, R&B stayed in the black neighborhoods, and white pop had the largest share of the field. We [white pop singers] covered them all. White singers had more avenues open than blacks, that's the way it was in America. God almighty, it was nothing to be proud of. It was dreadful, and that's the way it was until some Civil Rights laws were passed [in the 1960s]. It was nothing to be proud of at all.

Two of the black founding fathers of rock 'n' roll, Little Richard and Fats Domino, were great successes and sold millions of records. But their songs sold many more millions in the most tepid versions for their great white compromiser, Pat Boone.

Fats Domino/Rock 'n' Roll Piano New Orleans R&B

In the cradle of musical civilization, New Orleans has long been acknowledged as a birthplace of jazz. But the city was also one of the pillars in the building of rock 'n' roll, and the staunchest was Antoine "Fats" Domino.

Born into a French-speaking family, he started recording in the late 1940s, and in 1949 had his first hit, the self-caricature called "The Fat Man" that many credit as one of rock's direct predecessors. Teaming with bandleader and saxophonist Dave Bartholomew, Domino wrote and played on some of the most distinctive of rock's early classics: His first rock hit was "Ain't That a Shame" (originally listed on the label as "Ain't It a Shame"), characterized by his languid, pronounced French Louisiana accented singing and relaxed, rolling piano sound.

Domino's version peaked at No. 10 in 1955, a week after Pat Boone's tepid copy had reached No. 1. But like Little Richard, Domino's mastery of rhythm and his bluesy feeling struck teens the way Boone never could. A series of million sellers in 1956 to 1957 — "My Blue Heaven," "Blueberry Hill," "Blue Monday," "I'm Walkin'," and "I'm in Love Again" made Domino a huge star; and his one-of-a-kind charm netted him appearances in films like *The Girl Can't Help It,* one of Hollywood's best rock movies, starring buxom sex symbol Jayne Mansfield and a host of rockers, including Little Richard.

Domino would continue having hits into the 1960s. His "Walking to New Orleans" remains a beloved tribute to his now-devastated hometown. And he put a fresh, blues-rock spin on Hank Williams's classics like "Jambalaya (On the Bayou)" and "You Win Again." The Beatles piano-driven hit "Lady Madonna" was intrinsically a Fats Domino tribute, made clear by the ease with which Domino played and sang that tune in his own 1968 version.

New Orleans rock 'n' roll was invariably piano-based, and Domino was the best known of many piano-playing rock and blues musicians to come out of New Orleans. Domino brought a more distinctively rock 'n' roll beat to the sound developed by Professor Longhair (aka Roy Byrd). Huey "Piano" Smith's "Rockin' Pneumonia and the Boogie Woogie Flu" and "Don't You Just Know It" and Frankie Ford's "Sea Cruise" (featuring Smith's band) were among the national hits with a distinctive New Orleans feel. Decades later, an artist like Ernie K. Doe could attract as much attention at the annual New Orleans Jazz & Heritage festival as national stars like Bonnie Raitt.

Allen Toussaint, the most prolific songwriter, producer, and arranger from the Crescent City, is another musician who owes a debt to Domino's breakthroughs. In 2006, Toussaint recorded the acclaimed album *The River in Reverse,* a collaboration with Elvis Costello.

In 1971, New Orleans pianist Mac Rebennack made his national debut as Dr. John, the Night Tripper, on a self-titled album that mixed spooky voodoo incantations, trippy psychedelic tracks, and swampy R&B. The next year, as simply Dr. John, Rebennack released the influential album *Gumbo,* which introduced the classic New Orleans R&B of Professor Longhair, Huey Smith, and others to a new generation of curious rock fans. Among the songs he revived was pianist James Booker's "Junco Partner" (also associated with Professor Longhair), which was covered by the Clash on their 1981 album, *Sandinista!* The title song of Dr. John's 1973 album, *Right Place Wrong Time* was his only top-ten single.

In the 1980s, the Neville Brothers, from the first family of New Orleans rock and R&B, became a popular nationwide touring and recording attraction. In the early 1950s, as the Hawkettes, various Neville brothers sang on the local novelty *Mardi Gras Mambo.* The best-known brother, Aaron Neville, hit the pop charts in 1966 with the ballad "Tell It Like It Is," and teamed up with Linda Ronstadt in the late 1980s and early 1990s. Art Neville was the keyboard player for the Meters, which from the mid-1960s into the late 1970s were New Orleans' quintessential funky instrumental group. But it all began with Fats.

Pat Boone

If it's true that you are what you wear on your feet (or, as a sneaker commercial in the 1990s put it, "It's the shoes!"), then the blandly handsome Boone's preference was a dead giveaway. Elvis caused a ruckus singing about "Blue Suede Shoes," an assertion of nonconformity; Boone's trademark was symbolically appropriate as well: he wore white bucks.

While Presley maintained the earthy spirit of the originals, Boone squeezed the sensuality out of R&B hits and made them chaste. Though Presley was steeped in religion and southern gospel, Boone made his piety and purity the foundation of his appeal.

Boone had access to network TV shows to promote his records in a way that the black originators never did. Versions of Ivory Joe Hunter's "Since I Met You Baby," Fats Domino's "Blueberry Hill," and, most absurdly, the flamboyant Little Richard's "Tutti Frutti" nearly always outsold the originals. But history rewards authenticity, and it is Domino and Richard who are charter members of the Rock and Roll Hall of Fame, while Boone is unlikely ever to find his name on the ballot. But the major record companies were comfortable with Boone, who recorded for the Dot label. Fifty years later, he is the music expert for the Web site seniorsite.com. Here is an excerpt from his Web bio:

> With his trademark white buck shoes, perfectly combed hair and gleaming smile, Boone was the very essence of wholesome American values, and at a time when the rise of rock & roll was viewed as a sign of the apocalypse, he made the music appear safe and non-threatening, earning some 38 Top 40 hits in the process ... Of course, while Elvis — with his flashy suits, swiveling hips and suggestive leer — remained persona non grata throughout many corners of mainstream America, Boone was embraced by teens and parents alike; his music polished rock's rough edges away, making such madly rollicking songs as "Tutti Frutti" and such passionate New Orleans r&b hits as "Ain't That a Shame" palatable to white audiences who were raised on the soothing pop traditions of a vanishing era.[10]

That is certainly putting an interesting spin on what Boone accomplished. Boone himself has shown remarkable good grace, perhaps doing penance, in recording one of history's weirdest releases in the 1990s: *Pat Boone in a Metal Mood/No More Mr. Nice Guy,* an album of heavy-metal covers of songs by Alice Cooper, Metallica, AC/DC, and Ozzy Osbourne, all of which, in some way, have been accused of being "satanic" by the same people who held Pat Boone to be the epitome of Christian virtue.

Bill Haley & The Comets/ "Rock Around the Clock"

Elvis Presley was the first rock star, but "Rock Around the Clock" by Bill Haley & the Comets had its share of "firsts." It was the first worldwide rock 'n' roll hit; the first No. 1 rock 'n' roll record; and the first rock 'n' roll song played on a Hollywood movie soundtrack. It hit the top on May 14, 1955, and was No. 1 for eight weeks. In England it was an even bigger phenomenon, topping the chart there for more than four months in the fall of 1955. By some counts it is the top-selling 45 rpm single ever, with some 25 million copies sold worldwide, according to the Guinness Book of World Records. (Presley did not have his first No. 1 until "Heartbreak Hotel" in March 1956.)

"Rock Around the Clock" was anything but an instant sensation. In fact, it was a flop when it was first released in 1954, and would probably have remained obscure had it not been for an important 1955 movie about rebellious teenagers called *Blackboard Jungle.*

The movie was about an inner-city schoolteacher, played by tough but sensitive Glenn Ford. The incorrigible teenagers in his classes were feared by the public as "juvenile delinquents," teenage hoodlums increasingly cited by an anxious public and rabble-rousing press as America's No. 1 social ill.

Blackboard Jungle overflowed with teenage anger; sullen, impulsive behavior; and disdain for rules or order of any kind. The teachers are utterly demoralized: one is beaten, another sexually assaulted. In one famous scene, a teacher has brought some of his precious jazz records to play for one of his more advanced classes. The tough kids want to hear them; the teacher, at first, implies they aren't intelligent enough to appreciate them. Infuriated by the slight, the thugs take pleasure in destroying the collection, one record at a time, while the teacher watches helplessly.

Though the story and its message may seem dated or corny, *Blackboard Jungle* revealed some of the anger and resentment seething beneath the surface of the nation's supposed complacency. Adults were in denial, objecting to the movie's portrayal of class resentment and poverty being depicted with such dramatic realism. Ambassador to Italy Clare Booth Luce used her status as a powerful member of the establishment to block the exhibition of *Blackboard Jungle* overseas. For her, America was engaged in an ideological Cold War, and she believed "our enemies" would seize on images of schools in chaos as evidence of American decadence.[11]

Bill Haley & the Comets weren't in the movie, but the song "Rock Around the Clock" played over the opening credits. In theaters across America, teens went wild: sometimes, it was spontaneous dancing in the aisles; other times, fists would fly and theater seats would be torn from their moorings and tossed about in spasms of not quite comprehensible rage.

A year after its initial mediocre showing, the single "Rock Around the Clock" was rereleased. This time it became a phenomenon, and the importance of "Rock Around the Clock" can't be underestimated. It "created a dividing line between all that came before and all that followed … it was the beginning of the rock era."

Another essential movie of 1955, *Rebel Without a Cause*, had no music at all, but was just as important in establishing the alienated teenager as an icon. While *Blackboard Jungle* took place in the inner city, *Rebel* was set in the affluent suburbs. This landmark movie starred the young actor James Dean as an anguished misfit. His wealthy parents give him plenty of material comforts but none of their time, interest, or affection. He is constantly being shifted to new schools, and has a hard time making friends. Dean's sullen, charismatic rage made him the embodiment of the title, and the title embodied a new era. That image became eternal when Dean, twenty-four, crashed his new Porsche 550 Spyder sports car on a dark California road on his way to an auto race, and was killed instantly on September 30, 1955. *Rebel* was just Dean's third movie.

Rebel Without a Cause didn't feature any rock 'n' roll; it didn't have to. Dean was embraced by teenagers who were obsessed with what appeared to be his "live fast, die young" credo. And he had the look. Dean has been a character in more rock 'n' roll songs than you can count, from the Eagles' "James Dean" and David Essex's "Rock On," to Bruce Springsteen's "Cadillac Ranch." Between Dean and Elvis, a template was forged for rock 'n' roll's style and attitude.

"When rock and roll arrived and when you had two absolute symbolic teenagers suddenly appear in front of a nation (James Dean and Elvis Presley), everything fell into place. Then people had an image

Rockabilly (circa 1957)

A long line of talented southerners followed Elvis Presley into Memphis's Sun Studio. So many recordings were made there that Sun remains synonymous with this rock 'n' roll of the rural south known as rockabilly, which is what occurred when a hillbilly played rock 'n' roll. Emphasis was on the toe-topping rhythm and the "go-cat-go" guitar breaks. Some of the artists branched out and became stars in country music, and even crossed over to mainstream success, like Carl Perkins, Johnny Cash, Charlie Rich, and Roy Orbison. (Perkins composed Elvis's early musical calling card, "Blue Suede Shoes.") Others remained obscure except for perhaps one song known to collectors and rockabilly obsessives. These included Sonny Burgess, Carl Mann, Billy Riley, and Warren Smith.

Riley's 1957 record *Flying Saucers Rock 'n' Roll* stands as a pop-culture moment, when the juxtaposition of this way out music and the cool cats from outer space obsessing youth culture in science-fiction movies was clear. Smith's "Ubangi Stomp" may have taken its inspiration from Tarzan movies or some other film fantasies of darkest Africa, but its description of the denizens of this place were one of the rare lamentable instances in which an attempt at good ol' boy humor was instead a channel for racist name-calling.

There were many other important rockabilly artists that gave this music its stature. The brothers Johnny and Dorsey Burnette and Paul Burlison, known as the Rock 'n' Roll Trio, were originally from Memphis but made their records in Nashville, contributing tracks to the canon-like "Rock Billy Boogie" and "Rock Therapy." Their most influential recording was a version of Tiny Bradshaw's "Train Kept' a Rollin'." Before the session, Burlison loosened some tubes in his amplifier. As a result, his guitar playing sounded fuzzy and distorted. "With Burlison playing a deceptively simple series of bass-string octaves through his fuzzed-out amp, the record proved an instant sensation within the industry itself." The Yardbirds in the 1960s and Aerosmith in the 1970s revived the song, providing their own variations on the now-commonplace guitar technique known as fuzztone."*

Gene Vincent ("Be Bop-a-Lula") and Eddie Cochran ("Summertime Blues," "Twenty Flight Rock") were influential rock 'n' rollers whose records had the energetic simplicity of rockabilly. While Cochran's roots, like many rockabilly artists, were in country music, Vincent and his group, the Blue Caps, wore black leather jackets and projected teen gang menace. No wonder they were revered by British musicians, from John Lennon to Jeff Beck to Eric Clapton. In fact, a 1960 visit to England, where they were welcomed as conquering heroes, was fateful for Cochran and Vincent. They were riding together in a taxi when it crashed, killing Cochran and further damaging Vincent's leg, which had been mangled in a 1955 motorcycle accident. Cochran's "Summertime Blues," a profound testament to teenage boredom, is one of rock's essential songs. It was revived in 1968 by San Francisco band Blue Cheer, whose maniacal volume and stoner attitude made them among the first heavy-metal bands. And the Who made it a staple of their concert repertoire, with a bravura version on their 1970 *Live at Leeds* album.

But you can't talk about rockabilly — you can't talk about rock 'n' roll — without talking about Jerry Lee Lewis. The greatest rockabilly star of all is unique because unlike every other artist of the genre, he didn't play guitar: it was his sweeping, stomping, pummeling piano playing that gave Lewis his distinction, along with a reckless abandon matched

---

* "A Nashville Trio," by Daniel Cooper, from *The Nashville Scene* weekly newspaper, July 4, 1996. Archived at Rockabilly Net Web site http://www.rockabilly. net/articles/burnette.shtml.

to connect to, to try to live up to, to imitate," the rock historian Greil Marcus said in a 1997 interview.

Adult America was bewildered by this tribal teenage identity. You can see the ambivalence in the torrent of teen films that flooded out of Hollywood in the next few years. Elvis Presley, on the one hand, went from symbol of decadence to the All-American boy thanks to the power of Hollywood. A long-term contract with MGM studios guaranteed there would be Presley films on a regular basis. His debut, in the 1950s only by Little Richard. Jerry Lee's hits didn't hide behind sexual innuendo: "Great Balls of Fire," "Whole Lotta Shakin' Goin' On," and "Breathless" (1957–1958) were all Id, nothing hidden. Raised Pentecostal in Ferriday, Louisiana (he is related to the televangelist Jimmy Swaggart), Lewis is one of those artists without a filter between his art and his life; his performances sound like wrestling matches between God and the Devil.

Generally in these battles, Lewis lost. His rock 'n' roll career ended quickly in a kind of disgrace when his 1958 marriage to his thirteen-year-old cousin, Myra Gale Brown, was made public. Yet Lewis bounced back, becoming a successful country artist in the 1960s with classics like "What Made Milwaukee Famous Made a Loser Out of Me," and finding plenty of love on the rock oldies concert circuit. A volcanic personality, Lewis always seemed to be shooting off a gun, or his mouth, whenever he or the alcohol he was drinking suited him. Yet he has outlived Elvis, Johnny Cash, and Carl Perkins, the three other members of what was dubbed Sun Records' "Million Dollar Quartet." In 2006, nearing his seventy-first birthday, he released an album of duets cut with admirers like Bruce Springsteen and John Fogerty. It had an apt title: *Last Man Standing*.

Rockabilly has gone through numerous revivals. Its raw, primitive sound found favor during the punk rock era. Robert Gordon, the singer of New York punk band Tuff Darts, left that band to pursue a solo career as a rockabilly artist. With their pompadour hairdos and unwavering devotion to form, the Stray Cats, a trio from Long Island, made a big splash in the rockabilly-loving United Kingdom in 1981 before returning home to acclaim and platinum sales for their 1982 album *Built for Speed*. Guitarist Brian Setzer played the role of Eddie Cochran in the 1987 movie *La Bamba*. Bringing his passion full circle, Setzer released a 2005 album *Rockabilly Riot: A Tribute to Sun Records*.

Love Me Tender in 1956, featured the twenty-one-year-old as a romantic lead in a nineteenth-century love triangle. The title song, a slow ballad, was a huge hit, and served to transform the sex symbol into a more vulnerable love object. In *Jailhouse Rock*, he played a convict, doing time for manslaughter, who discovers his talent in jail. The title song is a marvelously choreographed musical production number that allows a little of Presley's rock 'n' roll animal to come across through the prison bars. *Loving You* (1957) relies almost entirely on Presley's charisma. As Marshall Crenshaw writes, "When he pulls up in his hot rod at the beginning of the picture, he's Brando, James Dean, and everyone else who's cool all rolled into one."[12]

Rosa Parks and Bobby Grier

In addition to the explosive growth of rock 'n' roll, 1955 saw the birth of the Civil Rights movement.

In his book *Race, Rock, and Elvis*, Michael T. Bertrand argues that Elvis Presley revolutionized race relations in the South by appealing to tens of thousands of working-class whites who were drawn to the same R&B he was. "Flocking to R&B clubs and, later, rock and roll venues, these young people challenged the prevailing racial norms. And in so doing ... they served as vanguards of the civil rights movement before there even was a civil rights movement."[13]

Within weeks of Elvis signing with RCA Records, an ordinary afternoon bus ride in Montgomery, Alabama, became a turning point in history.

Like almost everything else in the South — movie theaters, water fountains, coffee shops and restaurants, public bathrooms — city buses in Montgomery kept the races apart. Whites sat in the front, blacks in the rear. If there were enough white people, they were entitled to all of the seats; blacks would have to give up their seats to a white person and stand.

On December 1, 1955, Rosa Parks, a black seamstress, sat down in the front of a Montgomery bus. Parks sat down in the front of the bus. When the driver told her to move to the back, she refused.

The driver repeated the demand, and Parks would not budge. She was arrested and jailed. Later that night, she was released on a $100 bond.

It was not that Parks had snapped; behind the scenes, a group of Montgomery blacks had been seeking the opportunity to challenge this aspect of the segregation laws for some time. But she was the right person, at the right time, doing the right thing.

In the days immediately after Parks was bailed out of jail, an organization called the Montgomery Improvement Association formed to coordinate a response. It decided to protest Parks's arrest and the humiliation of segregation in public transportation by calling for a one-day boycott of Montgomery buses. The leader of the M.I.A. was the new young pastor of the Dexter Avenue Church: Martin Luther King Jr. Set to last one day, the boycott continued for 381 days. When it was over, an appeals court had ruled segregation in public transportation to be illegal, a decision upheld by the U.S. Supreme Court.

Parks's act of defiance traumatized some powerful Southern whites for whom segregation was not only a way of life, but the only way.

The day after that ruling, Georgia Governor Marvin Griffin vented about another affront to his belief system: a college football game in which the all-white Georgia Tech team was to play against the University of Pittsburgh. Pitt had one black player: Bobby Grier.

The two teams were scheduled to meet on January 1 in the Sugar Bowl in New Orleans. As the *New York Times* reported fifty years later, a black had never played in the Sugar Bowl. In 1941, Boston College played the Sugar Bowl without Lou Montgomery, the team's black star running back. Montgomery was not only forbidden by the authorities to play. He "was not even allowed to practice, or stay at the team hotel; he watched the game from the press box."[14]

To its credit, the University of Pittsburgh in 1955 was not as acquiescent as Boston College's administration and students were fifteen years earlier. The university administration, coaches, and team stood behind Grier, as the Georgia governor insisted that playing against a team with one black player would be the equivalent — literally — of the end of the world.

"The South stands at Armageddon," Griffin telegrammed the state board of regents. "The battle is joined. We cannot make the slightest concession to the enemy in this dark and lamentable hour of struggle."[15]

But something was stirring in the South, especially among the young people. Georgia Tech students held a protest rally at the Capitol in Atlanta — against Governor Griffin. "The governor acted like a horse's backside," a player for the 1955 Tech team told the *Times* in 2006. "The governor didn't reflect the attitude of the Georgia Tech football team at all."

The Pitt players stayed at Tulane University in New Orleans, because no hotel in the city would accept the entire team. But fraternities at local colleges, the *Times* said, held parties in Grier's honor. The game was played, and the world didn't come to an end, although segregation was at the beginning of the end. "I learned that things were going to change and that things were a' changin'," Grier told the newspaper.

Little Richard

If Georgia's governor could see Armageddon in a team from his state playing a college football game against one with a single black player, it's difficult to fathom what he made of one of his state's most illustrious citizens: singer, pianist, and songwriter Richard "Little Richard" Penniman.

"When I first started, it was all swing and sway with Sammy Kaye," Little Richard said.[16] "And there was nobody swaying in my [black] neighborhood. I started playing the piano and everybody started jumping around — that's when rock 'n' roll was born."

Little Richard may boast, but as a songwriter once said, "it ain't lying if it's true,"[17] and Richard tells the truth.

No fireball could match the heat and light exuded by a pompadoured black piano player and singer from Macon, Georgia. From 1956 into 1958, Little Richard knocked out nearly a dozen of the most frantic, appealing up-tempo rock 'n' roll records ever made. He was the Id of the rock revolution. Little Richard really drew the line between teenagers and their parents. To adults, Little Richard records like "Tutti Frutti" ("Tutti Frutti/Aw-rootie/A-wop-bop-a-loo-bop/A-wop-bamboom") were insanity multiplied by inanity. To teenagers, they sounded like anthems that carried the instinctive promise of freedom from the constraints of conformity.

Little Richard was a flamboyant, outspoken, transparently effeminate gay black man who wore rouge and red lipstick and carried on with the abandon of a drag queen. While Elvis created hysteria in the audience, Little Richard exuded hysteria from the stage, making the shedding of inhibition an art form.

In the prologue to his masterful book *Mystery Train*, author Greil Marcus describes an absurd but real get-together circa 1970 on Dick Cavett's talk show.

The guests were the snooty intellectual New York critic John Simon and the author Erich Segal, who though an academic himself, had just struck gold with a trite little novel made into a trite big movie called *Love Story*. And, there was Little Richard.

Simon and Segal were locked in a poisonous debate about "art" as Little Richard watched, waiting for his opening. When it came, Marcus writes, "that was it. Little Richard was the only artist on the set that night, the only one who disrupted an era, the only one with a claim to immortality. The one who broke the rules, created a form; the one who gave shape to a vitality that wailed silently in each of us until he found a voice for it."[18]

The keening wail, the whoops, the cascades of joy, the shouting, the hammerjack beat, drawn from gospel music and the patois of the black southern R&B subculture. That was the art.

Little Richard had been a veteran of the southern touring band the Upsetters in the early and mid-1950s. (When he went solo, his replacement was James Brown.) He was signed by Art Rupe's Specialty Records. The talent scout and producer for Rupe was named Bumps Blackwell, who understood perfectly how Little Richard's frantic style suited the burgeoning spirit of rock.

As Blackwell told Richard's biographer, Charles White:

> A singer could make a hit recording if he sang with a lot of feeling, regardless of how imperfect everything else might be... . You couldn't get a learned piano player to give you that simplicity, and put that much energy and excitement into it. And that was the rhythm people loved, and were dancing to, and were buying.[19]

Little Richard's claim to immortality was his first hit, "Tutti Frutti." After a fruitless early recording session in New Orleans, Blackwell and Richard were unwinding at a club called the Dew Drop Inn. During the entertainer's break, Richard went to the piano, where he started banging out a song whose bawdy variations were familiar to blacks in roadhouses and after-hours clubs. "Tutti Frutti, good bootie ..." It was a eureka moment. When they recorded it, Blackwell and Richard changed "good booty" to "aw-rootie"; Richard's wild-eyed exclamation, "Awop-Bop-a-Loo-Mop Alop Bam-Boom!" were nonsense syllables that nevertheless communicated a joyous catharsis.

To teenagers, it resounded as a release from restlessness, anger, and boredom. Life was so perplexing, so full of mixed signals and hypocrisy, they couldn't even think of the question. But in Little Richard's joyous dementia, they heard some kind of answer.

"Tutti Frutti" and Little Richard's other classics — "Long Tall Sally," "Lucille," "Slippin' and Slidin'," "Rip It Up," "Good Golly Miss Molly" — defined rock 'n' roll's appeal to the gut and the feet in their very titles. And they are the versions that shook the Beatles and other generations of rockers out of their teenage lethargy.

But it took some time for Little Richard to be accepted on his own terms. Although the practice of "cover records" was widespread enough to be considered almost universal, Pat Boone's whitewashing of Little Richard took the practice to a new level of absurdity. A few weeks after Little Richard's "Tutti Frutti" peaked on the pop charts in early 1956, Pat Boone's bland version sold more than 1 million copies. "The white radio stations wouldn't play Richard's version of 'Tutti Frutti' and made Pat Boone's cover No. 1," Bumps Blackwell said. Charles White generously suggests that despite being "a cruel larceny," that people who never heard rock 'n' roll before "turned on to the new sound."

Boone repeated the facsimile approach dutifully with "Long Tall Sally," on which he sounds, as White archly notes, "as if he is not quite sure what he is singing about."[20]

That insight seemed to be striking listeners as well: Little Richard's original of "Long Tall Sally," for what may have been the first time, did better on most pop charts than the imitation. Cover versions began to lose their mass appeal, as rock 'n' roll seemed to fill a teenage craving for undisguised emotions and vitality.

The social impact of Little Richard is also undeniable. "Richard opened the door. He brought the races together," said black musician, songwriter, and producer H. B. Barnum. "When I first went out on the road there were many segregated audiences. With Richard, although they still had the audiences segregated in the building [blacks in the balcony, whites downstairs, or separated by the center aisle] they were there together. And most times, by the end of the night, they'd all be mixed together."[21]

Little Richard had second thoughts about rock stardom: his hedonistic life style and sudden affluence contrasted with his religious upbringing as the son of a Seventh Day Adventist preacher. After a tour of Australia in 1957, a he decided to quit rock 'n' roll and entered a seminary. "I better hold on to that rock of ages, I've had that other rock," he said in 1984.[22]

He sang gospel music for a few years, and returned to rock in the 1960s and became a star of the oldies circuit. And of course, he was worshipped in England, where the Beatles began to develop their original style after mastering Little Richard's "whooo's!"

The British rock singer and composer Elvis Costello speaks about seeing Little Richard in 1993:

> He did "Good Golly Miss Molly," and it was three of the most exciting minutes of music I've ever heard. He must have done that song thousands of times, and although he had lots of extra showbiz padding, teasing the audience, when he hit it, it was terrifying. He just went … "whoooo!" Rock and roll is the only art, and that word can be attributed to Little Richard just as much as we're trying to do here, that is made in the moment that you hear it. When a painting is done, its done. The ear completes the music, but the execution is what puts it in the air in the first place.[23]

Or maybe let Little Richard tell it: "It was aw-rootie!," he said, recalling the "Tutti Frutti" recording session. "I was really desperate and determined… . I was singing at the top of my voice, I was screaming, you never seen a guy with a big head like me scream as loud as I was hollering. I made up this song and I screamed, and played, and banged on the piano; I think I almost tore that piano out of the wall. Everybody else was doing the trots and the foxes. I brought the rock 'n' roll in there."

Elvis Joins the Army

In 1957, nervous CBS network censors forced cameras to show Presley's performance on the Ed Sullivan Show from the waist up, lest his swiveling hips and grinding pelvis inspire overt sexual desire.

By 1958, his fans still swooned, but to many Elvis had ceased to be a symbol of rebellion. On that third and final appearance on *Ed Sullivan* (videos show him singing "Don't Be Cruel"), Presley could have used his enormous leverage to challenge the CBS network's "waist up" edict.

And though he may be swiveling at the end of the song (suggested by the screams of the studio audience), Presley went with the deal.

At the end of the performance, Sullivan, whose power as a star maker was unsurpassed until today's *American Idol* judges, waved Presley over for a firm handshake and a kind of secular blessing. "This is a real decent, fine boy," Sullivan said to both Presley and the 60 million Americans watching. "And wherever you go, Elvis, we have never had a pleasanter experience [on the show] with a big name. You're thoroughly all right."

"You're thoroughly all right." With those words, Elvis Presley was anointed a Good Person; it was safe to trust your teenage daughter with his records, posters, and movies. Presley's status as a rebel was further undercut when he was drafted into the United States Army in 1958. It was routine for celebrities like Presley to find some reason for deferment; the system was full of loopholes. He could have sought and would have been granted assignment to a military band, or served his two years entertaining his fellow soldiers. But then as now, the patriotic American South revered the military. And as a Southern male, Presley may have seen his service, especially in peacetime, as natural, and even desirable. It was also a fairly obvious and simple way for Elvis and his manager, the secretive, manipulative Col. Tom Parker, to change Presley's image. To those who had not already been won over by Presley's politeness, humility, and mainstream values, accepting his Army duty without complaint or special treatment, like any other citizen, gave the young star a new identity: the All-American boy. Presley was inducted into the Army at the Memphis draft board on March 24, 1958. There may not have been a newspaper or magazine in the civilized world that did not feature the famous photograph of Presley in the barber chair on March 25 at nearby Fort Chaffee, Arkansas, his long sideburns and glistening black coif shaved to a regulation G.I. crewcut. From there it was six months of basic training at Fort Hood, Texas, after which Private Elvis Presley was assigned to a U.S. Army base in Friedberg, Germany.

In August, Presley was granted emergency leave to be with his critically ill mother. On August 14, Elvis' mother Gladys died at age forty-six of hepatitis, a liver ailment. Few knew at the time how traumatic this was for Presley. A twin brother had died at birth. She was the closest person to Presley's heart. One concession to his stature: He lived in a house off-base in the town of Bad Nauheim with his father, grandmother, and some loyal friends and hangers-on who would become known as part of Presley's "Memphis Mafia."

Col. Parker (who had not, in fact, earned any military title; it was an honorary title he awarded himself, in line with his earlier career running carnivals) was prepared for Presley's absence from the scene. In a surge of pre-Army activity, there were plenty of movies and recordings in the can for steady release during Presley's tour of duty. But Presley's Army service dampened some of the hysteria. And rock continued to evolve, sometimes organically, sometimes manipulatively.

Meanwhile, in Outer Space ...

Even Private Elvis Presley, U.S. Army, could not prevent the United States from its most embarrassing "defeat" of the Cold War, and one of the many emotional blows to the national psyche that fed the U.S. neuroses during the 1950s.

On Oct. 4, 1957, the Soviet Union launched the first satellite to orbit the earth. Known as Sputnik I [the Russian word for "traveler"], it was "the size of a basketball, weighed only 183 pounds, and took about 98 minutes to orbit the Earth."[24] The launch set off "a wave of anxiety" in the United States[25] as Sputnik's success indicated that technologically and scientifically the U.S. had been surpassed by its archenemy. The Eisenhower administration viewed it as "a bitter disappointment"; rumors of an imminent Soviet expedition to Mars swept the country, although few paused to think about what such a space trip might actually accomplish. On a more concrete level, military observers feared that space satellites could and would be used by the Russians to launch ICBMs (Inter-Continental Ballistic Missiles) against the United States, possibly even with nuclear warheads.

The United States responded quickly, launching on January 31, 1958, its own satellite, the Explorer. This was not, however, before the Russians had successfully put Sputnik II into space on November 3, 1957. The second Sputnik carried a living creature into space for the first time: a dog named Laika. (Laika died during the expedition.)

Not quite coincidentally, the Tomorrowland exhibit at the original (and then only) Disneyland in Anaheim, California, also opened in 1957. People became obsessed with the future: Optimists focused on domestically useful developments, such as the toaster oven and other convenient time-savers for the home.

The more fearful, and there were many, feared that space travel could be a two-way street.

In the late 1950s, Hollywood and the United Kingdom rolled out dozens, perhaps hundreds, of movies in which space aliens were both metaphor for the Communist threat and personifications of the fear of ... space invaders.

Here are some film titles from 1958 alone:

Attack of the 50 Foot Woman
Attack of the Puppet People
The Blob
The Fly
Flying Saucer Daffy
Earth vs the Spider
Giant from the Unknown
Hare-Way to the Stars
Missile to the Moon
Monster from Green Hell
Queen of Outer Space
Night of the Blood Beast

Meanwhile, a series of "bomb" songs began to emerge. "Atomic" came to mean "powerful" in gospel music, and in rock became a code word for "getting it on," the explosion being an obvious guise for orgasm. "Atom Bomb Baby" by the Five Stars contains the illuminating notion, "little atom bomb, I want her in my wigwam." Rockabilly was especially taken with the idea of atomic power, as represented by songs such as "Uranium Rock" (Warren Smith), "Fujiyama Mama" (Wanda Jackson), and "Rock Old Sputnik" (Nelson Young).

One of the biggest hits of 1958 was a novelty record written and sung by the country singer and actor Sheb Wooley. "Purple People Eater" told the story of a "one-eyed, one-horned" flying creature who came out of the sky. Of course, the Purple People Eater did not come to Earth to destroy it. Asked by the singer why he came to land, he replied, "I wanna get a job in a rock and roll band."

"Purple People Eater" has become something of a standard among children's performers. It was not the only hit of the era appealing to younger end of the youth demographic. David Seville's "The Witch Doctor" introduced the world to Alvin and the Chipmunks, cartoon creations who've had a remunerative career ever since. The refrain: "Oo-ee-oo-ah-ah, ting, tang, walla-walla-bing bang" was bracingly entertaining nonsense: Little Richard for tots, a perfect rock 'n' roll primer for the beat crazy eight-year-old. It is also evidence to back up the adult attitude toward rock music as moronic and infantile.

Beat Generation: *Howl* and *On the Road*

The popular TV show host and comedian Steve Allen often featured rock 'n' rollers on his program (1957), including Jerry Lee Lewis and Fats Domino. But Allen, himself an accomplished amateur jazz pianist, used his withering wit to mock the rock. His dry recitation of the lyrics to Gene Vincent's "Be Bop a Lula" as if it were the work of a significant classical poet was one instance.

Ironically, poetry was one of the main areas of expression for rebellion in the 1950s. The poets and writers of the Beat generation, as it came to be known, were not rock 'n' rollers. They were of a slightly older generation and tended to prefer jazz: the bebop innovations of saxophonist Charlie Parker and trumpeter Dizzy Gillespie, the cool of trumpeter Miles Davis, or the unpredictable innovations of brilliant composers like bassist Charles Mingus and pianist Thelonious Monk drove their cultural engine.

But the Beats provided some intellectual cover for those feeling discomfort with the prevailing public social norms of the 1950s, as depicted by popular TV shows like *Father Knows Best, Leave It to Beaver,* and *Ozzie & Harriet*: a suburban land of rational normality, in which Dad could solve any problem with a few puffs of his pipe. The idealized couple played by bandleader Ozzie Nelson and his wife, former band singer Harriet Nelson, and their two real-life sons,

David and Ricky, at least acknowledged the existence of rock 'n' roll: the Elvis-handsome Ricky often sang a song and played guitar on the show. His numerous hit recordings, from 1957's "Be-bop Baby" to "Travelin' Man" (1961) showed him to be one of the more musically talented TV-created teen idols.

Real life was messier. To the bland vision of domestic tranquility, the poet Allen Ginsberg had one word: *Howl*. The first public reading of the poem that bore the title, in 1955 at an art gallery in San Francisco, is thought by many to be the first cannon shot of the Beat Generation. First published in 1956, *Howl* begins:

> I saw the best minds of my generation destroyed
>   by madness, starving, hysterical naked,
> dragging themselves through the negro streets
>   at dawn looking for an angry fix[26]

And it continues, page after page of "relentless rhythmic litany."[27]

"Nobody had ever heard anything like that before," said the poet Lawrence Ferlinghetti, whose City Lights Books published Ginsberg's epiphany. "When you hear it for the first time, you say, 'I never saw the world like that before.'"[28]

With many explicit references to sexual organs and sexual practices, not to mention illicit drugs and the then-torturous treatment of mental illness, it was not surprising that copies of *Howl*, printed in England, were seized by U.S. Customs officials and San Francisco police on the grounds that it was obscene.

A subsequent obscenity trial was brought against Ferlinghetti, the poem's publisher. Nine literary experts testified on the poem's behalf. Supported by the American Civil Liberties Union, Ferlinghetti won the case, the court deciding that the poem was of "redeeming social importance."[29] The judge was Clayton W. Horn, a Sunday-school bible teacher.

The publicity for *Howl* made Ginsberg and the Beat Generation famous; the City Lights books edition sold more than one million copies. The City Lights bookstore became the focal point for the San Francisco literary renaissance of the fifties, and has since been a shrine to the Beat Generation. (Ferlinghetti himself is one of America's great poets; his Beat-era "A Coney Island of the Mind" was nearly as influential and commercially successful as Ginsberg's masterwork.)

A year later, Jack Kerouac's *On the Road* was published for the first time, a nonstop, amphetamine-fueled semifictional account of a trip across America in search of kicks, chicks, and jazz, with fictionalized portrayals of Ginsberg and beat hero Neal Cassady. Reading it became a rite of passage for restless young people, and it became one of the essential parts of the literary canon of the 1960s. It still has some inspirational qualities, as one young reviewer wrote on an Internet message board:

> If you've ever been young and thirsting for what life is or what it could be you have to read this. If you strip away the time period which I think is cool in itself, It's really just about friends and the mind-blowing time of living in the moment. Of meeting new people faults and all, the experience of new places and seeing the good things in them and enjoying them. And how that precious time of living in the moment must ultimately come to an end. Whether it's 1947 or 2007 how we love our youth and our friends is timeless.[30]

And unexpectedly, Ginsberg became the link between the Beat generation and the rock 'n' roll baby boomers. He was a literary influence on Bob Dylan, appeared in Dylan's "Subterranean Homesick Blues" video, in the Dylan documentary *Don't Look Back*, and in Dylan's 1977 movie *Renaldo & Clara*. His participation in Ken Kesey's acid tests in the early 1960s forged a connection between the beats and the Grateful Dead, who provided the live soundtrack. A 1965 poetry reading at Royal Albert Hall in London was in some ways day one of the contemporary 1960s in the United Kingdom, giving a cultural significance to the music of early bands like Pink Floyd and Soft Machine.[31] And his friendship with the Clash led to his appearance on their last good album, *Combat Rock*, and he continued to support indie rock groups until his death in 1997.

1957–1959: Buddy Holly, Teen Idols, Gospel, and The Coasters

One reason rock thrived while Elvis was in the Army was the emergence of Buddy Holly and his band, the Crickets. (For contractual reasons, records released by these musicians on the Brunswick label were credited to the Crickets; those on the Coral label had the name Buddy Holly. Both were subsidiaries of Decca Records.) From Lubbock, Texas, Holly & the Crickets were rock's first self-contained band: one that played their own instruments and wrote most of their material. Holly started in country music, and it shows in his rock 'n' roll: Hits like "That'll Be the Day," "Peggy Sue," and "Oh, Boy!," all released in 1957, had a solid rockin' beat and just a dollop of twang. Strangely, at the time, enough people thought that the group sounded black that the group was booked at black theaters like the Howard in Washington, D.C., and the Apollo Theater, in New York's Harlem. The audience at the Apollo was reportedly "indifferent" at first, but Holly's version of "Bo Diddley" and the adaptation of the "Bo Diddley" beat to the original "Not Fade Away" won them over.[32]

Holly and the Crickets toured incessantly, which was unusual for rock performers at a time when there were not so many opportunities to play. In early 1958, they played Australia and made a triumphant debut on March 1, 1958, as the first rock stars to perform in England. It's no surprise that the Manchester, England, beat group, the Hollies, paid tribute to his name; and the name "Beatles" was a pun on the word "crickets."

The unusually wide appeal of Holly may have been based on his regular-guy persona: he wore thick, horn-rimmed glasses and had curly hair, the antithesis of the protypical teen idol of the day. And the songs Holly and the Crickets covered, like Bobby Darin's "Early in the Morning" and Paul Anka's "It Doesn't Matter Anymore" were performed with preternatural maturity and assurance.

But here's where the story ends, momentarily. Holly, along with Richie Valens, and the Big Bopper, died in a plane crash near Mason City, Iowa, on February 3, 1959. Valens was a young Mexican-American star who had shown his versatility with a two-sided hit — a ballad, "Donna," and a Spanish language rocker, "La Bamba." The Big Bopper (disc jockey J. P. Richardson), with his trademark line "hel-lo, bay-bee!" was touring behind his hit record, "Chantilly Lace."

There had been earlier, deeply felt rock 'n' roll deaths. In 1954, the R&B singer Johnny Ace, whose hit "Pledging My Love" was one of the first R&B ballads to be picked up by white teens, shot himself to death in a game of Russian roulette, backstage before a show. But it was the Holly/Valens/Big Bopper plane crash that traumatized the nascent rock 'n' roll generation. The tragedy was memorialized as "the day the music died" by folk singer Don McLean in the epic 1971 single "American Pie." Valens was just seventeen at the time of the crash; Holly was all of twenty-two. It's possible he might have taken a convenient turn into "adult" show-business fame. His music, however, revealed the potential to lead rock 'n' roll in new artistic directions. Instead, the music had to wait until the Beatles ("Words of Love") and the Rolling Stones ("Not Fade Away") took Holly's songs, and rock, to the next level.

Eventually, grown-ups began to get the picture—that rock 'n' roll was not a fad, and not going away as quickly as some of the fads of the 1950s.

It's not that all the new entrepreneurs understood what rock was about, but they were able to make some bucks by skimming the surface. Elvis Presley was in the Army; therefore, any sensible business executive would know there was an "Elvis" gap to be filled.

A few talented singers got their break because they sounded like Elvis. One was Mississippi-born Harold Lloyd Jenkins, and if you think that's no name for a rock 'n' roll star, you are right: in 1957, Jenkins changed his name to Conway Twitty.

Signing with MGM Records, he hit No. 1 on September 29, 1958, with "It's Only Make Believe," a mournful but affecting ballad done in Elvis's soft exaggerated baritone style. Twitty also had a top-ten hit in 1960 with "Little Boy Blue," a song Presley had recorded for the movie *King Creole* but had not released. In the mid-1960s, Twitty switched full-time to country music, where he became long-lasting with romantic songs like the 1973 crossover hit "You've Never Been This Far Before."

But the name Conway Twitty alone was such a marvelous invention that it caught the ears of Broadway composer Charles Strouse, lyricist Lee Adams, and bookwriter Michael Stewart. Their musical comedy *Bye Bye Birdie* (directed by Gower Champion) was about a clueless rock star whom they named Conrad Birdie, his manager, the manager's nagging mother, and his focused, driven fiancée. *Bye Bye Birdie* debuted on Broadway in 1960 and as a movie in 1963. It is one of the most-loved and still often-performed musical comedies.

There was much to parody in the "star-making machinery" of the late-1950s music business. In one instance, according to legend, Fabiano Forte was a really handsome fourteen-year-old sitting on a stoop in Philadelphia when he was spotted by Chancellor Records boss Bob Marcucci.

Launched through the friendly graces of Dick Clark on *American Bandstand,* the renamed hunk, now called Fabian, became a big star despite the fact that he couldn't sing a lick. But he could growl, and the growling gave at least some edge a few of his string of five hits in 1959: "Turn Me Loose" and "Tiger." The degree to which this pretty face was being sold as a new Elvis is apparent in his final top-ten hit, "Hound Dog Man," also the name of the good-natured Fabian's first movie.

A whole group of teen idols conveniently based in Philadelphia appeared around the time of Fabian. Frankie Avalon and Bobby Rydell had each been in a band called Rocco & His Saints before being discovered. Rydell, probably the best singer and most rounded entertainer of the bunch, recorded for Philly's Cameo label. Rydell's best records, like "Wild One" and "Swingin' School," were just a little wild and just as swinging. But their messages were utterly conventional. The vision of life promulgated by "Swingin' School" was that you go steady, marry your high school girl friend, and buy a house with a pool and have kids who will attend that very same high school.

Rydell appeared in the movie version of *Bye Bye Birdie* as the jealous local teen boyfriend of the girl who falls in love with Conrad. Those who've seen either the movie or stage show of the 1950s nostalgia show *Grease* know that the characters attend Rydell High School.

Avalon, like Fabian, recorded for Chancellor, and had lively teen-beat hits like "Dede Dinah" and "Ginger Bread" in 1958, and crooned his way to the top with the hit "Venus," No. 1 for five weeks in a dull 1959. The successful follow-up, "Bobby Sox to Stockings," typified the tugging-at-teenage-heartstrings tune that had overcome authentic emotion in many rock recordings.

Gospel Roots of Rock and Soul

In this generally quiet time, some black singers began evolving from their gospel music roots, performing R&B that was influenced by rock 'n' roll. Sam Cooke, a lead singer of the gospel Soul Stirrers from 1950 to 1956, laid one of the bricks of the foundation of soul music with his 1957 hit, "You Send Me." With a smooth, melodious delivery, Cooke elevated the pop standards he sang, such as "(I Love You) For Sentimental Reasons" with some of the subtle sighs and gliding repetition he brought with him from the religious background. In 1959, he quickened the tempo slightly and had three noteworthy hits. "Everybody Likes to Cha Cha Cha" was a novelty about the popular, genteel Latin-tinged adult dance craze of the late 1950s that worked on its own merits as rock 'n' roll. "Only Sixteen" captured attention as a epic teen romance. "Wonderful World" began with the lines that all too many teens (and others) have been proud to repeat over the years: "Don't know much about history," Cooke sang, and proudly reeled off the list of his other academic deficiencies ... All those were recorded for independent label Keen and might have been even bigger hits had they had the promotion that Cooke's subsequent recordings for RCA did. His first RCA hit, "Chain Gang," was in retrospect a real oddity: Cooke's entertainingly wily delivery made it easy for radio programmers and many listeners to overlook the story line about prisoners working on a chain gang, the typical brutal, dehumanizing punishment for blacks (and other criminals), especially in the South, convicted of even the most mild misdemeanors.

> In "My Memoirs of Georgia Politics," Rebecca Felton relates many disturbing memories that date from the turn of the century, including the story of a black man who spent 15 years on a chain gang for stealing a shotgun, and that of a 12-year-old black boy who was given 12 years on the chain gang for borrowing a horse to go for a short ride.[33]

The chain gang, oddly, was one of the few integrated institutions in the early-twentieth-century South. In an essay about Carson McCullers's "Ballad of a Sad Café," which ends with a chain gang singing, Margaret Whitt writes:

> McCullers must have known from the world as it existed around her in Columbus, Georgia, in the first half of this century, that the chain gangs, those groups of men in black and white striped uniforms who

worked the roadside swinging picks, digging ditches, laying pipes, picking up trash, were rare visual examples of integration in an otherwise segregated South. The irony that McCullers suggests through the men's song — that they must be chained to be together to find harmony — was not lost on her.

Cooke also wrote and recorded "A Change Is Gonna Come," which became an anthem of the Civil Rights movement, shortly before he was shot to death under murky circumstances by a motel clerk in 1965.

While Cooke was the personification of cool onstage, Jackie Wilson, a contemporary of Cooke's, was more visceral and emotional. A former gospel singer and boxer, Wilson had in 1953 replaced Clyde McPhatter in Billy Ward & the Dominos, one of the great R&B groups of the pre-rock era; their 1950 hit, "Sixty Minute Man," would have sold even more millions than it did if it weren't so racy. (Wilson sang on much tamer pop hits for Ward & the Dominos, such as "St. Therese of the Roses," a top-fifteen hit in 1956.)

Wilson's presentation was dramatic, even operatic: he hit with towering ballads such as "To Be Loved" and "A Woman, a Lover and Friend." (Another hit, "Night," was based on an aria by Saint-Saens.)

But he was most explosive on up-tempo tunes, such as the 1958–1959 hit "Lonely Teardrops" and "I'll Be Satisfied," both of which were written by Berry Gordy Jr. just before Gordy started Motown Records. Wilson's "Baby Workout" was one of the high-wire moments of 1963; by the time Wilson hit the top ten with "(Your Love Keeps Lifting Me) Higher and Higher," they were calling the music Wilson was making all along "soul music."

Ray Charles also made his crossover to the pop charts in 1959, with "What'd I Say (Part I)," whose call-and-response structure duplicated the most fervent, up-tempo gospel music. In the early 1960s Charles would establish himself as the most versatile, genre-bending artist in American music, with great R&B recordings like "One Mint Julep" and "Hit the Road, Jack" in 1961, and a year later he helped invent modern country music with "I Can't Stop Loving You" and "You Don't Own Me."

But the most sophisticated rock music of the late 1950s were the comic but biting insights into the frustrations of black urban males and white teenagers, a distillation pulled off by the vocal skills of a group called the Coasters and the production, writing, and arranging savvy of Jerry Leiber and Mike Stoller.

Enter the Coasters

"We formed the Coasters the way you'd form an acting troupe to do our material. We wrote for those voices. Sometimes you sit in a room, write a song, and say, who can we get to sing it? Frank Sinatra? Ben E. King, Bruce Springsteen? But we wrote specifically for their voices, and wrote the subject matter we thought they could handle, like gag writers," Leiber told me.

Though the Coasters wouldn't come together until later in the 1950s, their roots date back to the prerock days of Leiber and Stoller's career. One of Leiber & Stoller's earliest recorded songs was "That's What the Good Book Says," in 1951, by a Los Angeles singing group called the Robins.

In 1953, with Lester Sill, Leiber and Stoller formed their own label, Spark Records, and the Robins were among their first artists. The Robins and Leiber and Stoller combined for at least three of the great performances in early rock: "Riot in Cell Block #9," "Framed," and "Smoky Joe's Cafe." These songs featured lead singer Carl Gardner and bass singer Bobby Nunn, with just the right amount of zing and attitude to sell the white teen listener on these mini-plays based on ghetto life. "Riot in Cell Block #9" obviously is about a prison uprising; "Smoky Joe's Cafe" was about the violence that flares when flirting with the wrong girl in the wrong place; "Framed" was a typical story about any young black man arrested for being in the wrong place at the wrong time.

A guest artist, Richard Berry, does the deadpan narration on "Cell Block." Berry became a legend in rock 'n' roll history as the author of "Louie Louie," one of the great party rock songs of all-time. ("Louie Louie" was also among the most frequently banned; the FBI even launched an investigation into the song, whose indecipherable lyrics were suspected of being obscene; they were not.) "Cell Block" was one of the first rock records to use sound effects: the wail of police sirens, the rat-tat-tat-tat of machine guns.

"At rock bottom it was a pure traditional blues," the late music historian Robert Palmer wrote in the liner notes to the Coasters' 1982 Atlantic Records anthology, *Young Blood*. "That stop time figure the band plays was nicked from Muddy Waters, who was enjoying his greatest commercial success as an R&B singer in 1953 with a series of tough singles on Chess."

Only "Smokey Joe's Cafe" was a hit at the time. In 1955, Atlantic Records, now led by Ahmet and Nesuhi Ertegun and Jerry Wexler, was already establishing itself as the independent R&B label with a roster and history of success that gave it major label muscle. Atlantic bought the Sparks catalog. It also hired Leiber and Stoller as pop's first independent producers.

"Leiber and Stoller were making great R&B records," Jerry Wexler said at the time according to his autobiography, *Rhythm & the Blues: A Life In American Music*, written with David Ritz. "Very idiomatic records. Not only did the records have intelligent production, they were in tune, had a good beat, and were properly balanced. And the songs also had great penetration, social understanding."

When the Atlantic deal was made, the Robins split up, some joining another label. Gardner and Nunn stayed with Leiber and Stoller. "Comedy singer" Billy Guy and tenor Leon Hughes joined the group, now known as the Coasters, in honor of the West Coast. Interestingly, naming the Coasters coincided with Leiber and Stoller and the group recording at Atlantic's studios in New York.

The payoff was prompt. One of the Coasters' first cuts, "Searchin'," with "Young Blood" on the B-side, was a two-sided hit, a million-seller that peaked at No. 3 in May 1957.

"This one record made the Coasters pop stars in white America, along with Little Richard and Fats Domino and a few other black artists who had managed to cross over."

It also marked the flowering of Leiber's storytelling style set against Stoller's precise arrangements. "Searchin'" gave prominence to the detective heroes of radio plays and comic books in the 1940s and 1950s, with shout-outs to "Sgt. Friday, Charlie Chan and Boston Blackie." Only a lyricist as audacious as Leiber could get away with rhyming "hear me comin' and "Bulldog Drummond."

"The songs really started as fragments of stories," Leiber said. "I got a lot of these ideas out of radio, early radio; the machine gun blasts at the beginning of 'Riot in Cell Block #9' is right out of the beginning of the radio serial, 'Gangbusters.'"

The Coasters hit No. 1 and nailed down a future spot in the Rock and Roll Hall of Fame with "Yakety Yak" in the summer of 1958. But 1959 would be their best year, with "Charlie Brown," "Along Came Jones," and "Poison Ivy," all immediately popular, all recognized as rock 'n' roll classics.

"Charlie Brown," the voice of Dub Jones (who replaced Bobby Nunn at this point) was the nonchalant mischief-maker personified, while his classmates, Carl Gardner and Billy Guy, watch with worried admiration: "He's gonna get caught, just you wait and see," they sing, while Charlie, cool as ever, just wonders: "Why's everybody always pickin' on me?"

"Yakety Yak" identified what would become later known as the generation gap: Parents torment their lazy, wayward, sloppy teenager — the original slacker, perhaps — with demands to "take out the papers and the trash." And by the way: "You tell your hoodlum friends outside/you ain't got time to take a ride." With split-second timing, the only response the kid can get in is, "Yakety-yak," which is met by the immediate response: "Don't talk back."

"Along Came Jones" was modeled on Leiber's beloved cliffhanger radio serials, but its topic was contemporary culture: the total dominance of prime-time TV in the late 1950s by westerns. (Another hit of the era also spoofed the trend and borrowed the Coasters' style: "Western Movies" by the Olympics.)

While many rock songs seemed disposable, recorded in haste before their sound went out of style, the Coasters records achieved their lasting success because of the quality of every step of the process.

"Each seemingly off-the-cuff stutter [was] plotted to the millisecond," Palmer writes. King Curtis, perhaps the premier R&B saxophonist of the era, was heard in almost every Coasters song. But he wasn't just on sessions to play background fills and then do brief solos. Curtis would play saxophone fills specifically written out by Stoller, "witty comments on the action, announcements of scene changes, ironic asides — Stoller wrote most of them out, often on the backs of napkins at sessions."

Jerry Leiber was once quoted saying, "We didn't make great songs, we made great records." Mike Stoller believes the context may have been misunderstood.

"We treated being producers, which we became, to protect the intention of our songs," Stoller told me. "We treated our songs as one would treat a script, or a play, and it's not fulfilled in that sense," until it is performed.

"If we had turned 'Yakety Yak' to somebody else, it would never have been what they were, because when we were writing blues, we envisioned certain kinds of performances. We thought Big Mama's 'Hound Dog' was ideal, but if we played it for somebody at Capitol or Decca, they would go make a swing record, it would be all wrong. It would not be what we wanted. So we became producers. And they were songs. We're surprised that they've lasted, never assumed they would, and they were never written with longevity and posterity in mind. They were of the moment."

Peaking as they did in 1959, Leiber & Stoller and the Coasters provided the wit and quality control that kept rock alive; in other quarters, the music had been diluted, declawed, and disregarded.

Yet as the fifties were coming to a close, rock 'n' roll was really just getting started.

THE 1960s

Kennedy and the Twist

Ask fifty people old enough to have lived through the 1960s to describe that decade and you will get fifty different answers. The common denominator of the sixties was change.

The election of President John F. Kennedy in November 1960 was the first significant change. After the grandfatherly aloofness of the Eisenhower fifties, the forty-two-year-old Kennedy was the youngest president ever elected. One of his favorite words was "vigor," and vigor is what he, his wife Jacqueline, and their family brought to the spirit of the country. Eisenhower loved to play golf, and the sporting metaphor of his presidency was a foursome of older Republican white men taking care of, or ignoring, the country's business on the links. The youthful Kennedy encouraged a more active national lifestyle. Kennedy urged fifty-mile hikes and raised standards for physical fitness. The sports metaphor for the Kennedy years was his large Irish-Catholic family, brothers and sisters and cousins and nephews and nieces, men and women, boys and girls, playing touch football on the White House lawn.

The vigor even extended to the dance floor. In Eisenhower's White House, when people danced, they waltzed. An early symbol of the youthful Kennedy administration was the embrace of the energetic rock 'n' roll dance sensation, and the record that launched it, "The Twist" by Chubby Checker.

"The Ike-dominated fifties is Gale Storm celebrating the polka, and the media sanitizing R&B for the mainstream; the JFK-dominated sixties is Chubby Checker swinging his hips, and the media popularizing the release of inhibitions,"[1] critic Michael Sragow wrote.

Ground zero for dance fads of the time was Dick Clark's Philadelphia-based *American Bandstand* show. In the pre-, pre-MTV era, the five-day-a-week after-school dance program was must-see TV and one of the only national outlets for rock music on television.

Featuring attractive, well-dressed white teenagers from Philadelphia (*Bandstand* was de facto segregated, if not intentionally so), Clark hosted and the kids danced. One popular segment was the record-review board, in which three teens would grade new records as if it were a high school exam. Clark would ask his "reviewers" what they liked about the song, and the answer would invariably be, "It's got a good beat, and you can dance to it."

"The Twist" was written by the R&B singer Hank Ballard, the talented, controversial R&B singer responsible for the erotically transparent "Work with Me Annie." However, the origins of the dance itself are somewhat murky, although it appears to have developed out of parties and clubs in the black community. One historian has it emerging out of *The Buddy Dean Show,* a local teen dance program in Baltimore, fictionalized (as *The Corny Collins Show*) by director John Waters in his period comedy feature *Hairspray.*

Another story has Ballard writing "The Twist" after watching some young people perform the dance in Tampa. Ballard and the Midnighters recorded it, but it was put on the B-side of their R&B hit "Teardrops on Your Letter," and was, as a result, almost universally ignored.

But the dance, the Twist, began spreading, and soon the Philadelphia teens who danced on Clark's *American Bandstand* fell in love with it. According to the rock historian and chart scholar Fred Bronson, in the *Billboard Book of No. 1 Hits,* it was Clark who took the idea of someone recording "The Twist" to Philadelphia's hot Cameo-Parkway label. Cameo artist Ernest Evans, nicknamed "Chubby," was a skillful impersonator of other singers, and did a dead-on imitation of Fats Domino. It was Clark's then-wife Bobbi who came up with the catchy name "Chubby Checker."[2]

"The Twist" by Checker hit No. 1 on September 19, 1960, just a few weeks before Kennedy's election in a hotly contested race against the Republican candidate, Eisenhower's Vice President, Richard M. Nixon. The 1960 campaign was the first in which TV played a major role, as it was the first to feature a series of televised debates. In terms of content, Nixon tried to emphasize his experience and command of the issues. Kennedy sought to alleviate fears about his youth and his religion. Kennedy was the first Roman Catholic to be elected president.

The only other previous Catholic presidential candidate, Alfred Smith, the governor of New York, was defeated in 1928 at least partly due to opposition by even moderate Protestant groups, which feared it could not accept "the seating of a representative of an alien culture, of a medieval, Latin mentality, of an undemocratic hierarchy and of a foreign potentate [the pope] in the great office of the President of the United States."[3] In a speech before the Greater Houston Ministerial Association in September 1960, Kennedy was obliged to declare: "I do not speak for my church on public matters, and my church does not speak for me."[4]

But many believe that the election of 1960 was decided not on policy or religion, but by the television camera. On TV, Nixon looked jowly, sweaty, beady-eyed, and in need of a shave. Kennedy was bright, beaming, movie-star handsome, and charismatic.

The Kennedy White House became, in many ways, the center of American pop culture. A televised tour of the White House hosted by Jacqueline Kennedy in 1962 was broadcast live by two of the three networks (and on tape later in the week by the third) and was watched by three-quarters of all viewers. *The First Family,* a comedy album by Kennedy impersonator Vaughn Meader (who, like JFK, was from Boston), was No. 1 for twelve weeks in 1962 to 1963 and won the 1962 Grammy Award for album of the year. Kennedy once said his favorite contemporary writer was the British novelist Ian Fleming, who had begun writing a series of books about a flamboyant, debonaire super-spy named Bond — James Bond. As the macho hero who foils Russian plots to rule the world while drinking vodka martinis and bedding gorgeous women, Agent 007 was Kennedy's fictional doppelgänger.

The original Bond movies — *Dr. No, From Russia with Love,* and *Goldfinger* were the expertly entertaining first three of the now endless, banal series — starred the Scottish actor Sean Connery as Agent 007. Bond was sexy, and so was Kennedy. Today it is difficult to imagine that a president of the United States could also be one of the nation's top male sex symbols, but it was true of Kennedy. It is also difficult to imagine Marilyn Monroe (with whom Kennedy was rumored to have been intimate) singing "Happy Birthday" in her whispery, seductive voice, to any other world leader, as she did for Kennedy. In Madison Square Garden.

The Twist was the perfect dance for this era of rugged individualism and receding sexual repression. Wiggling your hips, wagging your tail, starting erect and corkscrewing yourself into the floor: the sexual expressiveness of the Twist could not be denied. And some religious figures found it could not be ignored. "Such dances have their origin in pagan fertility dances that were performed ... as a part of immoral religious rites. And just as they were designed to arouse the sexual emotions of the participants in the religious orgies, so their modern-day counterparts contribute to the loosening of moral inhibitions."[5] "The Twist" inspired a deluge of new dances and dance records. Checker himself had "The Hucklebuck," "The Fly," "Pony Time," and "Limbo Rock." Other artists had hits with songs constructed around dances like the "Mashed Potatoes," the "Hully Gully," the "Waddle," the "Popeye," and dozens of others.

The resilience of the Twist, though, was unusual for a fad. The uninhibited fun and ease of the dance allowed it to drift up the social ladder. In 1961, celebrities and social register types began showing up at a dive bar near New York's Times Square called the Peppermint Lounge, where the house band, Joey Dee & the Starliters, had a theme song called "Peppermint Twist" that was No. 1 for three weeks in December 1961.

When record buyers embraced Checker's "Let's Twist Again" in the summer of 1961, it was clear he was onto something special. So Cameo Parkway rereleased "The Twist," and toward the end of 1961 it was back at No. 1. It is still the only record in the history of the *Billboard* charts to repeat as No. 1 after having fallen off the charts completely.

By now the distinction between the Eisenhower fifties and the Kennedy sixties was clear. Before leaving office, as the twist was first becoming popular, Eisenhower called it "vulgar." Not long after Kennedy's inauguration in 1961, the Twist was danced enthusiastically at White House events. "The Twist" continued to have an unusual collateral effect. Dozens of acts tried to jump on the Twist bandwagon. And some made great records. The black rock singer and songwriter Gary U.S. Bonds had cut three of the great party records of 1960 and 1961: "New Orleans," "A Quarter to Three," and "School Is Out." (The carefree party atmosphere of "A Quarter to Three" has been sustained and celebrated as one of the favorite encore songs for Bruce Springsteen and his E Street Band over the last thirty years.) Bonds followed with "Dear Lady Twist" and "Twist Twist Señora" in early 1962, both records able to stand on their own even if you were sitting out the dance. But they were topped by perhaps the greatest of all twist records, the Isley Bros. "Twist and Shout," a hit in the spring and summer of 1962 and, it seems, forever since.

"Twist and Shout" was a delayed sequel to the Isley Borthers.[3] "Shout" (Part 1 and Part 2). The latter song, a big R&B hit in 1959 to 1960, took the call-and-response style of gospel churches and placed it in a whooping, rocking frame. The two parts went on together for nearly six minutes; at one point, the vocals trail off into whispers ("a little bit softer now, a little bit softer now …") until the record goes silent. Then it gradually builds back up, from a whisper to a shout. It was simple enough for any band to play at a high school dance, and it was guaranteed to generate excitement.

"Twist and Shout" was a little different, tighter, more focused, more rock 'n' roll–directed in its command to "shake it up, baby." In two years, everyone would know the Beatles' version.

These twist songs showed what clever songwriters and talented performers could accomplish with rock, commercially and artistically. Rock 'n' roll, as a format, was showing unusual flexibility and adaptability. And during these years of the early 1960s, it would begin to jell even further as popular art created in the recording studio as a collaborative effort between singers, songwriters, arrangers, and, most important, producers.

Producers and Writers: The Drifters, Phil Spector, the Brill Building, and Girl Groups

The Twist and *American Bandstand* made Philadelphia the land of a thousand dances, but the center of the rock universe in the early 1960s was clearly New York. Leiber & Stoller had moved there, and Atlantic Records, which had hired them as "independent staff producers" in 1957, if such a paradox is possible, was headquartered there.

The Coasters continued to have hits written and produced by Leiber & Stoller for Atlantic's Atco label into the early sixties, the last being the relatively racy song about a belly dancer, "Little Egypt." But Leiber & Stoller were increasingly focused on another important Atlantic act that was a similarly important bridge between black and white musical cultures: The Drifters. Actually, there were two different groups called the Drifters, and the group had hits with three different lead singers over its span from 1954 to 1966. The first was an R&B vocal group led by Clyde McPhatter; their hits in the African-American market, like "Money Honey" were frequently covered by white artists, and their doo-wop version of "White Christmas" is still a seasonal favorite. McPhatter left for a successful solo career, where he made good use of his soaring, gospel-trained tenor on "Treasure of Love" (1956), "A Lover's Question," (1958) and "Lover Please" (1962). Meanwhile, the other original Drifters soldiered on, but after complaining about pay, their manager, George Treadwell, fired the whole group and hired new singers. One of them was Ben E. King, and it was with King's Drifters that Leiber & Stoller began to work in 1959.

As Atlantic's co-owner Jerry Wexler wrote in his autobiography, *Rhythm and the Blues,* Leiber & Stoller were smart enough to realize that the cheeky, ironic style so successful with the Coasters was not suitable for the more traditional Drifters.

Unlike the Coasters, with which Leiber & Stoller perfected the art of storytelling in a three-minute song, the Drifters, a vocal group from New York, were their laboratory for innovations in sound. The first Drifters hit, "There Goes My Baby," is widely credited as the first rock hit to use a full-string orchestra as backing and an unusual, sophisticated Latin rhythm known as *bayo.*

Stoller says he first came across the bayo rhythm in the title song to the movie *Anna,* a 1953 hit by the Italian singer Silvana Mangano. "There was a song in the movie, a Brazilian group playing with a triangle and a tom-tom... I loved that, the rhythm and the tom-tom beat (boom bi-boom, boom, bi-boom). Then everybody started using it, [Phil] Spector and [songwriter/arranger/producer Burt] Bacharach, and people started thinking of it as a rock 'n' roll beat," Stoller said.

The string arrangement was based on a piano melody Stoller was playing in the studio. "It sounded like Borodin or Rimsky-Korsakoff, and Jerry [Leiber] said, it sounds like a string line, and I said, why not?" So they brought in violins, cellos, a drastic grafting of "black oriented music with Caucasian," as Stoller put it.

When they played the finished recording for Ahmet Ertegun and Jerry Wexler at Atlantic, their reactions were also extreme. "Jerry Wexler threw his tuna fish sandwich all over the wall. Ahmet said, 'you guys are great, but you can't hit a home run every time.'" Wexler has said the tuna fish sandwich is apocryphal, but it does accurately reflect his negative reaction to the record. "There Goes My Baby" became a million seller, hitting No. 2 on the pop charts in 1959 and the top of the R&B chart.

Leiber & Stoller found a songwriting team for the Drifters that had some of their own odd couple flavor. The team of Doc Pomus and Mort Shuman wrote "I Count the Tears," "Sweets for My Sweet," and "Save the Last Dance for Me" for the Drifters, combining the yearning gospel-rooted vocals, the smooth but assertive harmonies, strings, and that Latin-rock-pop polyglot rhythm.

Pomus and Shuman were like mirrors of Leiber and Stoller. Both were white guys with distinctive, even opposite temperaments obsessed with R&B. (Leiber & Stoller like to recall that it was once said of them, "Leiber has no brakes; Stoller has no motor.")

Lyricist Pomus (originally named Jerome Felder), the extrovert, had performed as a R&B singer as early as 1944; he was one of the first white R&B singers. Inspired by blues shouter Big Joe Turner, he wrote Turner's 1955 hit "Boogie Woogie Country Girl." Having contracted polio as a child, he performed on crutches, and, after an accident in the 1960s, was confined to a wheelchair. The classically trained Shuman was a pianist on some of Pomus's sessions.

Besides the Drifters, Pomus and Shuman wrote nearly two dozen songs for Elvis Presley, including his early 1960s hits "Surrender" (1961), "Little Sister," and "Viva Las Vegas." (Ironically, their early hits include most of the fabricated Fabian's Elvis-style hits such as "Turn Me Loose" and "Hound Dog Man.")

Pomus & Shuman and Leiber & Stoller were no doubt the role models for the ambitious young songwriters from Brooklyn, the

Bronx, and Queens who came up from the subway knocking on doors at music industry hothouses at 1619 and 1650 Broadway; the former, known as the Brill Building, was so packed with publishers, record companies, and studios that it gave name to both the scene and the era.

> When the Brill Building opened in 1931 during the Great Depression, three music publishers rented space there. By 1962, there were more than 165 music related businesses. "There you could write a song or make the rounds of publishers until someone bought it. Then you could go to another floor and get a quick arrangement and lead sheet for $10; get some copies made at the duplication office; book an hour at a demo studio; hire some of the musicians and singers that hung around; and finally cut a demo of the song. Then you could take it around the building to the record companies, publishers, artist's managers or even the artists themselves. If you made a deal there were radio promoters available to sell the record."[6]

This was a golden age for songwriters in New York, and an important transitional phase for rock 'n' roll. On the negative side, rock lost some of its free-wheeling frontier spirit. The plus side was that its permanence was sealed when these writers drew on the earlier tradition of American popular music, known as Tin Pan Alley, and applied it to rock 'n' roll.

> The influence of mainstream American popular songwriting, embodied by the conglomerate of professional composers and publishers dubbed Tin Pan Alley, on rock's early development is sometimes overlooked. While rock 'n' roll was to a significant degree a reaction against the overly professional, sentimental, and sterile conventions of pre-rock American pop, the best of Tin Pan Alley's melodic and lyrical hallmarks were incorporated into rock 'n' roll to raise the music to new levels of sophistication.[7]

The hottest publisher was Aldon Music, started by Don Kirshner and business partner Al Nevins. Kirshner started out wanting to be a songwriter and had some early success. In an extremely rare instance of someone other than Leiber & Stoller writing for the Coasters, Kirshner authored one of the Coasters' minor hits, "Wait a Minute," with his friend Bobby Darin. But Kirshner realized he had a better ear for hits than the ability to write them, and entered music publishing. Music publishers "own" songs, which they then license to record companies. Publishers receive a fee for every record sold and every spin on the radio or TV.

In 1958, Kirshner hired Pomus & Shuman and the team of Neil Sedaka and Howard Greenfield, both prolific, successful teams that made Aldon the place to be.

And so they came: working in cubicles furnished with upright pianos, they earned around $150 a week, which was then a reasonably decent wage, the great songwriting teams of the era were forged at Aldon: Carole King and Gerry Goffin, Jeff Barry and Ellie Greenwich, Barry Mann and Cynthia Weil.

These writers were more responsible for the sound of the early 1960s than many of the artists for which they wrote. Inspiration could be found anywhere. Goffin and King's babysitter would push the young couple's baby stroller or clean the house singing about "locomotion." Goffin and King not only wrote the song, "Do the Locomotion," but the babysitter, Little Eva, sang the hit record on Kirshner's Dimension label.

Appropriately, the years from 1961 to 1963 became known as "the girl group era." From the polished, soulful Shirelles to the bad-girl prototypes the Shangri-Las, girl groups were performing the most dynamic music of the era. Each style or faction seemed to be associated with particular labels: the Shirelles' recorded for Scepter, whose president (and founder), Florence Greenburg, was the first woman to own and operate a successful pop or rock label.

The Shirelles' combination of vulnerability and sophistication, the relentless yearning conveyed by lead singer Shirley Alston and the adroitly sung "sha-la-la-la-la's" behind her were the forces behind the Shirelles' impressive run of hits, from "Will You Still Love Me Tomorrow?" the first Goffin-King composition to hit No. 1, to "Dedicated to the One I Love," "Mama Said," and "Baby, It's You," culminating with the patriotic girl-misses-guy classic "Soldier Boy."

In contrast, the Shangri-Las pined for the deceased motorcycle gang leader in "Leader of the Pack." They were recorded by George "Shadow" Morton on Leiber & Stoller's Red Bird label. The dramatic cadence of "Remember (Walkin' in the Sand)" and the aggressive swagger of

"Give Him a Great Big Kiss" gave the Shangri-Las an image that owed as much to girl gang as girl group; the songs recognized that even good girls liked bad boys, and the performances made it apparent that most boys liked bad girls: the Shangri-Las injected their tunes with a taste of rebellion and lots of teased-hair attitude.

But the girl-group era was best defined by the recordings of producer/writer Phil Spector. Barely into his twenties, Spector could still identify with the unfulfilled longings and brief euphoria shared by an increasing number of teenagers in such records as the Crystals' "He's a Rebel" and "Da Doo Ron Ron," the Ronettes' "Be My Baby," Darlene Love's "(Today I Met) The Boy I'm Gonna Marry."

Spector, whose family moved to Los Angeles from the Bronx in 1953, had been a recording artist who wrote and sang on a No. 1 record before his eighteenth birthday, "To Know Him Is to Love Him." The single's title came from the inscription on the tombstone of his father, who committed suicide in 1949. The simple, wispy ballad, by the trio the Teddybears (Spector, Carol Connors, and Marshall Leib) was No. 1 for three weeks in December 1958. Spector, however, hated performing, and he decided to follow in the footsteps of Leiber & Stoller, then at a peak, as a producer and songwriter. He became a protégé of Leiber & Stoller's former partner in Sparks Records, Lester Sill. In 1960, Sill sent Spector to New York with an introduction to Leiber & Stoller. During a brief apprenticeship, Spector and Leiber cowrote the song "Spanish Harlem," the first solo hit (1961), for Ben E. King, after King left the Drifters.

Spector's records (many released on his own Philles label) sounded larger than life on the tiniest speakers. Using the best studio musicians in Los Angeles (including such later-to-be-famous artists as guitarists Glen Campbell, Sonny Bono, and jazz musician Barney Kessel, pianist Leon Russell, and drummer Hal Blaine), Spector used swelling orchestrations and powerful percussion to create what became known as his "Wall of Sound."

Spector simply massed more musicians into a small studio space than anyone had thought of doing. A typical early 1960s Spector session might feature three drummers, three bass players, various numbers of guitarists and keyboard players, a number of brass instruments, extra background singers, and percussionists (maracas, tambourine, triangle).[8] Virgil Moorefield writes,

A more complete definition of the Wall of Sound would add to the oblig-
atory massed instrumental and vocal forces the fact that it incorporates
an augmented R&B rhythm section ... playing particular patterns; as
well as the liberal use of echo chamber and tape echo effects ... the
technique was a celebration of sonic grandeur, achieved by both physical
and technological means.[9]

But Spector was at best a volatile and eccentric personality, and as he
lavished his professional and romantic attentions on Veronica Bennett, "Ronnie" of the Ronettes (with whom he would have a stormy
marriage), his string of hits eventually dissipated.

He would have more success in the mid-1960s with the "blue-eyed
soul" of the Righteous Brothers ("You've Lost That Lovin' Feeling").
But the moody Spector turned recluse when his proudest artistic
achievement, Ike & Tina Turner's "River Deep, Mountain High"
failed to make the top forty in the United States (it was more successful in the United Kingdom). Spector "retired," although he later produced the Beatles, John Lennon solo, and the Ramones, recordings
that did not stand with any of these artists' best work. (More recently,
Spector was indicted for the murder of actress Lana Clarkson, who
was shot to death in his Los Angeles mansion on February 3, 2003.
Spector has pleaded not guilty. After numerous delays, at the time of
this writing, his case had just gone to trial.)

Spector was not the only American rock personality who found
demand for his work evaporate shortly after New Year's Day, 1964. Good
rock artists like Del Shannon, Dion (DiMucci), and Gary U.S. Bonds
were unable to keep their rock careers in first gear; neither were vocal
groups, from the Drifters to Jay & the Americans to the girl groups.

They were all swept away by what became known as the British Invasion. Only one American rock band was able to sustain its momentum
from the early 1960s and compete head to head with the creativity and
popularity of the Beatles, and the intensity of the Rolling Stones not to
mention Americans like Bob Dylan. They were the Beach Boys.

The Beach Boys: From Surf
Sounds to Pet Sounds

While the East Coast was twisting, the West Coast was surfing, not to mention revving their custom hotrods and souped-up Detroit muscle cars up and down the wide straight boulevards of Southern California. Blasting the radio, carloads of guys checking out carloads of girls and vice versa, perhaps ending the evening at one of the drive-in hamburger restaurants that had started in California.

This was teen culture as butterfly, emerging incrementally from a totally self-absorbed, self-conscious but increasingly self-aware cocoon. Magazine stories on Southern California, with its emphasis on youth culture, fads, and a booming economy, enticed millions to the "Golden State."

This was something new. Until the beginning of the 1958 season, there were no major league baseball teams west of St. Louis. That year, the former Brooklyn Dodgers began playing ball in their own new stadium built over and through the Hispanic community of Chavez Ravine in Los Angeles; the New York Giants, with perhaps baseball's greatest centerfielder, Willie Mays, in tow, left their quaint Harlem stadium called the Polo Grounds and set up shop on a windswept crag of San Francisco called Candlestick Park.

California was no longer the other coast: it was in many ways the First Coast, and no chamber of commerce could create as alluring ambassadors for California life as the Beach Boys.

The Beach Boys were brothers Brian, Carl, and Dennis Wilson, cousin Mike Love, and friend Alan Jardine. They came from Hawthorne, California (bordered on the west by the 405 San Diego freeway, and the east by Crenshaw Boulevard), not far from Los Angeles International Airport. Beginning with "Surfin' Safari"/"Surfin' U.S.A." in 1962, the Beach Boys created an idyllic vision of teenage California life that the rest of the country adored. The Beach Boys, at first, were naively derivative: "Surfin' U.S.A." was little more than a rewrite of Berry's "Sweet Little Sixteen," with new lyrics applied. (A court later named Berry coauthor.) The Beach Boys also used the reverberating, echo-heavy hard twang of surf instrumental artists such as Dick Dale and the Deltones and the Ventures. The Seattle-based Ventures were one of a handful of instrumental-only rock bands to have hits, from "Walk Don't Run" (1960) to "Hawaii Five-O" (1969), the theme of a popular TV show.

A quick succession of Beach Boys hits about drag racing ("Shut Down"), hot rods ("Little Deuce Coupe"), and high school as center of teen life ("Be True to Your School") captured the sunny optimism and more or less wholesome fun of the 1960s before President Kennedy's assassination on November 22, 1963. (Coincidentally, the Beach Boys' first somber, reflective ballad hit, "In My Room," charted the week Kennedy died.)

The Beach Boys' kindred spirits, the L.A. duo Jan & Dean, reinforced surf music's popularity with hits like "Surf City" (Brian Wilson sang background of the delights of "Surf City," which included "two girls for every boy") and "Honolulu Lulu," also in 1963.

But even on the most throwaway songs (and there were many on the early Beach Boys' albums), Brian Wilson was honing his production, arranging, and composing skills. In terms of storytelling and instrumentation, Chuck Berry was an obvious influence. It was in the painstaking arrangements and production that Wilson set himself apart from the other Beach Boys, who seemed happy to settle for being the U.S.A.'s clean-cut party band.

But Wilson was intensely competitive. He was so obsessed with matching the grandeur of Spector's "wall of sound" recordings that the Beach Boys made their records in the same venue: Western Studios in Hollywood. Wilson's exhaustive experiments in the studio gave the Beach Boys a distinctive sound.

> That's how Phil Spector did it. That's what I learned from Phil Spector. To make songs echo and stuff like that, to combine piano and guitar to make one sound. Combine horns and strings to make another sound, strings with voices to make a sound. There's all kind of possibilities in the studio.[10]

Wilson even wrote the Beach Boys hit "Don't Worry Baby" for Spector's Ronettes to record as a follow-up to "Be My Baby." Spector wasn't interested.

Wilson was also competitive with the Four Seasons, the New Jersey–based vocal group. Frankie Valli's falsetto lead vocals gave the

Four Seasons some similarity to the Beach Boys sound, and the two battled for chart supremacy, as Four Seasons hits like "Sherry," "Big Girls Don't Cry," and "Walk Like a Man" were on the radio and in the shops during the same years as the Beach Boys. (The Broadway musical *Jersey Boys* showcases the music of Valli and the Four Seasons.)

"At the end of [album track] 'Surfers Rule,' we said in the fade out, 'Four Seasons, you better believe it … I did for competitive music was Jack LaLanne did for health," Wilson wrote in the 1990 liner notes to the *Surfer Girl* album.[11]

But the arrival of the Beatles while the Beach Boys were kings of American rock had a profound impact on Wilson's competitive juices.

"The British invasion shook me up an awful lot. They eclipsed a lot of what we'd worked for … eclipsed the whole music world…. we were very threatened by the whole thing."

Though not a major break with their past, the Beach Boys' first post-Beatles hit was one of their best, and carried a wallop: "Fun, Fun, Fun" featured surf-meets–Chuck Berry guitar, and a slice-of-teen-life story line about abusing the privilege of driving dad's sports car: "And we'll have fun fun fun til daddy takes the T-bird away," was full of energy and almost defiantly intense harmonies. "Fun-Fun-Fun" was a kind of innocent response to the Beatles' "yeah, yeah, yeah!"

Remarkably, the Beach Boys did stay competitive with the British groups, one of the only American acts to not just stand toe-to-toe, but to thrive in the midst of the expanding musical British Empire. The Four Seasons hung in pretty well, too, continuing to rack up hits through 1967. The oddest was done under a pseudonym. So as not to confuse their older, not-so-rebellious working-class fans, they recorded Bob Dylan's "Don't Think Twice" as The Wonder Who?[12] though Valli's voice and Bob Gaudio's production were unmistakable.

The Beach Boys at first didn't do anything dramatic at first to keep up with the Beatles. Their harmonies became more complex, perhaps. "I Get Around" and "Help Me Rhonda," the two Beach Boys singles that managed to interrupt the British hammer lock on No. 1 during 1964, are undeniably great records, but nothing to say, "You better believe it, Beatles."

In fact, it was the Beatles' "Rubber Soul," released at the end of 1965, that spurred Wilson to greater ambitions.

JFK Assassination / The Beatles

The day: Nov. 22, 1963.

The time: 1:45 PM, EST.

The place: A ninth grade classroom. Could be anywhere U.S.A., but in this case, in a suburb of New York City.

The public address system crackles. The speaker: the Assistant Principal, Mr. Sanford.

"An event has occurred of monumental importance, with repercussions for the entire world ..."

The AP's voice was somber, and in that pause, an electric jolt of fear, all of the fears, that had been inculcated in American school kids since the 1950s finally come to life: Had Russia attacked? Had we attacked Russia? Was this World War III? Was there an accidental launch of nuclear weapons? Was there time to get home to say goodbye to our parents and siblings?

The truth seemed as bad as those other options. Sanford was tearful and terse.

" ... President John F. Kennedy has been shot in Dallas. His condition is grave. School is dismissed: go home and pray for our President, and our country."

Students exited quickly and quietly, with none of the horsing around the lockers or displays of excess teenage end-of-school energy. Walking the few blocks home, we sensed an extraordinary stillness in the air. Even on a usually quiet suburban street, the silence seemed crushing.

President Kennedy was dead. Murdered by stunningly accurate shots from a high-powered rifle from a nearby building: the Texas Schoolbook Depository, a warehouse for school textbooks. He had been riding in an open limousine with the first lady, Jacqueline Kennedy, and the governor of Texas, John Connally and his wife, in a motorcade in Dallas.

Kennedy was not popular in Texas, although he won the state in 1960 by shrewdly choosing the powerful Senator Lyndon B. Johnson as his running mate.

A current of hatred and violence was bubbling over in the United States in 1963. The reaction against the Civil Rights movement in the South was spiraling into brutality and murder.

- April 1963: Martin Luther King arrested in Birmingham, Alabama, for leading a protest. King writes his famous "Letter from a Birmingham Jail," which asserts the moral right and responsibility to disobey unjust laws.[13]
- May 1963. Birmingham's city's chief law enforcement officer, Eugene "Bull" Connor, deploys fire hoses and police dogs to attack Civil Rights marchers. The televised brutality shocks many fair-minded Americans and boosts support for Civil Rights.
- June 12, 1963. Medgar Evers, the NAACP field secretary in Jackson, Mississippi, is murdered by a gunshot at close range. A white man, Byron De La Beckwith, is arrested, but goes free after two trials with all-white juries result in no verdict. Thirty years later, however, he will be convicted of the murder.
- August 28, 1963: Martin Luther King Jr. delivers his famous "I Have a Dream" speech in front of 200,000 people at the "March on Washington" in the nation's capital. Bob Dylan and Joan Baez perform. That night, recording devices illegally installed in King's hotel room by the FBI capture the civil rights leader in an extramarital affair.
- September 15, 1963. Four young black girls attending Sunday school are killed when a bomb explodes at the Sixteenth Street Baptist Church in Birmingham.
- October 24, 1963. In Dallas, just a month before Kennedy is killed, UN Ambassador Adlai Stevenson is spat upon and struck on the head with a sign carried by a woman picketing after he delivered a speech that was disrupted by 100 right-wing demonstrators who wanted the U.S. out of the United Nations. "Ironically, Mayor [Earle] Cabell suggested that the city had an opportunity to redeem itself from the Stevenson embarrassment when the president came to town."

American life froze in mourning during the days following the assassination. The beloved president was dead. A kind of mass enervation affected millions of young Americans, whose hero was gone. It was impossible to imagine that what would lift young America out of mourning and accelerate the transformation of every facet of society was the emergence of a four-piece rock 'n' roll band from Liverpool, England, called the Beatles.

Meeting the Beatles

During the four days between Kennedy's death and his televised funeral, music disappeared from the airwaves, as the nation mourned.

Not that there was much to miss: rock had bottomed out. The number one record for much of the fall of 1963 — in fact, the No. 1 single of the year — was an effervescent trifle called "Sugar Shack," by Jimmy Gilmer and the Fireballs.

Other hits at the time of the Kennedy Assassination included the Dixieland-tinted instrumental "Washington Square" by the Village Stompers; "Deep Purple," first a hit in 1939, and sounding like something from 1949, by the brother-sister team of jazz musician Nino Tempo and singer April Stevens; and, perhaps the longest long-shot novelty hit ever, "Dominique," by a young woman from a monastery in Belgium who went to No. 1 as The Singing Nun. "Deep Purple," won a Grammy Award as best rock 'n' roll record, even though it was not a rock 'n' roll record.

Amid these torpid tunes appeared a giddily up-tempo rock song so harmonically unusual, its guitar-attack so aggressive yet agreeable, that it didn't register the first time one heard it. The second time, however, it was unforgettable. One remembers running to the radio, turning the volume up as much as possible, and feeling a delirious shiver. The song was "I Want To Hold Your Hand" by a group called the Beatles.

The Beatles were already a sensation in England. The quartet from Liverpool sold 3 million records in nine months in the United Kingdom in 1963. But their records, on EMI's Parlophone label, went unreleased in the United States; executives at EMI's Capitol label (for which the Beach Boys recorded), didn't hear any potential for the U.S. market, and so passed on releasing the 1963 U.K. hits "She Loves You," "Love Me Do," and "Please Please Me."[14]

And why would they? Culturally, pop music had always been an American export, loved overseas, and especially in England, where rockers like Chuck Berry, Little Richard, Eddie Cochran, Gene Vincent, Buddy Holly, and the Everly Brothers remained popular even after their peak in the United States. Britain had one well-known rock star of its own: Cliff Richard and his group, the Shadows. Most Americans never actually heard Cliff, who was like an Elvis without the sex appeal, which made him to American ears and eyes, quite pointless.[15]

But "I Want to Hold Your Hand" sounded different; it was different. The electric guitars bristled with energy; the beat was relentless; the harmonies were thrilling. The singer seemed to be speaking directly to the listener, in an intimate, conversational way, from the first moment: "Oh yeah, I'll tell you something, I think you'll understand ..."

The chorus, in which the singer speaks of a touch that that makes him feel happy inside, didn't sound like the same old romantic gush, especially as the harmonies cascaded up the scale to a shriek that none, in those still proper times, would call orgasmic. But that is what it was. And while most romantic rock was about boys and girls, this song pleaded to the listener to "let me be your man." The signals seemed unspoken, but clear — the Beatles wanted something deeper, more intimate and exciting, than just holding hands. Teenage girls respond by screaming hysterically, unconsolably, just at the mention of their names. This reaction was given an appropriate tag: Beatlemania.

Beatlemania hit a crescendo with the appearance of the Beatles on *The Ed Sullivan Show* on CBS-TV on February 9, 1964. In the days before cable TV — in fact, at a time when many Americans owned TV sets that would broadcast only black and white — there were hardly a half-dozen TV stations available to those who lived in major cities, and those in smaller cities, or outside major metropolitan areas, had as few as three channel choices: the networks CBS, NBC, and, sometimes, ABC. *The Ed Sullivan Show*, a U.S. staple from 1948 to 1971, broadcast an hour of variety every Sunday at 8 p.m. EST. Each show might feature Chinese acrobats, stand-up comics, an opera diva, a ventriloquist and puppet, a trained animal act, a Shakespeare soliloquy, a song by a Broadway star and a pop singer, each given three or four minutes to do their thing.

Sullivan, whose cadaverous personality made him a favorite of the many comic impersonators who appeared on his show, did have one gift: the knack for knowing what people wanted to watch. He had overcome his own reservations about Elvis Presley. Bagging the Beatles was essential.

The Beatles drew more than 73 million viewers, nearly 40 percent of the United States population. Just as the nation sat as one and mourned John F. Kennedy on television, it shared a palpable sense of joy and revitalization with the appearance of the Beatles. Two weeks later, on February 23, the Beatles appeared again, the sensation undiminished.

The CBS Television office on West 53rd Street in New York was overwhelmed by more than 50,000 requests for tickets to a studio that held 703. During their appearance, the Beatles sang five songs: "All My Loving," "Till There Was You," "She Loves You," "I Saw Her Standing There," and "I Want to Hold Your Hand."[16]

Sullivan thought he had an exclusive, but late-night talk show host Jack Paar ran BBC newsreel and performance footage of the Beatles on January 3, 1964. An enraged Sullivan cancelled the Beatles. "Fortunately, a day or two later, Sullivan realized it would be a mistake to cancel the Beatles, and … cancelled the cancellation."[17]

Like many who found the Beatles to be oddities, Paar focused on the zaniness of their haircuts: "These guys have these crazy hairdos, and when they wiggle their head, and the hair goes, the girls go out of their minds."[18]

That was no understatement. In the first major article about the Beatles published by the Sunday *New York Times* magazine on December 1, 1963, there is a photograph of a policeman attempting to force back a virtual army of teenage girls rushing the stage at a Beatles concert in Manchester, England.

"One shake of the busy fringe of their identical mop-like haircuts is enough to start a riot in any theater in which they are appearing," Frederick Lewis wrote in the *Times*.[19]

In November, his reports sounded like dispatches from a small nation on the brink of Civil War.

- 400 girls battled police for four hours trying to get tickets for a show in Carlisle.
- Numerous broken bones were reported during the Beatles first visit to Dublin. "The mania descended into barbarism," said the chief of police.[20]
- During rehearsals for a show at the London Palladium, the Beatles were marooned for thirteen hours because the rioting girls made it unsafe, in the opinion of the police, for them to leave the building.
- In order to exit a mob in Birmingham, the Beatles had to disguise themselves as policeman, "complete with capes and helmets."

If they were stressed, the Beatles never showed it. Their shows were full of hilarious ad libbing. A penchant for skewering the pretensions of the establishment revealed itself early. At a Royal Family's annual charity benefit concert in 1963, John Lennon told the audience: "Those of you in the cheaper seats can clap your hands during the next number. The rest of you can rattle your jewelry."

The adoration of the Beatles by teenage girls perplexed many males, who thought the Beatles' haircuts to be effeminate. The hair softened the Beatles' Liverpool-bred machismo; it gave them a tool that provided a changing definition of what constituted masculinity, just one of many social and cultural mores the Beatles would affect.

How did they start? They were the first of a generation who had seen Elvis Presley on television and wanted to rock 'n' roll like that. During the 1950s, the most popular music craze in England was known as skiffle. It Anglicized American folk and blues, as well as drawing from the English Music Hall tradition. And in impoverished midcentury England, the equipment was cheap. "All that was needed was a Spanish guitar, a snare drum, a stand-up bass made from a broom handle attached to an empty tea-chest, and two chords."[21]

John Lennon started a skiffle group, the Quarrymen. Lennon said that the day he met McCartney, he asked him to join the band.[22]

More important, like many English teens, the Beatles were infatuated with the sound of American rock, and R&B from the 1950s: Chuck Berry and Little Richard, certainly, but also the Isley Brothers (whose "Twist & Shout" was a staple of the Beatles' repertoire). And there were the Shirelles. The Beatles recorded both the romantic "Baby, It's You," and the frisky "Boys" (the B-side to "Will You Love Me Tomorrow" in the states) was one of Ringo Starr's first of a number of occasional lead vocals. It is indicative of the Beatles' gutsiness and confidence that they did not change the gender of the song when recording it: the Shirelles were girls singing about how much they liked boys; the Beatles were men singing about how much girls liked boys. The Beatles were bold enough that they had no problem with the point of view at all.

The Beatles wrote most of their own songs, and that in itself was a breakthrough. (Presley did not compose any of his own material; if you see his name credited to a song, it is likely that the real songwriter had to give up some rights to Presley in order for him to record it.) Following the lead of 1950s rockers who did write their own songs, such as Chuck Berry, Little Richard, and Buddy Holly (whose band, the Crickets, was the basis of the pun that gave the Beatles their name), the Beatles stood apart with compelling originals from the very start.

There was no gradual momentum to the Beatles' takeover of the American rock scene: it was immediate, intense, all-consuming. Three different Beatles songs topped the charts for fourteen consecutive weeks in the winter and spring of 1964: "I Want to Hold You Hand" was followed by "She Loves You" and "Can't Buy Me Love."

Not knowing how long this Beatles bubble would last, Capitol and other labels, such as Vee-Jay and Swan, that had bought U.S. distribution rights to some of the 1963 U.K. Beatles hits, flooded the market with Beatles singles. And the market swallowed them all. The first week of April 1964, the Beatles held all of the top five positions on the *Billboard* Hot 100: "Can't Buy Me Love," "Twist and Shout," "She Loves You," "I Want to Hold Your Hand," and "Please Please Me." The following week, the Beatles had an unheard of fourteen songs on that Hot 100. And they were starting to bring some friends with them.

The British Invasion, 1964–66

Propelled by the Beatles, sweeping across the Atlantic Ocean with the cockiness that the British Navy once displayed as it colonized half the world, were the hundreds of rock bands — there were 300 or so in Liverpool alone at the time — to meet the frantic, insatiable craving for anything British.

Bands from Liverpool were especially welcome. There were Gerry & the Pacemakers, who romanticized their grimy hometown in "Ferry Cross the Mersey."

The Searchers, perhaps the best of the rest of Liverpool, literally followed the Beatles' footsteps, even performing in the Star Club in Hamburg, Germany. That was where the Beatles performed the rugged early 1960s residency that toughened them for the big time: six sets or more a night, in front of tough, sometimes violent, alcohol-sodden audiences forced the Beatles to forge their tight sound, and hone their survival skills. (Ringo Starr had not yet joined the group during the German boot camp; the Beatles' drummer was Pete Best, who was dismissed from the group on the brink of success because he didn't have the look, or provide the chemistry, that would have put the Beatles over the top.)

The Searchers had an excellent run of hits, mostly soft but savvy renditions of American R&B hits, including Pomus & Shuman's "Sweets for My Sweet" and Leiber & Stoller's "Love Potion Number 9." The capable Searchers also drew on Phil Spector associates Sonny Bono and Jack Nitzsche for their first U.S. hit, "Needles and Pins," and boosted the career of American songwriter Jackie DeShannon with their version of "When You Walk in the Room," both from 1964.

Groups aimed at the large younger, female segment of Beatlemaniacs were relentlessly hyped by top-forty disc jockeys and fan magazines like *16* and *Tiger Beat*. Such trivial bands included Freddie and the Dreamers; "I'm Telling You Now" was No. 1 for two weeks in March 1965. They had three more top-forty hits in the next six weeks, (including "Do the Freddie," a spazzy dance number), and then they were done.

Herman's Hermits, of Manchester, had a longer run of hits, into 1967, with well-crafted songs ("I'm Into Something Good," "No

Milk Today") as well as nonsensical novelties like the 1911 music-hall tune "I'm Henry VIII, I Am" and "Mrs. Brown You've Got a Lovely Daughter." The Hermits were built around their adorable lead singer, Peter Noone. (There was no one named Herman.) The Dave Clark 5 were one of the more underrated beat groups of 1964–1966. "Glad All Over" and "Bits and Pieces" had a pneumatic beat (Clark was the drummer), and their streak of fifteen or so short, snappy hits made them always welcome on the radio. The attractive, engaging DC5 even starred in a 1965 movie, *Having a Wild Weekend,* that elicited favorable if inflated comparisons to *A Hard Day's Night.*

While Herman's Hermits and Freddie and the Dreamers succeeded with typical pop songs, the more rugged and lasting English bands shared the Beatles' admiration and respect for the American blues and R&B acts who had been taken for granted or forgotten in their own country. The Animals, the Yardbirds, the early Moody Blues, and others introduced the mass American rock audience to their own culture. Even the two most original, distinctively British bands that formed in this era — the Who and the Kinks — gave their proper bow to R&B before their respective leaders, Pete Townshend and Ray Davies, developed their own personal, purely Anglocentric songwriting styles. Standing apart was a group from Ireland simply called Them, and they may have been the most robust of this new wave of R&B acts, behind the singing and harmonica playing of their irrepressible leader, Van Morrison.

The Animals, one of England's best blues-based bands and quite successful during the British mania of 1964 to 1965, first hit in 1964 with pianist Alan Price's arrangement of the frequently recorded folk blues standard "House of the Rising Sun." The gruff lead singer, Eric Burdon, was no delicate pretty boy, and he gave a forceful authority to songs by American black musicians, notaby John Lee Hooker ("Boom Boom"), Sam Cooke ("Bring It On Home to Me"), and Bo Diddley ("Story of Bo Diddley").

But one of their biggest hits, in the summer of 1965, was "We Gotta Get Out of This Place," a convincing song about the claustrophobia of poverty. That it was written by the husband-wife team of Barry Mann and Cynthia Weil showed how well even the Brill Building writers had become at composing contemporary R&B. Another great, angry

Animals track, "Don't Bring Me Down" (1966), was written by Carole King and Gerry Goffin. And while bands carrying the name of keyboard player Manfred Mann became renowned for popular, creative covers of Bob Dylan songs, they established themselves as the quintessential British Invasion beat group in 1964 with Jeff Barry and Ellie Greenwich's "Do Wah Diddy Diddy."

The Yardbirds were another British band that stayed as true as it could to the blues roots. The band is noteworthy for exposing and developing the three of British rock's greatest guitarists: Jeff Beck, Eric Clapton, and Jimmy Page. Those three went on to dominate the late 1960s and early 1970s British rock as leaders or key players of important acts. The Jeff Beck Group introduced a shy but gifted singer, Rod Stewart; Clapton formed the tempestuous, short-lived but influential improvisational blues-rock Cream; and Page, putting together musicians for a tour as the New Yardbirds, instead stumbled upon the creation and perfection of heavy metal with Led Zeppelin.

Beck, Clapton, and Page were the first to make the electric guitar player the focus of a band, the exemplars of a line of rocker that didn't exist before: the instrumental virtuoso. Their ability and flamboyance set the table for the emergence in 1967 of the greatest guitar hero of them all, Jimi Hendrix.

Another group that floated in on British Invasion stood apart from the Beatles and the rest, especially in terms of both talent and attitude.

They were among the devout followers of American blues and R&B. They weren't as adorable as the Beatles, but that was all right. The Beatles were charming enough to play before the Queen; the others were more likely to be guests of her majesty's hospitality — in an English jail.

They were the Rolling Stones.

The Stones — singer Mick Jagger, guitarists Keith Richards and Brian Jones, bassist Bill Wyman, and drummer Charlie Watts — were the bad boys to the Beatles' good lads. One of their most notorious stunts was Jagger, Richards, and Wyman getting arrested for urinating on the wall of an East London gas station. Of course, it was no coincidence that a London newspaper photographer just happened to be "passing by": It was one of many of the controversy-building publicity ploys of their manager and producer, Andrew Loog Oldham.[23] It helped create a mystique of menace that no other rock 'n' roll band has ever quite matched.

While the Beatles faced the press with wit and aplomb, the Stones were sullen, aloof, and angry. In a 1965 TV interview with the Canadian Broadcasting Corporation, interviewer Larry Zolf notes their "vulgar, obstinate and hostile behavior," and the Rolling Stones couldn't have agreed more, or cared less. [24]

But like the Beatles, the Rolling Stones earned their place in the rock pantheon with their music. Their first single, "Come On," in 1963, was a cover of a little-known Chuck Berry song. Jagger, from an affluent London suburb, sounded as if he'd been raised on the banks of the Mississippi River, so well had he internalized Chuck Berry's border-state drawl. And Richards, who would be known as Berry's greatest guitar acolyte (Richards would produce the 1987 Chuck Berry film biography/documentary *Hail! Hail! Rock 'n' Roll*) had learned the master's distinctive stroke and uncanny timing.

The second Stones single and first hit, "I Wanna Be Your Man," was written for them by Lennon and McCartney.

Soon the Stones were hitting the charts with songs by Buddy Holly ("Not Fade Away"), American R&B star Bobby Womack ("It's All Over Now"), and New Orleans singer Irma Thomas ("Time Is On My Side"). They also showed a devotion to Chicago's Chess Records sound (for which Berry recorded), and dipped deep into the catalog of the great Chicago blues composer Willie Dixon. For many Americans (and young Brits, no doubt), this was the first they had heard songs recorded by Muddy Waters and Howlin' Wolf.

Jagger and Richards tentatively began writing their own songs. One early semi-original was "Little by Little," written on a hallway piano in a London studio by Jagger with Phil Spector, who played maracas on the track. (The writer credits are Nanker Phelge and Spector; Nanker Phelge was the pseudonym for the earliest written work by the Stones and manager Oldham.)

Jagger and Richards became productive as a writing team in 1964, concentrating on bluesy ballads like "Tell Me (You're Coming Back)," their first U.S. hit, and "Congratulations," a sullen, sarcastic sulk that conveyed more than its weight of flicking-your-cigarette-butt machismo.

These are the songs that had the girls screaming for the Stones no less aggressively than they did for the Beatles. What was remarkable about both groups — and a key to understanding the creative ferment that was about to explode in the mid-1960s — was that they were solid, exciting, original rock bands from the very beginning. But no one imagined how much greater they and so many spirited colleagues and rivals, would become.

The Kinks

Depending on whom you ask, the Kinks are either the best, second best, third best, or fourth best British rock group spawned in the sixties. With the Beatles and Rolling Stones at the undisputed top of the heap, many consider the Who and the Kinks just a notch below in terms of artistic achievement and rock-historical importance. (A small but amusingly fanatical coterie of Anglophiles consider the Who and Kinks to be number one and number two, or number two and number one.)

The Kinks since 1964 have been built around the rhythm guitar, songs, and vocals of Ray Davies. The original band also included brother Dave Davies, lead guitar; Pete Quaife, bass; and Mick Avory, drums. Their first hit in 1964, the basic hard-rock rave up "You Really Got Me," is among the most celebrated anthems of the decade, a kind of "eureka" example of the potency of two primitive chords (G A G A) played in attack mode. As the Web site chordie.com writes of "You Really Got Me": "Words and music by Ray Davies; performance by any garage band in the world."

The similarly frantic "All Day and All of the Night" and the smart mid-tempo "Tired of Waiting" showed the Kinks to be hit-makers of the first order. But Davies kept raising his level of ambition. And "A Well-Respected Man" and its follow-up, "Dedicated Follower of Fashion" were sarcastic digs at British middle-class superficiality that were part of Davies's early blossoming as an acutely aware, ironic observer of the tragicomic details of British life.

The Kinks were unable to capitalize on these hits in the United States. Major management and record company misjudgments, a reputation for being difficult, erratic, and sometimes intoxicated onstage culminated with the Kinks being denied visas to perform in the United States for four years. But, as a detailed BBC biography points out, "away from summers of love, hippies and acid, Ray was able to concentrate on writing songs about the English way of life."[*]

And so he did, with sensitivity and skill. *Face to Face*, in 1966, was the first Kinks album consisting entirely of original songs. (Ironically,

---

[*] Excellent Kinks bio covering 1963-1970 on the BBC Web site http://www.bbc.co.uk/dna/h2g2/A11690994.

the Kinks were terrible at covering the American R&B songs most commonly used as filler on British Invasion albums; from the beginning their original tunes were invariably superior). The single "Waterloo Sunset" in 1967 may have been ignored in the United States, but it was a major hit in England. "Davies considered the song a professional milestone, where he managed to blend the commercial demands of a hit single with his own highly personal style of narrative songwriting."*

Brilliant as Davies's songs were, his cool, distant cynicism was not embraced by many young American rock fans in the optimistic days of 1966 to 1967. Young Americans, at the time, were engaged in ignoring, rebutting, or destroying the class system that trapped many Britons. Though the Kinks were among the earliest presenters of thematically cohesive concept albums — *The Kinks Are the Village Green Preservation Society* (1968) and *Arthur or the Decline and Fall of the British Empire* (1969) — their efforts were often trumped by the literally louder work of Brittania's thunderously brilliant the Who, who began 1968 with their own concept album, *The Who Sell Out*, a broad parody of advertising and commercialism. And while the rock opera *Arthur* was a solid piece of work, it had none of the grandiosity, ambition, and fury of the Who's breakthrough, *Tommy*.

After 1966, in fact, it was not until *Lola Versus Powerman and the Moneygoround, Part One* (1970) that a Kinks album even broke the top 100 again in the United States, led by the unlikely hit single "Lola," about a romantic encounter with a transvestite.

But America soon returned to its unfortunate habit of ignoring the Kinks; *Muswell Hillbillies,* considered by some to be their greatest album, was released in 1971 and peaked at an unmagical No. 100. This time, the concept was urban renewal in the London neighborhood where the Davies had grown up. "I was born in a welfare state ruled by bureaucracy," Davies sings in "20th Century Man," on which he presciently focuses on the dehumanizing effects of technology. "Ruing the present is a common Davies theme," critic and Kinks devotee Ira Robbins wrote in the program for the band's induction into the Rock and Roll Hall of Fame in 1989.

Though the Kinks continued to tour with theatrical presentations of concept albums (*Preservation Acts I and II* and *Soap Opera*), it was the artfully crafted, witty song albums like *Sleepwalker* (1977), *Misfits* (1978), and *Low Budget* (1979) that finally captured mainstream American rock fans. The Kinks' mordant, underdog world-

---

* Wikipedia entree on "Waterloo Sunset" seems credible backed by other research. http://en.wikipedia.org/wiki/Waterloo_Sunset.

view allowed the group to flourish and be, perhaps, one of the few sixties groups to be respected by the punks, especially by London-based stalwarts of the class of '77 like the Jam.

"Massive influence on me," Jam founder Paul Weller said. "I love the Kinks, love Ray Davies. He's just a fantastic English writer, man. He's one of the few people from the '60s who were actually writing about English subject matter. With the Beatles, it's more kind of universal themes you know. But Ray is very English and often very sort of London. He's a great man of melody as well."* The 1978 version of the Kinks' "David Watts" was released as a single and is one of the highlights of the Jam's *All Mod Cons* album. Interestingly, this was just around the time that for the first time, the Kinks were more popular in the United States than the United Kingdom. The same year, "You Really Got Me" was revived by the U.S.' newest mainstream hard-rock darlings, Van Halen, as the band's first single. Another Davies composition, the early Kinks tune "Stop Your Sobbing," was the first single by the Pretenders, in 1980. That was the year Davies and Chrissie Hynde began a love affair that lasted into 1983, when their daughter Natalie was born. The Kinks' biggest U.S. hit to date was "Come Dancing," from the 1983 album *State of Confusion*.

Davies published *X-Ray*, which he humorously described as an "unauthorized autobiography" in 1995, and was the debut artist in 1996 for cable channel VH1's "Storytellers" series. In 2006, Davies again avoided the spotlight with the album, *Other People's Lives*, which though favorably reviewed returned him to the highly public obscurity to which he had long been consigned.

---

* *Harp* magazine Jan./Feb. 2005 issue interview with Paul Weller of the Jam, speaking about the Kinks and Ray Davies, by Robert Baird. http://harpmagazine. com/articles/detail.cfm?article_id=2574

1965: Good Times, Bad Times

Perhaps no year in modern history contained the explosive brilliance of the music of 1965. The Beatles continued to confound their original doubters, and delight an increasing number of fans by increasing the sophistication in their songwriting without losing any of their charismatic appeal.

They had already left adult culture critics scratching their head in wonder with their delightful first movie, *A Hard Day's Night*, in 1964. Directed by Richard Lester, one of the United Kingdom's most gifted filmmakers, and shot in black-and-white, the movie was an often uproarious pseudo-documentary send-up of Beatlemania itself.

The startled reaction of *New York Times* movie critic Bosley Crowther, a man whose tastes and writing style were as starchy as his name, was typical. Calling it "a whale of a comedy," he admitted, "I wouldn't believe it, either, if I hadn't seen it with my own astonished eyes, which have long since become accustomed to seeing disasters happen when newly fledged singing sensations are hastily rushed to screen."

Yet Crowther found *A Hard Day's Night* to be "a wonderfully lively and altogether good-natured spoof of the juvenile madness called 'Beatlemania.'"[25]

He didn't understand the Beatles music: "To ears not attuned to it, it has a moronic monotony," he wrote. But into 1965 and certainly by 1966, many serious culture guardians had surrendered to the group's musical artfulness.

In fact, during a slight lull in Beatlemania (before they would shatter all records by selling out 55,000-seat Shea Stadium in August 1965), it was suggested their popularity was fading because they had become so accepted by adults and other responsible people.[26]

The Rolling Stones were one of the beneficiaries of such a swing, if it really existed. "The Stones, as they are called, have a rough, wild style in which everyone seems to go his own way, which is a far cry from the precise homogeneity of the Beatles," is the way one social critic put it.[27]

The Stones' expert mimicry of black styles brought to the surface the oldest question in American popular culture: What do white artists owe to their black predecessors? Are such cultural appropriations tribute or plunder, respect or exploit?

Irma Thomas's first reaction to hearing the Rolling Stones do "Time Is On My Side" reflects the longtime ambivalence many black performers feel about being covered and discovered by white artists. "At the time they did it, I was about 23 years old, very naive, and I was a bit miffed," Thomas told me in a telephone interview.[28] "My career was just starting to show some promise, and then came along the British invasion, and at that time, it didn't necessarily have to be good, as long as it was British ... We as American artists were darn good performers, and I felt my version of 'Time is on My Side' was far better than theirs, but I wasn't British, and I was black, so there were two strikes against me." Thomas paused to add: "Of course, over the years I've reconsidered, and I'm not so upset anymore."

Protest Music And Bob Dylan

One of the most left-field hits in the hyperfertile summer of 1965 was "Eve of Destruction" by Barry McGuire. The gravel-throated former member of the New Christy Minstrels (he wrote and sang lead on their up-tempo hit "Greenback Dollar") delivered this recitation of impending doom with fearful conviction.

Some listeners no doubt thought "Eve of Destruction," written by a twenty-year-old Los Angeles songwriter named P. F. Sloan, a kind of hilarious, over-the-top novelty. Others thought it perfectly dramatized the mood of a world in transition. In any case, it was unprecedented for a No. 1 record with a dirgelike beat to begin with such lines as:

> The eastern world it 'tis explodin',
> violence flarin', bullets loadin',[29]

As McGuire's Web site puts it, "Unlike the cheery tunes of the Christys, "Eve of Destruction" was a grave, prophetic warning of imminent apocalypse. It was a song that expressed the frustrations and fears of young people in the age of the Cold War, Vietnam, and the arms race."

"Eve of Destruction" also signified an emerging fissure in American society. The song was banned on some radio stations; its message of utter pessimism had never been so strongly conveyed on pop radio. McGuire and his writers were decried as traitors by some, naive Communist sympathizers who undermined the Vietnam War effort and were dupes of the alleged left-wing "agitators" resistant southerners blamed for the Civil Rights movement. A right-wing, patriotic response, "Dawn of Correction," was recorded by a group called the Spokesmen; it charted briefly in October 1965 before disappearing.

"Eve of Destruction" would have been impossible without Bob Dylan, even though Dylan in 1965 had moved beyond the topical folk anthems of the early 1960s and was on his way to becoming an unexpected king of rock 'n' roll, sharing the pantheon with the Beatles and Rolling Stones.

Dylan, born Robert Zimmerman, grew up in isolated Hibbing, Minnesota. He played guitar in some high school bands, and briefly made a name for himself in the "Dinkytown" coffeehouse section of Minneapolis, where he hardly bothered attending the University of Minnesota.

Like many folk singers in the late 1950s, Dylan headed to New York City's Greenwich Village neighborhood, where there was a burgeoning folk music scene. One of Dylan's heroes was the folksinger and activist Woody Guthrie, and one of Dylan's missions was to visit Guthrie, dying of Huntington's chorea, a central nervous system disorder, in a hospital near New York City, and play him an original composition, "Song for Woody."[30]

Dylan expresses a vision that would recur in his early tunes, singing about a world that is "sick an' it's hungry an' it's tired and it's torn," one that is "dyin' an it's hardly been born."[31]

"Song to Woody" was one of the few originals on *Bob Dylan,* his 1962 debut album for Columbia. But he wasn't just a Guthrie clone.

In the first volume of his autobiography, Dylan describes his ambition, in typically elliptical fashion:

> I needed to learn how to telescope things, ideas. Things were too big to see at once, like all the books in the library, everything laying around on all the tables. You might be able to put it all in one paragraph or into one verse of a song if you could get it right.[32]

Dylan was signed to Columbia Records by the legendary talent scout John Hammond, whose earlier signings included Billie Holiday and Count Basie, and later signings included Bruce Springsteen. Columbia at that time was known for elaborately orchestrated adult pop: Tony Bennett, Andy Williams, Jerry Vale. "His first album at Columbia didn't sell well and, outside of Hammond and a few others, most people at Columbia thought he was a freak," according to Clive Davis.[33] What set Dylan apart from the pack of New York folksingers was the explosive originality and incandescent power he could achieve with an acoustic guitar, a harmonica held in a brace, and the prophetic power of both his words and delivery. His topical songs made him famous. "Masters of War" seethes with contempt for those who profit by building weapons. "A Hard Rain's a-Gonna Fall" has an almost biblical cadence, as Dylan sings, "I heard the roar of a wave that could drown the whole world." And "Blowin' in the Wind," a sweetly sung pop hit for the folk trio Peter, Paul & Mary in 1963, became an anthem of the Civil Rights movement. The record's success was a hint of changing winds itself: a hit record about Civil Rights?

But Dylan was driven by a greater destiny. Asked to define "destiny," Dylan told CBS-TV's Ed Bradley it was "the picture you have in your mind of what you're about will come true."[34]

Being a controversial, if beloved, folksinger was not the destiny Dylan saw: "I was heading for the fantastic lights," he told Bradley. They would turn out to be the same lights that made a poor southern boy from humble roots into Elvis Presley, the same lights that four young men from Liverpool saw as they became not just a rock band, but the Beatles.

The Beatles had the same impact on Dylan as they did everyone else: He knew they had freed the genie, the bottled-up spirit of rock 'n' roll that had been missing since the first few months of Elvis Presley's career. The same age as the Beatles (Dylan was born in 1941, John Lennon in 1940, Paul McCartney in 1942), they were war babies, not baby boomers, a shared connection to a world dying yet hardly born.

On his March 1965 album, *Bringing It All Back Home,* Dylan began shaking up the distinctions between folk, rock, and blues. "Subterranean Homesick Blues" featured stinging guitar licks and rollicking keyboards, a swinging rhythm section, and Dylan's playfully surreal lyrics. (Unlike current rock performers, who release albums every two or three years, the biggest stars of the 1960s would release two or even three albums each year.) The album also included "On the Road Again," "Outlaw Blues," and "Bob Dylan's 115th Dream." It was an album containing, as author and Dylan scholar Greil Marcus writes dryly, "noisy rock 'n' roll songs ... along with others that were not noisy."[35]

A transitional album, if you will. But then again, everyone and everything were in transition in 1965. As Marcus points out, there were 27,000 American soldiers in Vietnam at the beginning of the year, 170,000 by its end.

On March 7, more than six hundred Civil Rights advocates attempted to march from Selma, Alabama, to the state capitol, Montgomery, for the right to vote. Led by the Rev. Dr. Martin Luther King, the marchers attempted to walk across the Edmund Pettus Bridge in Selma. They were met head-on by baton-swinging riot police and state troopers with bullwhips, tear gas, and attack dogs. The brutality of the confrontation, on the TV news, shocked white Northerners and shamed more than a few white Southerners.

1965: The Beatles, the Rolling Stones, Bob Dylan, and the Beach Boys Chase Each Other's Legacies

You wouldn't know it by looking at the charts, but the Beatles were in a rut. They had "Help!," the title song from their wonderfully entertaining second movie, and "Ticket to Ride," from the *Help!* soundtrack, which some found mildly disappointing because it had five instrumentals and just seven songs with vocals. The Beatles also caught listeners off-guard with "Yesterday," in which McCartney's singing and acoustic guitar is backed only by a string quartet. ("Yesterday" was on the U.K. version of the *Help!* soundtrack; in the United States, it was released as a single, with Ringo singing Buck Owens's country-music hit "Act Naturally" on the other side.) With its uncannily original melody and rueful lyrics, it marked a breathtaking step in the band's evolution, more complex than any of the wonderful, simpler Beatlemaniac tunes from a year earlier.

But the Beatles were keenly aware that summer of 1965 that Dylan was outwriting them, the Rolling Stones outrocking them. Even the Beach Boys were on their trail with increasingly spellbinding studio sounds. Like the Beatles would do in 1966, the Beach Boys' Brian Wilson had already stopped touring to concentrate on studio recordings. Rock 'n' roll was becoming a studio art, propelled by both the imagination of the artists and the technically savvy of their producers and engineers.

The Beatles had set off such an explosion of creative expression in pop music that had they not grown, they would have become irrelevant. The summer of 1965 was a pinnacle, for pop, rock, and soul:

never had so many records covering such a range of styles combined artistic excellence and mass popularity been issued in such a concentrated time period.

And there were new styles, or subgenres. One of the year's biggest hits was Phil Spector's production of "You've Lost That Lovin' Feelin'" by the Righteous Bros. The duo, Bobby Hatfield and Bill Medley, were clean-cut guys from Orange County in Southern California. They were regulars in the cast of *Shindig!*, one of the few TV programs spotlighting rock music in the sixties. Alternating lines, Hatfield's voice soared high; Medley's rumbled low: for choruses, their harmonies met in the middle. With its low, slow introduction, Spector built his "wall of sound" to new heights; the Righteous Bros. sang with so much gospel fervor that a disc jockey dubbed their sound "blue-eyed soul," a phrase used to describe any white act whose sound embraced R&B. Other exponents were the Rascals, and Mitch Ryder & the Detroit Wheels. The best-selling duo Hall & Oates was the quintessential blue-eyed soul group of the 1970s. The term didn't carry negative connotation; it was considered a compliment, though it did provide another example of the acuteness of racial awareness at the time.

"Soul music," was now the term to describe R&B. And 1965 was the year of soul music's great crossover, when it broke out of black neighborhoods and radio stations to mainstream America. Motown hit top-forty radio like a flood: "My Girl" by the Temptations, "Reach Out (I'll Be There)" by the Four Tops, and "Stop! In the Name of Love" by the Supremes were among the years great records, as were hits by Marvin Gaye ("I'll Be Doggone"), the Miracles ("Tracks of My Tears"), Jr. Walker & the All-Stars ("Shotgun"), and Martha & the Vandellas ("Nowhere to Run").

Beyond Motown, James Brown was riding high with the revolutionary rhythm of "Papa's Got a Brand New Bag" and "I Got You." Other gospel-rooted acts, such as Solomon Burke ("Got to Get You Off My Mind"), Wilson Pickett ("In the Midnight Hour"), the Impressions ("People Get Ready"), Sam Cooke ("Shake"), Fontella Bass ("Rescue Me"), and Little Milton ("We're Gonna Make It") were also heard on top-forty radio.

American musicians showed their creativity and enhanced their marketability by imitating British bands. Listeners thought that the Sir Douglas Quintet, from Texas, and the Beau Brummels from San

Francisco, were from the U.K. (Counterpunchers also surfaced, like Paul Revere and the Raiders, from the Pacific Northwest, and Jay and the Americans, from New York.)

Most people thought the Byrds were British, too, from the quaint spelling to the long hair to the mod clothing to the narrow-framed, rectangular glasses of leader Jim (later known as Roger) McGuinn. But the Byrds were the toast of Los Angeles, and they, too, created something entirely new by fusing styles that had not been paired before. "Before the Byrds recorded 'Mr. Tambourine Man,' there was folk music and there was rock music," Fred Bronson wrote. Plugging in his trademark twelve-string Rickenbacker guitar, and harmonies on top of the Bob Dylan song, McGuinn, with Byrds David Crosby, Gene Clark, Chris Hillman and Michael Clarke all providing harmony, created folk-rock.

The Byrds' next hit in 1965 was also a Dylan song. "All I Really Want to Do" sweetened with harmonies a sarcastic song Dylan had performed raw, solo and acoustically on his *Another Side of Bob Dylan*. The Byrds' third hit of the year was "Turn, Turn, Turn," their plugged-in version of a Pete Seeger folk song adapted from the Old Testament's book of Ecclesiastes. The Byrds, whose personnel seemed to change with the seasons, also evolved with the times. "Eight Miles High" in 1966 augured the psychedelic-rock era. Their 1968 album, *Sweetheart of the Rodeo* is one of the foundations of country rock, featuring two then-lesser-known Dylan songs, "You Ain't Goin' Nowhere" and "Nothing Was Delivered."

The New York folk-rock duo of Simon & Garfunkel found themselves stars almost by accident. In 1964, they had recorded an acoustic folk album called *Wednesday Morning, 3 AM* for Columbia Records. One album track was "Sounds of Silence," a hushed reverie about the gap between 1960s youth and adults, with precocious images. Its most memorable line: "The words of the prophets are written on the subway walls and tenement halls." (Simon composed the songs, played rhythm guitar, and sang harmony; Garfunkel was the lead singer with an angelic high voice.) When there was little reaction to the *Wednesday Morning* album, the group split up. After all, they had been working together since 1957, when, as Tom & Jerry, they had a minor doo-wop hit called "Hey Schoolgirl." After the split, Simon went to England to try his hand as a solo folksinger; Garfunkel returned to graduate school at New York's Columbia University, where he studied literature.

After a Boston radio station began giving frequent spins to "Sounds of Silence," however, Columbia Records had an idea: They took the master tape and had some studio musicians juice up the track, make that folk song rock a little. On January 1, 1966, the enhanced "Sounds of Silence" was the No. 1 record in the United States, and Simon returned home to continue working with Garfunkel. As a team, their recordings defined the literary side of folk-rock, New York intellectualism shaped into top-forty hits such as "Homeward Bound," " I Am a Rock," and "The Dangling Conversation." Their 1968 hit, "Mrs. Robinson," was from the soundtrack they composed for Mike Nichols' movie *The Graduate* and won two Grammy Awards, including Record of the Year.

The mass audience attracted to Simon & Garfunkel's rock-tinged folk and pop peaked in 1970 with the album and title song "Bridge Over Troubled Water." The hymnlike tune captured the need for spiritual replenishment and reconciliation after the harsh battles of the 1960s. But during its recording, Simon & Garfunkel had some bitter disagreements, and it was their last studio album together. They broke up in 1971.

Other rock groups found instant success with folk-rock versions of Dylan songs. The Turtles, another Los Angeles band that had previously been playing surf music as the Crossfires, made the top ten in the summer of 1965 with Dylan's "It Ain't Me Babe."

The Byrds and the Turtles paved the way for Dylan's own ascent to huge commercial success. By rounding some of the edges of anger of the Dylan originals, they softened up radio to accept more ambitious lyrics and defiant attitudes. In today's jargon, it gave the Dylan name a strong new brand identity, one that had parity with rock's until-then unchallenged kings.

The Beatles, like the rest of the British rock aristocracy, were in awe of Dylan. It was Dylan, after all, at the Delmonico Hotel in New York on August 28, 1964, who turned the Beatles on to marijuana for the first time. "Up until then, we'd been hard Scotch and coke men," McCartney said,[35] the "coke" referring to Coca-Cola and not cocaine. The event marks the beginning of the Beatles' musical evolution as well, because the marijuana, and later LSD, directed them toward "introspective and sensual moods."

While Dylan changed forever the way both musicians and listeners approached rock lyrics, the British rock stars who were galvanized by him drew on something more: his attitude, the sound of his voice, the texture of the music.

His engagement with the world, only on his own terms, was immensely appealing to the Brits, rock 'n' rollers on a kind of show-biz treadmill, trapped to some degree by their success. Dylan, meanwhile, was motivated by the Beatles to return to the rock 'n' roll that had engaged him growing up. The result: *Bringing It All Back Home.*

"'Bringing It All Back Home' was a bid for Beatle territory, for pop success," Greil Marcus writes.[35] The album was released in March 1965. The lead song from the album, "Subterranean Homesick Blues," was a joyous romp, a surreal rhyming delight, Chuck Berry anticipating Run-D.M.C., its cheery paranoia laced with offhand humor. It was Dylan's first top-forty hit, by the skin of its teeth: It peaked at No. 39, for one week, May 15, 1965.

Bringing It All Back Home was an evolution from the austere, serious, sometimes condescending culture of folk music to something more visceral, youthful, and popular. Many folkies, Dylan's original core audience, viewed rock 'n' roll as juvenile. And they would try to make him pay for his apostasy.

The Newport (R.I.) Folk Festival was their annual tribal gathering. In the previous few years, Dylan had emerged as "the biggest draw, the most mystical presence" among the greats of fifty years of folk, country, and blues traditions, as represented by Joan Baez and Peter, Paul & Mary, Mother Maybelle Carter, Mississippi John Hurt, and Pete Seeger.[36]

Some of their worst fears were realized when Dylan took the stage at Newport on July 25, 1965, backed by Al Kooper and members of the Paul Butterfield Blues Band, playing loud, fierce, and hard: "I ain't gonna work on 'Maggie's Farm' no more," Dylan sang defiantly, the sharecropper breaking free of his backbreaking responsibility to his overseers. That Dylan wore a black leather jacket was bad enough, the devout folkies thought; he also played a Fender Stratocaster electric guitar. The audience responded with a cacophony of sounds, most of them disapproving: a hailstorm of shouts, wolf whistles, anger, all kinds of mixed-up confusion. "The audience was booing and yelling, 'get rid of the electric guitar,'" journalist Paul Nelson wrote at the time.

It had been said that in the chaos Pete Seeger, paragon of nonviolent folk music, tried to chop the wires to Dylan's amplifiers with an axe. Rock 'n' roll to this crowd meant selling out, going Hollywood, becoming cheap and inauthentic. (One revisionist yet plausible theory decrees that the Newport crowd wasn't mad at Dylan per se; they were tormented by the volume and dissonance of the music, which had overpowered the festival's limited amplification capacity.)

The next concert, at Forest Hills Tennis Stadium in Queens, New York, Dylan opened with a solo acoustic set. After a break, he returned with a band, which now also featured Robbie Robertson on guitar and Levon Helm on drums: Members of the Toronto-based Hawks. With "Like a Rolling Stone" galloping up the charts, top-forty disc jockeys introduced both sets.

"Dylan," Marcus writes, "could not have been more provocative if he had appeared … riding in a solid-gold Eldorado, or for that matter on a golden calf, and people were ready to be provoked." And provoked many were: "Fury coursed through the crowd like a snake; the wails of hate are beyond belief."[37]

Those wails were a last hurrah for those who didn't get Dylan's new sound, or the credibility Dylan gave rock 'n' roll. His folk-purist detractors would soon get run over by history, on Highway 61. They would also get slapped silly by Dylan on his next single, "Positively Fourth Street," which seems to addresses these former fans with the line, "You've got a lot of nerve to say you are my friend …"

With both Dylan and the Beatles rewriting the rules for rock 'n' roll songwriting, the Rolling Stones were faced with a dilemma. "We'd been playing famous old black American jazz/blues tunes," Keith Richards had recalled. "'You can't survive playing other people's music,'" [manager Andrew Loog Oldham] said, and he somehow tricked us into the kitchen, locked the door, and said, 'Now, stay there until you've written a song.'"[38]

Richards and Jagger thought he was kidding, but they decided to humor him. They emerged with what Richards' calls "the very un-Stonelike" ballad, "As Tears Go By." Despite the vapid lyrics — "It is the evening of the day/I sit and watch the children play" — it was recorded by Mick's girlfriend Marianne Faithful. "A couple of weeks later it was in the top ten," Richards recalls. "That's when Mick and I looked at each other and said, 'maybe we can write songs.'"39

The Stones had kicked off 1965 with the stoic "Heart of Stone" before finding their voice, as writers and as a band, with the flamboyantly aggressive "The Last Time." They followed it with the only song to match "Like a Rolling Stone" in originality and bravado in the super summer of 1965: "(I Can't Get No) Satisfaction."

The lyrics cataloged the advertising world's phoniness and modern life's annoyances while somehow managing to make even sexual frustration sound like swagger. The repeated guitar riff that launches the song, one of the most identifiable and singular in rock history, was composed by Keith Richards during a sleepless night on a tour stop in Orlando, Florida. The Stones had very quickly lifted their game to the Beatles' level.

But Dylan was the Beatles' main rival. "Certainly, [Lennon and McCartney] were aware that with his tumultuously original singles 'Subterranean Homesick Blues' and 'Like A Rolling Stone' had expanded the horizons of the pop lyric in a way they must recognize and somehow must outdo."40

And it wasn't just Dylan. The Kinks, led by songwriter Ray Davies, had moved from catchy hard-rock riffs to whimsical, satirical observations of life such as "See My Friend," a British hit in 1965, while the Who were about to raise the stakes with their peerless youth anthem "My Generation," on which singer Roger Daltrey stutters out the defiant assertion: "I hope I die before I get old."41 And of course, Brian Wilson kept sneaking up on everyone.

Onstage, the Who would illustrate this symbolically. While bass player John Entwistle stood stoically aside, Roger Daltrey would lasso his microphone chord, manic drummer Keith Moon would kick over his drum kit, and guitarist Pete Townshend, concluding a series of broad, windmill strokes of his guitar, would jam the neck into a wall of amplifiers, creating a frenzy of feedback. Then he'd smash the guitar into the ground until there was nothing left but fragments.

A BBC radio interviewer at the time asked the Who how expensive the ritual guitar smashings were. "At least 6000 quid … we were looking for ideas that were big musically and visually. So we just kept doing it."[42]

The Who — four extremely distinct personalities whose only apparent bond was the music they played together — followed their own curious path, especially in the United States, where it took them a few years to catch on. It was not until their 1967 singles "I Can See for Miles" and "Happy Jack" (the latter perplexingly revived in a 2005 U.S. TV commercial for Hummer automobiles) that they received any airplay, 1968 until their album *Live at Leeds* charted in the United States, and not until 1969 and their "rock opera" *Tommy* that acclaim for what many believe to be one of the five greatest rock bands ever became universal.

The Doors

The Doors were not your typical Los Angeles beachgoing goodtime boys. Singer Jim Morrison met keyboard player Ray Manzarek at UCLA film school, which was appropriate considering that the band's dramatic approach separated them from the let-it-all-hang-out ethos of their contemporaries. In his black leather pants, with long, flowing brown hair, he was a seventeenth-century Celtic poet reincarnated on the Sunset Strip. While everyone else in the 1967 was enjoying the sunshine, both real and hallucinated, the Doors and Morrison, "the Lizard King," grasped the lurking darkness; even in their Summer of Love hit, "Light My Fire," there was an apocalyptic edge to the celebration. The line "Girl we couldn't get much higher" wasn't an expression of joy as much as a warning.

The Doors were ahead of the curve in acknowledging that free love sometimes came at a price. In the powerful "Soul Kitchen," one of their earliest songs, the singer is torn between staying all night and the impulse to go. The author Paul Williams, founder of the original *Crawdaddy* magazine, noted that the song's subtext is that "sexual desire is merely a particular instance of some more far-reaching grand dissatisfaction."

The author Joan Didion — novelist, journalist, screenwriter, native Californian — was not part of the sixties generation. With cool detachment, Didion captured some of the same skepticism about the ubiquity of "love" in a brief interlude with the Doors, which she wrote about in her collection of essays known as *The White Album*.

On the whole my attention was only minimally engaged by the preoccupations of rock-and-roll bands ... but the Doors were different, the Doors interested me. The Doors seemed unconvinced that love was brotherhood and the Kama Sutra. The Doors music insisted that love was sex and sex was death and therein lay salvation. The Doors were the Norman Mailers of the Top 40, missionaries of apocalyptic sex.[*]

The Doors' self-titled debut album in 1967 began with a distinctive rocker — in a world defined by guitars and sepulchral studio effects, their "Break On Through (To the Other Side)" used as its rampart the fierce, cutting keyboards of dominant musical force, Ray Manzarek. Guitarist Robbie Krieger and drummer John Densmore rounded out the band; they never really had a bass player as a full-time member. Besides the erotic tension of "Light My Fire," there was the taut version of Willie Dixon's "Back Door Man." Though not a blues-based group (Krieger had studied flamenco guitar, and you can hear that influence in his playing), their version replicated some of the menace of Howlin' Wolf's smirking boast: "The men don't know but the little girls understand."

Images of death pervade the Doors music, an anomaly in that 1967 Summer of Love. "Jim [Morrison] is fascinated with the concept of death," the band's producer, Paul Rothchild, said in an interview. "He's interested in spiritual deaths, conceptual deaths, more than physical deaths, actually, you'll find this theme in many of his songs ... [from "Crystal Ship"], 'the end of nights we tried to die.'"[†]

Their effortless handling of Bertolt Brecht and Kurt Weill's "Alabama Song" added a bit of intellectual luster to the album, but they really wanted to blow people's minds, which they did in the final track, "The End": eleven minutes of creepy but compelling psychodrama that peaked with the ultimate Oedipal nightmare. Stalking his home at night, the protagonist enters his parents' bedroom and declares: "Father, I want to kill you. Mother, I want to ..." the final word or words simply a scream of intolerable grief — and shocking release.

The Doors' next album, released later in 1967 was called *Strange Days*, and generated a dark hit single, full of nightmare imagery, "People Are Strange." Always distant from the happy hippie family

* Joan Didion, *The White Album*, New York: Simon & Schuster, 1979. p 21.
† Paul Williams interview with Rothchild, *Crawdaddy* magazine, 1967.

party of the summer of 1967, the Doors became more obsessed with alienation and fear: "Faces look ugly, when you're alone," Morrison sings in the opening verse.

With a third album, *L.A. Woman* in 1968, the Doors may have become the weirdest juggernaut in the history of top-forty music. While FM rock latched on to long Doors tracks like "The End" and the similarly epochal "When the Music's Over," the pop radio hits kept coming: "Love Me Two Times," "The Unknown Soldier," and "Hello, I Love You," through 1968. The Doors were shared by both teenyboppers and the emerging rock cognoscenti.

Another specialized interest group began taking interest in Jim Morrison: your local sheriff's office:

- December 1967. Morrison was arrested in New Haven for public obscenity at a concert.
- August 1968. Arrested for disorderly conduct aboard an airplane en route to Phoenix.
- March 1969. Arrested for "lewd and lascivious behavior by exposing his private parts and by simulating masturbation" in Miami.[*]

That arrest placed a financial toll on the Doors, who found it more difficult to get bookings, and increased psychological stress on its members. The group fragmented, as Morrison sought … something in Paris. As Manzarek writes of Morrison on his Web site:

"After his rampant drug use, erratic behavior and infamous obscenity bust in Miami all but scuttled the band, the singer perished in his bathtub while living in Paris."[†] Morrison died July 3, 1971; he was twenty-seven years old. The circumstances of his death were mysterious, though his resting place remains a shrine to those obsessed with Morrison, even generating an online "Paris Guide for Doors Fans," with all you need to know about his grave.[‡]

During the 1970s and 1980s, the phenomenon known as "tribute bands" burst onto the scene. Bands named after Doors songs, such as Crystal Ship and L.A. Woman, worked steadily in clubs as old

---

[*] Patricia Romanowski and Holly George-Warren, *The New Rolling Stone Encyclopedia of Rock & Roll*, New York: Fireside Books/Rolling Stone Press, 1983 and 1995. p. 282.

[†] Doors' keyboard player Ray Manzarek has been keeper of the band's flame. This at http://www.raymanzarek.com/DC21CPress072804.html.

[‡] Information about Morrison's grave from http://ww.geocities.com/SunsetStrip/Palladium/1409/jimparis.htm.

fans and those who missed seeing the Doors the first time around clamored for these precise copycat acts. In 1980, a Doors bio *No One Here Gets Out Alive*, by Danny Sugarman and Jerry Hopkins, made the best-seller lists and spurred a Doors revival; more Doors albums were sold that year than in any of the band's active career.* Morrison's murky death, exploited fully in the Oliver Stone's fictionalized screen bio, *The Doors* (1991), gave the band an extended and fruitful life beyond the grave. And every few years, there is another cluster of Doors books, boxed sets and DVDs. 2006 happened to be the fortieth anniversary of the Doors' formation, resulting in a new CD/DVD boxed set (*Perception*) and a lavish coffee table book promoted as "the first band autobiography," *Doors by Doors*.

---

* Romanowski and George-Warren, see*.

1966: The Beatles and Beach Boys: *Rubber Soul*, *Pet Sounds*, and *Revolver*

The Beatles raised their stakes with *Rubber Soul*, which displayed a new elegance and sophistication in the Beatles' writing. From the opening stroke, there are sitars and imagistic lyrics on "Norwegian Wood." The sitar, a string instrument used in Indian classical music, was brought to the group by George Harrison, who incorporated the musical and spiritual values of India into his life and music. The oblique lyrics of "Nowhere Man" generated comparisons to Dylan. "The Word" summoned some spiritual vision the Beatles hadn't experienced yet. Perhaps it even mocks know-it-all preachers: "Say the Word, and you'll be free/Say the Word, and be like me." The gorgeous "Michelle" had McCartney singing some French lyrics over one of the most beautiful romantic melodies the Beatles had written. And in "In My Life" they seemed in the full grip of nostalgia, sounding as if they were fifty-three, not twenty-three.

And in one of the few frank interviews they gave at the time, they were giddy about their evolving sound.

"People have always wanted us to stay the same, but we can't stay in a rut," McCartney told *Newsweek* reporter Michael Lydon. "No one else expects to hit a peak at 23 and never develop, so why should we? *Rubber Soul* for me is the beginning of my adult life."[43]

The Beatles' emerging brilliance was more apparent than ever. "Exchanging assault for seduction, they delivered the most serious love songs, exploring contingency, ambiguity, pleasure and guilt," Greil Marcus wrote. "Where before they took pop music by storm, here they remade it from the inside out."[44]

The Beatles were aware of their increasing influence on the culture. Lennon, the group's greatest wit and cynic, told a London newspaper in March that the Beatles were "more popular than Jesus now." Many Christian groups took offense; radio stations in parts of the South known as "the bible belt" stopped playing their records. Some churches called for the burning of Beatles albums. To some, this only underscored Lennon's contention that religion was failing to reach the young, who were searching for meaning, and finding it more readily in Beatles songs than in the Bible. To others it was an attack on religion. No matter what the point of view, some people see this as a kind of dividing line in the Beatles' history: the one in which they stopped being just a successful "pop group," and become lightning rods for the deepest fissures and controversies in our culture.

Soon the Beatles would acknowledge smoking marijuana, and enjoying it: they embodied the side of the debate that believed marijuana was safer than tobacco and not as damaging to the body or psyche as alcohol. Marijuana became the dividing line in the culture between young and old. Your parents drank whiskey; the young smoked pot.

Brian Wilson of the Beach Boys found his ambition fueled by *Rubber Soul*. "In December 1966, I heard the album *Rubber Soul* by the Beatles. It was definitely a challenge for me. I saw that every cut was very artistically interesting and stimulating."[45]

Like many ordinary music listeners, Wilson was moved by the cohesiveness of the Beatles' new album. Before *Rubber Soul*, rock albums were never more than a collection of songs. All of the songs might be great, or lousy, or mixed, but the work was considered track by three-minute track. On *Rubber Soul*, a rock album, for the first time, seemed greater than the sum of its parts... . "I really wasn't quite ready for the unity," Wilson said. "It felt like it all belonged together. 'Rubber Soul' was a collection of songs ... that somehow went together like no album ever made before, and I was very impressed. I said, 'That's it. I really am challenged to do a great album.'"

Wilson's next Beach Boys album, *Pet Sounds*, released in 1966, was exactly that: a great album many place among the top three, or ten, or twenty albums of the last fifty years.

With the first single, "Sloop John B," a gorgeous adaptation of a West Indian folk song, the Beach Boys took a quantum leap, sonically and harmonically.

And though *Pet Sounds* had another top-ten single, in "Wouldn't It Be Nice" and lesser hits in the beauties "Caroline No" and "God Only Knows," it was the way the album as a whole hung together, with instrumental-only tracks providing connective tissue, and "bicycle bells, buzzing organs, harpsichords, flutes, the theremin, and even dog whistles, on top of conventional keyboards and guitars."[46]

Some consider *Pet Sounds* a Brian Wilson solo album, since he had stopped touring, focusing entirely on experimenting in the studio. Most of the lyrics were by a new acquaintance, Tony Asher.[47] Wilson met Asher, an advertising copywriter, in a Los Angeles recording studio. Asher is said to have been modest about his input. "The general tenor of the lyrics was always [Brian's]," Asher later recalled, "and the actual choice of words was usually mine. I was really just his interpreter."[48]

The Beach Boys and the Beatles were now in a competition to blow each other's minds, a race augmented by the combination of genius, ambition, and drugs. For *Pet Sounds* drove the Beatles a little crazy, too.

Summer of 1965: Motown, Stax, and Watts

Top-forty disc jockeys and AM radio were still king in 1965, and they were more than tolerable. They could hardly go wrong with what they played in what was possibly the greatest year for pop music in any of the last fifty years. Besides the Beatles, Rolling Stones, Bob Dylan, and the Beach Boys, a vast number of black artists crossed over to pop with some remarkable records.

The leading edge was Motown Records. Founded in the late 1950s by a former Detroit autoworker turned songwriter named Berry Gordy Jr., Motown was the first black-owned entertainment empire.

Motown's first hit was "Money (That's What I Want)" performed by Barrett Strong and cowritten and produced by Gordy. Motown's first hit group was the Miracles, led by William "Smokey" Robinson. A brilliant songwriter and producer with one of the most beautiful voices in any style of music — broke through in late 1960 with the thrilling "Shop Around."

Robinson's effortless falsetto and compellingly clever lyrics made him and the Miracles a staple of pop R&B in the early 1960s. (In addition to recording "Money," the Beatles also did a version of the Miracles' 1962–1963 hit "You've Really Got a Hold on Me." Robinson's one-two punch of a first line — "I don't like you/But I love you" — made lyricists jealous on both sides of the Atlantic ever since. Bob Dylan was said to have called Robinson "America's greatest living poet," and even if it was one of Dylan's put-ons to the press, it happened to have the ring of truth to it.

Motown, whose other labels included Tamla and Gordy, was at the right place at the right time for the girl-group explosion. Robinson, as writer and producer, was responsible for a string of top ten hits by Mary Wells ("The One Who Really Loves You," "You Beat Me to the Bunch" and "Two Lovers"), the Marvelettes ("Please Mr. Postman"), and with Martha & the Vandellas ("Heatwave," "Quicksand," "Dancing in the Street"). These songs had a toughness, a firmer rhythmic kick, and just enough hint of blues; Motown's streetwise female contingent made Phil Spector's girl groups sound like, well, girls. But not *too* street.

Motown's slogan was "The Sound of Young America." Though most of his artists came from the black neighborhoods of Detroit and its metropolitan area, Gordy's vision was to appeal to black and white, young and old. Motown recordings had none of the salacious grit of blues and R&B. Instead, the emphasis was on an irresistibly danceable beat, a fat drum and bass sound, crisp horn arrangements, and polished vocals, all compressed to sound loud, immediate and powerful on 45 rpm singles and tiny transistor radios and car radio speakers. Virgil Moorefield writes, "There's almost always a sizzle to the Motown sound, a kind of subtle distortion that would be considered unacceptable in contemporary recording projects; it somehow projects performance energy, and it's also something that speaks well through small speakers."[49] In fact, while most record executives love to play back their wares through state-of-the-art audio equipment, Gordy had a Motown engineer run recordings through a tiny speaker to see how they'd sound coming out of a car radio.

In addition, Motown puts its performers through a kind of finishing school, tutoring them in choreography, stage patter, and the elements of style so that they could appeal to audiences anywhere: Ed Sullivan was especially fond of booking Motown acts, a guarantee of professionalism, and of good ratings.

There seemed to be no end to the talent that poured through its Detroit headquarters, "Hitsville U.S.A." There was the suave but rocking and soulful Marvin Gaye, the one Motown singer who drew most strongly on R&B's gospel roots. There was a twelve-year-old blind boy Gordy named Little Stevie Wonder, whose prodigious talents as a singer and harmonica player brought acclaim in 1963 with the No. 1 record, *Fingertips, Pt. II.*

There were male vocal groups such as the Temptations, who rose on Robinson's songs and production to become one of the most reliable brands in pop music for decades, as were the Four Tops, whose muscular singing provided a perfect vehicle for the songs of another in-house production team, brothers Eddie and Brian Holland and Lamont Dozier, known as Holland-Dozier-Holland.

The female trio the Supremes were the most dynamic result of Gordy's polish and Holland-Dozier-Holland's flair for the dramatic and romantic. Singer Diana Ross brought an effortless sensuality to a yearlong run of five consecutive No. 1 hits from the summer of 1964 through 1965, Beatles or no Beatles: "Where Did Our Love Go," "Baby Love," "Come See About Me," "Stop! In the Name of Love," and "Back in My Arms Again."

Meanwhile, these were also good times for a grittier form of black music that drew more directly from the well of southern R&B and gospel.

Stax Records in Memphis was one of the most daring labels of the era. The anchor for Stax was the four-piece house band known as Booker T. & the MG's, and they were integration personified: pianist Booker T. Jones and drummer Al Jackson were black; bass player Donald "Duck" Dunn and guitarist Steve Cropper were white.

The label was founded in 1959 by a white banker and part-time musician named Jim Stewart, who was an enthusiast of the Memphis music being made across town at the Sun Records studios. The Carla Thomas ballad "Gee Whiz" was Stax's first hit, in 1960. (It appeared on the Atlantic label; Stax was distributed by New York-based Atlantic, and in the 1960s the labels, artists, and recordings were often shuffled.) Her father, Rufus Thomas, was a hugely popular disc jockey at WDIA in Memphis. Stewart met Rufus while promoting the label's (first known as Satellite) first recording efforts. Rufus, a former comedian with a likeably growly voice, had had his own hit on Sun in 1953: his "Bear Cat," an answer song to Big Maybelle's "Hound Dog," was in fact Sun's first hit.[50]

Ten years later, in 1963, Rufus Thomas had a national hit with the irresistibly funky novelty "Walkin' the Dog." Although the dance — the dog — never became a craze, Thomas's hit was an R&B benchmark.

Tight, hard-swinging instrumentals such as "Last Night" by the Mar-Keys and "Green Onions" by Booker T. and the MGs both broke out of the South to become national hits. Stax scholar Rob Bowman writes, "What is significant here is that this relatively simple recording featured a racially integrated group sporting a walloping drum sound, an accent on the low end of the pitch spectrum, organ, and exceedingly prominent horns,"[51] ingredients "essential" to the sound of Memphis soul in the sixties."

Like Motown, a coterie of in-house songwriters, musicians, and producers gave Stax its consistency and durability. Especially notable was the work of the team of Isaac Hayes and David Porter, who wrote and produced hits that became rock/R&B standards for Sam & Dave including "Hold On, I'm Coming" (criticized by some more conservative churchgoing southerners as a direct lift from a beloved hymn turned into something entirely too worldly), and "Soul Man."

In 1965, the singer and songwriter Otis Redding brought soul music to another level. Redding, from Macon, Georgia, had been with Stax's Volt imprint almost since it began. His first songs were gospel-based ballads of unbearable romantic agony such as "These Arms of Mine" (1962), and "Pain in My Heart" (1963). His switch to a spirited, irresistible up-tempo mode for "Security" in 1964 had him poised for potential crossover from the R&B ghetto. Not a little thanks was due to the Rolling Stones, enormous fans, who recorded versions of Redding's "Pain in My Heart" and "That's How Strong My Love Is."

Redding, like the Stones, the Beatles, and Bob Dylan, was evolving in his writing and performing. Enjoying the success of "Security," he hit again with "Mr. Pitiful," which was suffused with joyous self-mockery. But in 1965, he would create his first masterpiece, a top-five R&B record called "Respect." Aretha Franklin's version in 1967 would break her career open as "Queen of Soul."

Redding recorded "Respect," his own composition, on August 15, 1965. The insistent beat of the music made the lyrics seem like a demand: "Show me some respect, give me some respect, all I want is a little respect ..." It was hard not to make the connection to that very moment in Los Angeles, where one of America's most devastating race riots was in its fifth day.

The Watts riots, or "insurrection," as some called it, was started by that most banal of daily activities: a white police officer (the Los Angeles police department, which had a long-earned reputation for harsh treatment of minorities, had zero blacks on the force in 1965) pulling over a black driver for some infraction. The driver was twenty-one-year-old Marquette Frye; the policeman thought he might be intoxicated.

While the officer was arresting Frye, a crowd gathered, taunting the policeman. A second cop arrived on the scene, and reportedly hit people in the crowd with his baton. The news spread through the neighborhood like an AOL instant message. It was as if everyone snapped at the same time. Fed up with police brutality, unemployment, crowded neighborhoods, and all the other frustrations of ghetto life, Watts erupted in fires and violence. The police were unable to quash the rebellion, perhaps a manifestation of writer James Baldwin's prophetic 1962 essay "The Fire Next Time."

The riot lasted for six days, and required 16,000 National Guard troops and police to bring under control. By the time it was over, 34 people were dead, more than 1,000 injured or wounded, nearly 3,000 arrested, and $200 million in property destroyed.

While many tried to blame "outside agitators" or neighborhood criminals, longtime Watts resident Johnny Otis wrote a book called *Listen to the Lambs,* his own observation about the Watts riots. He wrote about some of his friends, middle-class black adults, who found themselves arrested and handcuffed to a jail cell for six days. None of their families, friends, or lawyers knew where they were.

A report issued by the then Governor Pat Brown said, "The riots weren't the act of thugs, but rather symptomatic of much deeper problems: the high jobless rate in the inner city, poor housing, bad schools." Although the problems were clearly pointed out in the report, no great effort was made to address them, or to rebuild what had been destroyed in the riots.[52]

The Watts riot marked a turning point in the Civil Rights struggle, away from the goal of integration and in the direction known as "black power."

According to James Graham, "After 1965 blacks became increasingly disillusioned with a system that continued to marginalize them and allowed them only limited victories. In this environment black power's philosophy of black pride and self-determination of black affairs could only increase in popularity."[53] But much of the rest of the country was divided along racial lines about what such assertiveness meant.

> The Watts Riot was the first major lesson for American public on the tinderbox volatility of segregated inner-city neighborhoods. The riot provided a sobering preview of the violent urban uprisings of the late 1960s and helped define several hardcore political camps: militant blacks applauded the spectacle of rage; moderates lamented the riot's senselessness and self-destructiveness; and conservative whites viewed the uprising as a symptom of the aggressive pace of civil rights legislation.[54]

That same month, there was more revolution, musically. Soul singer James Brown, long the biggest solo star and most dynamic performer in R&B, finally had his first pop top-ten hit: "Papa's Got a Brand New Bag."

Until "Papa," Brown, a former boxer raised on the rough streets of Augusta, Georgia, was a raw, compelling singer with a lavish, neatly choreographed stage show. His 1963 album, *Live at the Apollo*, was recorded at Harlem's Apollo Theater in October 1962 and became the standard by which concert albums are measured. His audience was almost totally African-American at that point: "Please Please Please" and "Try Me" were wringing, emotional ballads hardly more than one degree of separation from the testifying one would hear in a storefront church in a city ghetto on any given Sunday. Besides secular lyrics, Brown managed to convey combustible excitement (his nickname at the time was "Mr. Dynamite") with precise musical arrangements. A blunt taskmaster, he was renowned for fining musicians who played a wrong note or missed a beat.

The surprise popularity of *Live at the Apollo* (it peaked at No. 2 on the *Billboard* Top Albums chart during its sixty-six-week run) showed there was an audience for this kind of powerful, deep-rooted rhythm 'n' blues similar to that which Little Richard discovered in the 1950s: suburban kids loved this passionate music as well. "James Brown was a 'truth singer,'" wrote British author Valerie Wilmer. "He reached back in time for his feeling, to lay hidden verities at the feet of his listeners ... When [he] sank to the ground or tugged at your soul it was as if some dreadful, long-hidden secret was being revealed at last ... After Brown has done a song, there's nowhere else to go ... the catharsis is absolute."[55]

Brown's "Papa's Got a Brand New Bag" more than lived up to the boast of its title. It really was something else in 1965, even to ears becoming attuned to Memphis soul and Motown swagger. It was a revolutionary record because of the rhythmic variation on the gospel-rooted soul music Brown introduced. It was the first funk record, and changed the way music would sound from that time on. Frank Kogan writes,

> Funk at its invention was *really* extreme; *everything* became rhythm, foreground became background and vice versa, nothing simply supported a "lead" instrument or singer. The vocals were drumbeats, the drums punctuated and completed the vocals. The horns and guitars were staccato percussion. The beats were not evenly spaced: Instead, even more

than in the rest of rhythm and blues, everything was in complementary note clusters, no instrumental part replicating another, each tumbling over the others in a perpetual-motion machine. Basically anything by James Brown from 'Papa's Got a Brand New Bag' onward (r&b number one, pop number eight, 1965) that wasn't a ballad fits this pattern.[56]

Hippie Roots: San Francisco and LSD

Monterey Pop Festival

Sgt. Pepper's Lonely Hearts Club Band

Dylan, (1966s) *Blonde On Blonde*;
The Basement Tapes; *John Wesley Harding*

The Beach Boys' *Smile*

When people talk about "the sixties" with a glint in their eyes, with rueful sadness, or through clenched teeth, what they mean is three, perhaps four years: 1966, and certainly 1967 to 1969. They really were the best of times and the worst of times, depending on who you were, where you were, or what day it was. Life moved so fast that it was impossible to see what was coming around the next corner. It was a time of so many extremes that it seemed like the world was pulling apart and that the center would not hold.

But at first, it was quite lovely. Beginning in 1966 into early 1967, the center of rock culture shifted to San Francisco. In a rundown neighborhood called Haight-Ashbury, where the Grateful Dead, Jefferson Airplane, and Big Brother and the Holding Company lived, a steadily increasing number of young people came seeking utopia on the city's hard streets.

The seminal event occurred January 14, 1967, when "A Gathering of the Tribes, for a Human Be-In" was held at Golden Gate Park. Posters around the city advertised LSD gurus like Timothy Leary and Richard Alpert; activist comedian Dick Gregory; poets Allen Ginsberg, Lawrence Ferlinghetti, Gary Snyder, and Lenore Kandel; as well as "flags, flutes, families, incense, chimes ..."; and "all San Francisco bands."

The be-in, as Paul Grushkin has written, was "a pivotal event in the history of hippie culture, it ushered in the 1967 'Summer of Love' when thousands of young people ... converged upon San Francisco to create a lifestyle that would transform social values across the country."[57]

The San Francisco scene began to coagulate around 1965. Long welcoming to beatniks, poets, and freethinkers of all kinds, such organizations as LEMAR, to legalize marijuana, and the Sexual Freedom League held meetings in the Blue Unicorn coffeehouse. Some have credited the San Francisco writer Michael Fallon as the first to describe these people and the communal lifestyle being developed as "hippies." (In 1963, the Philadelphia girl group the Orlons sang a tune that went, "Where do all the hippies meet? South Street, South Street"; that area is still the best place in Philly to eat a cheesesteak, but it had nothing to do with the developing counterculture.)

Bands began forming to play for the large-scale get-togethers that were beginning to occur. The bands, Jefferson Airplane, Grateful Dead, and Big Brother & the Holding Company, distinguished themselves from the rest of the rock world by disdaining, at first, the corporate music business, resisting the impulse to make concise, conventional songs suitable for top-forty radio, preferring to jam for hours, rarely performing the same song twice the same way.

Money, and how to get it, was almost nonexistent on the list of priorities in the Haight. A volunteer group called the Diggers trolled for food tossed out from fancy restaurants and supermarkets — the blemished but otherwise perfectly healthy tomatoes, the edible day-old bread that had to be gotten rid of for the next day's deliveries: they fed those who had come to the Haight without, literally, thinking about where their next meal was coming from. Young doctors, nurses, and medical students opened up the Free Clinic, where anything from sinus infections to sexually transmitted diseases like gonorrhea could be treated with penicillin, and where tranquilizers and friendly peer support could help some having bad LSD trips.

If you came to town not knowing anyone, chances are you'd find a place to "crash" — sleep — that night. And marijuana was not just cheap and plentiful, but ubiquitous. Like any shopping center or mall, the Haight had an anchor store: The Psychedelic Shop. There you could buy everything but the drugs: rolling paper for marijuana, pipes and screens for hashish, incense, black lights, posters — enhancements for the drug experience.

Marijuana was openly smoked and easily available. But LSD was the drug that defined this moment in 1967, having a substantial impact on rock's quantum leap into something more than entertainment. It was becoming part of what was being called a lifestyle.

LSD — d-lysergic acid diethylemide, or "acid" for short — was discovered by the Swiss scientist Albert Hoffman in 1943 while he was seeking a compound to treat blood ailments. In his lab notes, he wrote down impressions of his first experience ingesting LSD:

> I suddenly became strangely inebriated. The external world became changed as in a dream. Objects appeared to gain in relief; they assumed unusual dimensions; and colors became more glowing. Even self-perception and the sense of time were changed. When the eyes were closed, colored pictures flashed past in a quickly changing kaleidoscope. After a few hours, the not unpleasant inebriation, which had been experienced whilst I was fully conscious, disappeared.[58]

Proponents believed that a several-hour trip could open the "doors of perception" to a new dimension of not only visual and aural extravaganzas, but could even help one attain a state of intense spiritual well-being. (The British author Aldous Huxley, who wrote the essay collection *Doors of Perception,* first took LSD in 1955.)[59] The spiritual effects of LSD were comparable to those of natural hallucinogens that were sacred to some Native Americans and South American tribes: peyote, mescaline, and psylocybin or "magic mushrooms."

In the summer of 1964, a year after being dismissed from Harvard, LSD's great propagandist, Dr. Timothy Leary, and his associate, Dr. Richard Alpert, began holding LSD sessions at a house in exclusive Millbrook, New York In September 1966, Leary formed the quasi-religious League for Spiritual Discovery (LSD), whose most famous tenet, heard and seen almost daily in the summer of 1967, was "Turn on, tune in, drop out."

In the spring of 1965, Stanley Augustus Owsley began manufacturing LSD in the San Francisco Bay Area; the drug was legal in California until October 1966.

Your experience of LSD depended largely on the quality and quantity of the drug, the security you felt in the setting for the trip, and your previous psychological disposition. If you were happy, chances are you'd have an enjoyable trip. If you were prone to depression or anxiety, the trip could be a nightmare extension of those maladies. Those who used it wisely used it infrequently; those naive enough to think it an every day drug, like marijuana, may have found their personalities altered, rarely for the better.

Some rock musicians paid the price for excessive LSD use: Syd Barrett, a founder of Pink Floyd, and Roky Erickson of the Texas psychedelic band the 13th Floor Elevators, were among those whose ability to function were curtailed by the drug. Moby Grape, which had the potential to be the greatest of all San Francisco groups in 1967, had its potential greatly diminished by acid-enhanced personality problems.

The Beatles, on the other hand, especially McCartney, openly said they enjoyed LSD quite a bit. And the Grateful Dead and Jefferson Airplane both liked to take it, and liked to play for crowds who were taking it — which led to their music being called "acid rock," although the term was vague and often applied to any loud band that jammed a bit in the late 1960s.

Jefferson Airplane's hit "White Rabbit" from its 1967 acid-influenced *Surrealistic Pillow* album compared LSD to an "Alice in Wonderland" experience. In the grand finale, singer Grace Slick bellows: "Remember what the Doormouse said/Feed your head!"

"The political and social juggernaut of the 60s rolled on wheels of music, and that music owed both its aesthetic and ethical impetus to psychedelics. Eyes and hearts were opened — frequently by way of the ears — to fresh perceptions and utopian possibilities," Tom Robbins wrote. To downplay the importance of psychedelics in talking about the 1960s "would be akin to a panel on eggs that ignores or downplays the contribution of hens."[60]

While everyone else was tripping, the concert promoter Bill Graham was a professional who understood the music and musicians. His shows started on time; he had the best sound engineers, the first light shows, well-trained stage hands, theater managers; the sound was excellent, the venues orderly. Graham, more than anyone else, gave the performance of rock — which really until 1967 was an art form entirely defined by studio recordings — the professionalism it needed to thrive in the concert setting. At the Fillmore Auditorium in San Francisco, and by early 1967, the Fillmore East in New York, Graham also showed great imagination in putting two or three artists from different genres — jazz, blues, soul, rock, gospel — together on a single bill, helping his audience expand their own musical experience: The Doors /Chuck Berry; Jefferson Airplane/jazz guitarist Gabor Szabo, and Jimi Hendrix; Otis Redding / the Grateful Dead ... blues guitarist Otis Rush/Frank Zappa and the Mothers of Invention.

Also on the scene: KSAN, the country's first "free-form" FM rock radio station. Led by program director and air personality Tom Donahue, KSAN had laid-back air personalities who could play pretty much anything they wanted, with none of the frantic jabber of top-forty radio disc jockeys. KSAN and its "free-form" format were not out to entertain listeners for the purpose of selling advertising time. They made the radio station an inextricable part of the community.

By June 1967, transformation was in the air. The Monterey (California) Pop Festival, about ninety minutes south of San Francisco, held from June 16 to 18, was both a musical love-in and a gathering of the business tribes. Organized by John Phillips of the Mamas and the Papas and Lou Adler, founder of Dunhill and Ode Records, Monterey was noteworthy in a number of ways.

As a benefit for something called the Monterey International Pop Festival Foundation, musicians waived their fees. For another, it represented a merging of Los Angeles's ostensibly commercial pop music and San Francisco supposedly communal, theoretically noncommercial rock: "A temporary fusion between the purist, non-capitalistic Bay Area and heathen Los Angeles," Adler said, surely tongue-in-cheek.[61]

It was a remarkable assemblage. From Southern California came the Association, Buffalo Springfield, the Beach Boys, the Byrds, Johnny Rivers, and the Mamas and Papas — all, except for Buffalo Springfield (which included Stephen Stills and Neil Young) — major top-forty hit-makers, yet all with some artistic credibility.

Monterey really was a comprehensive showcase for the Bay Area bands: the Dead, the Airplane, Big Brother featuring Janis Joplin; the

Steve Miller Band, Quicksilver Messenger Service, Country Joe & the Fish, and Mike Bloomfield.

Five shows were presented over three days; the top ticket price was $6.50. New York's unofficial representatives were Simon & Garfunkel, the Blues Project, and singer/songwriter Laura Nyro. There were soul acts the Impressions, Booker T & the MG's, Lou Rawls, and Otis Redding; South Africa's Hugh Masekela and the great Indian classical musician, sitar player Ravi Shankar, performed the Sunday afternoon show. And, from England, the Jimi Hendrix Experience on opening night, and the Who closing the show Sunday night.

Unlike subsequent rock festivals, Monterey was not too crowded, with plenty of food, water, bathrooms, and sunshine. In the documentary film *Monterey Pop*, directed by D. A. Pennebaker, you see the well-prepared local police force, at first ready for action, uncertain about what a large influx of hippies would do to their idyllic community. Visibly impressed by the orderliness and gentleness of the crowd, the police spent most of the weekend faded into the background, wearing shorts and gladly accepting flowers from the happy crowds, even being introduced, and thanked by name, for being so groovy, from the stage.

A few performances were career-changing events. Soul singer Otis Redding was making one of his first appearances in front of a purely white audience, and he responded with a show-stopper set in which he giddily repeated: "Is this the love crowd?" And it was. It was a crossover moment unparalleled by any pure soul music artist, and Redding took advantage of it. He listened and learned from the Beatles' *Sgt. Pepper's Lonely Heart's Club Band*, expanding his writing palette and coming up later in 1967 with "(Sittin' On the) Dock of the Bay," a gorgeous, tender, and rueful song set in San Francisco. There was something haunting about the song, which was recorded on November 22, 1967, the fourth anniversary of the JFK assassination. It was released on December 8. But time was not on Redding's side. He died two days later in a plane crash outside Madison, Wisconsin, along with four members of his touring band, the Bar-Kays. "Dock of the Bay" was Redding's first and only top-twenty pop hit. In fact, it was No. 1 for a month in the chilly winter of 1968.

It was also Janis Joplin's breakthrough moment. Already a legend in the Bay Area but unknown in the rest of the country, the singer for Big Brother & the Holding Company sang, shouted, and screamed the blues like a woman possessed. "She didn't sing a song; she ravished it, tore it to shreds, made it explode," Clive Davis said.

Davis, the newly named president of Columbia Records in New York, came to Monterey to check out the action. As he continues in his autobiography, *Clive*:

> [Janis] was electrifying. She strutted up and down the stage banging a tambourine, and as the audience got turned on, she got more turned on, almost childlike in her exhilaration." Her bravura moment, and one of her signature tunes, was her near out-of-body experience in her exquisitely tortured version of Big Mama Thornton's "Ball & Chain."

Davis would sign Big Brother & the Holding Company to Columbia the following year (after protracted, expensive negotiations with a small company that had signed the band earlier). Big Brothers' first Columbia album, *Cheap Thrills* (1968) was both a major hit and came close to capturing the band's fiery, expansive spirit.

Joplin was an avenging angel to the multitudes like her who were not preppy, athletic, or beautiful, ostracized from the high school cliques in their narrow-minded hometowns (in her case, Port Arthur, Texas).

In the movie *Janis*, she is seen nervously returning to her ten-year high school reunion, just to get some revenge. "They laughed me out of class, out of town, out of state," she said. "That's why I want to go back."[62]

Yet some felt that the band's meandering jam style was holding Joplin back from being a star of the first magnitude. That may have been true, but outsiders may have underestimated how much her rapport with Big Brother grounded her, if she was grounded in any way.

But Joplin, like so many other rock stars of the time, could not make her peace with stardom. "I wasn't asked to the prom, and it still seems to hurt," she says in *Janis*. An omnipresent bottle of Southern Comfort, a sweet-tasting whiskey, was but one of her crutches. This heroine also had a taste for heroin. She died of a drug overdose on October 4, 1970, at age twenty-seven, just after completing recording her second and best solo album, the emotionally charged *Pearl*.[63]

Sgt. Pepper's Lonely Hearts Club Band

Asking rhetorically if there really ever was "a common culture of widely shared values and knowledge in the United States at any point between 1956 and 1976," the social critic Michael Berube answers affirmatively — but for one week only, in June 1967, the week *Sgt. Pepper's Lonely Hearts Club Band* was released.

It was played so incessantly, so ubiquitously, embraced so universally when it was released that it inspired the critic and scholar Langdon Winner to write:

> The closest Western Civilization has come to unity since the Congress of Vienna in 1815 was the week the *Sgt. Pepper* album was released... At the time I happened to be driving across country on Interstate 80. In each city where I stopped for gas or food — Laramie, Ogallala, Moline, South Bend — the melodies wafted in from some far-off transistor radio or portable hi-fi. It was the most amazing thing I've ever heard. For a brief while the irreparable fragmented consciousness of the West was unified, at least in the minds of the young.[64]

The cover was iconic, and has been imitated by art directors ever since. The then-mustachioed Beatles wore hot-colored, elaborate, vintage marching band uniforms with epaulets and tassels. They posed amid dozens of celebrities' faces pasted in cutouts, well known and obscure, from W. C. Fields to Karl Marx, Fred Astaire to Bob Dylan. Directly to the left of "Sgt. Pepper's" band were the Beatles in their 1964 look, matching suits and moptop hair, as they were portrayed for posterity in Madame Tussaud's Wax Museum. In front of all, an elaborate floral arrangement spelled out the band's name. Perhaps it was meant to suggest the funeral of the former Beatles, and the birth of a new Beatles.

The title song begins with trumpet fanfares and the sounds of a stadium crowd murmuring its approval and anticipation.

The album seems replete with drug references. Ringo gets the early spotlight with "A Little Help from My Friends," the refrain which goes, "I get high with a little help ..." Lennon sings "Lucy in the Sky with Diamonds," whose spacey vocals, ethereal echo chamber sound effects and trippy lyrics made it appear that the song was a testimony to the first letters of the three main words: LSD. Despite his reputation for brutal candor, John Lennon's lifelong insistence that he wrote the song about a drawing by his son Julian has never been accepted as the truth, the whole truth, and nothing but the truth. No one denied, though, what writer Sheila Whiteley later wrote in describing *Pepper* as a record that "encoded the acid experience through multilayered esoteric references."[65]

From the sitar on Harrison's "Within You, Without You" to the giggly orchestration on "Lovely Rita" (about a crush on a meter maid) to the rooster crowing on "Good Morning, Good Morning," *Sgt. Pepper* was a riot of effects, some of which only lasted for seconds but have lingered for decades.

One song that stands alone from this colorful pastiche is "A Day in the Life," which appears at the end of the album, after the reprise of the carnival-like title song. Spare and dramatic, it builds slowly, matter-of-factly announcing some of the day's tragedies read about in a newspaper. Each series of verses dissolves into a dissonant orchestration as the Beatles sing a hauntingly held refrain: "I'd love to turn you on." The lyrics and sound seemed again to mimic the hallucinatory drug experience, and as a result the song was banned by the BBC and some American radio stations as well.

Even in a cheery middle section, McCartney sings, "Went upstairs and had a smoke, somebody spoke and I went into a dream" followed by a billowing chorus of harmonies. The song fades with a single piano chord resonating for nearly a minute. Mysterious and wonderful, it achieved an unspoken Beatles goal: creating a song inscrutable yet appealing, as subject to debate and analysis about its meaning as anything by Bob Dylan.

* * *

There were doubters. The most influential was rock critic Richard Goldstein, who reviewed *Pepper* for the Sunday *New York Times*. "Like an over-attended child," he wrote, "*Sgt. Pepper* is spoiled … the obsession with production, coupled with a surprising shoddiness in composition, permeates the entire album. There is nothing beautiful on *Sgt. Pepper*."[66]

This was such an extreme minority view, so at odds with what the rest of the world was hearing, that it was immediately rendered irrelevant. Clearly, the mainstream press could not be trusted with something as precious as rock 'n' roll. In San Francisco, the ambitious young Jann Wenner convinced the dean of the Bay Area's music critics, the esteemed jazz writer Ralph J. Gleason, to back him in a biweekly magazine that would report and critique the burgeoning rock world respectfully but professionally. The magazine was *Rolling Stone,* and for at least its first few years was the most powerful arbiter of taste and opinion rock culture has ever had, with the authority and power to make or break bands, and to continue to bind this nationwide army of rock-music lovers as a unique counterculture.

Even before *Rolling Stone,* a magazine called *Crawdaddy* had begun publishing academic and pseudoacademic critiques of rock albums. And a number of weekly newspapers reporting on the youth/rock/drug culture and opposition to the war in Vietnam had begun sprouting up all over the country. The *Los Angeles Free Press,* the *Berkeley Barb,* the *East Village Other,* the *Real Paper* in Boston and dozens of others attracted talented young writers, artists, and photographers who rejected the bland "objectivity" and bloodless writing of the establishment newspapers. Collectively, these new publications constituted the underground press. Rock magazines such as *Fusion* in Boston and *Creem* in Detroit also played an important role in treating rock as a topic of legitimate discussion.

* * *

Coinciding with *Sgt. Pepper,* 1967 was the year an entire new regime of creative rock artists emerged or made their presence known on the scene.

The British folk singer Donovan created his distance from Dylan with two songs in early 1967 that captured the moment: "Sunshine Superman" and "Mellow Yellow." The latter was apparently about banana peels, a prank started by a *Berkeley Barb* writer who wrote that you could get a marijuanalike high smoking the stuff. Many tried; few succeeded in feeling anything but ridiculous.

Psychedelia wasn't really the Rolling Stones' strength, but they had to try to keep up with the Beatles. As journalist David Dalton wrote:

> It was the day after the release of *Sgt. Pepper* and ... Mick knew something was happening. Not to be outdone, and as a man who prides himself on being on time and in tune, Mick conceived a psychedelic satire on the Queen to be called *Satanic Majesties Request* (from the first line

in the front of British passports — "Her Britannic Majesty's Requests and requires ..."

Their *Satanic Majesties* was the mood of the times," Jagger said around that time. "You can't play or write outside the mood of the times unless you live on a mountain — and even in the south of France I wasn't that out of it ... it was flowers, beads and stars on yer face ... In fact, I'm rather fond of that album, and I wouldn't mind doing something like that again."[67]

The Stones never repeated that particular mistake, however. Dalton writes,

> Even taking into account that it was a year in the making, and recorded under very trying conditions (four busts; Brian was busted twice that year) and two trials — some found it hard to believe that the Stones were being serious. Was it really a parody of *Sgt. Pepper?* ... Less electric and flexible than the Beatles, the Stones seemed ill at ease with random experimentation of other musical forms, and they lacked the production polish of George Martin that had made the freakier parts of *Sgt. Pepper* stand up.[68]

Brian Wilson came closer to reaching *Sgt. Pepper's* grandeur, its musical variety and brilliance, and perhaps even its cultural impact. Yet between his perfectionism, his drug-induced mental illness and his competitiveness, *Pepper* drove Wilson a little mad.

He had already worked for months in 1967 on the next step beyond *Pet Sounds*. While that introspective album was considered a commercial failure in the United States, it was greeted rapturously in England, where it hit No. 2. The 1966 *New Musical Express* readers' poll named the Beach Boys the top musical personality in the "world" category. Paul McCartney, Eric Clapton, and the Rolling Stones manager/producer Andrew Loog Oldham all declared songs on *Pet Sounds* to be among the greatest ever made.

While the other Beach Boys toured (most triumphantly, in England), Wilson stayed in California refining "Good Vibrations," a single whose title alone captured more than any individual song the giddy possibilities of the era. Wilson deployed flutes, Jew's harp, piano, organ, cello, harmonica, layers of percussion and falsetto harmony, and a theremin, an electronic instrument that creates oscillating pitch and amplitude generated by waving ones hands over its antennas, to create his own wall of sound.

"Good Vibrations" (written by Mike Love and Wilson) and its follow-up single, "Heroes and Villains" (written with his new collaborator, Van Dyke Parks), were to be the core of *Smile*, which was expected to be Brian Wilson's defining epic. These daring singles unnerved the Beatles. Their producer, George Martin, said that "they were looking over their shoulders, seeing who was coming up on them along the rail." Wilson's music, Martin said, motivated them to "experiment more, and do rather more outrageous things" in the studio.

Meanwhile, the accolades were mounting. Leonard Bernstein, America's leading classical composer, conductor, and educator, had Wilson play "Surf's Up," another *Smile* track, on a TV show, declaring it was music that "claims the attention of every thinking person."

Yet as the sessions progressed, so did dissent and disintegration. The other Beach Boys, especially Mike Love, hated Parks's surreal and sometimes admittedly meaningless lyrics. Brian Wilson became more paranoid as the recordings went on. For a section called "Mrs. O'Leary's Cow" (which, according to legend, started the great Chicago fire of 1871), Wilson had musicians wear fire helmets and other gear, and filled the studio with smoke. Subsequent fires in a nearby section of Los Angeles convinced Wilson that his "teenage symphony to God" was somehow responsible. As Jeff Turrentine has written,

> Wilson's LSD-addled mood, already mercurial, hardened into a full-fledged bipolarity, marked by bursts of obsessive tweaking alternating with long periods of sulky inaction. He was acutely aware that with the release of *Sgt. Pepper's Lonely Hearts Club Band*, the Beatles were about to lay irrefutable claim to the title of Pop's Reigning Geniuses, and he was despondent at having lost the race to usher in the "new sound." By the time *Sgt. Pepper* came out, it was already sadly evident that *Smile* probably never would.[69]

And it wouldn't, for almost forty years.

It wasn't until 2004 that *Smile* was completed as intended, painstakingly re-created by Wilson and Van Dyke Parks. When it was released, it made the hype and anticipation of it its nearly forty-year interruption seem a minor miscue: As a single rock 'n' roll orchestral work, the 2004

Nonesuch recording of *Smile* places Brian Wilson in the ranks of great American composers, the work of a rock 'n 'roll George Gershwin.

As for Bob Dylan, he had withdrawn from the competition with the Beatles and Rolling Stones with an exclamation point — a motorcycle accident near his home in Woodstock, New York, on July 29, 1966, had nearly killed him; he suffered cracked vertebrae and a mild concussion.[70] Though the spin was that this was a near-death experience, Dylan biographers like Clinton Heylin believe his injuries to have been exaggerated. That he needed time off and away from his unexpected rock stardom was undeniable.

In the spring of 1967, Dylan began working with members of the Hawks, playing music every day with them in the pink house they had rented near Woodstock (in West Saugerties, New York) called Big Pink.

For six months every day that spring, summer, and fall, Dylan and the Hawks — Robbie Robertson, Richard Manuel, Garth Hudson, Rick Danko, and Levon Helm — met at the house at 1 p.m. and just played for their own enjoyment. Sometimes they'd spontaneously jam on rock classics or long-forgotten folk and country songs. Dylan wrote about thirty songs during the six-month period, including some that would stand with his best: "I Shall Be Released," "Tears of Rage" (cowritten by Manuel), and "This Wheel's on Fire" (with Danko), all of which appeared on the debut album by the Band (renamed from the Hawks), *Music from Big Pink*.[71] The informally recorded music would be known as "The Basement Tapes," and would remain unreleased (though available on the bootleg market) for many years.

When Dylan finally released an album in early 1968, it was another extreme change in direction. *John Wesley Harding*, was a reaction to the multitracked, multilayered music and multiple meanings of the psychedelic era, and his earlier work. With extremely spare, largely acoustic instrumentation, *JWH* nevertheless was as enigmatic and mystical as anything Dylan had recorded.

Dylan apparently decided he felt no need to compete with *Sgt. Pepper* and thought it was an "indulgent" album.

It could also be said that Dylan had "been there, done that." His two-record set *Blonde on Blonde*, released in the summer of 1966, was rock's surreal poetic classic. Dylan once said that individual tracks on

Blonde on Blonde were "the closest I ever got to the sounds I hear in my mind … It's that thin, that wild mercury sound. It's metallic and bright gold, whatever that conjures up."[72]

On *Blonde on Blonde*, Dylan had already stretched the boundaries of rock, blues, and freewheeling lyricism as far as it could go. Some songs were of epic length: the twelve-minute "Sad Eyed Lady of the Lowlands," the eight-minute-long "Visions of Johanna" and "Stuck Inside of Mobile with the Memphis Blues Again." There were also tighter pop songs, all of which became hits: "I Want You," "Just Like a Woman," and "Rainy Day Women #12 & #35"; its party-sound refrain, "everybody must get stoned" had suburban kids spending too much time wondering if it were true "rainy day woman" was some British slang for a joint. Much of the album was recorded in Nashville, where Dylan had become comfortable with the relaxed yet professional approach to recording.

Dylan, The Band, Eric Clapton

Dylan continued to confound admirers with the retrenchment that was *John Wesley Harding*, which is sparely arranged, with simple words touching on biblical imagery. Recorded in Nashville in fall 1967, it has a plainspoken directness not previously seen in Dylan's work, with running references to the Old and New Testament throughout the songs "I Dreamed I Saw St. Augustine," "The Wicked Messenger," "Drifter's Escape," "Dear Landlord," and "All Along the Watchtower" (the latter would quickly be adapted by Jimi Hendrix and become a bedrock part of his repertory). Dylan himself told *TV Guide* years later that *John Wesley Harding* was "the first biblical rock album."[73]

Dylan's final album of the 1960s was even more confounding to both folk and rock fans: *Nashville Skyline* (1969) was as its title suggested, a country music album, with appearances by Johnny Cash and Charlie Daniels. (It did yield the hit single, and one of Dylan's most recorded love songs, "Lay Lady Lay.")

At the time, the rock community regarded country, in its extreme, as the redneck music of Southern racists. But others saw Dylan's duet with Cash on "Girl of the North Country" a sign of rapprochement between the counterculture and Southern culture, a musical peace treaty signed and delivered to end this most tumultuous decade.

Dylan's imprimatur was also evident, and welcomed by fans, on *Music from Big Pink*. At a time when music was becoming louder, The Band's debut album was quiet, but heartfelt. The front cover was a primitive painting by Dylan of six musicians (maybe one meant to represent producer John Simon), and an elephant (perhaps Dylan's recognition that he was the elephant in the room). "I Shall Be Released," one of Dylan's most revered and hopeful ballads, closes the album; one of his most jolting rockers, "This Wheel's on Fire," written with Danko, is the penultimate song; "Tears of Rage," by Dylan and The Band's Richard Manuel, opens *Music from Big Pink*.

At the end of the 1960s, The Band's first two albums (their 1969 release was called simply *The Band*) were corrections, of course, that influenced other musicians in profound ways. Most notable among these was Clapton, who has said that the album changed his life.

In an era of guitarist worship, Clapton had few peers. He became an international superstar by moving away from the blues and into noisy, ego-driven improvisations with the trio Cream, which also comprised singer/bassist Jack Bruce and drummer Ginger Baker. Cream was a huge, but brief, success. All three had firm roots in the purist British blues revival earlier in the 1960s: Baker and Bruce had played in Alexis Korner's Blues Inc., Clapton and Bruce in John Mayall's Bluesbreakers.

Cream had a dual musical personality. Their own material, much of it written by Bruce and lyricist Peter Brown, could be witty, polished, politically progressive. Their signature commercial tune was "Sunshine of Your Love," whose rudimentary but addictive main riff would became a staple of hard-rock guitarists for decades to come. But live, they could take a blues standard like Willie Dixon's "Spoonful" and spend more than fifteen minutes bludgeoning it into submission. Some found this exciting; others found it tiresome, Clapton among them. Having heard an early pressing of *Music from Big Pink*, Clapton was taken by the spareness of the songs, the way the instruments — especially Robertson's guitar, Helm's drums, and Hudson's organ — blended so intuitively that the impact was intense without any solos. Clapton realized he was on the wrong track with Cream, which broke up in fall 1968. He quickly formed a group with the keyboard player and singer Steve Winwood and Baker, with good intentions but meager results.

As a sixteen-year-old Winwood had been the much-older sounding lead voice on the blues-rock hits "Gimme Some Lovin'" and "I'm a Man" in early 1967 by the Spencer Davis Group. (Davis, the nominal leader, was rhythm guitarist.) Winwood left to form the more musically elastic group Traffic with guitarist Dave Mason, drummer Jim Capaldi, and reed player Chris Wood. Drawing on everything from British folk music to American jazz, to blue-eyed soul to the melodic psychedelia embodied by their signature tune, "Dear Mr. Fantasy," Traffic moved at a steady, colorful pace.

Clapton was an admirer of Winwood and of Traffic, and at first he thought that Winwood might provide some grounding for Cream, not to mention act as a buffer between the mutually antagonistic Baker and Bruce. Winwood was not interested in Cream, so he, Clapton, Baker, and bassist Rick Grech formed the supergroup Blind Faith.

It lasted less than a year, launched and finished in 1969. It released only one album. The band could not avoid falling short of the oversized expectations drummed up by their U.S. record company, Atlantic. Audiences wanted to hear Clapton's thunder and Traffic's power surges. Blind Faith was more quiet and contemplative. One of the centerpiece songs was the hymnlike "In the Presence of the Lord," a place, at least musically, where Clapton was getting comfortable. 1970 would be his year to break out as a singer as well as a guitarist in control of his craft. A live album, *Delaney & Bonnie & Friends on Tour with Eric Clapton*, found him in a comfort zone with American rock and blues musicians Leon Russell, Bobby Whitlock, Carl Radle, and Jim Gordon. The headliners were a husband-wife team around which a large community of musicians had coalesced: Bonnie Bramlett was a fireball singer and dancer, Delaney Bramlett was songwriter, producer and singer. One of the spokes was singer Joe Cocker, the gruff-voiced working-class shouter from Sheffield, England, who had charmed Woodstock with his bellowing voice and spasmodic gestures on his version of the Beatles' "With a Little Help from My Friends." His 1970 tour featured Oklahoma-raised Russell, the piano-playing bandleader, fronting a musical menagerie that became known as *Mad Dogs & Englishmen*.[74]

That same prolific year, Clapton released two solo albums: the disappointing *Eric Clapton*, which for some reason downplayed his guitar playing, and *Layla and Other Assorted Love Songs* by the pseudonymous Derek & the Dominos: Clapton, Radle, Whitlock, and Gordon. The title track, featuring a heartfelt vocal and inspirational guitar duel with guest Duane Allman, is a cornerstone of modern rock. Clapton the rocker had one more brilliant set, *461 Ocean Boulevard* (1974), the address of the Miami studio at which it was recorded. The album featured Clapton's only No. 1 single, a jangly version of Bob Marley's defiant reggae tune, "I Shot the Sheriff." Later in the decade, Clapton would cement his preference for the restraint that has marked his recordings for the last thirty years with the laid-back *Slowhand*, beginning a successful musical relationship with the spotlight-shy songwriter and guitarist J. J. Cale ("Cocaine"), with whom Clapton cut a new album in 2006.

1967: Summer of Fire

A deep split was forming along generational lines in the Civil Rights movement. Martin Luther King and mainstream black organizations like the NAACP remained committed to nonviolence.

But the slow pace of progress in improving the lives of blacks was still causing anger and indignation in the cities. So did the violent repression of the Watts riots of 1965. And the Vietnam War was radicalizing many young blacks, who saw that a majority of those fighting and dying for America in Asia were the poor, blacks, and other people of color.

In 1966, the heavyweight champion Muhammad Ali (formerly Cassius Clay), refused induction into the U.S. Army and said he would not fight in Vietnam. The outspoken Ali became a lightning rod when he justified his stance, saying, "No Vietcong ever called me 'nigger.'" In 1967, he was stripped of his heavyweight title and sentenced to five years in prison for draft evasion. (His conviction was overturned in 1971.)

In fall 1966, Huey Newton and Bobby Seale started the Black Panther Party in Oakland, California. The most militant of organizations, the Panthers urged armed resistance against police.

The phrase "black power" was first used in a speech in 1967 by Stokely Carmichael, head of the Students Non-Violent Coordinating Committee (SNCC).

What did Carmichael mean by "black power"? He said it was an assertion of black pride and "the coming together of black people to fight for their liberation by any means necessary." The radical, confrontational rhetoric alienated many, black and white, who believed that nonviolent civil disobedience was essential to the cause of Civil Rights.[75]

More than 125 cities, including Cleveland and Washington, D.C., had substantial riots during the summer of 1967. But for rage and destruction, it was hard to match what happened in Newark and Detroit.

That summer, race riots consumed Newark (July 12–16) and Detroit (July 23–30). In Newark, the arrest and beating of a black cabdriver lit the fuse. During the ensuing week, twenty-six people were killed and all but two — a white detective and a white fireman — were black.[76] More than 1,000 were injured, and property damage ran to around $10 million.

The Detroit riot started when white police were making what was considered a routine raid at an unlicensed black after-hours club. Inside the club, however, were eighty-two people holding a welcome-home party for two black Vietnam veterans. The police called for reinforcements; a window was kicked-in.

Before it was over, the Michigan National Guard had to be backed up by the Army's 82nd Airborne division. When it was over, there were 43 dead, nearly 1,200 injured, and more than 7,000 arrested.

In both Newark and Detroit, looting and arson spread from the initial areas of concentration to wide swaths of the city. In both places, police harassment and brutality of blacks was persistent and widespread. In both cities, so-called "urban renewal" projects resulted in the bulldozing or planned destruction of homes in black neighborhoods to make way for a highway to the suburbs (Detroit) and a medical school (Newark).

What happened in Detroit was typical. "To build Interstate 75, Paradise Valley or 'Black Bottom,' … was buried beneath several layers of concrete. As the oldest established black enclave in Detroit, 'Black Bottom' was not merely a point on the map, but the heart of

Detroit's black community, commercially and culturally. The loss for many black residents of Detroit was devastating, and the anger burned for years thereafter."[77]

In both cities were grinding poverty, youth unemployment rates of more than 30 percent, the loss of factory jobs, and the enormous demographic change which in little more than a decade had created black majority cities whose citizens had little representation or control over the institutions that influenced their lives: city government, schools, police.

The number one single in June 1967 was Aretha Franklin's roof-rattling version of Otis Redding's "Respect." Franklin was the daughter of the Rev. C. L. Franklin, evangelist and pastor of one of Detroit's largest congregations, the New Bethel Baptist Church. Gospel greats James Cleveland, Mahalia Jackson, and Clara Ward sang regularly in the church; Aretha first sang solo there at twelve. Signed to Columbia Records in the early 1960s, she saw her gifts wasted as the label had her sing show tunes and utterly inappropriate material like "Swanee" and "Rock-a-Bye Your Baby with a Dixie Melody."

In 1967, Franklin began recording for Atlantic, which sent her to Muscle Shoals, Alabama, where the musicians and atmosphere were more attuned to soul music. "I Never Loved a Man (The Way I Love You)" struck gold right off the bat, Aretha playing gospel chords on the piano and letting her voice soar. "Respect" was awe-inspiring. And though the Otis Redding composition is putatively about a man and a woman, the demand for "R-E-S-P-E-C-T," as Aretha so clearly enunciated, suggested a partial, hopeful, simple solution to the tattered soul of black America that summer of 1967.

1968: The Year the World Fell Apart

Bookstores and library shelves are filled with books about 1968 for a good reason — it was at the very least, one of the most dramatic years of the twentieth century. The United States nearly broke apart in a generational civil war as deep and angry as the War Between the States slightly more than a hundred years earlier. Martin Luther King (April 4) and Robert F. Kennedy (June 6) were assassinated, ending hope that America would pursue a peaceful, progressive path at home and abroad.

The Vietnam War took a disastrous turn when the Viet Cong and North Vietnamese launched the Tet offensive on January 30, a broad attack on towns, cities, and military installations throughout South Vietnam. Though Tet did not achieve the goal of inflicting a quick military defeat of the United States and the South Vietnamese government, for the first time it became abundantly clear that despite our overwhelming advantage in numbers of troops, planes, bombs, weaponry, and pure military power, the United States appeared to be losing the Vietnam War.

Less than two weeks before Tet, on January 17, President Johnson asserted just the opposite in his State of the Union address. "The enemy has been defeated in battle after battle," he said. "Our patience and our perseverance will match our power."

The feeling that the United States government was simply lying to its people was widespread. Or, an even worse possibility: that the people in charge, from President Johnson to the military spokesmen in South Vietnam, actually believed the false or dubious information they were peddling as the truth.

The influential TV journalist Walter Cronkite, the fatherly anchorman of the *CBS Evening News,* gave vent to the frustrations of millions of Americans when he asked, "What the hell is going on? I thought we were winning this war."[78] Years later, the conservative humorist and commentator P. J. O'Rourke would say: "The Tet offensive was important because what sort of sunk in in the next month or two or three ... was that we were not going to win that war in Vietnam."

Rock music began expressing this sentiment in blunt terms. Country Joe & the Fish, from Berkeley, the main campus of the University of California and a town so liberal it was called "the People's Republic of Berkeley" by friend and foe alike, recorded the great protest song of 1968, the darkly comic "Fixin' to Die Rag." When Country Joe sang, "and it's one, two, three, what are we fighting for?" he was really asking a question that many Americans had no answer for. In search of Viet Cong, who blended easily into local populations, Army units would torch entire villages to the ground. The reasoning was typical, as one commander put it: "We destroyed the village in order to save it."

The war's moral bottom may have been reached on March 16, 1968, when five hundred Vietnamese civilians — old men, women, children, and babies — in the tiny village, or hamlet, of My Lai, were massacred by American soldiers.

In March, the Minnesota Senator Eugene McCarthy entered the New Hampshire Democratic primary as an antiwar candidate against President Johnson. College students and others cut their hair and put on jackets and ties in a "clean for Gene" door to door campaign, to help McCarthy attract voters in the conservative New England state. McCarthy was such a long-shot that polling a few hundred votes less than Johnson looked like a major victory. Robert Kennedy joined the race; at the end of the month, Johnson decided not to seek reelection.

But the chaos was only beginning, and it was worldwide.

On April 3, Martin Luther King Jr., in Memphis to support a strike by mostly black sanitation workers, gave one of his most inspirational speeches. King prophetically declared, "I've been to the mountaintop," that he had "seen the promised land. I may not get there with you, but we, as a people, will get to the promised land … I'm not fearing any man. Mine eyes have seen the glory of the coming of the Lord."

The next afternoon, as he stood on a balcony outside his Memphis hotel room, King was murdered by a rifle shot from a nearby window. A white man, a petty criminal with a racist pedigree named James Earl Ray, was convicted of killing King. But right until his death in prison in 1998, doubts about the extent of Ray's involvement resonated; even Dr. King's family doubted Ray was the assassin, or if he was, that he acted alone. Many believed he was the fall guy for other conspirators; that belief has never been proven. As Judge W. Preston Battle wrote in 1969 when sentencing Ray, the lack of sufficient evidence to indict co-conspirators is "of course, not conclusive evidence that there is no conspiracy."

Riots erupted in more than a hundred cities. One exception was Boston, where at the request of the mayor James Brown performed a televised concert, keeping people off the street.

Unrest was spreading from the nation's poorest streets to its most exclusive campuses. In April, protesters took over key buildings at Columbia University in New York, bringing classes on the Ivy League campus to a halt. A week later, the police were called in and dragged out the demonstrators with undeniable enthusiasm.

The Columbia disturbance did not resonate well with mainstream America — or even some nearby poor neighborhoods in adjoining neighborhoods like Harlem. "This wasn't throwing off the shackles of an oppressive and airless society," National Public Radio commentator Ray Suarez, who was growing up in an apartment building in the neighborhood, said years later. "It was people who were lucky, flaunting their luck … it was, look at these people who don't have to work their butt off like everybody I know does."

Students had broader support in France. On May 6, after running street fights with police in Paris, classes were canceled at the Sorbonne, the country's most prestigious university. In an alliance American leftists could only dream of, union members began a series of strikes in solidarity with the students, bringing France to a halt and nearly upending the government.

On June 3, Valerie Solanis shot the pop artist and Velvet Underground mentor Andy Warhol. She was an unbalanced former hanger-on who wrote the SCUM (Society for Cutting Up Men) Manifesto. Warhol recovered, but his death in 1987 after routine gall-bladder surgery may have been hastened by latent weaknesses stemming from the shooting.

The following day, June 4, Robert Kennedy won the California primary, and seemed well on his way to securing the Democratic presidential nomination in advance of the August convention. Shortly after making a touching acceptance speech at his headquarters at the Ambassador Hotel in Los Angeles, Kennedy was shot dead at point blank range by Sirhan Sirhan, a twenty-four-year-old Jordanian said to be upset by Kennedy's pro-Israel stance. Doctors worked furiously for many hours to save Kennedy's life, but he was pronounced dead early on the morning of June 6.

The murder of yet another American voice for peace and justice left the country bereft. The killing seemed to "break the year's back. Nothing good, one thought, could happen after that," *Time* magazine's Lance Morrow wrote years later.

By August, when the Democrats gathered in Chicago at their convention, the country seemed again on the brink of civil war. Thousands of protesters had gathered for what protest leaders Jerry Rubin and Abbie Hoffman called a "Festival of Life." Rubin and Hoffman had formed a political entity called the Youth International Party — the Yippies. The essence was guerrilla theater: one tactic included dropping money from the observation gallery onto the floor of the New York Stock Exchange.

Dozens of rock bands were invited to Chicago, but the aura of violence that permeated the summer kept most of them away. Paul Kantner of the Jefferson Airplane, whose music had evolved in a short year from songs about getting high to anthems of revolution, said before Chicago that "you were going up against a force that was not going to respond to you appropriately." The Airplane did not go to Chicago.

The MC5, revolutionary rockers from Detroit, did go to Chicago, but also anticipated trouble. "We knew it was going to be creepy as far as the Chicago police department went," guitarist Wayne Kramer said ... "There was going to be a clash."

The MC5 was set to perform in Lincoln Park on Sunday, August 25. The city had refused the protesters a concert permit, so the MC5 plugged into an electric outlet in a hotdog cart. Soon undercover policemen started fights in the audience; police on motorcycles stampeded through the crowd.

The next day, CBS reporters Dan Rather and Mike Wallace were both punched by Chicago policeman inside the convention hall. Anchorman Walter Cronkite called the police "thugs" and told the American people, "This convention belongs in a police state. No other way to put it."

In Grant Park, protesters chanting, "The whole world is watching" tried to fly the American flag at half-mast. The police attacked again, clubbing anyone in their path — senior citizens, pregnant women, journalists. Inside the convention hall, Connecticut Sen. Abraham Ribicoff was at the podium, staring at Chicago's omnipotent ruler, Mayor Richard Daley. Ribicoff denounced "Gestapo tactics on the streets of Chicago." The Mayor gave Ribicoff the finger. Everything was televised. Protest leader Rennie Davis noted that, "the brutality of the Vietnam War" was now coming home.

More than ever, rock 'n' roll was a mirror of the time. "The music got darker," said the late music journalist Timothy White. The war was certainly coming to rock 'n' roll. Not as protest music, but as commentary. The Doors' "Unknown Soldier" ("unborn living, living dead/bullet strikes the helmets head") from their 1968 album *Waiting for the Sun* made explicit the fear and paranoia that was being shipped back from Vietnam along with thousands of body bags. On "Five to One," the Doors boasted, "They got the guns but we got the numbers." As always, however, the guns ruled.

All three of the Jimi Hendrix Experience albums — *Are You Experienced, Axis: Bold As Love,* and *Electric Ladyland* peaked during 1968. Though he may have been concerned about his lack of popularity among blacks in the street, he was a favorite of soldiers in Vietnam (black and white). His music emanated throughout Vietnam from Armed Forces Radio like a black rainbow.

Other rock bands also had top 40 hits while exploring the dark side of the late 60s.

Creedence Clearwater Revival were masters of roots rock. Even though from El Cerrito in Northern California, singer/guitarist/songwriter John Fogerty's evocations of voodoo, hoodoo, and bayous made people think they were from the swamp. That's one reason American soldiers adopted Creedence as a favorite band — songs like "Suzie Q," released in the summer of 1968, sounded like it belonged in the humid, tropical Asian jungle, and their rendition of another fifties hit, Screamin' Jay Hawkins "I Put a Spell on You" sounded like a talisman to keep the nightmares at bay. (Fogerty had served in the Army reserves. Among the most lasting of their Vietnam-era hits was 1970's "Fortunate Son," a three-minute rock 'n' roll song that exposed the class differences that made the war so contemptible to many. Speaking as a soldier in the field, Fogerty sang: "It ain't me, it ain't me, I ain't no senator's son.")

Even the black gospel-rock group, the Chambers Brothers, hit an ominous note in 1968: Their ten-minute-long "Time Has Come Today" sounded like the arrival of doom. The 2006 version by *American Idol* runner-up Bo Bice lacks the prophetic fearfulness of the original.

The time had come: time had come for forces of oppression to crack down all over the world. During the Democratic convention in Chicago, Russian tanks rolled into Prague, Czechoslovakia, crushing a brief experiment with autonomy and liberalism that was known as "the Prague Spring." In Mexico City, soldiers killed as many as three hundred demonstrators on October, ten days before the Olympic games opened in the capital.

At the Mexico City games, two black American track stars, Tommie Smith and John Carlos won the gold and bronze medals, respectively, in the 200-meter run. As they stood on the winners box and "The Star-Spangled Banner" played, Smith and Carlos bowed their heads and raised black-gloved right fists in the air in a Black Power salute. Smith and Carlos were stripped of their medals and kicked off the U.S. Olympics team.

On November 5, in what was then the closest election in American history, Richard Nixon, preaching a "law and order" platform appealing to what he called "the silent majority," defeated Hubert Humphrey, the Democrat who could not shake off the stigma of Chicago, nor his support for the war as LBJ's too-loyal vice president. Former Alabama Govenor George Wallace, running as an independent, won five Southern states, which — with the exception of 1976, when Georgia Governor Jimmy Carter was elected — have been reliably Republican ever since. Nixon got 43.4 percent of the popular vote to 42.7 percent for Democrat Hubert Humphrey, and Wallace making a startlingly strong showing with 13.5 percent. Blue-collar audiences loved his baiting of protesters on the campaign trail. Showing contempt for their easy way with epithets, Wallace would say he had a few four-letter words for them: "W-O-R-K" and "S-O-A-P."

Among the memorable political/cultural events of 1968 was the feminist protest September 7 at the Miss America contest in Atlantic City. It was a "symbolic bra-burning," as one of the participants called it, though contrary to legend, no bras were set afire. But the impact was the same: women no longer wanted to be judged like cattle by demeaning male definitions of beauty.

Backing up this attitude symbolically were both Grace Slick of Jefferson Airplane and Janis Joplin of Big Brother and the Holding Company. They embodied a new stance for women in rock, replacing the coy, cute pose of previous white women performers with striking, bold assertiveness.

Oddly, it was a Broadway show that tried to explain to America what the sex, drugs, long hair, and rock 'n' roll was about. On April

29, *Hair,* known as the "tribal love rock musical" opened on Broadway, after a successful off-Broadway run and ran for 1,750 performances. Some were shocked by the brief yet complete frontal nudity in the show, and in some cities *Hair* was busted for obscenity.

Hair was a series of vignettes dealing with the conflict between generations, the war, sex, drugs, and all of the other elements of life that were bewildering to so many Americans. "*Hair* is the one current show which exactly reflects the temper of the times," one TV reviewer said the day after the opening.[79]

The theater notes described the point of the show: "The tribes are forming, establishing their own way of life, their own morality, ideologies, their own mode of dress, behavior, and the use of drugs, by the way, has a distinct parallel in ancient cultures, in tribal spiritual tradition, both east and west."

Even the conservative ideological godfather William F. Buckley, writing in his *National Review* magazine, seemed somewhat enchanted by *Hair*: "A great deal of energy — and talent — go into the production of this psychedelic extravaganza," he wrote.[80]

The irony is that however hard *Hair* meant to shock, it could not compete with the startling reality happening in the world beyond the theater doors.

Jimi Hendrix

Even in an age of monthly musical miracles, guitarist, singer, and songwriter Jimi Hendrix was special. As a guitarist, he was rock's first and still greatest virtuoso: a musician whose talent was as great as his imagination was unlimited. In the mid-1960s, Hendrix played guitar in bands led by Little Richard and the Isley Brothers, but chafed at having to play the same songs the same way night after night. "I was always kept in the background," he once told Melody Maker's Chris Welch, "but I was thinking all the time about what I wanted to do. I used to join a group and quit them so fast. I dug listening to top 40 R & B but that doesn't mean I like to play it every night."*

---

* David Dalton and Lenny Kaye, *Rock 100* (1977).

In 1965, the started his own band, calling himself Jimmy James and his group the Blue Flames. They had a regular showcase at the Cafe Wha? [sic] in New York's Greenwich Village. With most of the folk singers having moved on to Los Angeles, the Village clubs began booking adventurous rock bands: the Blues Project had a regular gig at the Cafe Au Go Go; Frank Zappa and the Mothers of Invention had a residency at the Garrick Theater.

Chas Chandler of the Animals saw Hendrix in the Village, became his co-manager, and brought him to England. Chandler's strategy was brilliant, as David Dalton and Lenny Kaye describe it. "Chandler and co-manager Michael Jeffrey put their pieces together carefully. The idea of a black guitarist breaking and entering white ranks could only be looked on as natural in England, in a country where American blues artists were lionized long after they'd been forgotten in their homeland: and Chandler-Jeffrey sweetened the mix further bv dressing Jimi and back-up musicians Noel Redding (bass) and Mitch Mitchell (drums) in all manner of exotic finery."[*]

The interracial band was an immediate sensation in London, creating a huge buzz in the United States. The Jimi Hendrix Experience, as the band was called, made its American debut at the Monterey Pop Festival, an appearance Hendrix climaxed by burning his guitar while playing his feedback-drenched adaptation of "The Star-Spangled Banner."

The debut album, *Are You Experienced?,* released in spring 1967, left listeners gaping in awe. "Purple Haze," "Foxy Lady," and "Manic Depression" took guitar rock and electronics to new frontiers. He used feedback, echo, and wah-wah, shifted between major and minor chords, unleashed dazzling runs of notes that were at once blues-based and a kind of audio science fiction.

"Electricity was never mere amplification for Hendrix," Dalton and Kaye wrote. "But rather the unfolding of an alien terrain to be roamed at will." He could also compose graceful melodies, as he did on oft-covered songs like "Wind Cries Mary" and "Angel." He was admired by jazz greats, from arranger Gil Evans, who recorded an album of Hendrix songs with an orchestra, to Miles Davis, whose jazz fusion breakthroughs like "Bitches Brew" might have never occurred had it not been for the influence of Hendrix.

And he was a masterful interpreter. His first single, "Hey Joe," was a bluesy, down-tempo version of a usually frenetic folk-rock standard in the repertory of numerous Los Angeles bands, including

---

* Ibid.

the Leaves, who had a top-forty hit with it, and Love, an immensely influential interracial group led by Arthur Lee. In concert, Hendrix would play everything from the Troggs' "Wild Thing" to Dylan's "Like a Rolling Stone" in ways that illuminated and expanded the original versions. Hendrix' version of Dylan's "All Along the Watchtower" is imbued a with lost-in-the-spiritual funhouse spirit that fills out some of the ideas for which Dylan himself may have been searching.

Hendrix was "a blues-based rock musician who had the same basic approach to his instrument as a jazz musician would have. [He] never played the song the same way twice. He was constantly inflecting notes with different resonances, getting different sounds out of his guitar, and he placed a high emphasis on improvisation."[*]

Two more albums with the Experience, *Axis: Bold As Love* and *Electric Ladyland,* named after the New York studio he built with engineer and producer Eddie Kramer, consolidated Hendrix's reputation, which needed no further burnishing. But he got it, anyway, at the Woodstock Festival in August 1969, where Hendrix and a new band closed the show.

Yet Hendrix's restlessness and unease with stardom were apparent. And in the "blatantly erotic arrogance" of his performances, he was a Rohrschach of a neurotic society's projections about race and sex.

In an era of black power and black identity, he was not embraced by a black audience. "In the Village people were more friendly than in Harlem where it's all cold and mean. Your own people hurt you more," he told Michael Lydon about his 1966 days in New York. "Anyway, I had always wanted a more integrated sound. Top-Forty stuff is all out of gospel, so they try to get everybody up and clapping, shouting, 'yeah, yeah.' We don't want everybody up. They should just sit there and dig it. And they must dig it, or we wouldn't be here."

There's little question that Hendrix would have continued to grow, take rock, jazz, and the rest of pop music in directions no one could have imagined. We'll never know. He was found dead September 18, 1970, in the London apartment of a girlfriend. Hendrix suffocated on his own vomit after taking an unintentional overdose of barbiturates.

---

[*] Craig Matthews, "Jazz Primer for Rock People" *Oculus Magazine*, November 1995.

The Beatles: *The White Album*

The Beatles released important albums in November 1968, songs that were written and recorded during this tragic, tumultuous, and almost unbelievable year. The Beatles record was untitled but known as *The White Album,* for its plain cover. It was a sprawling two-record set. For most fans, it was a great success, a record of enormous range displaying what appeared to be yet another creative growth spurt by the band.

And in the long run, it has been by far the group's best-selling album, certified for sales of more than 19 million by the Recording Industry Assn. of America (RIAA). The two hit singles collections — *The Beatles: 1962–1966* and *The Beatles: 1967–1970* have sold 16 million and 15 million, respectively. *Abbey Road* has sold 12 million, *Sgt. Pepper* 11 million.

If *The White Album* was the work of genius, it was the first and only Beatles album to exhibit individual genius rather than collective brilliance. For at this point, the four Beatles could hardly stand the sight of one another, and many of the tracks on the album were recorded by the individuals who wrote the particular song, with the others either not appearing at all or overdubbing their own parts in solitary detachment from the now-toxic chemistry.

There were many reasons for the mutual disdain. After four years of the most intense celebrity, fame had become a prison. And each was growing in different directions, causing resentment from the others. Lennon's consuming love affair with Japanese conceptual artist Yoko Ono might not have been so burdensome to the other Beatles if he had not unilaterally breached the band's solidarity by insisting that Yoko attend their recording sessions, an intrusion not before permitted. Harrison, for his part, had remained a devotee of all things from India, including the Maharishi Mahesh Yogi, the popularizer of what was known as Transcendental Meditation. The Beatles and their wives and girlfriends had all gone along with Harrison on a pilgrimage to India in 1967 to be with the Maharishi; only Harrison stuck with it.

Their longtime recording engineer, Geoff Emerick, wrote,

> It seemed from the start of the *White Album* sessions, the Beatles were bringing their problems into the studio for the first time. If John had made a nasty crack about the Maharishi that George resented, they would have a go at each other while gathered around a microphone to do backing vocals. If Paul criticized Ringo's drumming, Ringo would get moody; if George dared question any of Paul's suggestions, Paul would get into a

snit. And if any of the band members had done anything which an overly defensive John viewed as a potential slight to his new girlfriend — who sat by his side impassively the entire time they were making the album — he would be lashing out at all of them with his acid tongue."[81]

And yet … if the Beatles were feeling nasty, these were nasty times, and once again, the disparate collection of songs seemed to capture the moment. Just a year after the Summer of Love, there was violence everywhere. Just a year after *Sgt. Pepper,* the ultimate Beatles group statement, the Beatles were fracturing.

Among the standout songs, Paul's "Back in the U.S.S.R." was a parody of Cold War tensions, and a little wink at the Beach Boys, with its surfer harmony bridge and play on the California group's one-time dependence on Chuck Berry songs like "Back in the U.S.A.," to which the tune was an obvious tribute.

Lennon's scathing wit was evident in "Happiness Is a Warm Gun," another song whose music looked back to the early days of rock, with a mock doo-wop harmony arrangement. As usual, Lennon elided direct topical commentary for bitter satire; the wicked irony of "Warm Gun," written during the murderous year of 1968, had a little bit of the spirit of Jonathan Swift's scathing 1729 essay, "A Modest Proposal," in which he suggested, to avoid them being a burden to their families or society, that the Irish eat their own children.

One of Harrison's most lasting individual songs, "While My Guitar Gently Weeps" also starred on the *White Album.* The other Beatles, supposedly, were so uninterested in recording the song that Harrison invited Eric Clapton to play on the track, and it was Clapton who recorded the solo with the famously "weepy" tone, while Harrison played rhythm guitar and sang.

There were two songs called "Revolution"; "No. 9" was an eight-minute abstract sound collage, using tape loops, and special effects. This showed the influence of Yoko Ono, who had been affected by the music of experimental composers of John Cage and Karlheinz Stockhausen, whose work this resembles. The other "Revolution" also by Lennon, may have been the most controversial song on the album, as listeners parsed what seemed to be Lennon's most direct opinion regarding the shift in protests, from peaceful to rhetorically confrontational to violent.

The lyrics of the song can be interpreted as a cautionary response to the most extreme elements of the counterculture movement of the era, as Lennon outlines several limits to his support of political and social revolutionary action, in the most famous case rejecting violence:

> "But when you talk about destruction
> Don't you know that you can count me out."

So much did the rock culture of 1968 depend on the Beatles' support that the next line, "Don't you know it's gonna be all right," caused paroxysms of confusion and engendered heated debate in college dormitories and political protest meanings around the country. What does "it's gonna be all right" mean? Does it mean should we keep marching, or is he saying things will get better whether we march or not is he against destruction or "talk about destruction"?

Strangely, and sickeningly, well-intended though perplexed young people weren't the only ones seeking messages in songs on the *White Album*. A charismatic sociopath ex-convict named Charles Manson had collected a cult of misfits and runaways he called The Family, who lived on the fringe of the Southern California desert. In his twisted imagination, Manson believed that the songs on the *White Album* were a virtual instruction manual to carry out his apocalyptic visions.[82] "Helter Skelter," one of McCartney hardest-rocking songs ever (he was said to be inspired to try to match the sound and fury of the Who), was thought by Manson to signal the coming of a race war. Just after midnight on August 9, 1969, four members of the Manson family (three of them women) entered the posh Bel-Air home of the pregnant actress Sharon Tate, wife of director Roman Polanski, who was in Europe shooting a movie. Tate and three others in the house with her were murdered in a frenzy of stabbing and terror — 102 stab wounds altogether. The word "pigs" was written in blood; the next night, in a similar raid at another Los Angeles home, Leno and Rosemary LaBianca were brutally stabbed to death. On their refrigerator were written the words "HEALTER SKELLTER" (sic). Prosecutor Vincent Bugliosi wrote a best-selling book about the trials and conviction of the Manson family: It was called *Helter Skelter,* indelibly entwining the Beatles' song with one of the sickest ritual murders in American history.

1969: Year of the Rock Festival
Woodstock and Altamont

1969 was the year of the rock festival. Two stand out, for very different reasons. The Woodstock Music & Art Fair at rural Bethel/White Lake, New York, in August and the Rolling Stones free concert at Altamont Motor Speedway sixty miles from San Francisco in December provide almost too neat bookends to describe rock's developing mass culture at its kindest and most life-affirming and its descent into brutality, chaos, and death.

The ideal of Woodstock was stated in its advertisements: "Three Days of Peace and Music." The idea was to find a site near Woodstock in Ulster County, New York, long home to artists, folk musicians, and other bohemian types that had become newly chic as home of Bob Dylan. The promoters, all in their twenties, found a site in nearby Walkill, New York. But negotiations with the local authorities continued to bog down, and Walkill pulled out altogether a month before the scheduled show.

Max Yasgur had a large dairy farm on the other side of the Catskill Mountains in Bethel, in Sullivan County, seventy miles from Dylan's home. (Despite personal pleas, Dylan was never on the lineup and did not perform.) Woodstock Ventures leased six hundred acres of his land for $75,000. It was a bucolic setting and just right for a concert: a kind of hill for the stage, then a sloping bowl for the audience, and a scenic lake behind that.

Right up to the last minute there was resistance from some local politicians, building permits withheld. But 180,000 tickets had been sold. And despite the obstacles, and not counting Dylan and the Beatles, the promoters had succeeded in booking every major and minor rock and folk act they could find: Jimi Hendrix, Jefferson Airplane, Janis Joplin, the Who, Creedence Clearwater Revival, The Band, Crosby, Stills & Nash, Santana, Janis Joplin, Joan Baez, Sly & the Family Stone ... the list went on and on. The imagination of America's rock-loving young had been captured, and they came. And came, and came. Crowds descended on the tiny Catskills hamlet a full day before the official kick-off of the music at 5 p.m. on August 15, continuing into Monday August 18 with the early morning performance by Jimi Hendrix and his new band.

Two and a half time times the 180,000 filled the narrow two line road leading to the site. Traffic jams were 20 miles long; people just dumped their cars and hiked.

Though state and local authorities were prepared for a crowd, no one expected the nearly half a million — 450,000, by most counts, who showed up. Just the sheer mass of people caused the fences to go down; for those who came without tickets, it was a free concert.

There wasn't nearly enough food, water, or toilet facilities to provide basic comforts for so many people for three days and nights. And, to top it off, it rained like crazy from almost the moment the concert began. The then-right-wing *New York Daily News* gloated on its famous cover for Saturday, August 16: "HIPPIES MIRED IN SEA OF MUD."

But what made Woodstock special was that the vast majority of people did not seemed to mind. The adverse conditions resulted in a remarkable display of comradeship, sharing blankets, tents and limited food and drink, not to mention plenty of marijuana, which added to the generally peaceful mood.

All the musicians showed up, and seemed captivated, and motivated, by the enormous crowds and the united spirit of the fans. Many who attended felt that the event was the pinnacle of their lives.

The moment was captured in song by Joni Mitchell, whose composition "Woodstock" became a hit for Crosby, Stills and Nash.

Ironically, Mitchell was one scheduled performer who never made it to the event.

"We had played in Chicago on Friday night (with Crosby, Stills and Nash), we got out to the airport, found out Woodstock was a disaster area ... I had to do a TV show in NY Monday morning,[83] so the managers and agents ... it was deemed by the bosses, 'Joni, be a good girl and go to New York.' I became one of the fans that missed it," Mitchell told the BBC.[84]

Mitchell doesn't believe she could have written the song if she had been there, backstage. "It was the audience that was the phenomenon, the sharing, that mass spirit, no other festival had that. Woodstock [was] a kind of modern miracle."

The *Village Voice*, a New York weekly that was then the most journalistically professional and distinctive representative of the alternative press, captured what Woodstock meant to many of the individuals attending. As their onsite reporter, Steve Lerner, noted,

> Although in the beginning the music was good enough reason for the gathering at White Lake, ... one got the feeling something larger was at stake. Indeed, most of the people who made the trip seemed to be looking for a kind of historic coming out party for the East Coast freak population. Many of the longhairs who walked up to 10 miles to the fair grounds after abandoning their cars were the only hippies on their block or in their hometown, and the mass rally served as a confirmation of their lifestyle after months of sitting alone counting their psychedelic beads.[85]

Just weeks after Woodstock, the second annual Isle of Wight festival was held in the United Kingdom. Bob Dylan, the Band, the Who, the Moody Blues, and Joe Cocker, drew nearly 200,000 people to a large and largely peaceful gathering reachable by ferry in southwest England. The Isle of Wight fest, which had started in 1968, became an annual affair, and the Who's headlining performance at the 1970 get-together was released on DVD in 2005 and captures one of England's greatest bands at the peak of its force and fury, performing a good chunk of *Tommy*, the rock opera.

Three months after Woodstock, the mighty Rolling Stones, who didn't play at the festival, were pressured by the self-righteous San Francisco musical/political community, which wanted a Woodstock of its own.

In late October or early November, the Stones played a smashingly good, sold-out concert at Oakland-Alameda County Coliseum, continuing to show their support for blues, and R&B by featuring the great blues guitarist B.B. King, and the Ike and Tina Turner Revue, the hottest R&B act in the country, as opening artists. Tickets cost around $7.

But the Bay Area wanted a free concert, and the Stones somehow felt obliged. First it was set for Golden Gate Park, but the city refused to grant the necessary permits. A site was found in the nearby suburbs, at Sears Point Raceway in Sonoma. A stage was even built at the site. But that, too, did not work out. Desperate, with famed San Francisco attorney Melvin Belli manning the phones, a last minute switch was made, and on December 6, 1969, the concert was held at the Altamont Motor Speedway, about sixty miles west of San Francisco.

The images of this nightmare were captured for posterity in the movie *Gimme Shelter,* by the noted documentary directors Albert and David Maysles and Charlotte Zwerin, who'd been shooting the Stones' otherwise successful 1969 tour.

At the advice of the Grateful Dead, which had good relations with the Hell's Angels, the Stones hired the notorious motorcycle gang to provide "security" for the concert, for a fee of numerous cases of beer.

The weather was overcast and cold: 30 degrees that morning. No buffer separated the Stones from the crowd pushing toward the stage. People on weird drug trips found their way to the stage. Neither the Angels nor the Stones were pleased. But the Stones didn't come packing pool cues and knives; the Angels did. One hapless fan knocked over one of the Angels' bikes, and was beaten mercilessly. Marty Balin of Jefferson Airplane was punched during that group's set. The Stones came on and were performing "Sympathy for the Devil" when indeed, hell broke loose. The Angels were beating and kicking people. A wave of paranoia gripped the crowd. The Stones, for the first and perhaps last time, stopped playing in the middle of the song as Jagger pleaded for calm. "Hey, people … sisters, sisters and brothers, brothers and sisters. Everybody just cool out. Everybody be cool now, come on … All right … Something very funny happens when we start that number."

Things got worse. During "Under My Thumb," things came to a halt again, and Jagger quickly discovered, to his own everlasting chagrin, that he had no power to control the situation. "Who's fighting and what for?" he repeated. As it turns out, a very stoned black man named Meredith Hunter was fighting with a Hell's Angel. The documentary crew cameras capture the scene: a Hell's Angel with a knife in his hand, using an overhand motion, stabbing the other man repeatedly. The light catches a silver reflection from the other man's pocket. Apparently,

Hunter had a gun. (For that reason, a jury later found the Angel inno-cent of all charges; the knife-killing was ruled self-defense.)

The crowd is aghast. The Stones don't know what to do. They rush their way through "Street Fighting Man" and run for their helicopter.

It would seem intuitive to say that Woodstock was the start of something positive, and Altamont the end — a symbolic, violent end for the rock 'n' roll sixties. But some counterintuitive ideas should be considered.

One is that Woodstock was not really the beginning of an era of visionary creativity in rock culture, but its end. True, Woodstock showed that rock could be a unifying, galvanizing force for an incipient youth culture. Woodstock turned corporate America on to rock as a commodity to be exploited, the rock fans a burgeoning, powerful con-sumer force. Woodstock made rock too big and important for radio station owners and managers to ignore. The competition for advertis-ing dollars based on ratings points caused the end of progressive, free-form radio. Rather than relying on the taste, passion, and expertise of the disc jockey, the tight playlists of post-Woodstock rock stations were dictated by program directors, who in turn were programmed by a handful of consultants who removed all spontaneity and personality from both the radio stations and the music that they played. Wood-stock led to the homogenous, faceless "corporate rock" that dominated rock radio in the 1970s.

Casting rock musicians as heroes with almost mythological power was not good for the health of the rock star, either. The mortality role of those who died relatively soon after Woodstock, from drugs, alcohol, suicide, accident, or misadventure, is frightening: Hendrix, Joplin, Paul Butterfield, Tim Hardin, Keith Moon of the Who, Al Wilson of Canned Heat, Richard Manuel, and later Rick Danko of The Band.

Meanwhile, the Rolling Stones never lost a step after Altamont or even in the nasty prelude to the fateful autumn. The band's cofounder, Brian Jones, the guitarist who was the charismatic rival to Jagger, had been tossed from the band on June 8, 1969. Despite his great musi-cal gifts — he played everything from slide guitar to sitar — Jones had been on a drug-induced, self-destructive spiral for years; one can imagine just how deep into such drug-induced depravity one would have to fall before it became too much for even the other Rolling

Stones to deal with. Jones was found dead in his swimming pool on July 3, 1969. The circumstances of the death are invariably preceded by the word "mysterious," and some not entirely credible books and articles say that he was murdered by some of the resentful workmen on his estate, who in some angry prank that got out of control were alleged to have held his head underwater until he expired. Jones, like Hendrix, Joplin, and Morrison, was just twenty-seven when he died.

Jones was replaced by Mick Taylor, whose skills on guitar and other string instruments and relative absence of addictions made him a strong addition to the Stones musically. In fact, a free concert at July 5 at London's Hyde Park was meant to introduce Taylor as a full-time member of the band; instead, it was more of a memorial to Jones. Jagger began the concert by dedicating a reading of Shelley's "Adonais" in honor of Jones; thousands of butterflies were released but, somewhat ironically, they hadn't been cared for properly in the preceding days, and many were dead on arrival.

The new Stones album at the time of Altamont was *Let It Bleed*. The essential song from the album, "Gimme Shelter," almost anticipated the tragedy that was about to happen, the confusion of hippie wistfulness and violent reality: "Love … is just a shot away," Jagger sang.

The run of four albums — *Beggar's Banquet* and *Let It Bleed* in 1968 and 1969, *Sticky Fingers* and *Exile on Main Street* following immediately thereafter — are the evidence on which the Rolling Stones have been able to deservedly claim the mantle of "World's Greatest Rock 'n' Roll" band. The Beatles had broken up, Dylan had semiretired and played around with country music, the Beach Boys had splintered and Brian Wilson temporarily cracked up, the Who were making rock operas … all this time, the Rolling Stones' were alone, perfecting rock 'n' roll, both for their time and for ages to come. Altamont was, historically speaking, a hiccup.

Rock In Transition: The Velvet Underground, Lou Reed, the New York Dolls, T-Rex, Roxy Music

In March 1967, the Beatles' "Penny Lane" was No. 1, sunny in the United States, a sunny precursor to the Summer of Love. That month, a debut album called *The Velvet Underground & Nico* was released by the least hip of the then-major record companies, MGM Records. The cover featured a peel-off banana peel and the large signature of its designer, the group's mentor and patron, the artist Andy Warhol. The Velvet Underground was singer, guitarist, and songwriter Lou Reed; John Cale, the Welsh-trained electric viola player whose solo and production work have been influential since the 1970s; Sterling Morrison, who eventually received a Ph.D. in medieval literature; and Maureen Tucker, the first woman to be the drummer of a rock band of any consequence. Nico was a German model and borderline-capable singer Warhol inserted into the band and credited as "chanteuse."

The Velvet Underground & Nico reached a chart peak of No. 171 on The *Billboard* Top Album chart in April 1967. Such commercial failure was understandable, in retrospect, a fate consigned to those as detached from the mainstream currents of their time as the Velvets were. While the West Coast and England were providing the soundtrack for utopian marijuana epiphanies and the curative powers of love, the Velvet Underground's songs were about hard drugs ("Heroin"), sadomasochism ("Venus in Furs"), and paranoia ("I'm Waiting for the Man").

Compare the sunny optimism of that spring's Monterey Pop Festival with this description of a Velvet Underground performance as part of Warhol's multimedia show, The Exploding Plastic Inevitable. Author Victor Bockris describes the scene:

> Two of Warhol's films were projected side by side on a floor-to-ceiling white wall behind the band. The Velvets, all dressed in black, often turned their backs to the audience. Nico, all in white, sang under a single harsh spotlight. In front of them, two Warhol dancers in black leather ... one often brandishing a whip, acted out images from the songs. Over the stage, Warhol hung a spinning mirrored ball. From a balcony at the other end of the hall, Warhol focused colored strobe lights on the stage ... Combined with the loudest rock music ever heard at the time, [it] disoriented the audience, with mixed messages of love, peace, hate and revenge.... Warhol's show filled the space with images as disturbing and abrasive as Reed's songs.[86]

The Velvets, relieved of Nico, built their underground reputation with albums *White Light, White Heat* (1967), *Velvet Underground* (1969), and *Loaded* (1970). The denouement of *White Light, White Heat* is the seventeen-minute, twenty-five-second "Sister Ray," described by MTV's Kurt Loder as "an unprecedented explosion of pure squall-and-thrash noise" with Reed, in his effectively affectless monotone, singing about "a smack-fueled orgy featuring drag queens, sailors and God knows what else. Predictably, the record-buying public did not want to know about such stuff."[87] Cale left to pursue a prolific career as solo artist and producer; he was replaced by a more conventional musician, Doug Yule, for the 1969 album *The Velvet Underground*. "Pale Blue Eyes," and "Beginning to See the Light" showcased Reed's maturation as a song craftsman, though the mainstream-shunning experiments ("Murder Mystery," the nearly nine-minute "audio montage") continued.

Loaded was the last studio album by the Velvets, the one with the most commercial focus and two of the great rock anthems ever recorded: "Sweet Jane" and "Rock & Roll." The Velvets were so estranged from any kind of meaningful relationship with the radio industry by this point that "Rock & Roll," a tribute to the healing powers of hearing the music on the radio, received almost no airplay. Maybe it was lines like "despite all the amputations/you could still dance to the rock 'n' roll station" that made programmers feel that they were being damned with faint praise.

Though the Velvets didn't connect with the collective imagination back then, their influence has been so pervasive that it has often been said that not many people heard the Velvet Underground, but that everyone who did started a band. Their expressions of nihilism inspired many a punk rock band, while their assertion of rock as a living art form gave intellectual cover to many of the more experimental acts of the 1970s onward.

Reed, still one of rock's most vital contrarians, made his influence felt as a solo artist in the 1970s. Reed grew up in suburban Long Island, New York, and played in local bands as early as the late 1950s. His earliest recorded work was as a member of a group called the Jades, which recorded "Leave Her for Me" and "So Blue" in 1958 for producer Bob Shad's Time label; as Lewis Reed, he recorded "Your Love" and "Merry Go Round" in 1962, also for Shad, but not released until they appeared in 2000 on the U.K. CD *Rockin' on Broadway: The Time Brent Shad Story.*

While a literature major at Syracuse University studying with the noted poet Delmore Schwartz, Reed kept his rock 'n' roll inclinations — especially an infatuation with doo-wop — under wraps. After college and before the Velvets, he was a staff songwriter for Pickwick Records, a budget line label known for putting together cheap knock-offs of whatever pop trend was popular at any given time in the early and mid-1960s.

Reed's solo breakthrough was his second album, *Transformer* (1972), produced by David Bowie and Spiders from Mars guitarist, Mick Ronson. The opening song, "Vicious," sung in Reed's sarcastic monotone, is deliberately bitchy: "You hit me with a flower … oh, you're so vicious." The back cover featured a gorgeous drag queen in one photo and a prototypically macho gay hustler with what seemed like a very long flashlight outlined from zipper to thigh on his blue jeans.

Transformer contained one of rock history's most unlikely top-forty hits, "Walk on the Wild Side." Reed recounts the tics of some of the Warhol characters he had once hung out with; there is a clearly enunciated, utterly unambiguous reference to oral sex. A few years before, or a few years later, it certainly would have been banned from the radio: why it wasn't at the time is still a kind of delightful mystery. The song's popularity, though, helped bring glam out of the closet.

Glam has been defined as "extravagantly showy glamour"[90] and the music of glam, also known as glitter rock, as "rock music characterized by performers wearing glittering costumes and bizarre often grotesque makeup."[88]

Glam's other U.S. avatars were the New York Dolls. One of a number of bands that attracted attention in seedy, late-night shows at the Mercer Arts Center in the early 1970s (another was Kiss), the Dolls, like the Velvets, also seem to have skipped the counterculture part of the 1960s: they took the girl-group sound of the early part of the decade and a fondness for R&B music and added booze, drugs, cross-dressing, and good-natured menace. Their presentations evoked a loopier, less disciplined vision of the Rolling Stones, with singer David Johansen and guitarist Johnny Thunders expanding on the Mick Jagger/Keith Richards elegantly wasted template; their New

York swagger and knowing streetwise humor generated enormous excitement in their home town. The Dolls didn't travel well beyond New York; they were often drunk, drugged, or sloppy at important gigs. At an anticipated concert in Detroit, then a bellwether for rock in the United States, they barely made it onto the stage hours late, then went about deliberately antagonizing their audience.[89] This was especially unfortunate, as "they were more in the mode of the Detroit high-energy scene (Stooges, Mc5) than rock-as-art, though ... they dolloped in the gritty urban surrealism of the Velvets."[90]

England might have made them, and eagerly anticipated crowning a new star. But while on tour in November 1972, Dolls drummer Billy Murcia died of an overdose involving heroin and alcohol in their London hotel. (Bowie sang of Murcia's death in his song "Time" on *Aladdin Sane*.) Murcia was replaced by drummer Jerry Nolan; Egyptian-born guitarist Sylvain Sylvain and bass player Arthur Kane rounded out the group.

Despite the adoration of critics, the music industry was reluctant to take a chance on the band until rock critic Paul Nelson, who was working as an A&R executive for Mercury Records, signed the band to a recording contract. Their 1973 debut, *New York Dolls*, is a rambunctious masterpiece featuring such signature tunes as "Trash," "Personality Crisis," "Subway Train," and a head-spinning rendition of Bo Diddley's "Pills." Some credit producer and studio master Todd Rundgren for "a great-sounding document with all the chaos intact."[91] The second album, *[In] Too Much Too Soon* (1974) was produced by George "Shadow" Morton, who was behind the recordings of girl-group prototypes the Shangri-Las. The album reaffirmed the rootsiness beneath the veneer of lipstick, mascara, rouge, and platform shoes: heavy harmonica blues (Sonny Boy Williamson's "Don't Start Me Talkin'"), Philadelphia soul reinvented (Archie Bell & the Drells' "[There's Gonna Be a] Showdown,") and a a high-wire version of the Cadets' 1950s doo-wop musical comedy skit, "Stranded in the Jungle." Yet the second album's title was a self-fulfilling prophecy, and the Dolls broke up shortly after its release.

Among the disappointed must have been Morrissey, the future leader of the Smiths, who was at one time president of the Dolls' U.K. fan club. In 2004, now an elder statesman of British rock, he persuaded the surviving Dolls to perform, for the first time in nearly thirty years, in London. Original bassist Arthur Kane, who had straightened out his life and become a member of the Church of the Latter-Day Saints, died shortly after the show. In 2006, survivors Johansen and Syl Sylvain recorded a new album as the New York Dolls their first in thirty-two years; the record, *One Day It Will Please Us to Remember Even This*, made many end of the year ten-best lists.

After the Dolls, Thunders, with Nolan, formed the Heartbreakers, another influential prepunk band that carried on and off over the years; Thunders managed to sustain his drug addiction for many years, but was found dead of a heroin overdose in a seedy New Orleans hotel room in 1991. Nolan died of a stroke a few months later, in 1992.

Johansen has had an interesting post-Dolls career. He released some tight and charming solo albums, including *In Style* (1979), and adopted the stage persona Buster Poindexter, who became a New York nightlife staple. Poindexter's 1988 album featured the Caribbean-tinged party hit "Hot Hot Hot."

While glam was influential, though not successful, in the United States, it was a major phenomenon of U.K. rock from 1971 to 1975, where it operated in a variety of styles. It was four-square stomping teen music, typified by the hard-rock soccer-stadium chant-alongs of Slade ("Cum On Feel the Noize"), a No. 1 record in England that didn't make the U.S. charts; it was catchy bubble gum (the Sweet's "Ballroom Blitz").

Glitter rock's biggest U.K. phenomenon was T-Rex, led by Marc Bolan. Known first as Tyrannosaurus Rex in the late 1960s, the band initially blended acoustic folk, psychedelia, and British folklore and mythology. When they changed the name to T-Rex and replaced the pastoral sound with buzzsaw guitar riffs, songs like "Bang a Gong (Get It On)" and "Telegram Sam" became huge U.K. hits. Bolan, "with his Botticelli face and curls and whimsically glamorous image," created a Beatles-like mania in England in the early 1970s.[92] Often described as "elfin," Bolan had a boundary-breaking beauty: "Girls wanted to get close to him, boys wanted to be him," as one fan site said. But "T-Rex mania" did not cross the Atlantic, and one reason was Bolan's self-destructive impulses. "I was living in a twilight world of drugs, booze and kinky sex," Bolan told *Rolling Stone* magazine.[93] Bolan died in a car accident in 1977.

Roxy Music, a kind of prog-art-glam band, stood apart from others of the era, visually and musically. Their cool, wry, tuxedo-clad lead singer Brian Ferry was complemented by the warm brass of sax player Andy Mackay and avant-garde riffing of guitarist Phil Manzanera. Like T-Rex, they were a mass phenomenon in England, but a minority taste in the United States. Unlike T-Rex, they did not have an appeal that rested on hit singles; like a self-consciously sophisticated Velvet Underground, they saw rock as art and the album as canvas. Their most productive period was 1972 to 1974, when they released their first four, and best, albums, including *Stranded* and *Country Life*. Their conceptual approach was evident in the song "Do the Strand," whose title suggests it's a dance song, but for a dance that never existed. Yet they also offered moments of visceral pleasure, with punchy songs like "Street Life" and "Love Is the Drug," as appealing and interesting as anything on the radio on either side of the Atlantic.

Their original keyboard player, Brian Eno, developed into one of the most influential producers and conceptual artists of the era, collaborating with David Bowie, Talking Heads, U2, and other independent-minded acts. His own records included such adventurous, song-focused albums as *Taking Tiger Mountain by Strategy* and more sonically experimental collections like *Music for Airports*.

Ferry had a fruitful solo career, focusing on stylized interpretations of familiar rock, folk, and pop songs: A version of Bob Dylan's "A Hard Rain's Gonna Fall" epitomized the solo Ferry's paradoxical approach, campy yet sincere.

THE 1970s

How could you tell the sixties were over?

Wars raged in 1970, both in the jungles and cities of Southeast Asia and the streets of the United States. Jimi Hendrix and Janis Joplin died of drug overdoses. The Beatles broke up. And the idea of rock 'n' roll as a unifying force of a worldwide youth culture splintered with them.

Even the phrase "rock 'n' roll" itself "broke up." It came to refer to the music of the 1950s and the guitar-based hard rock of sixties bands like the Rolling Stones. It was replaced in popular consciousness with the term "rock." The catchall referred to any kind of up-tempo or midtempo music by or for young people. In the 1970s, "rock" could be soft or loud, smart or dumb, pretentious or natural, fast or slow, with guitars or synthesizers, contrived or spontaneous. From this point on, for simplicity and sanity, "rock" and "rock 'n' roll" are used interchangeably.

The Beatles split was undertaken in a typically public way, their sour bickering revealed to the world in the 1970 documentary *Let It Be,* also the title of the group's final album. McCartney announced the formal end of the Beatles on April 10. The title song and "The Long and Winding Road," both ballads by McCartney, were both No. 1 singles that spring. Though these songs are favorites of some, admirers of the Beatles as a rock 'n' roll band view sees these pretty but sentimental tunes as evidence the Beatles had chosen the right moment to make their exit. Oddly, one of their most engaging later albums, *Abbey Road,* was released in 1969 but recorded after *Let It Be,* but because it was released last, and has the feel of a farewell, *Let It Be* is considered the final Beatles album.

The death of Hendrix on September 18 and of Joplin on October 4 also underscored just how much had been lost from the brief but intense optimism of the 1960s. Aside from the obvious loss of brilliant, creative talent, their passings had substantial symbolic importance. Both had exemplifed "sex, drugs and rock 'n' roll," which had been a boast of generational pride, the hedonistic triad that was supposed to distinguish the young from their repressed, uptight, whiskey- and martini-swilling elders. Marijuana, for most, and LSD, for some, had helped realign values and elevate consciousness. The heroin, pills, and hard liquor that killed Joplin and Hendrix were not part of the deal. When Jim Morrison of the Doors died the following year on July 3, 1971, in Paris, the official cause was heart failure. The heart failure was "aggravated by heavy drinking,"[1] according to a doctor's report.

The novelist Tom Robbins describes the benign aspect of drugs in the sixties as "a fleeting moment of glory, a time when a significant chunk of earthlings briefly realized their moral potential and flirted with their neurological destiny; a collective spiritual awakening that flared brilliantly until the brutal and mediocre impulses of the species drew tight again the thick curtains of meathead somnabulism."[2]

By spring 1970, the meatheads were in charge on all sides of the political culture.

"The atmosphere in the country had grown toxic with hate," wrote Phillip Caputo, a journalist, author and Vietnam veteran.

> The Black Panthers hated whites, the white Weathermen hated American society, the cops hated them all, and each Friday night Walter Cronkite announced the weekly toll in Vietnam, which everyone hated. The tension was more than palpable — you could practically smell it, hear it in the pop music of the day — the angry, jarring riffs of Jimi Hendrix's amped-up guitar, in the death-haunted lyrics of songs like [Creedence Clearwater Revival's] "Fortunate Son" and "Bad Moon Risin'":
>
> "Don't go out tonight,
>   it's bound to take your life
> There's a bad moon on the rise."
>
> "And there was. A bad moon, a bad mood, one of ominous expectancy. There seemed to be a yearning in the national psyche — if there is such a thing — for a catharsis. America was ready for a tragedy, and on May 4, 1970 it got one."[3]

David Bowie

David Bowie, originally named David Jones, was as out of place in the 1960s as a character he played later in the movies: "The Man

Who Fell to Earth." He recorded the albums *The Man Who Sold the World* and *David Bowie* (aka *Space Oddity*) in 1969. But although United States astronauts walked on the moon in 1969, it was not yet Bowie's time.

Confusion over ownership of his recordings kept his career off-balance until he signed with manager Tony DeFries in 1971. DeFries signed Bowie to RCA in the United States. The label hadn't exactly missed the rock revolution — having the Jefferson Airplane meant someone there was paying attention. But this very middle-of-the-road label hadn't had a rock star since Elvis, and eventually, Bowie filled the bill.

His first RCA album, *Hunky Dory,* caused a terrific buzz in 1971. There were songs about Bob Dylan and Andy Warhol. And the mid-tempo anthem "Changes" was one way of signifying the changing of the guard Bowie was about to preside over.

In 1972, with the release of *The Rise and Fall of Ziggy Stardust and the Spiders from Mars,* Bowie went from being an oddity to the man who owned the world, or at least that high-profile, rock 'n' roll part of it. *Ziggy* was a concept album, with a storyline that had to do with a rock star's sudden fame, his glamour, his decline, and ultimate death. Some saw it as a parable about Jimi Hendrix. But what was interesting was that Bowie had succeeded in becoming the pinnacle of the glam-rock style at virtually the same time that he was inventing it.

Long, lean, and handsome, onstage and off, Bowie attracted both men and women. He and his wife, Angela, made bisexuality a kind of moral imperative, the most desirable of all orientations.

Bowie was also generous to those whose music he admired. The Stooges, led by the self-destructive wild man Iggy Pop, were a Detroit band that forged a synthesis of punk and heavy metal before either style was really formed; but their tense songs like "1969" and "I Wanna Be Your Dog" and Iggy's uninhibited stage performances made them influential. Bowie produced and cowrote Iggy's solo album, *Raw Power.* Regrettably, *Raw Power* wasn't a hit, but it gave Iggy Pop an identity and authority that allowed him to develop a successful solo career that, to everyone's surprise, has lasted for decades.

Bowie also produced Mott the Hoople, a good but hard-luck British band that had all the tools for stardom except success. Bowie provided Mott with their finest moment, the song "All the Young Dudes," a spectacular anthem of that glam-rock moment.

Bowie was relatively open about his bisexuality at a time when many artists who would later come out as gay (such as Elton John) remained in denial, or closeted. More than any other figure of his era, he made gay life chic, and he emboldened many people to explore both sides of their sexuality.

Bowie defined himself by never defining himself. Every album and tour was a reinvention, a new alter ego, a new musical style, a new stage show.

Ziggy Stardust was the first, and best. His appearance was aptly described by Irvin Stambler in his *Encyclopedia of Pop, Rock and Soul*: "Wearing a tight, glittering metallic costume with high, laced hunting boots and orange tinted hair, he presented an almost unreal appearance, as though he had come from outer space. Onlookers were impressed with the feeling of psychological change that seemed to flow from Bowie's act."

Although *Ziggy Stardust* made Bowie a star, the album was peculiarly unsuccessful at the time of its release. It never rose higher than No. 75 on the *Billboard* chart, though it sold steadily enough to become gold for sales of more than 500,000 in 1975.

Bowie again was a little ahead of his time; people eventually caught up. He recorded eight more albums during the 1970s, all hits. After Ziggy, *Aladdin Sane* went deeply into struggles with sexual identity. A review in *Rolling Stone* magazine seemed to resent Bowie's interpretation of the Rolling Stones' "Let's Spend the Night Together," as "one of the most ostensibly heterosexual calls in rock is made into a bi-anthem."[*]

In *Young Americans* Bowie anticipated the era of celebrity and scored his first No. 1 record in the United States: "Fame," written with

---

[*] Rolling Stone, July 19, 1973. Review by Ben Gerson.

"Four Dead in OH-IO"

On April 20, 1970, President Nixon went on television to announce that "Vietnamization" was succeeding, and that 150,000 American soldiers would be brought home by the end of the next year. Ten days later, Nixon went back on TV to say that the United States was invading nearby Cambodia, ostensibly to destroy Viet Cong and North Vietnamese supply bases and camps. In this famous speech, Nixon insisted that the United States would not be a "pitiful, helpless giant." The next day, Nixon, in an off-the-cuff remark, referred to college students who were against the war as "bums."

John Lennon, who knew something about the subject. On the 1976 album *Station to Station,* he made the feint toward disco and racked up another hit, "Golden Years."

Burned out by the work and the focus on celebrity, he moved to the then least-hip city in Europe, Berlin, where he recorded *Low* and *Heroes* in 1977. These were early expressions of what has become known as "ambient music."

Those low-key albums and sojourn in Berlin allowed Bowie to make a transition away from the spotlight, and eventually into the footlights: Bowie's theatrical rock presentations made his acting potential clear, and he has had a prolific, if not quite as triumphal, career as a stage and screen actor. In 1980, he won critical accolades performing on Broadway in the title role of the drama *The Elephant Man.*

First acclaimed for playing the title character in the 1976 science-fiction film *The Man Who Fell to Earth,* Bowie otherwise avoided roles too similar to his rock personas. Top dramatic roles included *The Hunger,* and *Merry Christmas Mr. Lawrence* (both 1983) and *Basquiat,* in which he was deftly cast as Andy Warhol. In 2006, he starred as Nikolas Tesla in *The Prestige,* a drama about the inventor and eccentric genius.

During the 1980s he sought anonymity as a member of the adequate and unoriginal rock band Tin Machine, whose great failing was the desire for Bowie to be just another one of the musicians in a band of supposed equals. A regular guy was one role beyond Bowie's grasp. He married the Somalian-born model Iman in 1992.

Protests against the expanding war sprang up on campuses around the country. It was no longer just the elite universities with activist reputations that had quarrelsome protests. On May 1, the ROTC building at Kent State University in Ohio was burned. The Republican Governor James Rhodes, a Nixon supporter, called out the Ohio National Guard to quell the demonstrations. On Monday, May 4, groups of students assembled on the green for a peaceful, if noisy, demonstration. Standing not far away were another group of youths approximately their age: members of the Ohio National Guard. Nervous and poorly trained, the guard opened fire: four students were killed.

Less publicized was the killing of two students at the predominantly black Jackson State College in Mississippi, who were also protesting the war.

The Kent State killings shocked the country. The mood of the time was summed up in a famous photograph of a young woman bending over one of the dead on the Kent State green moments after the shooting, her arms thrust in the air, her mouth open in a scream, her face expressing the utter bewilderment of the tragedy.

Protest music wasn't dead, yet. Neil Young, shifting roles between solo artist (often accompanied by the band Crazy Horse) and fourth member of Crosby, Stills and Nash, delivered with the latter group a scathing bit of musical reportage, in a song called "Ohio": "Tin soldiers and Nixon coming ... Four dead in O-hio."

But "Ohio" was an exception, at least among white artists. "Teach Your Children," another CSN hit from 1970, was more indicative of the direction music was going. The song indicated a retrenchment from confrontation, and was an assertion of family values, expressing the hope that parents would pass on the positive values learned in the sixties to their kids.

Exhausted by protest, by death, by the relentless war, young people and the pop-music culture began to turn inward. It was the era of the singer-songwriter.

Singer-Songwriters

Today's listener who first hears such singer-songwriters as James Taylor and Carole King, two massively popular artists of the 1970s, might be right to wonder, What does this music have to do with rock?

Taylor's breakthrough album, 1970's *Sweet Baby James,* was a prototype singer-songwriter album. Taylor's hit, "Fire and Rain" was an autobiographical tale of dread and hope, presented tenderly, with an irresistibly hummable melody and handsomely crafted arrangements by some of the best studio musicians Los Angeles had to offer. (One of them, guitarist Danny Kortchmar, had been in a band called the Flying Machine with Taylor in 1967; coincidentally, Kortchmar was also in a band called City with Carole King.)

Taylor was already somewhat well known by the time *Sweet Baby James* was released. After the Flying Machine broke up because of Taylor's heroin addiction,[4] he moved to England in 1968, where he was the first artist signed by Apple Records, the ineffective and short-lived money-pit of a label started by the Beatles.

In London, Taylor met producer Peter Asher, who was the A&R chief at Apple. Asher had had his own brief moment of success as a recording artist. The wispish-sounding pop duo Peter & Gordon — Asher and Gordon Waller — had a number one record, "A World Without Love," in 1964. If it sounded like Beatles-lite, it was for good reason. Paul McCartney wrote it for them, a kind of favor to the family: Peter's sister, Jane Asher, was McCartney's girlfriend during the Beatlemania era.

Peter Asher found his calling on the other side of the recording industry, as a record producer and manager. James Taylor was his breakthrough client, but soon his stable also included Linda Ronstadt and others of the L.A. school of laid-back million sellers.

It was almost impossible in 1970 and 1971 to walk through any college or university dormitory or sorority house without hearing Taylor's plaintive melodies emanating from a stereo system, on the albums *Sweet Baby James*, and *Mud Slide Slim and the Blue Horizon*.

Taylor's early lyrics often dealt with addiction and depression, but soothingly so. The warmth of his voice made it seem like he was a friend listening to your problems, rather than the other way around. Taylor's shyness was an asset. His songs and singing conveyed intimacy and humility; his No. 1 version of Carole King's "You've Got a Friend," made you feel that he was your personal pal. Too soft for some tastes, Taylor was refreshingly unpretentious, and perhaps history's quietest rock star. Both King and Taylor won Grammy Awards in 1971: Taylor for Best Male Pop Vocal Performance, King for Song of the Year.

Despite his own reticence, Taylor became a high-profile celebrity when he married another former child of wealth and privilege, the pop star Carly Simon, in 1972, a marriage that dissolved in the early 1980s.

The tall and striking Simon, from a prominent New York family, was a top pop/rock hit-maker with "That's the Way I've Always

Heard It Should Be" (1971), "Anticipation" (1972, and later famous in a ketchup commercial). At the end of '72, she had her biggest hit, "You're So Vain." It was a parlor game to guess which of Simon's many famous supposed lovers the song was addressed to: the actor and lothario Warren Beatty? Mick Jagger, who sings background on the record? Perhaps it was Bond, James Bond: Simon sang the 1977 hit theme song "Nobody Does It Better" from the Roger Moore-as-Bond movie, *The Spy Who Loved Me*. Simon and Taylor had a duo hit, a cover of Inez and Charlie Foxx's 1963 hit "Mockingbird," a steamy variation on the folk song at the root of "Bo Diddley." Some could carp that the Simon & Taylor rendition was comparable to Pat Boone covering Little Richard. But Simon and Taylor were rock-culture royalty, and it was a 1974 hit, nevertheless.

Taylor's musical success was sustained throughout the 1970s on such top-ten albums as *Mud Slide Slim and the Blue Horizon* (1971), *One Man Dog* (1972), *Gorilla* (1975), and *JT* (1977). Taylor's consistency and low-key demeanor helped him survive the fracturing musical trends of the next few decades, and he is still a performer who can sell out concerts to multiple generations of fans. His voice is so distinctive that an attentive ten-year-old listening to Taylor sing his hit "Country Roads" in 2004 could say, "Isn't this the same guy that sings 'Jelly Man Kelly'"? To a generation raised on *Sesame Street*, he certainly is.

Carole King

Carole King and Gerry Goffin, whom she would marry and divorce, were among the most successful of the Brill Building songwriters in the 1960s. Under the radar during the British Invasion, Goffin & King continued to develop, writing songs of soulfulness and sophistication. With producer Jerry Wexler, they wrote Aretha Franklin's great 1967 hit "(You Make Me Feel Like a) Natural Woman."

King's *Tapestry* album in 1971 featured a song called "I Feel the Earth Move," and indeed it did, right along with her. The biggest hit from *Tapestry* was "It's Too Late," a declaration of a woman who was not going back to her guy. It was as gentle as it was assertive, melodic and meaty, the gift that allowed *Tapestry* to sell more than 15 million copies. It was evident that King had gone through the same kind of consciousness-raising that many women did between the early 1960s and 1970s: early in her career, she and Goffin had written a song called "He Hit Me (And It Felt Like a Kiss"). Even though it was produced by Phil Spector and recorded by the Crystals, most radio stations, even in that unenlightened time, found it over the line.

It was no coincidence that while *Tapestry*, with its clear message of female empowerment, was topping the charts in 1971, *New York* magazine came out with a one-shot special issue of a magazine for women called *Ms. Magazine*. *Ms.*'s one-shot was so successful it began publishing on a regular schedule in the summer of 1972. A few months later the Australian pop singer Helen Reddy became a phenomenon, as her feminist anthem "I Am Woman" topped the pop charts in November 1972, indicating that at least some of the message of the women's liberation movement was filtering into the mainstream.

Tapestry was the No. 1 album for 15 weeks on the *Billboard* Top Albums chart, and King won four Grammy Awards. It was the No. 3 selling album of the seventies, just behind Fleetwood Mac's *Rumours* and the soundtrack to *Saturday Night Fever*.

Singer-songwriters kept coming, it seemed, from everywhere: Cat Stevens, Jim Croce, and John Denver were three of the most popular, but their styles were more aligned with pop-folk than even the loosely redefined "rock."

What follows are some snapshots of some of the important singer-songwriters of the 1970s who did, in fact, rock.

Elton John

Born Reginald Dwight, Elton John was everything a pop star was not supposed to be. He was short and plump, wore thick eyeglasses, and what hair he had would usually not behave. From 1966 he was a member of the British band Bluesology, playing under the tutelage of the preeminent U.K. blues aficionado, Long John Baldry. In 1969, Elton John embarked on a solo career. A hard-pounding pianist with a gift for composing melodious rock tunes as well as ballads, he formed a partnership with lyricist Bernie Taupin that was one of the most successful of the seventies. Beginning in 1970 with "Your

Song," and through 1976, John, Taupin, and producer Gus Dudgeon released nearly two dozen hit songs, many of which are staples of various radio formats, from classic rock to adult contemporary. The signature tunes include the midtempo "Rocket Man" and powerful ballads like "Goodbye Yellow Brick Road," "Don't Let the Sun Go Down on Me," and "Someone Saved My Life Tonight." John's exuberant piano style on up-tempo tunes gave his music vast appeal: "The Bitch is Back," "Crocodile Rock," "Honky Cat," and "Saturday Night's Alright for Fighting" gave him rock 'n' roll credibility. The low-key but invigorating "Bennie and the Jets" (1974) and the souped-up soul song "Philadelphia Freedom" (1975) made John's appeal universal, and his 1974–75 hit version of the Beatles' "Lucy in the Sky With Diamonds," featuring John Lennon playing the reggae riffs on guitar, confirmed John's multidimensional ability.

Though some years passed between hits, John has remained prolific. He appeared on the No. 1 1985 AIDS benefit song "That's What Friends Are For," featuring Dionne Warwick, Stevie Wonder, and Gladys Knight. In 1997 he had the biggest hit of his career with a revised version of his 1987 song "Candle in the Wind," which he and Taupin originally wrote about Marilyn Monroe. The new lyrics were a tribute to his friend Princess Diana, who died in a car crash earlier in 1997. The single has sold more than 35 million copies worldwide, with its proceeds going to a variety of charities. At the end of 1997, for both his musical and charitable contributions, John was knighted by Queen Elizabeth II and may now be addressed as Sir Elton.

Billy Joel

Billy Joel was another piano-playing rock 'n' roller who was gathering his sea legs as Elton was at the peak of his roll.

Joel grew up in suburban Long Island, the source and setting of many of his songs. He was well known in the Long Island band scene as a member of the Hassles, which achieved headliner status in local clubs and sometimes backed larger touring acts. Around 1970, he cut his first solo album, *Cold Spring Harbor,* about a sedate and lovely town on Long Island's expensive North Shore. But the album was mastered at the wrong speed, making Joel sound a bit like a chipmunk. Naive in the ways of the record business, he had signed a disadvantageous contract that gave away his music publishing rights, left him with minimal record sales royalties, and essentially made him an indentured servant of the music world.

Bitter, angry, and still in his early twenties, Joel dropped out of sight. He could be heard in seedy Los Angeles piano bars, under the pseudonym Billy Martin — an appropriate name, for Martin was the often-hired, often-fired manager of his favorite baseball team, the New York Yankees, with a volatile personality Joel had to admire, if not echo.

His song about his experiences, "Piano Man," was his first for Columbia Records, which paid handsomely to extricate him from his earlier contract. With a hard-nosed manager, his wife Elizabeth, Joel was ready to create, and he seized the moment. In 1977, a love song to his wife, "Just the Way You Are," became not just a million-selling single but the slow dance of choice at wedding receptions the world over.

Joel, like Elton John, also had a rock 'n' roller inside him. Joel drew on his background among working-class Long Islanders and wrote songs about dating habits ("Scenes from an Italian Restaurant") to assertions of independence ("My Life," "Movin' Out" [Anthony's Song]") to seduction moves ("Only the Good Die Young"), all hits from multimillion-selling albums *The Stranger* (1977) and *52nd Street*, which won the 1979 Album of the Year Grammy Award. As of 1994, *The Stranger* had sold more than 9 million copies; *52nd Street*, 7 million.

Joel was always a master of pastiche, able to distill music from sources as diffuse as George Gershwin, Ray Charles, and the Beatles into his own pungent style. His 1980 album, *Glass Houses*, featured a number of strong songs, anchored by "It's Still Rock and Roll to Me." The song was an amusing critique of the nature of "flavor of the week" stardom and the new hair and clothing styles that seemed to be the required uniform of some "new wave" acts at the time. The song was Joel's first number one, and *Glass Houses* sold more than 6 million copies. And as he grew older, Joel continued to write about the lives of his generation, the dashed hopes and grand ambitions of blue-collar baby boomers. *The Nylon Curtain* (1982) was his most powerful album, full of songs of struggle and loss, whether dealing with factory closings ("Allentown") or the emotional and physical struggles of a Vietnam veteran ("Goodnight Saigon").

For reasons not always understood, many critics, most prominently at *Rolling Stone*, were dismissive of Joel's more rocking efforts. It was as if the same person who wrote and sang a ballad as pretty as "Just the Way You Are" could not be an "authentic" rocker, although few had the same problem reconciling the Paul McCartney of "Yesterday" with the McCartney of "Helter Skelter." There was also the matter of Joel's new celebrity, as he married the swimsuit and fashion model Christie Brinkley in 1985, after a few years of dating. One of his most popular albums, *An Innocent Man* (1983) was a stylistic throwback to the pre-Beatles era. It featured tributes to Brinkley like "Uptown Girl," a spot-on update of the Four Seasons falsetto-harmony style, and the Drifters'-style R&B of the title song.

In the summer of 1987, Joel and his band played six concerts in the former Soviet Union: three in Moscow, and three in what was then known as Leningrad, which has since reverted to its pre-revolutionary name, St. Petersburg. The Soviet head of state was premier Mikhail Gorbachev. Though head of the Communist party, which, as always, *was* the government of Russia and the rest of the Soviet Union, Gorbachev was engaged in loosening some of the restrictions of the tightly wound society. The words heard everywhere that summer were *perestroika* and *glasnost*. *Perestroika* referred to an economic restructuring that would allow a modicum of private enterprise to exist within the rigid confines of the state-run economy. *Glasnost*, which translates as "public voicing," allowed a certain amount of free expression in the tightly government-controlled media and among the populace. Rock was still in theory a disapproved form of expression, although some government-authorized acts, such as Time Machine, thrived. Their shows were held in elegant concert halls, and albums released by the state record label, Melodiya. "Unauthorized" local bands like Televisor (Television) still had to promote their shows by word of mouth on the day of the event and perform in out of the way coffeehouses or small theaters. On the other hand, an open-air heavy-metal concert featuring Russian bands in the middle of Moscow's lush Gorky Park could not have taken place without the support and approval of the government. Within two years, Communism would fall in Russia; the atmosphere around the Joel tour was unmistakable: the times were a-changin' here, too.

Fans never stopped believing that Joel's best songs eloquently dramatized the soundtracks of their lives. The bond he created with them has been so enduring that in 2006 he set a record for New York's Madison Square Garden, selling out twelve nearly consecutive shows. *Movin' Out*, a stage musical choreographed by modern-dance diva Twyla Tharp based on Joel's songs, debuted on Broadway in 2003 and was both a critical and popular success.

Paul Simon

The quintessential sixties folk-rocker with Simon & Garfunkel, Paul Simon had a solo career in the 1970s that was immediately successful and liberating. He began enlivening his compositions with varied musical influences: he used Jamaican reggae on "Mother and Child Reunion" (1972), gospel music on "Loves Me Like a Rock" (1975), and Latin music on "Late in the Evening" (1980). His most memorable tracks of the seventies, "50 Ways to Leave Your Lover" and "Still Crazy After All These Years" (1976) showed Simon's knack for creating phrases that would become part of the American vernacular.

After the mixed critical and commercial response to his 1980 movie and album, *One-Trick Pony*, Simon (who wrote the screenplay) kept a low profile in the earlier part of the 1980s. But he roared back in 1986 with one of the most innovative and important albums of the rock era, *Graceland*. Inspired by the various pop-music styles of black South Africa, *Graceland* blended impressionistic lyrics and inspired melodies with the rhythms and harmonies of Soweto and other black "homelands." The project brought international attention to South African musicians like Ladysmith Black Mambazo and guitarist Ray Phiri. The musical combinations were rich and complex: the title song uses steel guitar played by a member of King Sonny Ade's band from Nigeria, a kind of West African/country music fusion. Lyric bits and musical phrases from fifties rock emerge as touchstones: bits of the Del-Vikings' doo-wop classic "Whispering Bells" and lyric traces from the Penguins'

"Earth Angel" and various Little Richard songs can be heard amid the Zulu harmonies and "township jive" rhythm arrangements. And the last two tracks are not cut with the blend of South African and American musicians that appear on the rest of the album, but feature the Louisiana zydeco band Rockin' Dopsie and the Twisters ("That Was Your Mother") and the then-little-known Los Lobos, Mexican-American roots rockers from Los Angeles ("All Around the World or The Myth of Fingerprints"). Most important, *Graceland* helped open a window into the oppressively segregated "apartheid" of South Africa.

Simon continued to pioneer what is now known as "world music" while keeping the spirit of rock 'n' roll's foundation in *Rhythm of the Saints* (1990), focusing on Brazilian drumming and locally made instruments while not eschewing the toast to Frankie Lymon & the Teenagers (on "Obvious Child") and other rock originators. He embraced those doo-wop roots, along with salsa music, in *Songs from The Capeman* (1997), a stand-alone album of tunes from Simon's Broadway musical set in 1950s New York.

The Sound of Southern California: The Eagles

The Eagles/Their Greatest Hits 1971–1975 is the best-selling album of all-time in the United States. It has been certified by the Recording Industry Assocation of America for sales in the United States of more than 28 million copies as of June 20, 2005.

By comparison, Michael Jackson's *Thriller* has sold 27 million; Pink Floyd's *The Wall*, 23 million; *Led Zeppelin IV*, 22 million. (AC/DC, Billy Joel, and Shania Twain all have released albums that sold more than 20 million; Fleetwood Mac's *Rumours* and the Beatles' top-seller, *The Beatles* (aka *The White Album*) are at 19 million.

It is worth mentioning because the Eagles have a distinction none of the other artists have. They are the band that critics have most loved to hate. "Critics (mainly East Coast/Detroit) hated the Eagles because they epitomized the supposedly smarmy self-satisfaction of El Lay — pretty-boy looks, neat blue jeans, mirror shades and suntans — at a time when punk's nihilistic post-Velvets/Stooges trash aesthetic was taking form," says Barney Hoskyns, the U.K. critic and author of *Hotel California: Singer-Songwriters & Cocaine Cowboys In The L.A. Canyons, 1967–1976.*[5]

This image of Los Angeles and its entertainment industries as a kind of land of the living brain-dead was most savagely depicted in Woody Allen's best film, *Annie Hall.* The movie, released in 1977, won four Academy Awards, including best picture, best director, best original screenplay, and, for Allen's costar Diane Keaton, a best actress nomination. Arguing with Annie to return with him to New York after she's hooked up with a hotshot L.A. music producer (played with relish but against type by Paul Simon), Allen's Alvy Singer character cries that the only cultural advantage Los Angeles has over New York is the freedom to make a right turn on a red light.

The Eagles were at the epicenter of the large community of musicians who had begun gathering in Los Angeles around 1964. "The whole scene was still very sweet and innocent at this point," recalls Tucson native Linda Ronstadt, the most popular woman rock singer of the 1970s. "It was all about sitting around in little embroidered dresses and listening to Elizabethan folk songs."[6] They came for the opportunity to sing and strum at clubs like the Ash Grove and the Troubadour. But for these musicians, the Beatles changed everything. As they did for Bob Dylan, "the Beatles validated rock and roll," says Lou Adler, then an L.A. producer and label-owner ... All of a sudden young folkies like David Crosby saw that you could write your own songs, draw on rock and roll, rhythm and blues, and country music and still be stampeded by young girls."[7]

The particular Los Angeles stamp these musicians placed on the music in the 1960s was folk-rock, and the Byrds, formed in 1964 by guitarists Jim McGuinn, David Crosby, bassist Chris Hillman, Gene Clark, and drummer Michael Clark, made folk-rock a phenomenon. Hillman and Gene Clark were accomplished bluegrass musicians; McGuinn and Crosby and Clark's harmony singing had special chemistry. In June 1965, when their sweetly electric version of Bob Dylan's "Mr. Tambourine Man" became a No. 1 hit, a genre known as folk-rock was launched. (The coyly olde English spelling of the Byrds helped the band gain the British Invasion affiliation, which, however tenuous, was required at the time.)

The same year, John and Michelle Philips teamed up with Cass Elliott, an overweight earth mother with a splendid voice, and Denny Doherty, her former partner in New York's short-lived band the Mugwamps, to form the Mamas and the Papas. Their hit from late 1965 to early 1966, "California Dreamin'," was a folk-rock milestone, and a kind of musical chamber of commerce invitation to musicians all over America (and England) to forget the winter chill and come to the warmth of the California sun.

Stephen Stills and Richie Furay met up with guitarist, singer, and songwriter Neil Young. They formed a band called Buffalo Springfield, a band of only partly reached potential, to create a folk-country hybrid.

Stills and Young were both talented songwriters beginning a decades-long, occasionally codependent relationship. After three underachieving albums, Buffalo Springfield split. Furay started a pure country rock band called Poco. Stills teamed up with David Crosby and a mellow, down-to-Earth Englishman, Graham Nash, who had already tasted top-forty success as a member of the British Invasion band the Hollies.

Ronstadt and some friends formed a country/pop/folk band called the Stone Poneys, and had a big hit in the late winter of 1967 called "Different Drum," written by Mike Nesmith of the Monkees. But Ronstadt understood her potential as a solo artist. In 1971, she pulled together four guys from the L.A. scene to be her backing band. They were Glenn Frey, from Michigan, Don Henley, a Texan, and Randy Meisner and Bernie Leadon. Meisner had been a founder of Poco; Leadon was in the most rootsy of the California country-rock bands, the Flying Burrito Brothers. Henley and Frey found common ground as songwriters. Quickly moving away from Ronstadt's shadow, they became the band known as the Eagles.

The Eagles first hit, "Take It Easy," was written by another star of the scene, the strikingly handsome Jackson Browne from nearby Orange County ("The OC"). Browne came to typify a kind of West Coast sensibility similar to that of James Taylor as the "sensitive" singer-songwriter of the 1970s. His early albums *For Everyman* and *The Pretender* took introverted expression to a new level of artistic achievement and popularity. Though an opposite in terms of style, Browne acknowledges Bob Dylan's impact on the nascent L.A. scene.

"Dylan exploded the universe of folk songwriting," Browne said. Suddenly there was a whole wealth of ideas out there, and you could discuss anything in a song."[8]

But like Browne, most Southern California writers chose to write about what they knew, or thought they knew — their feelings. "Take It Easy" verified what people liked about this music and confirmed what they disliked. It was melodious, harmonically beautiful, crisply sung and played. It was impeccably arranged and engineered. And the lyrics, heard one way, were about taking a load off your mind, enjoying fast cars and beautiful women. Listened to another way, it was a paean to self-absorption and a rejection of the community spirit of the 1960s. And about that impeccable sound: critics, at least, found it too clean, the singers too comfortable, too disconnected from the pain, or bluesiness, of what some considered the rough-edged working-class roots of country music.

The Eagles' reputation with critics took a steep drop with their second and least-successful album, *Desperado*. The song cycle comparing rock stars to cowboy gunfighters was seen as not only pretentious, but also smug, arrogant, and self-delusional. In retrospect, they may agree with some of that point of view. "The metaphor was probably a little bullshit," conceded Henley. "We were in L.A. staying up all night, smoking dope, living the California life, and I suppose we thought it was as radical as cowboys in the old West."[9]

Insulated from day-to-day life by their driven, aggressive, protective manager, Irving Azoff, the Eagles kept perfecting their sound, which increasingly reflected a conflict between accomplishments and insecurity.

Their best and best-selling individual album, *Hotel California*, was a vision of the dark side of the California dream. The No. 1 title song was shot through with paranoia; its famous last line sounds like a promotional slogan for a horror movie: "You can check out anytime you want, but you can never leave."

The other No. 1 hit, "New Kid in Town," represents, Hoskyns suggests, their fear of being overtaken by the next big thing, whatever it might be. In this case, it is Bruce Springsteen who is the new kid in town. If Hoskyns's theory is correct, then the Eagles were even more insecure than could have been imagined.

Consider that the Eagles' "One of These Nights" was No. 1 for five weeks in the summer of 1975, and Springsteen's breakthrough album, *Born to Run*, released that summer, never even hit the top (it peaked at No. 3). Springsteen wouldn't rack up Eagles-level sales numbers until 1984's *Born in the U.S.A.* But Springsteen had the respect and adoration of the critics the Eagles craved.

Maybe it was the drugs. The enormous wealth and the protected lifestyle allowed drugs, especially cocaine, to take its toll on the California scene. The mix of cocaine and rock-star egos was a disaster for the Eagles. Hoskyns writes, "Cocaine was ubiquitous in the L.A. music scene by mid-1973. The perfect drug for the unbridled rock ego, it gave musicians and scenesters alike a temporary sense of omnipotence. It also deadened much of the emotional rapport that music requires."[10]

Or maybe they were not capable of emotional rapport. The songs of most of these members of the once very world-conscious rock community rarely wrote about anything that occurred outside the canyons of Los Angeles. During these peak years of L.A. rock, U.S. troops left Vietnam; the Watergate scandal resulted in the resignation of President Richard M. Nixon on August 9, 1974, less than two years after he had been reelected to a second term in 1972, on a strong "law and order" platform. Nixon had carried forty-nine of the fifty states, history's greatest landslide. But like the Eagles, no amount of success could provide him with security or a sense of well-being.

A few Southern California artists from this insular scene nevertheless stood out. Randy Newman wrote biting, satirical songs so dark that you could almost see the dirt under his fingernails as he played. Singing in a laconic, nasal Southern accent, Newman can thank Bob Dylan for stretching the boundaries of what pop audiences would accept from a singer; Newman's voice was marginal, and the unmitigated irony of his songs was too much for mass consumption. (Yet smoothly produced versions of Newman songs, like "Mama Told Me Not to Come" became hits for seventies pop groups like Three Dog Night.)

Newman was both an outsider and an insider; he grew up in a Jewish family in New Orleans during World War II. (He tells the story of his family's emigration to Los Angeles, while his father, a doctor, was serving in World War II, in the marvelous song "Dixie

Flyer.") Though bespectacled, shy, and unathletic — not exactly your natural California outdoors golden boy — he was nevertheless related to Hollywood royalty: his uncles Alfred, Emil, and Lionel Newman were among the great film composers of the 1940s and 1950s. So he had insights to the foibles of that set as well. His one odd novelty hit, "Short People" (1977), which poked fun at prejudice but outraged the height-and-humor deficient, featured his high-flying friends Glenn Frey of the Eagles and their songwriter comrade J. D. Souther. The Eagles had also appeared on his album *Good Old Boys*, a cutting satire about the South and mutual ignorance, in 1974.

Ronstadt and Mitchell were the two leading ladies of the time. Ronstadt, with the smart, delicate hand of Peter Asher as producer, was developing into powerful, emotive singer with great taste in both songs and arrangements. Her hit streak began in earnest in 1974 with the album *Heart Like a Wheel* (with the hit "You're No Good") and continued to have hits with intelligent and moving interpretations of songs by Roy Orbison ("Blue Bayou") and Buddy Holly ("It's So Easy") on her 1977 blockbuster *Simple Dreams*.

Though not a songwriter, she was always evolving, segueing into new-wave rock with "How Do I Make You" and "Get Closer" in the early 1980s. Later, she performed in New York in Gilbert & Sullivan's operetta *The Pirates of Penzance*, and started her generation's infatuation with the great American songbook revival with some classic albums by the venerable Frank Sinatra arranger Nelson Riddle on *What's New* (1983) and *Lush Life* (1984).

She revisited her Mexican-American heritage on two sets of *Canciones* and cut a great pure country album, *Trio*, with Dolly Parton and Emmylou Harris. She remains a vital artist, and her musical curiosity allows her to rock if she chooses to, but to otherwise act her age.

Perhaps the best work of the seventies in any form of rock came from two outsiders from Canada: Joni Mitchell and Neil Young. Mitchell had already been known as a songwriter; folk singer Judy Collins had a 1968 hit with Mitchell's lovely but frail "Both Sides Now." Mitchell also wrote the song "Woodstock," which became a hit for her buddies Crosby, Stills, and Nash.

The temperamental Mitchell flirted constantly with both greatness and the boys. Confessional songs about her relationships with David

Crosby, Graham Nash, and John David Souther are woven through her early seventies albums, such as *Blue*.

Her peak was *Court & Spark* (1974), a richly detailed sophisticated rock album with singles like "Free Man in Paris." The song is about her own pop-star burnout, in which she sings of "Stokin' the star-making machinery behind the popular song." Often thinking of herself as a painter (indeed, there have been gallery showings of her work, and in unguarded moments she has compared herself to Picasso), Mitchell has followed her muse to wherever it led her, with the less-than-linear "Hissing of Summer Lawns" (1975) and the aptly titled "Don Juan's Reckless Daughter" (1978) and finished out the decade with *Mingus*, her interpretations of songs by the ambitious and enigmatic jazz composers. Charles Mingus died in January 1979, shortly before the album's release.

That Neil Young ultimately couldn't get along with Stephen Stills (or Crosby or Nash) for very long turned out to be his advantage — he has had the most praiseworthy, artistically ambitious solo career of any of his peers. The 1970s were his finest and most prolific years: a dozen albums from 1970 through 1979, including an album with Stills as the Stills-Young Band (*Long May You Run*, 1976) and a 1979 concert album, *Live Rust*, released just a few months after *Rust Never Sleeps*. One of Young's finest albums, *Rust Never Sleeps* showed Young to be the only one of the Southern California singer-songwriters to come to an accommodation with punk rock, to feel its urgency and grasp its relevance. In the opening song, "Hey Hey, My My," he sang about the implosion of the Sex Pistols: "The King is gone but not forgotten/this is the story of Johnny Rotten." In the late 1970s, only a musical intellect as curious as Young's would find something uplifting about the Sex Pistols' brief, violent, drug-and-publicity-addled existence: "It's better to burn out than it is to rust," Young sang.

With his plaintive voice and instrumentation that usually blended country, folk, and rock elements, Young's 1970s albums conveyed the awkward transition from the optimism of the counterculture to its depressing downward spiral by the end of that decade. *Everybody Knows This Is Nowhere, After the Gold Rush*, and *Harvest* were all best-sellers that exuded Young's pain, humor, outrage, intimacy, and the conflicting desires of withdrawal and engagement.

A trio of mid-1974 to 1975 albums, *On the Beach, Tonight's the Night*, and *Zuma* plumbed the plunging spirit of Los Angeles, the United States, and Young's personal life. The depressive masterpiece *Tonight's the Night* was like a coroner's inquest into the death from heroin overdoses of two close friends: Danny Whitten of Crazy Horse and Bruce Berry, a road manager. Life, like rock, could be messy; not for Young the crystal purity of the Eagles, or for that matter, the harmonies of Crosby, Stills, and Nash, with whom his volatile relationship continued intermittently into the 1980s.

In the eighties, Young also followed his muse to the point where he would occasionally infuriate those who operated the "star-making machinery" of the music business. During a brief period with Geffen Records (he had been with Reprise before and since), he was sued by the label for intentionally delivering albums with little commercial potential, such as the 1983 synth-rock album *Trans* and, the same year, a faux-rockabilly album, *Everybody's Rockin'*. You could understand David Geffen's chagrin at these works, which were artistically subpar as well as unsellable. But he should not have taken it personally. Young continued his wayward ways when he returned to Reprise with *This Note's for You*, a mediocre blues record.

Young remains one of rock's most productive artists. His music wears like a favorite pair of jeans and flannel shirt. In 2001, he recorded a song called "Let's Roll," the words of some passengers who fought back against the hijackers on one of the four planes on September 11, 2001. His 2005 album *Prairie Wind*, recorded in Nashville, is a solid country-rock work that looks back with being overwhelmed by nostalgia.

If the Eagles had a composite opposite, it would be Steely Dan. Walter Becker and Donald Fagen started Steely Dan in 1972 in Los Angeles and somehow found that their quirky pop songs had hit potential: "Do It Again" and "Reelin' In the Years," from their debut album, *Can't Buy a Thrill*, both became hits in 1973.

Deciding that their singular artistic ambitions could best be accomplished in the studio, they shed the members of what had been their band and began recording with studio musicians, especially L.A. and New York pros comfortable with inventive chord changes that created a very hip niche between jazz and rock. They quit touring in 1974, adding a layer of mystique to their already reclusive personalities and inscrutable lyrics.

On their hit "Any Major Dude Will Tell You" from what may be their best album, *Pretzel Logic,* radio listeners had to be scratching their heads as Fagen sang the line, "Have you ever seen a squonk's tears? Well, look at mine." "Rikki Don't Lose That Number" underscores Fagen and Becker's infatuation with bebop jazz chord changes: Its introduction is a salute to pianist Horace Silver's "Song for My Father." Though based in Los Angeles for most of the seventies, neither Fagen nor Becker was ever seen sporting a tan, nor did they socialize with the Southern California rock royalty. And their songs were laced with irony, not the favored literary device of the "Take It Easy" gang.

Steely Dan, wrote L.A. writer Chris Willman, "mellifluously ravaged the post-counterculture landscape with brilliantly veiled sarcasm and revolutionary lack of sentimentality."[11]

Their second album, *Countdown to Ecstasy* (1973, as was the debut album), featured a track called "Show Biz Kids" that mocked the pretensions and superficiality of the glam kids on Sunset Strip; it was also seen as a bit of a sneer directed at the cocaine cowboys of the Eagles and their circle.

In fact, in a Steely Dan song about a loud argument called "Everything You Did," the man sarcastically tells his girlfriend, "turn up the Eagles, the neighbors are listening." The hypersensitive Eagles were thought to have been replying to this mild put-down by including a line in the song "Hotel California": "They stab it with their steely knives but they just can't kill the beast."

In one way they were similar to the Eagles — both toiled endlessly in the studio, seeking the perfect sound on every note in every song. They became so polished that songs on masterful late-1970s pop-jazz albums like *Aja* and *Gaucho* became adult contemporary or smooth-jazz standards, much to Fagen and Becker's everlasting ambivalence. And, oddly, they were long managed by Irving Azoff, architect of the Eagles' high-flying career.

Fleetwood Mac

Fleetwood Mac began as an English blues band, led by drummer Mick Fleetwood and bass player John McVie. John's wife Christine McVie joined as a singer/keyboard player in 1970. The band muddled through the early 1970s, frequently dropping and adding other musicians. Settled in Southern California in 1975, they hooked up with American guitarist/singer Lindsey Buckingham and his girlfriend, singer Stevie Nicks, who had recorded as Buckingham Nicks.

The musical chemistry was instantaneous. The first album by that fivesome, *Fleetwood Mac* in 1975, sounded deliciously fresh; its beautiful pop songs rocked forcefully, were deftly played and elegantly sung. "Over My Head," "Say You Love Me," and Nicks's bewitching showpiece, "Rhiannon," were all deserved hits, as different from one another in mood and tone as they were from everything else on the radio in the mid-1970s.

Fleetwood Mac was very much a band of its cultural moment. Great success, easy availability of cocaine and sexual temptations put strains on the two couples — John and Christine McVie, and Buckingham and Nicks — at the core of the band, as well as Fleetwood, who was going through a divorce. Their relationships were imploding as *Rumours* was being written and recorded, adding a layer of dramatic recognition to Buckingham songs like "Go Your Own Way" and "Second Hand News." The album was No. 1 for thirty-one weeks, and delivered four top-ten singles, including "Dreams," "You Make Loving Fun," and "Don't Stop." The latter song had a significant afterlife: a favorite of baby boomer President Bill Clinton, "Don't Stop" ("thinking about tomorrow") became the optimistic semiofficial theme song of his successful 1992 and 1996 presidential campaigns.

Led Zeppelin and the Birth of the Heavy

Listening again to the first few bars of "Communication Breakdown," the opening track from Led Zeppelin's self-titled debut album, is to listen in slack-jawed astonishment at the evolution of rock 'n' roll entering the 1970s. Guitarist and band founder Jimmy Page plays faster, harder, louder than he ever had as a member of the Yardbirds, the U.K. finishing school for blues-rock guitarists. (Eric Clapton and Jeff Beck had also been Yardbirds; Page had been in the band when it decomposed around 1968.)

With drummer John Bonham pounding the drums like a roomful of inmates rioting in a prison cafeteria, and John Paul Jones playing bass as adeptly as he had done in hundreds of London sessions during the 1960s, you knew you were hearing something new. And that was before the voice of Robert Plant made its entrance.

While most British rock singers emulating the blues tried to sound Southern low-down and dirty, as if they came from Mississippi rather than the Midlands (as Plant did), Zeppelin's singer moaned and wailed in the high registers, scatting and improvising, bending words into shrieks and back again — not a pure and pretty voice, but something other-worldly and very effective.

The overall effect was heavy, but they massaged their noise with textures. Alternating bucolic acoustic passages with ear-shattering steel-hard riffs, Led Zeppelin was setting the template for heavy metal and hard rock for the next quarter-century.

The band was going to be called the New Yardbirds, and was born out of necessity. Page's Yardbirds had broken up, but they still had some touring obligations in North America.

When Page, Plant, Jones, and Bonham got together for their first rehearsal, "a basement in Gerard Street in what is now Chinatown," as Jones recalled — the song they played was the Yardbirds' "Train Kept a Rollin'."[12]

"The whole room just exploded," according to Jones. "Silly grins. We knew it was going to work from the first number."

But it didn't sound like the Yardbirds, which was fine with Page. "I had in my mind exactly what I wanted to try, I was searching for the right personnel," Page told an interviewer in 1990. "To sort of expand on the Yardbirds … Areas of improvisation, some things I had come up with on my own, some passages and movements … acoustic work, along with the blues."

Plant, meanwhile, had grown up sneaking into folk and blues clubs, soaking in everything from British coal-miners' songs to American R&B, about which he has an encyclopedic knowledge and remarkable memory for artists, songs, and labels. (In a conversation with the author in 1993, Plant identified the label of a record by 1950s Bronx doo-wop group Dion & the Belmonts, as a casual fact. "Sure, on Laurie," Plant told me, meaning, correctly, the Laurie Records label.[13]) In the 1980s, he formed a band called the Honeydrippers that played exclusively jump R&B tunes from the 1940s and 1950s, as had Joe

Liggins and the Honeydrippers — who, as Plant could tell you off the top of his head, recorded at first for the Exclusive label, then for Specialty.

Jones had been one of London's most in-demand session players on bass guitar. He could, and would, play anything, with anyone. "Rolling Stones, the Everly Brothers, French and German rock sessions, Tom Jones, all in the same day, quite often."[14]

And Bonham was simply rock's most powerful drummer, give or take the Who's Keith Moon.

Zeppelin was not immediately loved, especially by the developing coterie of rock critics who, having discovered the blues on an album by the Yardbirds, the Rolling Stones, or Cream, became very serious and proprietary about it. Zeppelin was accused of exploiting the blues, or "da blooz," as the heavy, British style was called, to distinguish it from the authentic Southern sharecropper variety.

"Decadently exaggerated, bowdlerized blues-rock," Amazon. com writes of that debut album. And, the review continues, they pumped up "blues classics such as Otis Rush's 'I Can't Quit You Baby' and Howlin' Wolf's 'How Many More Times' into near-cartoon parodies."[15] Of course, that's true only if you listen to *Led Zeppelin* as a blues album; as rock 'n' roll, it is masterful. What is most troubling about Led Zeppelin's relationship to the blues is the band's willingness to claim authorship on some of these classic blues tunes, having changed but a few words or a chord or two, if at all.

Led Zeppelin also boasted "Dazed and Confused," which became the title of director Richard Linklater's coming-of-age movie about stoners in the seventies. It was an appropriate title, because there was no coming of age for most American high school and junior high students that decade without Led Zeppelin as a kind of personal soundtrack.

Interestingly, as their popularity grew, so did their mystique. Post-concert, hotel-trashing bacchanals were common, and an event in a suite in Seattle featuring a groupie and a live salmon fresh from Puget Sound is one of rock's most grotesquely perverse legends.

Their music kept evolving, both simpler ("Whole Lotta Love") and more complex ("Kashmir"), adding North African strains, medieval echoes, and Celtic mysticism to the blues-based rock 'n' roll. Their pinnacle, and a defining benchmark for the era, was the 1971 release of the untitled album known as *Led Zeppelin IV* and the song "Stairway to Heaven." Though it was never released as a single and is eight minutes long, it has become one of the most-played radio songs ever. Throughout the 1980s and into the 1990s, it has been regularly voted the No. 1 or No. 2 song of all-time by listeners voting in classic-rock radio station polls.

"Stairway to Heaven," critic Chuck Eddy wrote, "was the most famous rock song in Western civilization in the '70s because it was the best rock song in Western civilization in the '70s. No one has equaled Led Zeppelin's accomplishment: the marriage of hard rock and this sort of corny medievalism. It's tremendous."[16]

"Stairway" was so dominant a cultural moment that academics gave it serious attention. Not since the Beatles' *Sgt. Pepper's Lonely Heart's Club Band* had a rock recording been so carefully studied. *Sgt. Pepper* was just four years old, but Led Zeppelin made it seem a relic from an earlier generation.

One of the most interesting interpretations was by musicologist Dr. Robert Walser,[17] then at Dartmouth College. Walser, who had been known to illustrate lectures with his own capable hard-rock guitar playing, begins by noting the chord progression: A minor, A minor 9th/G sharp, A minor 7th/G, F major 7th, G, A minor.

> Such details are important, for the choice of one note rather than another can make a tremendous difference in how a song makes us feel … [Yet] such details function in a larger context — lyrics, timbres, visual images; the histories of the band, the music, the world — that makes them meaningful in particular ways. That chord progression, for example, signifies rather differently when George Benson plays it in 'This Masquerade.'

Indeed it does. Walser goes into detail describing the various strategies within the song that make it so powerful. On the one hand, he writes, there is a

> "folk/pastoral/mystical sensibility; on the other, desire/aggression/physicality. The song begins with the gentle sound and reassuringly square

phrases of an acoustic guitar, complemented by the archaic hooting of recorders, suggesting a pre-industrial refuge of the folk. Soon, Jimmy Page trades in his acoustic for the twangy punch of an electric [guitar] and, eventually, the raucous roar of heavy distortion. After a Hendrix-like guitar solo (blues-based, mildly psychedelic), Robert Plant's voice rises an octave, wailing over countless repetitions of a two-measure pattern, propelled by the band's frantic syncopations. The apotheosis/apocalypse breaks off suddenly, and the song ends with Plant's unaccompanied voice, a return to the solitary poignancy of the beginning.

Blending the "sensitive (acoustic guitar) and the aggressive (distorted electric guitar)," Walser notes, became a consistent approach of heavy-metal bands. The approach also suited later bands, such as Metallica, whose eighties speed-metal offered slow passages, and Nirvana, which used alternating soft/hard sections in "Smells Like Teen Spirit" In fact, all of the various shards of metal rock splinter off from Led Zeppelin in general and "Stairway to Heaven" in particular.

Black Sabbath, featuring vocalist Ozzy Osbourne, drummer Bill Ward, bassist Terry "Geezer" Butler, and guitarist Tomy Iommi slowed metal to the speed of a lumbering giant, and were the first really popular band to dwell on a horror-movie depiction of the afterlife as their subject matter. Osbourne not only talked the talk, he walked the walk, so to speak, biting off the head of a bat during a concert in Des Moines.

Black Sabbath's contribution, especially in the early 1970s, shouldn't be underestimated. Songs like "Paranoid," "War Pigs," "Iron Man," "Sweet Leaf," and "Children of the Grave" created the template for heavy metal, without the complications of Led Zeppelin's virtuosity. Don Kaye writes, "Sabbath not only perfected the crushing rhythms, juggernaut riffs, and wailing, haunting vocals of metal, but the band codified the image and attitude — a dark, cynical, often sinister worldview that provided bitter relief from the false optimism of so much pop music." The minimalist purity of the music, listened to in the twenty-first century, makes it sound almost like folk music.[18]

Of course, as the evolution of rock has shown, the outrageous eventually gets sucked into the mainstream. A TV reality show, *The Osbournes* — at home with Ozzy, wife Sharon, and the brood — was one of MTV's most popular programs around 2003 to 2004. (In 2005, Osbourne's annual heavy-metal summer package, Ozzfest, in its tenth year, was one of the most successful package tours ever.)

The phrase "heavy metal," as used in rock 'n' roll, stems from the hard-rock band Steppenwolf's 1968 classic, "Born to Be Wild," a rumbling theme song for motorcycle gangs everywhere.

Blue Oyster Cult mixed the Steppenwolf motorcycle sensibility, nihilistic World War II imagery, and rarefied lyrics by rock critic R. Meltzer and punk poet Patti Smith to make metal for smart people. Alice Cooper and Kiss took the comic book/horror movie sensibility to the stage, where they became major concert attractions. Kiss performed in trademark costumes, and indeed became stars of their own comic book. Cooper's stage act included simulated blood, dismembering dolls, guillotines, and hangman's nooses.

Cooper and his original band from 1971 to 1975 also cranked out some witty satires about teen life, "Eighteen" and "School's Out," that made them deservedly popular.

The Australian band AC/DC added huge power chords and a singer, Bon Scott, who could out-shriek Robert Plant. AC/DC apparently never toyed with ballads, tempo changes, or other subtleties. The simple, balls-to-the-wall appeal of AC/DC is represented by their album *Back in Black,* which has sold around 20 million copies.

The oddest Zeppelin-influenced musical event of the 1970s was the bewildering popularity of Grand Funk Railroad. The trio from Flint, Michigan, had no great musicians, mediocre songs, and little radio play, and yet it struck a chord with working-class males who couldn't quite relate to whatever else was available. Grand Funk's legions stunned the rock intelligentsia of magazines like *Rolling Stone* and *Crawdaddy* — many of his writers were now in their ripe mid-twenties — by selling out more than 50,000 seats in ballparks like New York's Shea Stadium.

Grand Funk Railroad was a breakthrough, in another way. They were one of the first massively popular bands that drew absolutely nothing from blues, R&B, country music, or early rock: No sight of Chuck Berry, Little Richard, the Beatles, or Rolling Stones anywhere near them.

The popularity eventually got critics, especially those aligned with the populist *Creem* magazine in Michigan, to give another listen, and

Creem ran a somewhat enthusiastic appraisal of the 1971 album, *Survival*. Robert Christgau (whose Consumer Guide columns originated at the *Village Voice* but also appeared in *Creem*), was apparently referring to such revisionism when he wrote of *Survival*:

"It Americanizes Led Zeppelin with a fervent ingenuousness that does justice to the broad gestures of mass art. But now I read where various men of taste, having reached similar conclusions, claim in addition actually to like the stuff. That's going too far."[19]

They were undoubtedly prolific: eleven albums between late 1969 and 1975. In 1973, firing their controlling producer/manager Terry Knight, they signed on with producer Todd Rundgren and finally made an album (*We're an American Band*) that didn't cause nonfans to grind their teeth. And the title song was a great radio record, catchy and anthemic in the style of their contemporaries Bachman-Turner Overdrive (BTO), a Canadian band. BTO, as it was known, was one of the top radio bands of 1974, with hard-rolling hits like "Takin' Care of Business" and "You Ain't Seen Nothing Yet."

With so much average music in its wake, "Stairway to Heaven" still evokes mixed feelings in its cocreator, Robert Plant, who composed it with Jimmy Page. In 1993, Plant told me:

> It's embarrassing, really, for me. Because I enjoy the song, but it seems very strange that there's nothing to go beyond that. Twenty years later, no one's come up with an alternative sort of plot … it is confirmed and celebrated for its commercial implications — for the radio stations, and their voters (contests), the phone-ins, to keep the interest going: Is "Layla" number two, or will it be "Bohemian Rhapsody" by Queen? I mean, really, 'In the Still of the Night' or 'A Thousand Miles Away' or 'There's a Moon Out Tonight' by the Capris or 'Tossin' and Turnin' " by Bobby Lewis, I would vote for one of them.[20]

Aerosmith

The most unlikely survivor of the 1970s was Aerosmith, which, as this is being written, is still recording and touring successfully with most of its original lineup intact.

Aerosmith split the difference between Led Zeppelin and the Rolling Stones. Their signature tune, 1972's "Dream On," was a clear derivation of "Stairway to Heaven," without the inscrutable Celtic mythology.

At first, despite a rabid fan base in their home, Boston, and nearby New England, "Dream On" and Aerosmith were flops. The competition was too rich. In 1972, Led Zeppelin still ruled, and their fifth album, *Houses of the Holy* (1973) some consider their best. The Rolling Stones had just followed one of their great albums, *Sticky Fingers* (1971, with a zipper cover designed by Andy Warhol) with their dense, yet masterful two-disc set, 1972's *Exile on Main Street*.

But in the next few years, Led Zeppelin would "begin to outgrow itself," as Christgau wrote, and the Stones would start their decline with *Goats Head Soup*, the 1973 release in which Christgau would accurately note, the performance was "slovenly ... I don't mean sloppy, which can be exciting, but arrogant and enervated, all at once."

To the teens who started, say, junior high in the early 1970s, the Rolling Stones had little relevance. Their 1972 tour attracted high-society types like Princess Lee Radziwill, author Truman Capote, and Andy Warhol.

Meanwhile, Keith Richards's use of heroin and other drugs was at a peak. He hit bottom in 1977 when he was arrested in Toronto for possession of heroin and cocaine, and faced a long stretch in a Canadian prison. "That was the watershed, the crunch," he said.[22] "That was the point, even in my condition after 10 years, that I suddenly realized this is it. I can't do this anymore."

Richards' heroin addiction nearly tore the Stones apart. "I'd keep the band waiting weeks before the start of rehearsals for a new tour, because I couldn't set up my 'French connection' or whatever. That was the first. First the dope, then the world could start revolving again, and I could get involved."

Aerosmith, meanwhile, were young, hungry, and had the insolent swagger of the Stones. (They wouldn't develop their own very serious substance abuse until a few years later.)

There was even a physical resemblance: Singer Steven Tyler, with his oversized lips and ever-present scarves, was the Jagger figure; Joe Perry, the talented guitarist, had gaunt, angular features similar to those of Richards. (Aerosmith's singer is the father of actress Liv Tyler.)

And while they had one foot into heavy metal, the other foot was in R&B: On their first album, *Aerosmith* (1972), they even covered Rufus Thomas's "Walking the Dog," as had the Stones.

After two albums, Aerosmith still hadn't clicked. The third album, *Toys in the Attic*, fit a comfortable theory at the time — that a typical rock band would hit its peak on the third album. It was certainly true with Aerosmith.

Toys was full of raunchy rockers like "Back in the Saddle," "Sweet Emotion," "Adam's Apple," and "Walk This Way," rich with double entendre and thick with hormonal glee. Aerosmith wasn't subtle: they didn't record Bullmoose Jackson's "Big Ten Inch Record" for its melody. Asked, in 1976, to explain the appeal of Aerosmith, Mick Jagger told me, succinctly and sarcastically, "it's cock rock, mate."[23]

Different Strokes for Different Folks: Sly and the Family Stone

It has been said that "There are two kinds of black music: before Sly Stone, and after Sly Stone."* The first major multiracial, multigender rock band, Sly & the Family Stone had a run from 1967 to 1975 that parallels the racial, political, and social environment of the era, from optimism to despair.

But those first four years were unparalleled. "In his heyday, Sly had the pop sense of a Lennon-McCartney, the backing band of a James Brown, and a multiracial lineup that looked liked Bobby Kennedy's America," Matthew Weiner wrote in 2003.[†]

Sly Stone was born Sylvester Stewart and grew up in the San Francisco Bay Area. As a producer and songwriter for the local Autumn Records, he was behind such hits as "C'mon and Swim," a 1964 dance hit by Bobby Freeman, and he recorded some of the earliest white San Francisco rock bands, including the Beau Brummels, the Mojo Men, and Grace Slick's Great Society, forerunners of the Jefferson Airplane.

Sly Stone was also a popular disc jockey on a high-energy San Francisco R&B station, KSOL, from 1963 to 1967. Though the call

---

* [book description of Sly & the Family Stone: An Oral History [For the Record series] by Joel Selvin and Dave Marsh, http://www.amazon.com/Sly-Family-Stone-History-Record/dp/0380793776].

† http://www.stylusmagazine.com/reviews/sly-and-the-family-stone/the-essential-sly-and-the-family-stone.htm

letters described the station's format (soul music), Sly would mix in music from white artists, from the Beatles to blue-eyed soul stalwarts like the Young Rascals. Even as a disc jockey, his quick patter carried a message: "Everybody dig, everybody dig, do not burn, baby, burn, [but] learn, baby, learn so you can earn, baby, earn," he would say in the few seconds allotted between records.*

In 1967, Sly & the Family Stone's live performances had also become one of the Bay Area's biggest buzz bands. While the region's celebrated rock acts — the Airplane, the Grateful Dead, Country Joe & the Fish — considered flamboyance to be as unhip as top forty, Sly & the Family Stone were a carnival of bling. Sly, with his towering Afro, was "an outrageous showman whose style was a combination of Fillmore district pimp gone stone crazy and Fillmore Auditorium optimism with a point to it."†

The band, built around Sly's keyboards and vocals, also included his brother Freddie on guitar; sister Rosie on vocals and piano; a cousin, Larry Graham, on bass; a horn section comprised of a black woman, Cynthia Robinson, on trumpet, and former rival bandleader Jerry Martini on sax. Martini, like drummer Gregg Errico, was Italian-American.

The group's debut album for CBS's Epic label, 1967's *A Whole New Thing,* sold poorly, but the title song of the 1968 album *Dance to the Music* was a breakthrough, a mass of soul horns and psychedelic guitar, of call-and-response between a controlled bass singer and ecstatic shrieks and wails of the chorus, of disciplined ensemble playing and free-for-all solos. It was something entirely new, and audiences responded across the board.

By the beginning of 1969, Sly & the Family Stone were No. 1 on both the pop and R&B charts with their signature tune, "Everyday People." The song held the promise of a utopia of tolerance and acceptance — it introduced the phrase, and the idea, of "Different strokes, for different folks." There couldn't be an audience more open to that message than the 400,000 or so who saw and heard the band at Woodstock in the summer of 1969, and surging anthems like "Stand!" and mellower workouts like "Hot Fun in the Summertime"

---

* [http://airchexx.com/?p=164; Sly Stone on KSOL San Francisco/1967, an 8 minute, 28 second aircheck (an aircheck is a demonstration recording, a radio personalities version of a resume, to show off the talent of an announcer or radio disk jockey to a prospective future employer.

† Greil Marcus, Mystery Train, page 81.

made Sly & the Family Stone emblematic of Woodstock's message of unity and harmony through music.

The hits kept coming, as Sly kept emphasizing the "fun" in the funk masterwork "Thank You (Falettinme Be Mice Elf Agin)"; the feel-good Aquarian-age anthem "Everybody Is a Star"; and the ecstatic "I Want to Take You Higher."

The politics may have been implicit, but the hope and good feeling in Sly's sound rewarded those like Greil Marcus, who sought and found a deeper message. "A smash with black kids and white, these records had all the good feeling of the March on Washington and the street cachet the march never had," Marcus wrote.[*]

Sly Stone was living large, buying mansions and vintage cars, able to afford any indulgence, including drugs. In 1970, the impact of the drugs — cocaine, heroin, and PCP, better known as angel dust — started to become evident. He would show up hours late for concerts, if he showed up at all. An aura of menace and violence, bodyguards, and guns became pervasive. Looking back in this context, a song like the popular "Don't Call Me Nigger, Whitey," a track from the 1969 album *Stand!* was a sign of cynicism shredding the Family Stone's optimism.

It is a testament to Sly's genius that when that cynicism became as toxic as an overdose, he was able to put it to music. The 1971 album *There's a Riot Goin' On* is widely regarded as one of the bleakest, most despairing rock recordings ever made. *The Rolling Stone Encyclopedia of Rock & Roll* notes, "Its darkly understated sound, violent imagery and controversial militant stance were a sharp contrast to the optimism of earlier works."[†] Tempos are sluggish; chords assert themselves, then fade away; the once exuberant singing is now a kind of muttering. "Dyin' young is hard to take/Sellin' out is harder," one revealing but wounded couplet goes.

Strangely, this most difficult of albums was Sly & the Family Stone's only No. 1, boosted by the brooding but eloquent hit single "Family Affair." It's hard to think of an artist at a simultaneous artistic high and emotional low — unless you go back to Robert Johnson and the other Delta bluesmen of the 1930s, who transmuted their misery into music for the ages.

Sly did a slow fade: a brief bounce back to funk with the 1973 album *Fresh,* and a festive 1974 concert at Madison Square Garden at which he married his girlfriend. Since then, however, it seems as

---

* *Mystery Train*, 82.
† Pareles and Romanowski, *Rolling Stone Encyclopedia of Rock & Roll*, 510.

if he has appeared more often in court than on stage. His musical output has been minimal. In 2005, a tribute album, *Different Strokes,* featured current such current hip-hop stars such as will i am and OutKast, underscoring the importance of Sly's rhythms as a foundation of black music. Sly made an extremely rare public appearance on keyboards during a tribute to his music on the 2006 Grammy Awards telecast, with a bizarre Mohawk haircut. But the appearance presented more questions than answers, and underlined the likelihood that Sly Stone is the most tragic drug casualty in rock 'n' roll. Not because he died, but because he didn't die and has had to live all these years as the epitome of musical brilliance squandered. Yet more than any other individual, Sly may be responsible for the profound shift toward rock 'n' social awareness that black music took in the 1970s.

Black Album Rock In The Seventies: Stevie Wonder/Marvin Gaye/Isaac Hayes/Curtis Mayfield/Parliament-Funkdelic

For his twenty-first birthday in 1971, Stevie Wonder sent Motown Records a letter declaring his contracts void. (Wonder recorded for Motown's Tamla imprint.) Blind since birth, he had been one of the label's most consistent hit-makers since he began recording as the harmonica-playing prodigy twelve-year-old "Little Stevie Wonder."

His range of interests, and successes, was enormous, from his first hit, the surreally intense live hit recording of "Fingertips Pt. 2" in 1963. The string of hits that followed were noteworthy for the versatility, quality, and universal appeal, from the rousing "Uptight (Everything's Alright)," to the laid-back version of Bob Dylan's "Blowin' in the Wind" (perhaps the first version of a Dylan song to top the R&B charts), from the knockout swagger of "I Was Made to Love Her" to a swinging version of the standard "For Once in My Life."

Wonder often cowrote his hits, and on 1970's *Signed, Sealed and Delivered* album he had already begun producing his records as well.

But except for the No. 1 novelty of *Little Stevie Wonder — The 12 Year Old Genius,* his albums didn't sell and didn't chart. Motown, like most labels that specialized in R&B music, promoted singles, not albums; the routine was to include one or two hits and leave the rest to chance. And for all the hits, Wonder, like many artists of his era, didn't feel his earnings were commensurate with his sales.

"It's not just Motown," Wonder said many years later.[*] "You could talk about Atlantic … all the different companies. You can talk about black artists, you can talk about some of the rockabilly people. They didn't have great representation [in negotiating their original recording contracts], either." A voracious listener and versatile musician who would eventually play every instrument on many of his records, Wonder's first entirely self-produced album was *Where I'm Coming From* (1971), which addressed racial and antiwar themes as well as generating a melodically beautiful and rhythmically driving hit single, "If You Really Love Me."

Music of My Mind (1972) and *Talking Book* formed the first wave of Wonder's unprecedented creative and popular surge, the beginning a four-year period in which three of the albums for which he composed, produced, sang, and played many of the instruments would be critically hailed as well as Grammy Album of the Year winners: *Innvervisions* (1973), *Fulfillingness' First Finale* (1974), and *Songs in the Key of Life* (1976).

Wonder's fecundity was no doubt enhanced by a recent technological development: the Moog synthesizer. Invented by the music lover and engineering physicist Robert Moog in 1964, the Moog synthesizer is a keyboard instrument that "transformed electronic currents into sounds that could be almost infinitely modified, sparking a revolution in how music is created."[†]

Rock musicians immediately embraced the Moog; in this era of experimentation, it was a simple weapon that greatly diversified their sonic arsenal. Bands from the Beatles to the Monkees, from the Doors to Frank Zappa, were early adapters. In 1968, Walter Carlos performed classical music on the Moog, resulting in the Grammy Award–winning album *Switched-On Bach,* which brought the Moog synthesizer to "spectacular prominence." [‡] [§]

The music, production, and engineering team of Robert Margouleff and Malcolm Cecil used the name Tonto's Expanding Head Band for their album *Zero Time* in 1971. (TONTO is an acronym for The Original New Timbral Orchestra, as well as the name of the instrument.) Margouleff and Cecil became associate producers, engineers, and

---

[*] c 2005 Barney Hoskyns, *Rocks Back Pages,* http://rocksbackpages.com

[†] Karen Grigsby Bates, *Day to Day,* August 22, 2005, http://www.npr.org/templates/story/story.php?storyId=4810029

[‡] http://news.bbc.co.uk/1/hi/entertainment/music/4696651.stm

[§] Carlos had a sex-change operation and has been known as Wendy Carlos since approximately 1982.

programmers for most of Wonder's albums, from *Music of My Mind* through his soundtrack to the Spike Lee film *Jungle Fever* in 1991.

Writing in *Keyboard Magazine* in 1984, John Dilberto asserted that "... this collaboration [Wonder, Margouleff, and Cecil] changed the perspectives of black pop music as much as the Beatles' *Sgt. Pepper* altered the concept of white rock."

Marvin Gaye

Marvin Gaye was the closest thing to a solo male sex symbol Motown had in the 1960s. Growing up singing in his father's Apostolic church, he was once a member of the doo-wop group the Moonglows, whose lead singer, Harvey Fuqua, became a prominent Motown producer/ writer/executive. From 1963 he had an unbroken string of hits, exciting dance tracks that retained more of the emotional gospel roots of R&B than many Motown records. They included "Hitch Hike" and "Can I Get a Witness," both covered by the Rolling Stones. He made towering records that stood out even during the English Invasion and the summer of love: the same month *Sgt. Pepper's Lonely Heart's Club Band* was released, Gaye and a duo partner, Tammi Terrell, hit the charts with their monumental performance of "Ain't No Mountain High Enough," the first of a half-dozen sparkling hits they made together. Gaye's intensity was so dominating that even though fellow Motown act Gladys Knight & the Pips had a huge 1967 hit with "I Heard It Through the Grapevine," less than a year later, Gaye's version sounded revolutionary. Writer Dave Marsh, in his book *The Heart of Rock & Soul: The 1001 Greatest Singles Ever Made,* declares Gaye's sublime recording to be the best.

In 1970, however, the already moody and erratic Gaye was traumatized when Terrell collapsed in his arms and died onstage. Gaye spent a few months in seclusion, and emerged with some intensely introspective music. Motown wouldn't release it. Gaye threatened never to record again if it wasn't released, so Motown reluctantly relented and put out the single "What's Going On," which was not just an immediate hit but helped change the esthetic of urban music. The song, and the album that it gave title to, was a litany of urban and personal woes, a song cycle addressing poverty, the Vietnam war, crime, and ghetto life. It was both deeply pessimistic and naively hopeful at the same time. Rather than tightly constructed Motown tracks, the album had a flowing, jazzy ambience. The three big hits from the album, "Mercy Mercy Me," "Inner City Blues," and "What's

Going On," made it clear that R&B could be topical and still appeal to a mass audience, could be airy and romantic and still have impact. It was an emotionally complicated record, as the British writer Vivien Goldman pointed out, calling Motown's first "concept album" a "compelling, impassioned, brain-and-soul searching cry for reason in a world that was … burning itself up through greed, wastefulness, callousness and ignorance."

Gaye continued to morph spiritually through the 1970s, creating masterpieces ("Let's Get It On," 1973), and then disappearing into silent exile in Europe to escape drug and financial problems. Moving over to Columbia in 1982, he was back at the top of the charts with "Sexual Healing," one of the most seductive tracks ever recorded. He didn't live long to build on the renewal the song and album (*Midnight Love*) provided. On April 1, 1984, Gaye was shot to death by the minister father after whom he was named, a day before the singer's forty-fifth birthday.

Curtis Mayfield

As songwriter, producer, musician, and lead vocalist for the Chicago-based vocal group the Impressions, Curtis Mayfield was long putting spiritual messages about black pride into his music. Impressions tunes like "Keep on Pushing," "Amen" (1964), and "People Get Ready" (1965) were the soundtrack for the nonviolent Civil Rights movements. As the country descended into rioting and chaos in 1968, Mayfield's songs with the Impressions maintained their harmonious sound while the lyrical message jacked up in intensity: "We're a Winner" and "This is My Country" provided a musical link between black pride and black power, as did the uplifting but direct "Choice of Colors" (1969) and the really odd "Mighty Mighty (Spade and Whitey)"; the latter title, in a nutshell, said it all about the confusing race relations of the time, the tug between integration and separation, between the desire for brotherhood and the venting of mutual contempt.

Mayfield went solo in 1970, scored with another topical hit that, against all odds, reached the top thirty and gained substantial radio play. Shocking listeners with the opening that shouted: "Sisters! Niggas! Whiteys! Jews! Crackers! …" Don't worry, Mayfield sang, because "If There's a Hell Below We're All Gonna Go."

In 1972, Mayfield released his most memorable, controversial album, the soundtrack to the movie *Superfly*.

Superfly was one of the most successful "blaxploitation" movies of the 1970s. The trend started in 1970 when filmmaker/actor Melvin Van Peebles raised the money for an independent film called *Sweet Sweetback's Badass Song.* Culture critic Nelson George wrote that Van Peebles was "the first film director to understand that black audiences (and many whites as well) wanted their black heroes rebellious, to mirror the romantic revolutionaries one saw on the evening news."* Van Peebles also knew that the audience for these films wanted to hear street-smart music on the soundtrack; he commissioned the then-little-known Chicago-based jazz/funk band, Earth, Wind and Fire, who would become superstars in a few years with songs, arrangements, and an arena-sized stage show that appealed across racial and age lines.

Soon Hollywood was onboard, releasing a torrent of films filled with ghetto hyperrealism — telling it like it is from a cynical, pessimistic point of view. In *Shaft* (1971) the protagonist was a black private eye, "caught in a struggle between black and Italian mobsters for control over organized crime in Harlem."† Isaac Hayes composed the soundtrack, including the hit theme from *Shaft.* Hayes and former partner David Porter had been the production and writing team at Stax Records in the sixties behind hits like "Soul Man"; in 1969, he emerged as a solo artist and a new kind of soul man, whispering to his lover in the extended orchestrations of *Hot Buttered Soul.* Hayes's deep baritone became a meal ticket years later as the voice of "Chef" in the animated TV series *South Park.*

The *Shaft* soundtrack contained only three songs with vocals; it was Mayfield in 1972, with *Superfly,* who fully integrated hit songs with singing into the movie plot. The protagonist was a midlevel cocaine pusher trying to close out one last big deal, but both the cops and the drug kingpins have other plans for him. Songs like "Freddie's Dead," "Pusher Man," and the title song drove the action.

"The storyline breaks down the ghetto situation, the drugs, the crime … they sell cocaine and hustle their way through life. They are looked at as princes of the ghetto because they live off it," Mayfield said at the time.‡

"Superfly was the culmination of Mayfield's long career," George wrote. "It summed up his social concerns with the most aggressive

---

* Nelson George, *The Death of Rhythm & Blues* (New York: E.P. Dutton, 1988), 122.

† Ibid., 123.

‡ Interview with Roger St. Pierre, *Let It Rock* magazine, October 1972.

music he ever wrote." Mayfield was paralyzed in a freak accident when a lighting tower fell on him before a 1990 outdoor concert in Brooklyn; he died in 1999.

Mayfield went on to write many other soundtracks, but the influence of blaxploitation music was heard throughout the culture. "It encouraged all R&B musicians to expand their sound and ambition," George wrote, citing Norman Whitfield's psychedelic soul 1972 production of the Temptations' "Papa Was a Rolling Stone" (1972). Whitfield, cowriter of "I Heard It Through the Grapevine" and producer of Gaye's version, was also the auteur behind the paranoid sound of the Undisputed Truth's hit "Smiling Faces Sometimes."

In fact, hard edges were being heard throughout black music. At Philadelphia International Records, producers Kenny Gamble and Leon Huff created a sound that was simultaneously street-smart and sophisticated. Some of the most dynamic records were made by the O'Jays, whose song about casual betrayal in the 'hood, "Back Stabbers," was a chart-topper and club favorite in every neighborhood. (The follow-up, the No. 1 "Love Train," had a more positive message and thirty-three years later is a theme song for a Coors Lite beer advertising campaign.)

Having gotten the hang of thematically coherent albums, a number of self-contained R&B acts began doing stage shows. The tradition in R&B performance had been for a solo artist or group to be backed by an anonymous large band or orchestra. During the 1970s, bands that played their own instruments and material began hitting arenas doing rock-style stage shows, with sophisticated lighting, grandiose sound systems, and special effects. The Commodores were successful with both funk-rock ("Brick House") and ballads sung by lead singer Lionel Richie ("Easy").

From the West Coast, the group War emerged. After backing former Animals' singer Eric Burdon on some eccentric albums (*Eric Burdon Declares 'War,' The Black Man's Burdon*) in 1970, they stepped out on with a Latin groove and a knack for fresh-sounding radio hits ("Low Rider," "Gypsy Man"). Their peak moment was the No. 1 album *The World Is a Ghetto*, released in 1972.

But Parliament/Funkadelic, or P-Funk, was the great R&B rooted arena rock band of the 1970s. "P-Funk" was a melding of two groups, both led by hipster-visionary George Clinton. "The Parliaments" were a doo-wop group formed by Clinton in Newark as early as 1955; moving to Detroit in 1967, the group had evolved into a standard soul vocal quintet, and had a hit that summer with the decent but unspectacular "(I Wanna) Testify." A year later, Clinton created Funkadelic based around the Parliament rhythm section and keyboard player Bernie Worrell. The crew also featured Fred Wesley and Maceo Parker, James Brown's top two horn men, who had formed their own band, the JB's, and brought with them to P-Funk the Collins brothers: Phelps "Catfish" Collins, and the high-wattage bass player/singer/writer William "Bootsy" Collins.*

Clinton's conceptual brilliance was partly a business stroke: Parliament and Funkadelic shared the same personnel, but were signed to two different labels. Artistically, there was a distinction that eventually overlapped, but Parliament was initially the more conventional R&B band with tighter, punchier, horn-driven songs, while Funkadelic, as the name implied, was more of an experimental, guitar-centric rock band.

Under either name, Clinton's groups made magnificent music, which went from earthy and political (Parliament's *Chocolate City,* 1975), to Funkadelic's inspirational party jams (*One Nation Under a Groove,* album and title song, 1978) to the territory that would today be considered part of the Cartoon Channel's *Adult Swim,* like the 1979 album *Aqua Boogie (A Psychoalphadiscobetabioaqudoloop).* Cartoon drawings were in fact part of the brand: illustrator Pedro Bell drew comic book-style "liner notes" on many P-Funk albums; some of these albums told fairly amusing, over-the-top stories, which were usually about recapturing missing or stolen funk (1977's *Funkentelechy vs. the Placebo Syndrome*).

P-Funk concerts in the 1970s were events that could feature as many as forty musicians on the stage. No expense was spared on stagecraft: the set for the 1976 Mothership Connection tour cost $260,000 and was designed by Jules Fisher, who also did high-tech sets for David Bowie, Kiss, and the Rolling Stones.† Though wildly inconsistent (how could they not be?), P-Funk's blend of guitar rock, soul horns, weirdly snaking keyboard lines, and dizzying choral chants (by female backing groups like the Brides of Funkenstein) put them in a matchless class of their own — a whole new thang, as George "Dr. Funkenstein" Clinton would have called it.

---

* The author is grateful for Joel Whitburn's *Billboard book of Top Pop Singles 1995–2002,* p. 535, for helping with the who's who.

† By Wayne Robins, "Halloween Mutants Invade Louisiana," *Rolling Stone* magazine, Dec. 30, 1976.

Punk

Punk rock began in the United States in 1976 not as a rebellion against authority or government or as a political or fashion statement. Punk rock was a rebellion against rock music itself.

"We were a reaction to all the pretentiousness, mediocrity and superficialness that was going on at the time," said Joey Ramone, singer of punk rock's most indispensable band, the Ramones.[24]

The Ramones mission was to rescue rock 'n' roll from the staid, conformist, and predictable music on the radio in the mid-1970s. Rock had become a commodity; it had lost the edge, innovation, and daring that made it such a revolutionary force the previous decade. Typical was journeyman rocker Peter Frampton, who was No. 1 for ten weeks in 1976 with his two-disc concert recording, *Frampton Comes Alive*, which served a vast constituency that wanted to be soothed.

Paul McCartney was becoming by far the most commercially successful of the former Beatles, with a band called Wings (featuring his wife Linda on backup vocals and keyboards). McCartney couldn't deny that his music wasn't much more than silly love songs, since that was the title of one of Wings' biggest hits.

There was a group called Boston, whose leader, Tom Scholz, an engineering whiz used the most pristine studio techniques to showcase his guitar solos, efficient melodic runs with a knack for finding the sweet spot. Scholz was augmented by the late Brad Delp, whose keening voice on "More Than a Feeling" brought romantic crooning to hard rock, a manifestation of the radio-friendly big rock song known as the power ballad. The 1976 debut album *Boston* sold 15 million copies; *Frampton Comes Alive* moved 10 million. And the Eagles and Fleetwood Mac were selling similar numbers.

But the connection to rock 'n' roll's antiauthoritarian roots had snapped. For inspiration, some were attracted to the dark nihilism of late 1960s Velvet Underground and to the manic stage show and minimalist raw ruckus of Detroit's legendary band the Stooges, featuring Iggy Pop.

Others were inspired by simple, hard-nosed roots rock styles like rockabilly, and even surf music. The rock writer, historian, and nascent guitar player Lenny Kaye in 1972 was behind the influential compilation

Nuggets: Original Artyfacts of the First Psychedelic Era 1965–1968. The two-disc set provided a new context for what was also known as the "garage band," era, which featured derivative, sometimes amateurish, but raw and spirited records like *I Had Too Much to Dream Last Night* (the Electric Prunes), *Dirty Water* (Standells), and *Pushin' Too Hard* (the Seeds).

According to the liner notes to "Nuggets," by Kaye,

> Most of these groups (and by and large, this was an era dominated by groups) were young, decidedly unprofessional, seemingly more at home practicing for a teen dance than going out on national tour. The name that has been unofficially coined for them — "punk-rock" — seems particularly fitting in this case, for if nothing else they exemplified the berserk pleasure that comes with being on-stage outrageous, the relentless middle-finger drive and determination offered only by rock and roll at its finest.[25]

Kaye's definition of punk rock described a rock 'n' roll revolution that was simmering even as he typed the words. (And little did he know that he would soon become one of the participants as the guitarist for the Patti Smith Group.)

Punk rock started in New York, where crime, recession, inflation, strikes, and sky-high interest rates had caused real estate values to plummet. Young people with artistic inclinations surged into neighborhoods like the East Village, where cheap apartments were plentiful. (Even in now-long-gentrified neighborhoods like Chelsea, a one-bedroom apartment in a converted brownstone could be had for under $200 a month; on the Lower East Side or East Village, less than that.) A struggling saloon on the northern end of the Bowery, nearly edging into Third Avenue just below Bleecker Street was called CBGB and OMFUG. The oblique initials stood for Country, Bluegrass, Blues, and Other Music for Uplifting Gourmandizers, according to the club's longtime owner, Hilly Kristal.

With not much going on, and nothing to lose, Kristal's dive became a place where local bands could get their stage legs in front of whoever might be curious enough to walk in the door. Tom Miller, aka Tom Verlaine, was one of the first. He and fellow guitarist Richard Lloyd led a band called Television; their first CBGB gig was March 31, 1974. Word began to get around the relatively close-knit network of creative young people in lower Manhattan that there was a bar with cheap beer, low or no cover prices, and live music played by an odd but potentially interesting rock band.

People started showing up. Verlaine's friend Patti Smith, already known as poet, writer, and muse with roots in the area's bohemian art scene, was an early regular. The charismatic Smith recited her rock 'n' roll poetry backed by a guitar player — Lenny Kaye. CBGB started filling up whenever she played. Soon she went from writing poems steeped in rock 'n 'roll to forming a band, the Patti Smith Group, whose 1975 album *Horses* is a landmark, in which every sound — especially the show-stopping version of Van Morrison's 1960s garage-band classic "Gloria" — implied that spiritual trans-formation was still possible through rock 'n' roll. Neither Television nor Smith played anything resembling either the top-forty or album-oriented rock (AOR) being played on the radio and popular among the mass of rock fans outside this slice of New York enclave. The singing may have been unrefined, but it was passionate. In Televi-sion, Verlaine and his coguitarist, Richard Lloyd, were ragged and unpolished, but they played with an out-of-tune intensity that was riveting. They conveyed a spirit of agony and uplift. It was deeply personal and highly expressive, intense, and combustible, and soon there were bands by hundreds sharing this do-it-yourself esthetic.

Debbie Harry of Blondie asked rhetorically,

> What makes any scene happen? What made it happen in San Francisco [in the 60s] or London? A bunch of people all there at the same time. One of the magnetic things that made it possible was that New York always had a music scene. But one of the groups that turned on alot of the groups that came later was the New York Dolls. They were really caught in a time warp. They were a glitter band, but they were too punk to be a glitter band, and too New York–ish. They paved the way for a lot of bands.[26]

These new punk rock bands came in all forms and sizes.

Some were preppy, like Talking Heads, who approached rock like one of their art projects at the Rhode Island School of Design. Origi-nally a trio (singer/guitarist David Byrne, bassist Tina Weymouth, and drummer Chris Frantz) played a kind of jerky, cubist funk; when guitarist/keyboard player Jerry Harrison joined, the band's sound began fleshing out; in the 1980s, the funk became authentic as Bernie Worrell, formerly of Parliament/Funkadelic, joined the band and played on their urban jungle showpiece, *Speaking in Tongues* (1983), and in director Jonathan Demme's visually arresting Talking Heads concert movie, *Stop Making Sense.*

Blondie updated the girl-group sound of the 1960s, emphasizing the trashier end of the style, the Shangri-Las with guitars and keyboards. Others feasted on revving up 1950s rockabilly, like Robert Gordon's Tuff Darts. Richard Hell & the Void-Oids had a sharp guitar attack and a way with metaphor ("Love Comes in Spurts"). The Dead Boys played out the hoodlum/nihilist act, while others, like Mink DeVille, sought a safe harbor in early 1960s R&B of groups like the Drifters.

Then there were the Ramones.

The Ramones typified the CBGB ethos. They were not pretty: lead singer, the beanstalk Joey Ramone, wore thick glasses, had shaggy, messy long hair, and may have been the homeliest young man to seek his fame on a rock 'n' roll bandstand. The Ramones pretended to be brothers: Joey, DeeDee, Johnny, and all took the stage surname "Ramone." They dressed identically: in black leather jackets and tight jeans. Joey was really Jeffrey Leigh, a Jewish kid from the middle-class borough of Queens, where the group was formed.

They played their own two-minute songs at breathtaking speed, with a relentless, consistent, brain-pounding beat. Their lyrics were epiphanies to family and psychiatric dysfunction: "Beat on the Brat," "Pinhead," "I Wanna Sniff Some Glue." So fast, hard, and strange were their songs that it was a year or two before even their devotees realized that behind the hard facade was a rock 'n' roll fantasy as romantic as that of the Beach Boys, whose chords were echoed in such Ramones songs as "Rockaway Beach."

But that year or two was essential, since that is the time it took for the Ramones to change the world. The trend-crazy weekly British music press — *Melody Maker, New Musical Express,* and *Sounds* — went Ramones-beat crazy, and found a deep well of stories in the New York punk scene. And of course, the British were charmed. "We may not be the brightest guys in the world," Dee Dee Ramone told *NME* at a soundcheck at London's Roundhouse club. "But I don't think I'm no mutant weed, either."[27]

Among all the bands, it was the Ramones who inspired the Clash and the Sex Pistols and the Damned and a hundred other young Brits. The medium was the Ramones' message, and that medium was punk rock, distilled to its essence.

The Sex Pistols took the insolent stance of the Ramones and turned it into musical juvenile delinquency. They had the look: the spiky hair, the torn and tattered clothes, the nihilistic attitude, the gobbing (spitting), the drugs, as embodied in the look and short, sick life of their inept but symbolically essential bass player, Sid Vicious. And of course, the ranting lead singer, John Lydon, had the stage name that will forever remain punk rock's most significant brand: Johnny Rotten.

The Pistols received a bounteous amount of publicity and attention even before their first album was released. Their look, their attitude, and their anti-everything promotional campaign was the brainchild of fashion entrepreneur Malcolm McLaren, who essentially created the group from customers and hangers-on at Sex, the trendy London clothing store he ran with designer Vivienne Westwood.

After the free-swinging 1960s, when London was an epicenter of music and style, England had settled back into its gray, prim self. To a young person in Britain in the mid-1970s, conformity was as stifling as it was in the United States in the 1950s. It was even worse, because while the American teen foresaw an optimistic future, British youth saw "no future," in the words of the Sex Pistols' defining tune, "God Save the Queen."

Merely the title "God Save the Queen" was enough to shock the timid mainstream British media. And when Johnny Rotten sang, "God save the Queen/she ain't human bein'," the song was immediately banned. Censorship in a democracy is often the quickest way to spread a provocative message. Alert for controversy, the BBC had the Sex Pistols on TV to discuss the song. They were warned against vulgar language, which was like ordering an infant not to drool. Rotten spat and used four-letter words, which again, banished the group.

McLaren and company were, of course, delighted, since the backlash against the Pistols led to a similarly forceful backlash against those who would deny the Pistols. The controversy sent "God Save the Queen" to No. 1 immediately. And despite the obvious limitations of Sid Vicious as a musician, their ferocious debut album, *Never Mind the Bollocks, Here's the Sex Pistols,* was a defining moment in Anglo-American rock — blunt, crude, concise, and inspiring in its proof that rock 'n' roll still had the capacity to enthrall and offend.

But the Pistols' attempt to alienate the establishment was too successful. Fear of malicious behavior got the Sex Pistols blackballed from almost every city and town in the United Kingdom: they had no place to play. And that enabled the Clash — a more serious, musical band — to stake its place as the great band of British punk, and more.

Their debut album, *The Clash,* was released in the United Kingdom by CBS Records in 1977; it was so raw that the company initially refused to release it at all in the United States. In 2003, it was hailed by British music monthly *Mojo* as "searingly evocative of dreary late '70s Britain, but still timelessly inspiring."

The record company wanted something more "American" sounding to release in the United States. The result was "Give 'Em Enough Rope," released in 1978. A bit of a mess, it was produced by Blue Oyster Cult's Sandy Pearlman, a match made in corporate boardroom hell. (The album went to No. 2 in the United Kingdom, but didn't make the Top 100 album charts in the United States.)

In 1979, the Clash released their masterpiece, *London Calling,* a two-LP set that established them as not just punk, but a world-class rock 'n' roll band with a bold, expansive vision. Featuring hoarse-throated shouter Joe Strummer, and a solid guitarist in Mick Jones, the Clash mixed and matched their talents with everything from the reggae that had always been a part of its London multicultural stew to New Orleans R&B, from the unsentimental romantic yearnings of "Train in Vain" to the apocalyptic title song.

For a time, they were rock's best, but internal dissension, and the contradictions of succeeding as capitalists while pitching a socialist worldview caused them to gradually disengage. The three-disc set *Sandinista!* (named for the left-wing Nicaraguan rebels engaged in a civil war with the U.S.-supported right-wing Somoza government) showed some of the overreaching ego which they had once appeared to shun. But it had some great moments, including "The Magnificent Seven," which dabbles in hip-hop's earliest roots. 1982's *Combat Rock* featured the hit "Rock the Casbah," a prescient vision of the West's culture clash with Islam that retains its incendiary power to this day.

The Buzzcocks, Gang of Four, the Mekons, Wire, the Slits, and X-Ray Spex are some other British bands from the seventies worth further attention.

Los Angeles also developed its own lively punk scene, from the rowdy roots rock of X to the condensed fury of Black Flag to the nihilism of the Germs to the sleaze of the aptly named Weirdos. But like their New York counterparts, they could not catch a break with radio.

"Radio, when they get locked into something that sells advertising, that's what they're going to feed back to record companies," Debbie Harry said. "Record companies are going to say [of a punk band] well, they (radio) can't sell them, they can't market them, they're not compatible to airplay or selling advertising."

Disco

On August 9, 1974, Richard M. Nixon, about to be impeached by Congress for obstruction of justice, became the first U.S. president to resign from office. He was taken down by his efforts to cover up the June 17, 1972, burglary, ordered by his minions, of the Democratic National Committee in the condo/office complex on known as Watergate in Washington, D.C.

The Vietnam War ended in defeat for the United States and its South Vietnamese allies. The capital, Saigon, fell to North Vietnamese troops on April 30, 1975, uniting the country under Communist rule. The war had lasted more than ten years; approximately 58,000 Americans and more than 2 million Vietnamese died. Faith in institutions such as the military and the presidency fell to an all-time low.

It was time to dance.

But disco wasn't just about dancing. The epicenter of the disco world was Studio 54. Mick Jagger, Liza Minnelli, Bianca Jagger, and Margaret Trudeau (wife of Canada's prime minister Pierre Trudeau), Andy Warhol and his entourage, athletes, movie stars, politicians … all came to Studio 54 to dance, to be written about in gossip columns, to have near-public sex and engage openly in snorting epic amounts of cocaine, the drug that fueled the seventies party. Such was the prestige of attending Studio 54 that implacable doormen Marc Benike and Haoui Montaug became celebrities themselves.

But disco was a multicultural way of cutting loose. Gays, blacks, and Latinos enjoyed the disco scene with their own clubs, drugs, and style. Disco had another crowd: urban whites, who worked in blue-collar jobs during the week and saved their money to go to discos in their neighborhood boroughs: Odyssey 2000 in Bay Ridge, Brooklyn, was one such spot. A *New York* magazine article about the scene by British writer Nik Cohn was called "Saturday Night Fever," and it became a movie. It's an awkward coming-of-age tale about a working-class kid named Tony Manero, whose dancing ability opens his eyes to the world beyond his neighborhood. But mostly, it was about John Travolta as Manero dancing his way to superstardom in a gaudy white suit, and the music. *Saturday Night Fever* is the best-selling movie soundtrack of all-time (more than 25 million sold); it was No. 1 on the *Billboard* Top Pop Albums chart for an astonishing twenty-five weeks, beginning in November 1977. Numerous acts contributed hits to the soundtrack: Yvonne Elliman's "If I Can't Have You," "A Fifth of Beethoven" by Walter Murphy, "Disco Inferno" by the Trammps, and "More Than a Woman" by Tavares. But the Bee Gees dominated the soundtrack, not just by writing the Elliman and Tavares hits, but performing three consecutive No. 1 singles from the album: "How Deep Is Your Love," "Stayin' Alive," and "Night Fever."

The Bee Gees were one rock group that grew in stature thanks to disco. Raised in the United Kingdom and Australia, the initials stood for "the brothers Gibb": Barry and twins Maurice and Robin. They came up in 1967 with the Beatles-channeling psychedelia-with-strings hit with the unlikely (and meaningless) title, "New York Mining Disaster 1941 (Have You See My Wife Mr. Jones)." They had a run of soft-rock hits including "To Love Somebody" through 1971's "How Can You Mend a Broken Heart." Nothing else seemed to click for them until 1975, when they hit No. 1 with the semifunky dance hit, "Jive Talkin'." For better or worse, they will always be the one band that personified disco, one of the few that gave the style a face.

Another was Donna Summer, one of the few disco artists with recognizable talent, stage and studio presence, and the ability to transcend the format. Working with producer Giorgio Moroder, she broke through with "Love to Love You Baby" at the end of 1975. Mixing sensual moans with a propulsive synthetic beat that had been introduced by the German studio band Kraftwerk, her records were among the best sounds to come out of the radio in the disco era. She was believable, whether impersonating streetwalkers on "Hot Stuff" and "Bad Girls," giving a writhing disco twist to Jimmy Webb's "MacArthur Park," or bringing Barbra Streisand into the moment on the duet "No More Tears (Enough Is Enough)."

But Bee Gees and Summer aside, disco was the era of one-hit wonders, and overrated ones at that. The nadir was the hit of the summer of 1978 known as "Boogie Oogie Oogie," which consisted of little else but that phrase repeated over a seductive dance track. The National Academy of Recording Arts & Sciences (NARAS, known since 2004 as the Recording Academy) bestowed on the group that sang the song, known as Taste of Honey, the Grammy Award for Best New Artist. The group was heard from briefly in 1981 with a remake of the Japanese pop song "Sukiyaki," then disappeared for good. It was the success lavished on such nonentities that irritated critics of disco.

Disco was such a hot fad in the late 1970s that many acts found it desirable to cut disco records, no matter what genre they came from. Rod Stewart, with "Do Ya Think I'm Sexy" had commercial success at the expense of their artistic credibility. Even the Rolling Stones gave the disco ball a spin, and a worthwhile one it was with the 1978 track "Miss You," one of their better cuts since the early 1970s.

Many rock fans not only disliked disco — they despised it with an active passion. The metal-rock band Twisted Sister became stars in the New York metropolitan area with a single they pressed themselves called "Disco Sucks." That catchy phrase was also taken up by Chicago rock disc jockey Steve Dahl. Major-league baseball had been looking for ways to fill seats and attract a younger audience, so the Chicago White Sox allowed Dahl to hold a "disco sucks!" rally between games of a twi-night double header at Comiskey Park on July 12, 1979. Admission was 98 cents and one disco record. Dahl was going to burn the disco records in a dumpster in the outfield. More than 50,000 people showed up, and thousands more were outside unable to enter. The mayhem was predictable, as thousands of fans ran onto the field, lighting bonfires and tearing up the outfield grass. The White Sox had to forfeit the second game (against the Detroit Tigers). It may have been coincidence, but disco did indeed begin to fade just around that time.

Rod Stewart / The Jeff Beck Group/ The Small Faces/The Faces

With four consecutive sets of "The Great American Songbook" series becoming best-sellers among middle-aged music buyers in the 2000s, it may be hard for some to believe that Rod Stewart was once among rock's greatest singers and songwriters.

Stewart toured Europe as a folk singer in the early 1960s, and joined Long John Baldry's blues group, the Hoochie Coochie Men, in 1964. Stewart was able to give up his day job as a gravedigger before becoming the voice of the Jeff Beck Group from 1967 to 1969. Beck, along with Jimmy Page and Eric Clapton, was one of the acclaimed British blues-rock guitar heroes to come out of the Yardbirds. "Beck stood head and shoulders above his competitors (including Eric Clapton), with blinding speed and inventive use of feedback and distortion. He continued to demonstrate his astounding mastery of the instrument on a long series of solo records, culminating in a highly successful jazz fusion period during the mid-70s."[*]

Beck was a virtuoso, but if there wasn't a lick he couldn't play, he also couldn't sing a lick. So then-journeyman Stewart signed on as lead singer with Ron Wood (bass) and Mick Waller (drums). Beck, Stewart, and Wood strengthened their reputations on two good but spotty Beck Group albums: *Truth* (1968) and *Beck-Ola* (1969). The group's early live performances at the Fillmore East in New York were inspirational musically, but odd to watch: Stewart was so stricken with stagefright that he hid from the audience behind amplifiers or kept his back to the audience for almost the entire show. [†]

Songwriting was another Beck weakness. But he and the band played a daringly wide range of material, and those two albums showcased Stewart's ability to sing almost anything with ease and conviction: the Jerome Kern/Oscar Hammerstein II standard "Ol' Man River" from the Broadway musical *Show Boat*; a remake of the Yardbirds' "Shapes of Things" that Stewart bent into his own shape; the folk-rock standard "Morning Dew" that the Grateful Dead had popularized; and such raucous blues as Howlin' Wolf's "I Ain't Superstitious." (The instrumentals included "Greensleeves" and the guitarist's take on Ravel, "Beck's Bolero.") *Beck-Ola* burnished Stewart's credentials

---

[*] Wilson and Allroy's Record Reviews, http://www.warr.org/beck.html

[†] I was at this show at the Filmore East in New York in 1968, the Beck Group was opening for the Grateful Dead. Stewart's shyness or stage fright is also noted in the liner notes to the Faces box set, *Five Guys Walk Into a Bar …* (Warner Bros./ Rhino Records, 2004).

as an interpreter, as he successfully reworked "Jailhouse Rock," one of the best-known Elvis Presley hits written by Jerry Leiber and Mike Stoller. (Commissioned in 1957 to write songs for the film, which then had the working title *Ghost of a Chance,* Leiber & Stoller wrote "Jailhouse Rock," "You're So Square, Baby I Don't Care," "Treat Me Nice," and "I Want to be Free" in a single afternoon.)[*]

In 1969 Stewart and Wood left Beck to join Ronnie Lane (guitar and bass), Ian McLagan (keyboards), and Kenney Jones (drums) from the Small Faces, which from 1965 through 1968 was among the most popular and influential bands in the United Kingdom. British critics still worship the Small Faces as the great working class R&B band, "Booker T and the MGs meet the Who."[†] Americans found the comparison to the great Memphis soul instrumental group to be specious at best. The Small Faces had just one U.S. hit, "Itchycoo Park" in 1967 to 1968, a simple but catchy depiction of a psychoactive drug experience. (The inspiration for marketing their best-known U.S. album, *Ogden's Nut Gone Flake* apparently came from a similar vision — this piece of appealing but instantly dated sixties Brit-rock was packaged in a round cardboard cover, like the pipe-tobacco tin that was its design inspiration.)

On New Year's Eve 1968, Marriott walked offstage during a Small Faces concert and announced he was starting a band with a guitarist, Peter Frampton, called Humble Pie, a harder-rocking aggregation.

And the Faces became a totally different band. Stewart, Wood, Lane, McLagan, and Jones turned out to be famous drinking buddies: their recording sessions would involve meeting in the studio, heading to the pub, coming back to the studio, then back to the pub …

The Faces didn't get a lot done, but what they did have was the informal spontaneity of some very talented blokes who enjoyed playing together in every sense of the word. Loose, tough, and raucous, the Faces were a bracing antidote to the increasingly seriousness of rock during their 1969 to 1975 run.

While with the Faces, Stewart was able to continue to record as a solo artist. (The Faces recorded for Warner Bros.; as a soloist Stewart was with Mercury/Phonogram.) His solo debut, *The Rod Stewart Album,* drew minimal attention, but his second album, *Gasoline*

---

[*] *PR Newswire*, March 18, 2004. Distributed by PR Newswire on behalf of Leiber & Stoller, who were protesting news of a London theatrical production called 'Jailhouse Rock' used without their permission.

[†] Nigel Williamson in the DVD *Small Faces Under Review*.

Alley (1970) established him as an emerging personality and critic's favorite. His sealed his deal with stardom with the near-perfect 1971 album *Every Picture Tells a Story,* and was named *Rolling Stone's* "rock star of the year."

Just as Stewart's career veered between the delightful sloppiness of the Faces and the more focused solo albums, so did he evolve into a powerful songwriter and masterful interpreter. The dual careers were more cohesive than they might have seemed, since on the first four Mercury solo albums Stewart was backed by the Faces.

His first No. 1 was his own "Maggie May" in 1971, though this bittersweet tale of a young man's sexual initiation with an older woman was not the first choice for a single. It was the B-side to Stewart's heartfelt rendition of Tim Hardin's often-covered "Reason to Believe." The up-tempo, refreshingly original "Maggie May" was pure enchantment, and it was No. 1 for five weeks in the fall of 1971. And the 1972 album *Never a Dull Moment* sealed Stewart's stature as the both the best and most popular rock singer of his time. Except for "Maggie" (written with Martin Quittendon), his best original songs were written with Ron Wood, who left the Faces to join the Rolling Stones in 1975.

Stewart had shown the knack to put his own mark on even well-known songs by other artists: the Rolling Stones' "Street Fighting Man," Jimi Hendrix's "Angel," the Temptations' "(I Know) I'm Losing You," an array of Bob Dylan songs, R&B singer Etta James ("I'd Rather Go Blind"), and a number of tunes by his musical idol, Sam Cooke, including "Twistin' the Night Away" and "Shake."

He had also shaken the shyness of his early career. Like his friend Elton John (whose "Country Comforts" Stewart recorded on "Gasoline Alley"), Stewart learned to overcompensate by becoming a fearless, outgoing showman, finally able to attach his slightly gravelly

The Prog Impulse of the 1970s

At a moment when fragmenting community of rock fans was uniting behind styles and avoiding others, what is now known as prog rock was one of the most popular yet widely derided genres.

Basically, it was rock music by people who didn't mind letting you know they had taken piano lessons and done very well with them. Almost all the major prog purveyors were from the United Kingdom. Musicians like Rick Wakeman, the keyboard player for Yes, or Keith Emerson, first of the Nice and then Emerson, Lake and Palmer, voice to the (near-) professional athlete's physical grace. (He was a talented soccer player.) He became a relentlessly crowd-pleasing entertainer, and has been for the last thirty-five years, still selling out sports arenas throughout the world.

It's a lucky thing for Stewart, since in the mid 1970s, his reputation took a nosedive when he moved to Southern California. Like many British expatriates, he loved Los Angeles, and L.A. loved him back, and he showed more interest in the celebrity life — especially the highly publicized relationships, beginning with the Swedish actress Britt Ekland and numerous other actresses and models — than he was in protecting his artistic reputation. The bottom, in terms of his critical cachet, is agreed to be the self-parodying disco record *Do Ya Think I'm Sexy,* which was nevertheless a huge hit in 1978–1979.

"It was a period I regret a bit, because I was reading all my own press and believing it," Stewart told me in a 1993 interview.* "I got a lot of slagging off from critics, which I thought I fairly deserved. I think Greil Marcus in *Rolling Stone* wrote: 'Rod Stewart has one of the finest instruments, rock 'n' roll voices, of the 20th century, and he's completely wasted it.' I read that and said, 'God, he's so right.'"

Stewart has regained some of his critical reputation, if for no other reason than those forgettable gaffes carry much less weight than the overpoweringly good body of work that really defines him. And though the critics might not care much for Stewart's take on American pop standards, he still enjoys performing, critics be damned. Something he said in 1993 still holds true:

"When I'm up there singing for people, when my voice is working, and it's working really well, it's the finest drug in the world."

* Wayne Robins, "Facing the Music," *Newsday*, May 23, 1993

might have been saying, "roll over, Chuck Berry — and dig the way we blast out Mussorgsky."

Those who loved flamboyant displays of the piano technique of Wakeman and Emerson, amplified to heavy-metal volume, believed this was rock coming to maturity. Others thought such symphonic airs and virtuosic displays were self-indulgent and against rock's populist values.

The Moody Blues had begun as one of the more likeable English Invasion bands, with the fondly loved hit "Go Now." But the Moodies evolved. Their *Days of Future Passed* album in 1968 with the London

Symphony Orchestra was one of the first full-blown meldings of rock and classical musical. Although it was hugely successful thanks to some well-placed allusions to the psychedelic experience, some found it the equivalent of spinach laced with sugar cubes. A single from the album "Nights in White Satin" became a major hit in 1972. Moodies albums like *A Question of Balance* (1970), *Every Good Boy Deserves a Favour* (1971), and *Seventh Sojourn* (1972) benefited from the development of the (Moog) synthesizer, which made it possible for rock bands to approximate orchestral sounds with a keyboard instrument.

Genesis was among the earliest and, at times, most creative progressive rock groups, formed in 1967 under the leadership of singer Peter Gabriel. Other key members were Tony Banks (keyboards), Mike Rutherford (guitar and bass), Steve Hackett on guitar, and Phil Collins on drums.

In a genre based on sci-fi or pastoral fantasies and transcendent visions, Gabriel was the rare artist who really was visionary, as his compelling 1980s solo albums and innovative videos later proved. In the early 1970s, though, Genesis scored mostly among Anglophiles, who couldn't get enough of the Britspeak of "Selling England by the Pound" and tracks like "The Battle of Epping Forest," which used "military and sports terminology as metaphors for gang warfare."[28] Some found the two-disc concept album about a New York street urchin, or gang member, or some roustabout to be a work of great breadth and interest; others thought it just wordy. It was also Gabriel's last album with the group. Phil Collins became the lead singer, and steered the group toward pop; the payoff was the 1986 album *Invisible Touch*, which sold more than five million copies and delivered five top-five singles. And Collins has since, of course, been one of the most popular middle of the road artists in pop, a recent staple of adult contemporary radio formats and composer of soundtracks for Disney movies.

Pink Floyd may have been prog's most popular and defining group. It began as England's most prominent acid-rock band as early as 1965, featuring the songs of Syd Barrett. Their debut album, *Piper at the Gates of Dawn*, with Barrett on guitar and Roger Waters on bass and vocals, Richard Wright on keyboards, and Nick Mason on drums, is a fascinating curio of the acid-rock moment in England, where it reached No. 5 on the charts; it didn't even make the U.S. top 100. Songs like "Astronomy Domine" and the instrumental "Interstellar Overdrive" captured the swirling disorientation of an LSD trip as well as any band did, and they remained lucid enough to include one permanent addition to the list of England's great singles of the 1960s, "See Emily Play."

After one more album (*A Saucerful of Secrets*), it was evident that Barrett had become deeply incapacitated by overuse of LSD. David Gilmour replaced Barrett in 1968 as the band's following grew in Europe and the United Kingdom, and their excursions into other galaxies continued with albums like *Ummagumma*" (1969) and *Atom Heart Mother* (1970), with its famous counterintuitive cover (perhaps mocking those hippies now seeking the rustic life): a close-up photo of a rather homely cow with its large butt to the camera.

The breakthrough album was *Dark Side of the Moon*, which dominated the seventies like no other record. It was the band's first top-forty record in the United States, and went to No. 1. Once it hit the charts, it stayed for 741 weeks, nearly fifteen years. With music mostly by Gilmour and lyrics by Waters, it was a concept album dealing with what *Q* magazine called "the simple, often trivial pressures of daily life that can lead to insanity."[29] Over the years it has sold more than 23 million copies worldwide. There is no truth to the rumor, however, that it the soundtrack is perfectly synchronized with the movie of *The Wizard of Oz*, although those who have tried this stunt insist it is credible.

The members of the group did not seem to be the best of chums. "In theory we were all producing," David Gilmour told *Q*'s David Sinclair. "But in practice it meant that Roger (Waters) and I would argue considerably about how it should sound." Chris Thomas (who later produced The Pretenders, The Sex Pistols, and others) was called in at the mixing stage as a "neutral party" to try and resolve the internecine wrangling.

Still, the group continued to have other successes, building elaborately staged tours around concept albums like *Animals*, which was perhaps inspired by George Orwell's *Animal Farm*, and *The Wall*, in 1979, an epic about totalitarianism and the whole ball of wax of post–World War II life and politics. Punk-rockers, of course, found Pink

Floyd as insufferably overblown as glam-rockers had found Yes and Genesis. And the loathing was mutual. But in the seventies, there was room for just about everything.

Queen, for example. The British band (Freddie Mercury, vocals; Brian May, guitar; John Deacon, bass; and Roger Taylor, drums) was a pastiche of prog, metal, and glam with colorful costumes and explosive effects-laden stage shows. Their peak years were 1975 to 1980, but their 1977 hit "We Will Rock You"/"We Are the Champions" has made them a permanent part of the pop-culture landscape. The first segment is heard chanted at everything from football stadiums to wrestling matches on both sides of the Atlantic; the latter part seems to be on the soundtrack to every TV sports championship event. The 1980 album *The Game* also had two especially durable hits, the rockabilly-flavored "Crazy Little Thing Called Love" and the disco-influenced "Another One Bites the Dust."

Their most unusual career accomplishment was having the same recording, "Bohemian Rhapsody," make the top ten sixteen years apart. The quintessentially over-the-top recording, with its operatic passage "mama mia, mama mia," peaked at No. 9 in 1976. It burst to life again in the 1992 movie *Wayne's World,* in which the main characters ride around their hometown of Aurora, Illinois, with Mike Myers and company hilariously lip-synching "Bohemian Rhapsody" while it plays on the car radio. The *Wayne's World* rediscovery made "Rhapsody" a bigger hit than before, and helped spark a revival of Queen's catalog with two successful greatest-hits compilations that year. The Queen revival sparked intense emotion, as it occurred quickly and coincidentally after the Nov. 24, 1991, death of singer Mercury, the most major rock star to die of AIDS.

Rush was Canada's contribution to prog majesty. For many smart high-schoolers of a certain era (late 1970s, early 1980s), a Rush concert is stamped in memory as their first rock concert. That may be because of Rush's nonstop touring and willingness to play the kinds of smaller markets that other rock bands find beneath their dignity.

Though they never had a U.S. top-twenty hit, songs like "The Spirit of Radio" and "Tom Sawyer" have been staples of classic-rock radio since they were released in 1980 and 1981, respectively. The trio is an anomaly in some ways, as the drummer, Neil Peart, writes most of the band's lyrics, and guitarist Alex Lifeson is one of the most laid-back personalities in all of hard rock. The singer, Geddy Lee, was known early for a continuous, keening banshee wail, but by 1992, he said in an interview, he had discovered his middle range, "experimenting with different keys, different approaches to singing. It's a physical thing ...to survive a tour these days, you've got to know your limitations physically."[30] Evidently he had learned them well, since Rush had a thirtieth anniversary tour in 2004 and is still active.

One can't discuss prog without mentioning Jethro Tull. Led by Scotsman Ian Anderson, Tull started promisingly enough, with the 1968 album *This Was,* on which Anderson's jazzy flute-playing was as refreshing as it was prominent. Albums like *Thick As a Brick* (1971) and *Aqualung* (1972) made Tull the top prog brand until Pink Floyd put everyone else on the dark side of the moon in 1973.

Southern Rock: Fatalism Boogies

After English rockers rediscovered the blues for Americans in the 1960s, it turned out there were a whole bunch of young American musicians with a firsthand feel for the music. The style of music, blending bluesy vocals with multiple guitars that often went off into extended jams, became known as southern rock.

The man behind the movement was Phil Walden, who started Capricorn Records, the label home for all but a few Southern rock bands, in 1969. Walden, from Macon, Georgia, started out booking fraternity concerts in the early sixties. He had earned respect as the manager for soul great and Macon-native Otis Redding.

With offices and studios in Macon, Capricorn was able to develop its own identity and sound. Upon starting the label, he signed Duane Allman, a session guitarist for Atlantic Records. Allman was part of the studio band at Muscle Shoals studios in Alabama, and played on some of the great soul records of the 1960s by Aretha Franklin and Wilson Pickett, among many others.

Allman moved from Florida to Macon at Walden's request; Duane called up his keyboard-playing brother and singer Gregg Allman to start a band. (The two had been together in such regionally popular Florida bands as the Almond Joys and Hour Glass.)

The Allman Brothers Band had a unique lineup. In addition to Gregg on keyboards and Berry Oakley on bass, there were two lead guitars (Duane and Dickey Betts), and two drummers, Butch Trucks and Jai Johnny Johanson (aka Jay Johnny Johnson). The first two studio albums, *The Allman Brothers Band* (1969) and *Idlewild South* (1970) sold marginally.

In 1970, however, Duane Allman's fame spread from his sublime, extended guitar duel with Eric Clapton on the recording of "Layla" by Clapton's band Derek and the Dominos.

Their 1971, double-disc live album, *At the Fillmore East,* captured what everyone who had heard them do a concert knew — this was one of the great bands of its era, with all of its charismatic appeal drawn from the virtuoso solos anchored by extraordinary ensemble playing. And the follow-up, *Eat a Peach*, contained two discs: one of more tracks from the Fillmore East (including the thirty-three-minute "Mountain Jam") and a collection of studio tracks. But for Duane Allman, it was a posthumous release: he died in a motorcycle accident on Oct. 29, 1971, just twenty-four years old. Just a year later, on November 11, 1972, Berry Oakley also died in a motorcycle accident not far from where Duane had died. He was also twenty-four.

Somehow the band regrouped around Gregg Allman. It added a second keyboard player, Chuck Leavell, and bass player Lamar Williams, and in 1973 scored the biggest hit of its career, *Brothers and Sisters*, featuring the quintessential hit single "Ramblin' Man." Though the Allman's have since split up and changed personnel many times, the band, built around Gregg Allman, has been one of rock's great ongoing concert attractions.

There were numerous other southern rock bands of note — Wet Willie, the Elvin Bishop Group, the Marshall Tucker Band, and the Charlie Daniels Band, among them. But the great Southern rock band, besides the Allman's, was Lynyrd Skynyrd.

Skynyrd was also blessed with excellence but cursed by tragedy. Singer Ronnie Van Zant and guitarists Allen Collins and Gary Rossington started the band while in school in Jacksonville, Florida. (The band name is a tricky spelling of the name of their gym teacher, one Leonard Skinner.)

They were discovered by Al Kooper. Kooper had been in the Blues Project and started Blood, Sweat and Tears after becoming famous at twenty-one for playing organ on Bob Dylan's "Like a Rolling Stone." Kooper, on sojourn in Atlanta, signed them to his fledgling Sounds of the South label.

Collins and Rossington gave Skynyrd that trademark Southern rock twin-lead guitar attack; with the addition of Steve Gaines, they had three guitars upfront.

Those guitars are what carry Skynyrd's 1973 "Free Bird," its signature tune and such a staple of rock radio that it has become something of a joke, especially among alternative rock fans, who see it as a massively indulgent cliché. But it's a better song and performance than that, a ballad about a guy telling a girl he can't settle down that evolves into seven and a half minutes of Allman-style twin guitar buildup.

It became the band's sad coda after the 1977 plane crash that took the whole band down, killed Ronnie Van Zant, Stevie Gaines, and his sister, backup singer Cassie Gaines. Many of the others were critically injured. In 1987, Rossington re-created the band with some old and new members, along with Johnny Van Zant, Ronnie's brother, who had his own Southern rock band, .38 Special, as lead singer. Closing the show with "Free Bird" as they always did, however, the refurbished band played it solely as an instrumental, the microphone stand up front and unattended, although either a cowboy hat or Confederate flag might hang from it.

It was their assertion of pride as southerners that gave Lynyrd Skynyrd its cultural resonance. Their signature tune, "Sweet Home Alabama," was a retort to two Neil Young songs: "Southern Man," which suggested spiritual retribution was in store for the sins of white southerners against blacks, and "Alabama," which reinforced the widely held northern view that the state was backwards. After all, this is the state whose most dominant politician, Governor George Wallace, defiantly vowed in his first inaugural address on January 14, 1963: "Segregation today, segregation tomorrow, segregation forever!"

In "Sweet Home Alabama," Lynyrd Skynyrd, neither defending or apologizing, tells Young to mind his own business. With the

Confederate flag part of their stage set, Skynyrd embodied the complexities of the emerging South, one difficult for non-Southerners to comprehend. Southern historian Hal Crowther explains this common misunderstanding in his book "Gather at the River: Notes from a Post-Millenial South." He writes:

> As long as popular culture persists in presenting them as incestuous hillbillies, church-burners, mule-beaters and randy evangelists, Southerners will dip snuff and fly Confederate battle flags just to make New Yorkers wince. This unlikely mixture of defiant pride and self-mockery is a joke Northern liberals never grasp ... Sly and impertinent, the South has preserved its self-respect at the expense of its public relations.[31]

Bruce Springsteen

John Hammond, the patrician talent scout for Columbia Records, had perhaps the most enviable track record of any A&R person in history. His signings including jazz greats Benny Goodman and Count Basie and blues greats Bessie Smith and Robert Johnson. Independently wealthy (he was a scion of the Vanderbilts, one of America's richest families), he became a champion of equal rights for all. His "Spirituals to Swing" concert in 1938 was the first event to feature black and white musicians, not to mention integrated bands, on the stage of Carnegie Hall.

Hammond had a special sensibility that allowed him to hear the potential that others couldn't. Mitch Miller, the head of A&R at Columbia Records in the 1950s, was used to the gifted singers and classic songs of his artists Frankie Laine, Tony Bennett, and Johnny Mathis. When Hammond played him a tape of Bob Dylan, he was unimpressed. But Hammond had the clout to sign Dylan himself; when he did so, in 1961, Bob Dylan was known around Columbia Records' New York headquarters as "Hammonds folly." History, obviously, proved otherwise, reinforcing Hammond's reputation as a talent scout par excellence.

But by 1972, the aging Hammond had been shuttled aside by a new generation of A&R and marketing specialists at Columbia who, like generations before them, thought they knew it all. Hammond hardly needed his salary, but he loved music and was often around the office. So in 1972 or 1973, when Hammond developed an enthusiasm for a scruffy newcomer named Bruce Springsteen, the smart alecks snickered, here, again, was Hammond's folly.

Springsteen came to Columbia's publicity offices for press bio that would accompany the debut album, *Greetings from Asbury Park, N.J.*

With a scraggly beard and mustache, thin as a whippet but with a loosey-goosey confidence in his walk, Springsteen first thought about rock stardom was pretty much like everyone else's of his generation: When he was nine years old, he saw Elvis Presley on TV. "Anybody who sees Elvis Presley and doesn't want to be like Elvis Presley has something wrong with him," Springsteen told me at the time.[32] A disinterested student, Springsteen and his buddies made a lifestyle of hanging around Asbury Park, a Jersey Shore beach town that had been in decline since the 1930s.

His first band was the Castiles, which was not only the best band on the Jersey Shore between 1965 and 1967; it traveled as far as San Francisco, where it was well received at the Fillmore West. After the Castiles broke up, he was in a hard rock band called Steel Mill: "A Les Paul [guitar] and a big Marshall amp. You come out with no shirt and yah, zam, you know how they do it, whomm!" he said, acting out the brutal chords on air guitar. He fronted a motley multipiece band called Dr. Zoom and his Sonic Boom.

In the summer of 1971, the Bruce Springsteen Band was formed, performing his songs like "Blinded by the Light." Words spilled out of Springsteen as if from a broken neon beer tap.

When Columbia was about to release "Blinded by the Light" as a single, company president and record business legend Clive Davis stunned the Ivy Leaguers in Brooks Brothers suits at the weekly singles marketing and promotion meeting by asking for quiet and reciting,[33] unaccompanied, the approximately twenty-eight verses, bridges, and choruses in the song.

Greetings from Asbury Park, N.J. was loved by critics, but ignored by the public. In typical fashion, Springsteen and the E Street Band were sent out on a tour of arenas with the popular top-forty horn band Chicago, a mismatch not quite as bad as Jimi Hendrix opening for the

Monkees in 1967, but close. It was the last time Springsteen played a tour as an opening act.

The week of July 18 to 23, Springsteen played at the 200-capacity club New York club Max's Kansas City with another act little known at the time: Bob Marley and the Wailers. Word spread among the cognoscenti that both acts were quite special. A second album, *The Wild, the Innocent and the E Street Shuffle* was released in the fall of 1973, with radio still resisting and critics still enthused.

This time the critics were right. You couldn't hear a song like "Blinded by the Light" and "Spirit in the Night" and not know a special talent was at work, one with the rare ability to absorb the reality and atmosphere of a time, place, and people and turn it into dream theater.

Rock critics generally have little impact on an act's success or failure. People get to hear the music on the radio, or, since the early 1980s, on videos and since around 2000, by Internet file-sharing. Fans will buy a record no matter what a critic says; by the time a critic reviews a concert, the performance has usually been long sold-out, and the act has moved on before the review is published. (The United Kingdom is a little different, as the national weekly music magazines such as *Melody Maker, Sounds,* and *New Musical Express* had enormous influence on trends in the 1970s, and were known for their fickle inclination to build up an act and then tear it down.)

It is likely that only once in rock history did a published article change the course of an artist's career, and of rock 'n' roll itself. That occurred in the May 22, 1974, issue of the *Real Paper,* an alternative weekly published in Boston. The rock critic Jon Landau had seen a Springsteen performance at the Harvard Square Theater. Landau was the most brilliantly analytical of rock critics, and as a frustrated guitar player through his college years at Brandeis University he could actually write about the technical aspects of the music in detail, while most rock critics tended toward sociological descriptions. He was one of the first writers for *Crawdaddy,* the wildly inconsistent but often exciting magazine that in the 1960s, under founder Paul Williams, was the first periodical to take rock seriously as an art form.

Landau usually kept his overwhelming passion for the music in check, explaining his erudite opinions with firm intellectual distance and control. But bored with what the seventies were offering and attempting to break into film criticism, he felt himself losing his obsessive interest in rock.

Then he saw Springsteen. After a Springsteen show at the Harvard Square Theater, Landau wrote a revealing autobiographical piece called "Growing Young with Rock and Roll" that laid his passions and disappointments bare.

"I'm 27 today, feeling old, listening to my records and remembering that things were different a decade ago," he wrote. Three-quarters of the way through this lengthy memoir, he finally came to a turning point: "Last Thursday, at the Harvard Square theatre, I saw my rock 'n' roll past flash before my eyes. And I saw something else: I saw rock and roll future and its name is Bruce Springsteen. And on a night when I needed to feel young, he made me feel like I was hearing music for the very first time."[35]

The Columbia Records publicity department seized on the "I saw rock 'n' roll future, and its name is Bruce Springsteen," and plastered it everywhere. The future arrived in 1975, with the release of *Born to Run*, his third and most fully realized album at the time, was released, the world was ready for Springsteen. The buzz was so enormous that he was on the cover of both the *Time* and *Newsweek* issues dated October 27, 1975.

Why Springsteen? Because those who heard and identified with him knew that he was one of the few at this time whose music connected both consciously and spiritually with rock's foundation, both wide and deep: rooted in Elvis Presley and Chuck Berry, James Brown and Jackie Wilson, and Leiber & Stoller and Phil Spector and Pomus & Shuman, the Drifters and the Shirelles, and then the next generation, drawing not only from acknowledged masters Bob Dylan and Van Morrison, but also briefly passing top 40 stars like Del Shannon and the Shadows of Knight and the Dave Clark 5. Rock that could be serious and escapist at the same time.

A number of elements made Springsteen a rare musician for his time. His style did not descend from the Beatles. Since the Beatles, rock had been utterly guitar dominated; Springsteen's musical framework was a throwback, featuring two piano players and one dynamic saxophonist in the E Street Band. Vocal harmonies were secondary, where they existed at all. There was no trace of psychedelia or studio effects, nor any of the sturdy machismo, the male dominant/female submissive strutting of the Rolling Stones.

Instead, on *Born to Run,* there were people like him — just past high school, who didn't last long at college, whose jobs were unfulfilling, who struggled with the present while longing to reclaim the freedom of youth for just one night, "that one endless summer night … and there's all these stories on one long summer night."[36]

From the start he sang his own original songs in a distinctive voice. There is a slight Southern twang to Springsteen's singing that doesn't have anything to do with Mick Jagger's self-aware, vaudevillian blend of rural American black and affected working-class British. It's a lot like his speaking voice, which lacks the typically harsh consonants of the classic New Jersey accent. Springsteen's friend and biographer Dave Marsh gives a hint about this in his book *Glory Days,* where he describes the place Springsteen grew up, Freehold. His father struggled from job to job: cab driver, bus driver, mill worker, and, according to Marsh, Springsteen grew up on what was literally the poor side of the railroad tracks that divided Freehold. His neighborhood contained families who'd lived in the same place for generations, along with "transplanted Southerners and recently arrived blacks," for jobs at a rug mill, a candy factory, and other low-wage, no-satisfaction jobs. There were so many Southerners in his area, Springsteen once said, that they called his neighborhood "Texas."

The publicity attending *Born to Run* was, as in most cases, a two-edged sword. Springsteen wasn't seeking an anointment. He sensed he was at the beginning of what would be a long, constantly evolving career. Such ambitions had been stunted by less intense publicity. There was a very real danger that the media attention — the hype — would cause a backlash that would turn off the millions who had not yet even heard his music.

And some other hitches to the career surfaced immediately. A dispute over management and production and music publishing contracts he had signed kept lawyers busy for years and kept Springsteen out of the studio and off the stage. But his songs kept turning into hits. English Invasion star Manfred Mann, probably the only artist to have hit songs written by Jeff Barry and Ellie Greenwich ("Do Wah Diddy" 1964) and Bob Dylan ("Mighty Quinn [Quinn the Eskimo]"

1968), had his second No. 1 record with Springsteen's "Blinded by the Light" in 1977. In 1978, punk priestess Patti Smith had her only hit record with Springsteen's "Because the Night."

Shortly thereafter, Springsteen's fourth album, *Darkness at the Edge of Town* was released, produced by Springsteen and Jon Landau, who was then (and is still) Springsteen's manager.

The title song sets the tone for Springsteen's emerging style. He and his Jersey Shore banditos have gotten a little older. The troubles of the decade — high inflation, unaffordable mortgage rates, unemployment — were hitting the average American hard.

Springsteen maintained his focus on people rather than politics. He wrote about the effect decisions made in Washington, in Trenton, and in corporate boardrooms, had on people he knew. Usually the news was not good. This is important, because of the depth it gave his songs: the world's greatest party band, Bruce Springsteen and the E Street Band, was not just providing escapist entertainment. His songs were emotional, philosophical, and in their portrayals of the over-matched individual against the odds, often profound. In "Badlands," the protagonist spends his life "waiting for a moment that just don't come." In the title song of "Darkness at the Edge of Town," he sings "Everybody's got a secret, Sonny/Something they just can't face," and warns that unless they cut it loose, it will "drag 'em down."

Springsteen's political consciousness evolved slowly, deliberately. In 1979, he played the "No Nukes" concert at Madison Square Garden along with Jackson Browne, Stephen Stills, David Crosby, Graham Nash, James Taylor, Carly Simon, Tom Petty, Bonnie Raitt, and John Hall, one of the benefit organizers, from the group Orleans. (The organization was MUSE: Musicians United for Safe Energy.) [The film, also called "No Nukes," appeared in 1980].

"Springsteen is an extremely cautious man, and he'd always been extra careful not to speak out about issues he didn't fully understand," Marsh writes[37] as a partial explanation for why Springsteen was the only artist not to make a statement about nuclear energy in the concert program. On the other hand, he was the only artist to light a musical fire that night, and it's quite evident in the film.

"Compared to the general blandness and air of self-satisfaction here, it's no wonder Bruce was hailed as the savior of rock 'n' roll," wrote a reviewer of the film who agreed with neither the politics nor much of the music in the film, on the Internet Movie Database.[38]

By the dawn of the eighties, he was ready to take a wider look at America and a deeper look into himself.

THE 1980s

Ronald Reagan, Bruce Springsteen,
John Mellencamp, Tom Petty

The murder of John Lennon on December 8, 1980, roiled the music world with intense, long-lasting grief. Lennon had just returned home to the Dakota apartment building at West 72nd St. and Central Park West when he was shot at close range by Mark David Chapman, an obsessed Beatles' "fan." The news was broken by sportscaster Howard Cosell, as the shooting occurred toward the end of a *Monday Night Football* game. Lennon and wife Yoko Ono had just released *Double Fantasy*, a kind of comeback for Lennon, who hadn't released new material since the 1974 *Walls and Bridges* album. (A Phil Spector–produced collection of standards, *Rock 'n' Roll* had been released in 1975.)

Rock radio stations stopped their regular programming, and played Beatles songs for days. In a typical spontaneous reaction, present and former staff of New York rock station WNEW-FM descended spontaneously on the station's studios, talking all night, trying to vent their sadness. An area of Central Park across the street from the Dakota became a shrine to Lennon called "Strawberry Fields," named after the Beatles' song. Pilgrims from all over the world still come to Strawberry Fields to sing and mourn.

Lennon's death was like the final, saddest stroke of the 1970s, a decade of disappointment and disillusionment. Ronald Reagan, the former movie actor who had become a conservative Republican icon as governor of California, never had a role that suited him as well as that of president. Elected just a month before Lennon's death, his presence and policies dominated the 1980s and, in an unintentional way, inspired a rebirth of mainstream American rock.

Reagan came to office as a strong antilabor reputation, and proved it immediately. When the 13,000 members of the air traffic controllers union did not return to their jobs after twenty-four hours, Reagan fired them. Nonunion replacements were quickly hired, trained, and put to work.

The irony of the Reagan years is that while such actions did much to undermine the strength of labor unions in the United States, many union workers, once loyal Democrats, supported Reagan. His appeal to construction workers, factory laborers, truck drivers, and those in other "hardhat" jobs dated back to his two terms as governor of California (1966–74). He won the governorship by one million votes in 1966 while making a strong stand against the protesting students and supposedly liberal faculty that made the main campus of the University of California, in Berkeley, synonymous with political activism. In the campaign, he declared that "a small minority of beatniks, radicals and filthy speech advocates have brought such shame to ... a great university."[1] Reagan's election sent an early signal that there was a backlash against the demonstrations, riots, and civil disorder.

Reagan's policy — cutting taxes and lowering government expenditures for everything but the military — defined modern conservatism. Though his tough negotiations with Soviet leader Mikhail Gorbachev helped reduce cold war tensions, his reflex anticommunism led the country down some dangerous paths in Latin America.

Reagan, though born in rural Dixon, Illinois, may have claimed to represent the values of the mainstream America. But his economic policies benefited the wealthy. The same may be said of every modern president, but during the 1980s, the accumulation of wealth itself was seen as a desirable goal. "Greed is good," says the fictional corporate raider Gordon Gekko in the 1987 movie *Wall Street*. Consortiums of investment banks would buy large companies with under-achieving stock prices, and then sell off the pieces or merge them with other giant companies. The bankers and lawyers involved in such deals could earn tens of millions of dollars in fees, while as a result of these mergers and acquisitions, tens of thousands lost longtime jobs and pensions.

A number of rock musicians, including Bruce Springsteen, John Mellencamp, Bob Seger, and Tom Petty, responded to the era of greed by presenting music that focused on mainstream American values. Some called it "heartland rock," but it was mass-appeal music, rock 'n' roll storytelling with meaningful verses and singalong choruses.

It wasn't a throwback to the protest music of the 1960s, by any means. But rock musicians saw a responsibility to stand out for the underdog in ways that politicians had forgotten and business leaders rarely understood. Their music reflected an awareness that all were not sharing America's bounty equally during the Reagan years.

Bruce Springsteen

Springsteen began the decade with *The River* (1980), a two-record set about what critic Robert Christgau calls "the small victories and large compromises of ordinary joes and janeys whose need to understand as well as celebrate is as restless as his own." The quintessential song here is "Hungry Heart," which shows the meticulous balance of Springsteen at the top of his craft: It is an anthem, with a singalong chorus that could elicit paroxysms of joy in a concert hall or on the radio. And yet its story is tragic: "Got a wife and kid in Baltimore, Jack/I went out for a ride and I never went back."

The struggle for dignity amid the psychic burdens of the past and the economic frustrations of the moment pervades the 1982 *Nebraska,* Springsteen's most unusual album to date. Recorded alone at home on a four-track reel-to-reel tape recorder, the music has a spareness that is reinforced by the lean storytelling, "songs of complete despair," as biographer Dave Marsh called it; "bitter tales of late capitalism," as Robert Christgau called it. The title song puts a twist on the "thrill-killer" Charlie Starkweather; another, "Highway Patrolman" — the story of a cop and his brother on the other side of the law — zeroes in on the complex relationships between family loyalty and responsibility to one's job. One song written from the set of gloomy recordings was "Born in the U.S.A.," which didn't fit, but which would find its place.

Being "the kind of artist who could describe life's most brutal moments of defeat and frustration and still find a way to turn those songs into affirmations,"[2] Springsteen rearranged "Born in the U.S.A." It was partly inspired by "Born on the 4th of July," the book (and then an Oliver Stone movie starring Tom Cruise) by Ron Kovic, a gung-ho all-American boy who went to Vietnam and came back a quadriplegic and an outspoken opponent of the war.

America liked its war heroes victorious; Vietnam was the first war the United States outright lost, and the U.S.A. does not celebrate its losers. Vietnam veterans were not embraced by organizations like the Veterans of Foreign Wars (VFW), then dominated by unquestion-ingly patriotic World War II veterans who had little in common with the younger generation.

By 1984 it was time to release *Born in the U.S.A.,* the album that would make Springsteen bigger than ever. By the end of 1985, it had sold more than 10 million copies in the United States. (It has since topped 15 million, according to the RIAA). Of the twelve songs, a remarkable seven became top ten singles. One of the great rock 'n' roll albums ever, it has hymns of disappointment ("My Hometown"), despairing yet romantic, MTV-embraced escapism ("Dancing in the Dark"), songs of lust ("I'm On Fire"), and songs of fear ("Cover Me"). It also boasted two anthems, both easily misunderstood: the rollick-ing "Glory Days" and the title song.

In the early 1980s, it's as if Springsteen knew how big he was about to become, and wrestled with the hopes and fears that represented. *Nebraska,* in its way, was a deliberate time-out, a record that would have moderate appeal, would not ignite a media or fan frenzy, and allow him to examine what was going on inside and around him.

Springsteen had spent much time pondering the fate of Elvis Pre-sley, who so inspired him as a youth. "It was like he came along and whispered a dream in everyone's ear and we dreamed it," Springsteen once said.[3] Like everyone else who loved rock 'n' roll, Springsteen was appalled by the way Elvis exited for the last time Aug. 16, 1977: fall-ing off the bathroom throne, full of pills, his heart stopped and spirit sapped, bloated and irrelevant.

"I think about Elvis a lot and what happened to him. The demands this profession makes on you are unreasonable. It's very strange to go out and have people look at you like you're Santa Claus or the Easter Bunny."

The answer, Springsteen decided, was to "stay healthy — mentally, physically, spiritually — all under a lot of pressure." Springsteen was an anomaly among rock stars — he never smoked a joint, never took a pill to get high or distort consciousness, and drank alcohol in small amounts infrequently.

And so he was balanced for the extra trajectory of fame and fortune that came with *Born in the U.S.A.*, which was the number-one album for much of the summer of 1984. Springsteen was equally temperate in responding to Reagan's praise during campaign stop in Hammonton, New Jersey. Reagan said:

"America's future rests in a thousand dreams inside our hearts. It rests in the message of hope in the songs of a man so many young Americans admire: New Jersey's own Bruce Springsteen."[4]

Neither Reagan nor his speechwriters had evidently paid any attention to what the song actually said: The verses were hopeless cries of a homeless Vietnam veteran whose life started on a downbeat and has now bottomed out. "I think people have a need to feel good about the country they live in," Springsteen later told *Rolling Stone*.[5] "But what's happening, I think, is that that need — which is a good thing — is getting manipulated and exploited. You see in the Reagan election ads on TV, you know, 'It's morning in America,' and you say, 'Well, it's not morning in Pittsburgh.' "

Springsteen chose Pittsburgh carefully as an example, for the one-time hub of American manufacturing had been going through particularly hard times in the Reagan years. Springsteen announced support for the union food bank created by Local 1397 of the United Steelworkers of America. During his second Pittsburgh show, during one of his many fondly listened to story-length preludes to songs, Springsteen waxed serious: "We're slowly getting split-up into two different Americas. Things are gettin' taken away from people that need 'em and given to people that don't need them, and there's a promise being broken … I don't think the American dream was that everyone was going to make a billion dollars, but it was that everybody was going to have an opportunity, and to live a life with some decency and some dignity and a chance for some self-respect. So I know you gotta be feeling the pinch down here where the rivers meet." He dedicated the song, "The River," to "Local 1397, rank and file."

John Mellencamp

John Mellencamp, from Seymour, Indiana, in the heart of the Midwest, had a similar gift for observing the struggles of ordinary people and telling their stories in catchy three or four minute songs.

Mellencamp emerged as a big star in 1982 with the album *American Fool*. The album, his sixth since 1976, was the last one billed to "John Cougar," an insufferable stage name given to him by his first manager, Englishman Tony DeFries, who somewhat deliriously envisioned the Midwesterner as a glam-rock star in the mold of his most famous client, David Bowie. In order to keep his audience from becoming too confused, he recaptured his own name for the 1983 album *Uh-Huh* as John Cougar Mellencamp. By the end of the 1980s, he was able to drop the "Cougar" altogether.

In such hits as "Jack and Diane" (1982) and "Pink Houses" (1983–84), Mellencamp emerged as the bard for disenchanted baby boomers, young people whose dreams become deferred or derailed by the mundane realities of adult life. On his 1985 album *Scarecrow,* Mellencamp matched musical muscle with social awareness more completely than ever, attacking the farm crisis ("Rain on the Scarecrow"), hunger, and deprivation ("Face of the Nation") while extolling the virtues of his rural roots ("Small Town").

With Willie Nelson and Neil Young, Mellencamp founded Farm Aid, to help family farmers. The first concert, on September 22, 1985, in Champaign, Illinois, starred the three founders plus Bob Dylan, Tom Petty, Billy Joel, Loretta Lynn, and others. It raised $80 million, seed money for an ongoing full-time organization.

In 1987, Nelson, Mellencamp, and a group of family farmers successfully lobbied Congress to pass the Agricultural Credit Act, which prohibited the government's mortgage lender, the Farmer's Home Administration (FmHA) from foreclosing on family farms unless foreclosure would bring in more money than investment in the farm to make it profitable.

Mellencamp was not enchanted by the politicians he met.

"It's not a secret that some people are there because of their egos," he told me. They want to be in a position where they legislate, vote on laws, things that affect people's lives, and they do it like you or I would be brushing our teeth. It's no big deal to them. I guess I'm real naive, but it's awfully hard to have a conversation with a man who's got three aides talking to him the same time you're talking to him. And I found that to be the rule, rather than the exception."[6]

Mellencamp continued to thrive in the eighties, writing human-scale, topical songs that challenged the popular assumptions of the Reagan era. On the 1987 album *Lonesome Jubilee,* a song called "Down and Out in Paradise" was a kind of open letter to the President, written in the voices of a white-collar worker who lost his job when his company relocated; a homeless woman who once had some of life's advantages; and a grade-school student, worried about both war and the anger engulfing her parents' marriage.

The Lonesome Jubilee, despite its heavy country instrumentation (dobro, fiddle, accordion), was Mellencamp's most personal album at the time. Talking about it, he offered a definition of the difference between "pop" and "rock."

"If you hear music, and you don't learn anything about the artist, it's 'pop' music," Mellencamp said. "When you hear songs and you learn about the artist, it's rock music."[7]

That's a very personal distinction, but for Mellencamp, it's a legitimate one.

Tom Petty

Tom Petty was yet another kid whose life was changed by seeing Elvis Presley. But it wasn't seeing Elvis on TV — it was meeting the King himself that inspired Petty's transformation.

"My aunt pulled up one day, I was sitting in my yard under a tree. I was at that age where you wonder: Now what? I was too old to play cowboys, and now what? She pulled up and said, 'Would you like to go see Elvis? Your uncle is working on a film about 30 miles away with Elvis Presley.'"

So began an obsession with music for the eleven-year-old from Gainesville, Florida. As a teen, he formed a band called Mudcrutch with high school buddies Mike Campbell (guitar) and Benmont Tench (keyboards). Moving to Los Angeles, Petty got a record deal, and immediately hired Campbell and Tench as the core of the band that became Tom Petty & the Heartbreakers, along with Ron Blair (bass) and Stan Lynch (drums).

It was not a long, drawn-out struggle for success. With years of experience, the Heartbreakers had an instinctive feel for one another. "They kind of know what they're going to do before they do it," said Jeff Lynne, coproducer of the albums *Full Moon Fever* (1989) and *Into the Great Wide Open* (1991, the former credited to Petty as a solo album).[8] The high level of excellence and comfort as a performing band allowed Petty & the Heartbreakers to reach their thirty-year anniversary in 2006; the other key element has been the same high level of excellence and consistency in Petty's songwriting. Petty's songs always have a strong point of view, though the clarity of the titles — "Don't Do Me Like That," "You Got Lucky," "I Won't Back Down" — belies the subtlety of his lyrical touch. Sometimes stubborn, sometimes defiant, yet never self-indulgent, Petty's songs never lose their veneer of hope. And he can show a wry sense of humor. An astute observer of the fast friendships and backhand dealings of the record business (some of his dozen hits in the eighties detailed his angry impasse with his record company at the time), Petty had a gift for tightly compressed narrative that is effectively expressed on "Into the Great Wide Open," which he wrote with his frequent collaborator Lynne. It tells the story of the modern music industry in four verses. It's about a guy who dreams of becoming a rock 'n' roll star, goes to Hollywood, meets a girl, gets a record deal, and has a hit, in the first three verses, before the forces of Hollywood gravity take over.

Rock Video, Michael Jackson, Madonna and Cyndi Lauper Hair Bands

In 1981, cable television, was, if not in its infancy, still in its preschool years, available or utilized in just a fraction of U.S. homes. So it seemed of little consequence that on August 1 a new cable channel appeared in a handful of homes in a few dozen cities.

An executive appeared onscreen and pronounced the words, "Ladies and gentlemen, rock and roll." The station played its first video clip, a promotional video paid for by the record company as another means of promoting a song or artist. The group was called the Buggles; the song was "Video Killed the Radio Star"; the station, formally known as Music Television, become known as MTV.

Created by the Warner Amex Satellite Entertainment Company (WASEC), MTV was launched after exhaustive market research revealed a potential market for such a channel. It didn't hurt that the programming cost almost nothing: record labels understood that making videos available to MTV for free was worth the expense in the promotional value of exposure.

Before MTV, there had been no steady place to see rock music on TV. In the 1950s and 1960s, there was *American Bandstand*; in the mid-to-late 1960s, weekly network shows like *Hullabaloo* and *Shindig* featured rock, folk, and pop performers. From 1973 to 1981, *Don Kirshner's Rock Concert* ran at 1 a.m. EST and provided exposure to dozens of rock and soul acts. Kirshner was a charisma-deprived and seemingly charm-free host, and the late-late show time reflected how little the TV networks had learned about the power and appeal of rock 'n' roll. Late-night talk shows, now routine stops for rock artists, were more comfortable with middle-of-the-road performers. One exception was Dick Cavett, who had Joni Mitchell, Jefferson Airplane, and Crosby, Stills and Nash on his show the morning the Woodstock festival ended.

Other TV shows featuring rock included *Midnight Special*, hosted by celebrated radio disc jockey Wolfman Jack. And when *Saturday Night Live* went on the air in 1975, with its hip ensemble comedy skits featuring young actors like John Belushi, Chevy Chase, Gilda Radner, and (in a few years) Eddie Murphy and others who would become household names, it always featured one trendy musical guest.

But rock music on TV 24/7? MTV was another step entirely. As Gary Burns wrote in an essay that appears on Chicago's Museum of Broadcast Communications Web site:

> MTV presented one video after another in a constant "flow" that contrasted with the discrete individual programs found on other television networks. Clips were repeated from time to time according to a light, medium, or heavy 'rotation' schedule. In this respect MTV was like top 40 radio (it even had video jockeys, or vjs, similar to radio djs). Moreover, it soon became apparent that MTV could "break" a recording act (move it into prominence, even star status), just as radio had done for decades.[10]

MTV grew slowly in its first year and a half. Many cable systems were skeptical about the channel and its format. Showing the genius for brand identity and self-promotion that would make it a worldwide phenomenon with multiple channels on six continents, MTV encouraged those without the channel to tell their parents to demand of their cable companies, "I Want My MTV." They even enlisted musicians such as Boy George, David Bowie, Pat Benatar, and Billy Idol to appear in such commercials.

The Rock Video

MTV's timing was fortuitous. At the end of the 1970s, the music business acted like the compulsive gambler that had already been its tendency and bet on disco, soundtracks, and melodic California rock — to rake in enormous profits — but did not know when it was time to cash in its chips and move on to another game. The assumption was that their luck would never change. As the eighties hit, after a reckless binge of spending, the labels had to trim expenses.

Many companies stopped subsidizing tours by new or upcoming acts. So MTV provided the consumer the chance to "see" an act that might not be able to appear in their town. "It's the only thing we have that represents us," said Carole Pope of the Canadian band Rough Trade. "It's good to be seen as well as heard."[11]

Rough Trade (no relation to the U.K. record company) made a straightforward performance video for only $5,000. Others spent considerably more: the manager of guitarist Pat Travers donated his Jaguar to be blown up as part of the storyline for his artist's video for "I'd Rather See You Dead," video director Ken Walz told me in a 1983 interview.[12]

The results for bands favored by MTV were immediate. The British group Duran Duran had had little success in the United States with its first album, *Planet Earth*. But the photogenic band's scenic videos from exotic locales on expensive videos such as "Hungry Like the Wolf" quickly made them major stars.

The British hard-rock band Def Leppard had the same positive result from video. Their second album, *High 'N Dry*, was released in July, 1981 and peaked at a respectable but hardly overwhelming 250,000 copies. In 1982, a video clip for the album track "Bringing On the Heartbreak" went into regular rotation, which meant multiple daily screenings, on MTV. Album sales soon doubled, and in December 1982 it was certified gold for sales of more than 500,000.[13] (The video was reshot in 1983.)

The video exposure set the stage for Def Leppard's *Pyromania* to live up to its name in the United States (where the British band has always been more popular than it is at home) and for the multimillion selling *Hysteria* (1988), which featured four U.S. top-ten singles, all represented by high-impact videos. (According to the official Def Leppard Web site, the band has made thirty-nine video clips.)[14]

Michael Jackson

MTV's explosive success and enormous influence led it into several early controversies: the most serious was that the absence of videos by black artists represented an institutional racism.

John Sykes, then the twenty-seven-year-old director of programming for MTV, defended his station. "We play black musicians, such as Prince and Joan Armatrading," Sykes said.[15] "We don't play rhythm and blues. We play format. We don't play race. We're aimed at a specific audience: The rock 'n' roll music audience. You won't see [punk group] Siouxsie and the Banshees on the Nashville Network."[16]

But Michael Jackson was different. Jackson had been a star since he was ten years old. With four older brothers, he was leader of the Jackson 5, who cut some of the most exciting pop records of the early 1970s, including the peerless "I Want You Back." They were so popular among all ages and races that they were characters in their own Saturday morning cartoon show.

Michael's first solo efforts in 1972 were tentative: an immensely likable version of Bobby Day's hit "Rockin' Robin" and a strange ballad, "Ben," the title song of a movie about a rat.

But in 1979, Michael found his adult groove. "Don't Stop 'Til You Get Enough" thrilled old fans and brought in a vast contingent of new fans: it was a great dance record at the end of the disco era, but it wasn't disco. It was a rockin' R&B album with sass, punch, and polish, produced by one of the most gifted musicians in contemporary music, Quincy Jones.

It was a record for all formats. Both the title song and its follow-up, the lilting "Rock with You," were No. 2 pop hits and R&B hits. Another hit, "Off the Wall," was a top-ten pop hit.

So Jackson was in no way ghettoized: his music had always been popular across the board. And it was about to become the most popular music on the planet.

Thriller came out in 1982. It's first single was a safe bet, perhaps too safe: "The Girl Is Mine," a duet with Paul McCartney. Cute, but nothing special.

"Billie Jean," though, was something else. With a kinetic groove, it was Michael Jackson's with a defiant lyric that — about a stalker, a girl who claims the singer is the father of her child — allowed Jackson to project an emotional assertiveness that hadn't been heard from him before. The video featured Jackson's tour-de-force dancing, the element that connected him to the great multitalents of black crossover entertainers, back through James Brown and Jackie Wilson to Sammy Davis Jr. and Cab Calloway.

Sykes's argument that somehow Michael Jackson was too pop or too R&B for MTV did not convince the executives at CBS Records, the parent company of the Epic imprint, for which Jackson recorded. CBS had clout, and wasn't afraid to use it.

"I did holler. Yes, I did intercede," Walter Yetnikoff, CEO/president of CBS Records, told me at the time.[17] It was said that CBS would withhold all videos from its enormous roster if MTV didn't play "Billie Jean." Yetnikoff did not confirm the notion of a CBS boycott, but said, "There was some initial unreceptiveness [on the part of MTV]. But it was not a stonewalling, 'fuck you' resistance. I think they rethought their position." MTV finally agreed. And to its surprise, not only did "Billie Jean" explode — so did MTV's audience.

The next video single made it easy for MTV. Jackson and Quincy Jones, again producing, had shrewdly figured that a really rock 'n' roll cut, with a burning-rock guitar solo, would widen Jackson's constituency further. "Beat It" featured an essential guest appearance by Eddie Van Halen, the most virtuosic and powerful guitarist of the moment.

In 1983, Jackson's version of "Beat It," on the TV special "25 Years of Motown," stole the show; in his performance, he introduced his trademark dance move, The Moonwalk. That show introduced Jackson to an even wider swath of America, and the *Thriller* album was unstoppable. Jackson's excitement and grace as a dancer also helped make him pop's biggest star.

The *Thriller* album, already hot, was selling in the neighborhood of 800,000 copies a week. (In 2005, only the top superstars of rock, rap, or country might sell in that neighborhood its opening week.) The album topped the *Billboard* chart for thirty-seven weeks, and sold more than 24 million copies in the United States, shattering all records.

Prince

Prince always defied categorization. The singer/musician/songwriter/producer came out of Minneapolis in the late 1970s. His unabashed carnality was reflected in the title of his third album, 1980's *Dirty Mind,* which led logically enough to the title of its successor, *Controversy,* the following year.

Decades seemed to have passed between the time Sly & the Family Stone's multiracial band created a universally pleasing sound in the late 1960s and early 1970s; and there hadn't been a black guitar player since Jimi Hendrix died in 1970 with the ability, drive, or will to rock a mass audience.

Dirty Mind broke barriers, becoming the strip-club music of its time in much the way that Southern hip-hop has become the strip-club music of the mid-2000s. *Dirty Mind* didn't deploy double-entendre. Prince let the taboos all hang out on the incestuous "Sister," and on the salacious "Head," he doesn't mince words: he seduces someone else's bride before her wedding, and they pleasure each other. By the end of the song, they've gone all the way — but Prince has replaced the groom, and they end up doing each other happily ever after.

The lasciviousness would not have counted for much if Prince's music had not been so intoxicating. Records like *1999, Little Red Corvette,* and *Delirious* were bouncing baubles of joy through 1982 and 1983, setting the foundation for Prince's world-domination move: the movie and soundtrack *Purple Rain.* The thin, semi-autobiographical plot took a backseat to the volatile performance footage of a favorite haunt, the First Avenue nightclub in Minneapolis. The film was a box-office hit, and the soundtrack matched *Saturday Night Fever* with its twenty-four weeks at No. 1 in 1984. And Prince became one of the most in-demand songwriters of the decade. "When You Were Mine" was recorded by both Cyndi Lauper and Detroit rock legend Mitch Ryder (in a production by John Mellencamp). The love song "Nothing Compares 2 U" was a No. 1 hit for Irish singer Sinead O'Connor in 1990.

Artists from Art of Noise with Tom Jones ("Kiss," 1988) to Mariah Carey, Foo Fighters, Ani DiFranco, Patti Smith, and School of Fish, not to mention many jazz and R&B musicians, have covered Prince's material. As a songwriter, his wish stated in his song "Controversy" — "I wish there was no black or white, I wish there were no rules" — seemed to have come true.

But it was as a performer that Prince clinched the deal with the public. On a good night he was among the best there ever was: he had the dancing explosiveness of R&B greats like Jackie Wilson, the sexual arrogance of rock greats like Mick Jagger, the exhibitionism of Madonna, and the funky bump of Parliament/Funkadelic.

Even on a so-so night, as at a concert at Long Island's Nassau Coliseum in 1988, he was still pretty good. The silly parts — doing calisthenics and simulating sex with bikini-clad dancers on a huge bed that was the center of his round stage, set in the middle of the arena — were pure spectacle. And his merging of the sacred and the secular was as bold, if more explicit, than anyone since Ray Charles took a sanctified gospel song and turned it into the squeals of pleasure of "What'd I Say." "God is alive!" Prince exhorted from the stage. "The news is coming like a dog in heat."

Because Prince has lasted so long and made good music in between, history has forgiven the egotistical self-indulgences that may have sunk a less-gifted artist. His subsequent movies were difficult to sit through: *Under the Cherry Moon* (the music from which was featured on the 1986 album *Parade,* or the inscrutable and unappealing *Graffiti Bridge* (1990).

Madonna and Cyndi Lauper

If Michael Jackson was already made for video, another major artist of the decade invented herself for video. The one artist who truly grasped the image-making and career-building potential of MTV was Madonna. Born Madonna Louise Ciccone in 1959 in Detroit, Madonna had a background in modern dance. What this means is that Madonna knew something about movement and performance beyond the typical disco-dance artist. (Before making it big on her own, she sang backup on Patrick Hernandez's disco hit "Born to Be Alive.")

If Prince could not sustain his musical superiority, neither did he ever bottom out. However, his set of songs for Warner Bros.' first big-budget *Batman* movie in 1989 and the single "Batdance" were a rare example of corporate synergy paying off, as each project helped raise the profile of the other. In 1990, Prince introduced a new band, which appeared with him on the platinum album *Diamonds and Pearls* (1991), and the symbol-titled album in 1992.

It was here that Prince's behavior became less easily understood by fans and press alike. From the beginning, he used what is now the core of instant messaging shorthand in his song titles and written lyrics: "I Would Die 4 U," "U Got the Look."

In 1993, Prince changed his name to an unpronounceable glyph that combined male and female symbols, and asked to be referred to in print as "The Artist Formerly Known as Prince," and later simply "The Artist." In the year 2000, he announced that he would resume using the name Prince. But the eccentricities matched the inconsistent output of the 1990s.

But Prince was shrewd. He started an online music club at a time when most major record labels had yet to even come to terms with the Internet. And during his 2004 tour, he simply gave away his album *Musicology*, as a bonus along with the purchase of a concert ticket. Both the album and the tour were his biggest hits in years.

Unhappy with the way major labels were handling his business (he regarded his relationship to longtime label Warner Bros. as that of a "slave"). Prince stopped signing longterm contracts. When he needs the distribution power of a major label, he signs a one-album deal. Prince continues to flourish: His 2006 release, *3121* (the title is intentionally enigmatic), was regarded by many as his best in 20 years, and it debuted at No. 1 on the *Billboard* album chart the week of release.

Instinctively provocative, her sell-out concert tours featured Madonna reenacting onstage the risqué, and clearly intentionally controversial, content of her videos. The 1984 "Like a Virgin" is quintessential Madonna: quintessential video, quintessential song, quintessential first No. 1 record.

The coauthor of "Like a Virgin," Billy Steinberg (who wrote it with Tom Kelly) said, "Like a Virgin" was a simile for "that great feeling of optimism and hope when beginning what feels like a good new relationship."[18]

Madonna had different ideas about the song. She performed it for the first time on September 18, 1984, at the first MTV Video Music awards. "Wearing a wedding dress and a belt buckle that said 'Boy Toy,' she sang a sultry version of this, ending with a simulated orgasm. The show was live. Madonna was convinced she missed a note while performing this on the show, but if she did, no one seemed to care.[19]

In their December 7, 2000, issue, *Rolling Stone* named this No. 4 on their list of the greatest pop songs since the Beatles era. The top three: "Yesterday," "Satisfaction," and "Smells Like Teen Spirit."[20]

Cyndi Lauper actually preceded Madonna as a video favorite. "Girls Just Want to Have Fun" was her first single as a solo artist from her album, *She's So Unusual*. (She released an album in 1981 as a member of the group Blue Angel.)

The video, which ran in heavy rotation on MTV, featured the professional wrestler Captain Lou Albano as Lauper's father. It won the first-ever award for Best Female Video at the 1984 Video Music Awards. Albano was also in her next video, for the now-standard "Time After Time."

"Girls" became an anthem for female attitude. Multicolored streaks of dyed hair and colorful thrift-shop clothes, an exaggerated Queens accent that made her sound like Betty Boop, and the songs' suggested assertion of female independence combined to make Lauper the personality of the moment.

Lauper also had a beautiful, powerful multioctave voice, and the ability to impart deep emotions into both party songs like "Girls …" and mature ballads such as "Time After Time."

She was on the cover of *Newsweek* and was named one of the "Women of the Year" by the influential feminist magazine *Ms.*, representative of the newly empowered women in rock. "Lauper was among the first women of the MTV generation to draw a distinct female following, one that paralleled the male fan base traditionally devoted to (male) rock stars."[21] Yet the honor from *Ms.* was controversial: Some women objected to the use of "girls just want to have fun" after so many years of struggling to be called "women." Lisa A Lewis heralded Lauper in her influential 1991 book, *Gender Politics and MTV*. Lewis argued that "Girls Just Want to Have Fun" was literally liberating both for women and especially, adolescent girls, described as a "very regulated and marginalized group." Lewis, in fact, finds that Lauper, Madonna, and other important female rock singers of the era, including Pat Benatar and Tina Turner, "appropriated music video as a vehicle of feminist expression and have reinterpreted the signs of a gender-typed culture — clothing, dance, the use of the street as public space, and even musical instruments."[22]

The wisdom at the time was that Lauper would be the female superstar of her era, and Madonna a popular dance music performer without much significance. (Madonna's first hits, such as "Holiday," were just that, well-produced pop dance tunes without much character.)

Why did it happen the other way around? For Lauper, her identification with Albano proved to be a disastrous career move. He appeared in numerous Lauper videos; and the singer "managed" pro wrestlers. For a short while, this helped Lauper ride a wave of popularity that turned out to be wide but thin. The public promptly tired of the wrestling gimmick. Lauper made some good records during the 1980s and is respected today as an excellent singer, but she never recaptured what many felt was her enormous potential.

Madonna, with her "boy toy" fetishes, and sexual teases, turned out to be the one with the iron discipline and white-hot ambition to become one of the late twentieth century's most recognizable women. Firmly in control of her career — it was clear that her managers worked for her, rather than the other way her around — she continually managed to reinvent herself, create controversies, make movies, and develop an accomplished, if occasionally contrived, body of work. Her stage shows, with frantically choreographed dance routines (some of which made it appear likely that she was lip-synching, or at least singing along to prerecorded or enhanced musical tracks), were adventurous entertainments filled, like her songs and videos, with sexually and religiously provocative imagery. (One of Madonna's most successful follow-ups to "Like a Virgin" was "Like a Prayer.") Her public relations were so finely tuned and masterfully manipulated to keep Madonna, her husbands, boyfriends, even celebrity girlfriends in the gossip columns, news pages, and TV.

Like many rock stars, Madonna craved a film career. She got off to a strong start in the 1985 indie film *Desperately Seeking Susan*. But her appearances in big-budget Hollywood films such as *Dick Tracy* (1990, with Warren Beatty) and *Shanghai Surprise* (1986, with her then-husband, Sean Penn), were disasters. She showed her resilience both with the provocative documentary *Truth or Dare* (1991), an intimate look at her "Blonde Ambition" tour, and her appearance in the fine ensemble work *A League of Their Own* (1992), with Tom Hanks, about a short-lived women's professional baseball league. Madonna has continued to masterfully adapt to changing styles and control the public's image of her, even as she stirred controversy by her enthusiasm for Kabbalah, a strain of Hassidic Jewish mysticism, and her concert in Rome in 2006, where she appeared onstage in a Crucifixion pose, to the distress of the Roman Catholic Church's hierarchy in nearby Vatican City.

Hair Bands

With MTV's influence so pervasive, a backlash was inevitable. Dire Straits' 1986 hit, "Money for Nothing" (the first song played when MTV Europe went on the air that year) was a sarcastic take on the video era's star-making machinery. Of course, Dire Straits and MTV had it both ways — the song became a big hit for Dire Straits thanks in large part to its video's exposure on MTV. MTV was delighted to take criticism, especially if the critique made it seem that the corporation had 1) a self-deprecating sense of humor that helped maintain its self-image of "edginess," and 2) you mentioned the name of the channel so that the song, whatever the content or message, simply became an extension of the MTV brand.

But MTV could only be as edgy as the music and videos that came its way. And the channel began to falter around 1986, as rock's creative musical elements seemed to dry up with so much focus on the visuals. Resistance to MTV was also fueled by the music programming that began to dominate around 1986 through the end of the decade.

The bands, almost all male, shared certain characteristics. They maintained an aura of machismo while sporting incredibly teased –and and blow-dried hairdos and absurd clothing that recalled the worst design sensibilities of the glitter/glam era.

The music these bands played was hard, sort of; heavy, sort of; and melodic, mostly. The definitive work explaining the phenomenon of hard/heavy 1980s "poufy-haired" rock bands is Chuck Klosterman's *Fargo Rock City*.[23] Klosterman was a North Dakota farm kid in 1983 when Mötley Crüe's *Shout at the Devil* was released. Describing his rural world and its time and place as "a deeply underwhelming place," Klostermann writes: "Mötley Crüe was made to live in this kind of world. *Shout at the Devil* injected itself into a social vortex of jaded pragmatism; subsequently, it was the best album my friends and I had ever heard."

One of the significant cultural contributions of Klosterman's book is its deft and thorough analysis of this music, which was often mis-named heavy metal. "Since there was so much loud guitar rock in the 1980s, describing a band as metal was about as precise as describing a farm animal as a mammal."[24]

Some of the loud guitar bands, many from or formed in Southern California, had the advanced musicianship, original songwriting, and grandiose vision to at least occasionally make great rock 'n' roll. They included Guns N' Roses and Van Halen, both of which featured bril-liant guitarists and flamboyant lead singers (Slash and Axl Rose, and Eddie Van Halen and David Lee Roth, respectively).

There was a second level of bands typified by Mötley Crüe. They were noteworthy for their musical adequacy, and a combination anti-authoritarian behavior and the tattooed pretty-boy image that made their posters required decor on the walls of junior high school boys. (It is a long tradition: Mötley Crüe's Nikki Sixx told me he grew up worshipping a poster of Kiss in his own bedroom at home.) It is an indication of the crossing the line between image and reality that when Vince Neil of Mötley Crüe was drunk behind the wheel in a car accident that killed his passenger and friend, Razzle Dingley of Hanoi Rocks, in 1985 in a sick way it enhanced Crüe's stature. Rob Reiner's 1984 faux-documentary movie *This Is Spinal Tap* cleverly satirized the distorted, hermetic world of the third-rate rock band, a British act much less successful and lucky than Crüe and its cohorts.

Other bands in the Crüe tradition were Poison, Ratt, Faster Pussycat, Cinderella, L.A. Guns, W.A.S.P., and Skid Row. Lean-ing more pop were Whitesnake, White Lion, Dokken, Britny Fox (which is a group, not a girl), Twisted Sister (also all males), and the neither-quiet-nor-riotous Quiet Riot, although the distinctions are not all that clear.

As Klosterman writes,

> I read an interview Nikki Sixx gave after the release of the unremarkable Crue reunion LP "Generation Swine," and he was bemoaning the fact that a magazine listed Motley Crue, W.A.S.P. and Twister Sister in the same sentence. He seems to think Motley Crue was far better, and far different, than those other groups, which is absolutely insane. Oh, they were better, but they certainly weren't different.[25]

And that sameness bored and irritated the heck out of rock fans, musicians and even ever-fearful-of-boredom MTV. A new style and scene was needed, and at the dawn of the 1990s, one was found, in Seattle.

Metallica/Megadeth/Slayer/Anthrax: Thrash/Speed Metal

Punk rock continued to morph in the early 1980s. Its effect on heavy metal was a surprise, since many punk bands saw themselves in rebellion against the bloated caricatures of 1970s metal. But rock 'n' roll is constantly evolving, and the artists that propel that evolution are those who create new hybrids without regard to categories. Metallica played as fast or faster than any punk band. But while punks found virtue in one, two, three, four brevity, Metallica stretched out songs for five, six, seven, eight minutes, with long, testosterone-fueled guitar solos and lyrics of struggle against material and spiritual oppression. Like many metal acts, Metallica had songs about demons; what made their songs so compelling is that the demons were not typical cartoon visions of Satan. The demons were inside them, and they were real. Formed in 1981 in Los Angeles (they later moved to the Bay Area), the lineup that first gained acclaim consisted of drummer Lars Ulrich, guitarists James Hetfield and Dave Mustaine, and bassist Cliff Burton. Mustaine's behavioral problems exacerbated by drugs and alcohol dragged on the other three, and he was dismissed from the band just before the recording of the Metallica debut album, *Kill 'Em All* in 1983. Mustaine started his own heralded band, Megadeth. He was replaced by Kirk Hammett. In 1986, shortly after the release of their metal masterpiece *Master of Puppets*, Burton was killed in a bus accident in Sweden, and was replaced by James Newsted.

With Newsted aboard, Metallica's star soared. They were fourth out of five on the bill on the 1988 "Monsters of Rock" tour, behind Van Halen, the German hard rock band the Scorpions, and Dokken, and ahead of only short-lived Led Zeppelin clones Kingdom Come. At a tour stop at RFK Stadium in Washington, D.C., Metallica went on at around 3 in the afternoon, powered by a 250,000-watt sound system. They were apparently in such synch with the audience that it seemed odd that hundreds, if not thousands, headed away from the stage before the set was quite over. A few minutes later, what had happened was clear: almost everyone, it seemed, had bought a Metallica T-shirt. "Everyone's saying we're kind of stealing the show," Hetfield said backstage before the band went on.[*] In August 1988, the band released its commercial breakthrough album ... And Justice for All, which eventually sold more than 8 million copies in the United States. They even released their first video, for the track "One," which became Metallica's first hit single.

In 1991, Metallica released an album with a black cover, sometimes called The Black Album, or Black, or Metallica. By any title, it sold 14 million copies. It marked a significant artistic evolution for the band as well. It was produced by studio pro Bob Rock, and it seems that Metallica realized that if it slowed down a drop, accentrude melody and an extra chord there, it could put Led Zeppelin numbers on the scoreboard.[†] At a concert at Nassau Coliseum, Hetfield berated the audience for not screaming and yelling enough. In fact, the audience was paying rapt attention to the substantial new songs, like "Enter Sandman."

Metallica has sold more than 90 million albums, clearly the gold standard for heavy-metal bands. But success did not come without its strains. In 2000, it was the first band to sue the popular free musical file-trading service Napster. Many fans were upset, but others in the music industry were pleased that an influential act was standing up against the piracy of their recordings. In a press release, Lars Ulrich said: "We take our craft — whether it be the music, the lyrics, or the photos and artwork — very seriously, as do most artists. It is therefore sickening to know that our art is being traded like a commodity rather than the art that it is. From a business standpoint, this is about piracy — a/k/a taking something that doesn't belong to you; and that is morally and legally wrong. The trading of such information

---

* Interview with the author, Newsday, June 26, 1988.
† Wayne Robins, Newsday, December 20, 1991.

— whether it's music, videos, photos, or whatever — is, in effect, trafficking in stolen goods."*

The 2004 documentary *Metallica: Some Kind of Monster* follows the group as it struggles to record its album, *St. Anger,* and the fragile chemistry of what is now a phenomenally successful business entity. What separates this movie from typical rockumentaries is the therapy sessions with a therapist hired by Metallica's management.

Ulrich and Hetfield, the two founders, are "like a long-married couple who find themselves bored, dissatisfied and on the rocks," *New York Times* critic A. O. Scott wrote in his fascinated review. "For nearly 20 years, Mr. Ulrich, Mr. Hetfield and their various band mates have channeled the basic adolescent experiences of alienation, frustration and rage into melodramatic, at times self-consciously mythic squalls of sound. One of the insights 'Some Kind of Monster' offers is just how much work this transformation requires, perhaps especially when it is undertaken not by teenage rebels but by family men in their early 40's," Scott writes. [NYTimes, July 9, 2004.]

As an example of how throughly Metallica's once-extreme music has entered the mainstream, "Enter Sandman" was the theme song for the New York Mets star relief pitcher Billy Wagner when he joined the team in 2006. This provoked a controversy, because "Enter Sandman" was also New York Yankees pitcher Mariano Rivera's psyche-up song as he walked from the bullpen to the pitcher's mound. A quick study by New York sportswriters found that Wagner had been using the song since he was a member of the Houston Astros in 1996, and in either case, Rivera didn't mind sharing the song: He said he prefers Christian music.

Megadeth: Though less successful commercially than Metallica, the band formed by Dave Mustaine and bass player Dave Ellefson has had four million-selling albums and has sustained a career that continues through today. The 1984 independent release *Killing Is My Business ... And Business is Good* and 1986 Capitol Records album *Peace Sells ... But Who's Buying?* unveiled a sound even faster and attitude more nihilistic than Metallica's. Despite distractions from heroin addiction and treatment, Mustine and Ellefson's band hit a popularity peak in the early 1990s with pitilessly explosive records like *Countdown to Extinction* and *Youthinasia*. Mustaine's livelihood was threatened when a nerve injury to his arm diagnosed in 2002 rendered him unable to play guitar. By 2004 he

* Wired News, April 13, 2000. http://www.wired.com/news/politics/0,35670-1
  .html?tw=wn_story_page_next1

had recovered, and Megadeth established its own annual traveling roadshow called "Gigantour" in 2005.

Slayer: When heavy metal is not heavy enough, hardcore punk is not hard enough, and even Metallica starts to sound like something for your sweetheart on Valentine's Day, there is Slayer. Savagely loud, insanely fast, with the most apocalyptic lyrics, Slayer also came out of California in the 1980s, and is the third of the big four speed/thrash metal bands. Their 1986 album *Reign in Blood* is ranked with Metallica's *Master of Puppets* as one of the great speed/thrash bands. Produced by Rick Rubin, who has recorded every Slayer album since *Reign in Blood,* it has a clarity and presence foreign to most bands of this subgenre. Other highlights have included 1990's *Seasons in the Abyss,* which with eerie prescience seemed to anticipate the first Persian Gulf War. While the graphic imagery of Slayer's songs is disturbing, the songs illuminate, rather than endorse, the horrors of war. "When victory is a massacre, the final swing is not a drill, it's how many people I can kill," vocalist Tom Ayala sings in "War Ensemble." Another song, "Skeletons of Disaster," is a nightmare vision of ecological ruin. Kerry King and Jeff Hanneman drive the furious double-barrel guitar assault. The replacement of drummer Dave Lombardo by Paul Bostaph in 1996 was virtually the only personnel change in Slayer for more than twenty years, a remarkable continuity for such a volatile musical field. Their 2006 album *Christ Illusion* is as tight, brutal, and cutting as anything they'd ever recorded. Among the institutions indicted for the rotten state of the world is the mass media: "The cameras are whores for the daily bloodshed." The usual complaints were made by religious authorities, who objected to the title of the album, but for Slayer, whose songs have included "Anti-Christ," "Hell Awaits," "Mandatory Suicide," and "Behind the Crooked Cross," such discussions are hardly bumps in the road.

Anthrax, from Queens, New York, are an excellent balance of punk and metal. Its message is largely positive and politically progressive; its best album may have been 1988's *State of Euphoria.* With songs urging compassion for the homeless and struggling against prejudice, they were and are the thinking person's speed/thrash band.

1985: Live Aid: Rock's Good Works

Though the 1960s are remembered as a decade of political activism, the 1980s will be remembered as the time when musicians put their mouths where the money was and raised millions of dollars for issues ranging from African famine relief to human-rights organizations.

"The Concert for Bangla Desh is rock reaching for its manhood. Under the leadership of George Harrison, a group of rock musicians recognized, in a deliberate, self-conscious, and professional way, that they have responsibilities," Jon Landau wrote in *Rolling Stone* on February 3, 1972. But it took some years for rock benefits to become a habit.

The "No Nukes" concerts of 1979 were undertaken by an organization called MUSE (Musicians United for Safe Energy). Jackson Browne, Crosby, Stills & Nash, the Doobie Brothers, John Hall, Graham Nash, Bonnie Raitt, Gil Scott-Heron, Carly Simon, Bruce Springsteen and the E Street Band, James Taylor, and Jesse Colin Young performed a series of concerts to work for a "non-nuclear future." The timing was more than coincidental. In 1978, a nuclear power plant known as Three Mile Island unit 2 went online in Harrisburg, Pennsylvania. In March 1979, a combination of human error and technical failure resulted in the near-meltdown of the reactor, the worst nuclear accident in American history. Ironically, a popular Hollywood movie about just such an accident, *The China Syndrome*, had just started appearing in theaters when Three Mile Island occurred.

1981: The Secret Policeman's Ball. U.K. concerts for Amnesty International featuring the great names of British humor including Monty Python and some musical guests. The Secret Policeman's Other Ball, a sequel, was more music oriented and featured Sting, Eric Clapton, Donovan, Pete Townshend, and Bob Geldof.

1985: Live Aid. The biggie. As a prelude, Geldof, a member of the fading punkish Irish rock band the Boomtown Rats, was one of many Britons horrified by 1984 BBC TV news reports that graphically displayed people starving to death in Ethiopia. With Midge Ure of Ultravox, they arranged a charity single called "Do They Know It's Christmas." More of the UK's top pop musicians showed up to donate their time and talent in a studio November 25, 1984: Duran Duran, Culture Club, George Michael, Spandau Ballet, and many others. Geldof called the group's recording Band-Aid, and were pleasantly surprised when the single was one of the UK's fastest sellers ever and raised more than 8 million pounds.

Emboldened, Geldof set about arranging simultaneous concerts July 13, 1985, at Wembley Stadium in London and JFK Stadium in Philadelphia. Largely through his determination and insistence, every big star in the world signed on for one or both concerts: Phil Collins performed earlier in the day in London, then flew on the Concorde to New York and by helicopter to Philadelphia to appear at both concerts, which were televised worldwide (and via a satellite TV hookup connecting the two stadiums). Queen, U2, Sting, Elton John, the Who, the Pretenders, Bryan Ferry, and Paul McCartney were among those at Wembley. In the U.S., Madonna, Bob Dylan, Tom Petty, Neil Young, the Cars, Robert Plant, Jimmy Page and John-Paul Jones of Led Zeppelin, and Mick Jagger and Tina Turner (as a duo) maintained the star wattage. The level of cooperation was high. As Page said, "All these bands going on and no one's overrunning. That's a statement in itself."

Some will always question whether the message would get lost in the entertainment, and certainly, the hundreds of thousands in the two stadiums and others around the world were there to be entertained. But Live Aid was, as Landau had said of "Bangladesh," a mark of rock's maturity, a way to use the assets of stardom in the cause of something good. As Midge Ure said of himself and Geldof: "If two tossers from Ireland and Scotland can get off their butts and do something, maybe other tossers will do the same."[26]

Earlier that year, about fifty top American artists also came together to do a charity single for Africa and the starving in America. At the peak of his enormous popularity and influence, Michael Jackson and Lionel Richie wrote a song called "We Are the World." The producer was Quincy Jones, who famously told the celebrated contributors as they entered a Los Angeles recording studio to "check your egos at the door." It appears they did. Stevie Wonder, Ray Charles, Cyndi Lauper, Billy Joel, Springsteen, Bette Midler, Diana Ross, Willie Nelson, Paul Simon … the list goes on. And though in retrospect some acknowledge that the song sounds like a soda commercial, it represented the greatest gathering of pop and rock performers for a brief, altruistic purpose.

The PMRC: Rock Must Be Restrained

If the rock community was behaving so splendidly, why was the music under unprecedented political attack in 1985?

A group of influential women who claimed to be rock fans with young children started the Parents Musical Resource Center (PMRC), requesting that rock music have a ratings code something like that of the movie industry. The PMRC saw its goal as to alert the public to "lyrics that are sexually explicit, excessively violent, or glorify the use of drugs and alcohol." The women of the PMRC had significant clout: its two protagonists were Susan Baker, the wife of the Reagan administration Secretary of State James Baker, and Tipper Gore, wife of then-Senator Al Gore (D-Tenn.).

Tipper Gore said it was a shock to bring home Prince's *Purple Rain* and hear the song "Darling Nikki," with its graphic references to masturbation. The Gore family also sat down to watch some videos on MTV, and Tipper said she was offended by the sex and gore in such videos as Van Halen's "Hot for Teacher," the Scorpions' "Rock You Like a Hurricane" and Mötley Crüe's "Looks That Kill."

They also found songs that indicated that some artists "seem to encourage teen suicide." The objectionable examples were Ozzy Osbourne's "Suicide Solution," Blue Oyster Cult's "(Don't Fear) The Reaper," and AC/DC's "Shoot to Thrill." As their public-relations offensive took off (appearances on TV talk shows, a sympathetic cover story in *People* magazine), PMRC's suggestions became more brazen. One staffer said Bruce Springsteen's "I'm on Fire" was inappropriate for young children because it was too sexually suggestive.

The PMRC wanted ratings stickered on albums: X for sex, V for Violence, D/A for drugs or alcohol, and O for occult, the latter a favorite boogeyman of Christian conservatives.

Opposition to the PMRC was led by artist manager Danny Goldberg and the American Civil Liberties Union. Goldberg called his organization "the Musical Majority," a clever twist on the name of one of the more influential right-wing family-values groups, the Rev. Jerry Falwell's Moral Majority.

Los Angeles Mayor Tom Bradley, the former police officer who was the city's first black mayor, was one of the few politicians to stand with the Musical Majority against the PMRC. After attending and enjoying a Springsteen concert at the L.A. Forum, Bradley held a press conference and asked, "What do Elvis Presley and Bruce Springsteen have in common? Both have been targets of small groups of people who want to impose their standards of all American families. Fortunately, would-be censors have lost nearly every round against popular music."[27]

After Congressional hearings in which colorful rock musicians like Frank Zappa and Dee Snider of Twisted Sister mixed it up with some clearly clueless politicians, a settlement between the PMRC and the Recording Industry Association of America (RIAA), which somewhat tepidly defended free speech, was reached. The result was a voluntary "parental advisory" sticker each record company could decide to put on what they determined might be potentially objectionable material. When they did so, it was usually to alert the buyer to the appearance of a dirty word. "I decided," Goldberg wrote, "to hold my nose and declare victory."[28]

The Alternative Mainstream

The college town of Athens, Georgia, about seventy miles east of Atlanta is an unlikely spawning ground for the best American rock of the 1980s. The University of Georgia campus is relatively liberal — for Georgia — which means pretty middle of the road, a town where Georgia Bulldogs football is the autumn obsession and fraternity-row beer blasts are always in season.

Yet like any campus there is always an artsy contingent, and from that sector in the late 1970s rose the B-52's. The two-man, two-woman quartet band dressed campy — the girls with beehive hairdos, the guys stylish but freaky. The inspired amateurism of their late 1970s novelty "Rock Lobster" put new-wave dance music and Athens on the map.

Other bands followed: the tightly coiled, hypnotic rhythms of Pylon, the southern surf-guitar fusion of the instrumental group Love Tractor, the Side Effects, the Method Actors ... "The thing here was to pick up an instrument, tune it a weird way, and go out and present art," Bill Berry told me.[29]

REM

REM was different. Drummer Berry and bassist Mike Mills were trained musicians, who grew up playing in bands together in Macon, Georgia. That gave R.E.M. a professional advantage that separated them from the arty bands. Peter Buck, a punk-rock aficionado with a huge record collection, was the guitarist. And on vocals was a strange, shy, moody esthete named Michael Stipe. "We became popular over night in Athens; we played one party, then sold out every show, he told me."

The garrulous, impatient, pragmatic rocker Buck and the ethereal, reticent Stipe made for an interesting combination. "People paint that Michael's really arty and I'm rock and roll, but we meet on a common ground," Buck told me in a 1988 interview. "It's not that I want to make a Led Zeppelin record, and Michael wants to do a [Brian Eno] record. It may seem that he ameliorates some of my rock and roll influences, and maybe I give him more rhythmic grounding, but that's just the way we like to work."

The band formed in 1980. For the first number of years R.E.M. recorded for independent I.R.S. Records making intriguing albums, full of jangling guitar sound that came to typify alternative rock in the 1980s. The records, and R.E.M.'s early concerts, were noteworthy for Stipe's appealing mumbling of lyrics that defied easy understanding. It is not without reason that the first R.E.M. album was *Murmur* (1983).

"They're difficult records," Buck said with a laugh. Referring to the song "Harborcoat," from the 1984 album *Reckoning:* "I don't know what that (song) is about, can't figure that out."

Stipe's art at first was communicating mood rather than message, allowing R.E.M.'s records to connect on both an intellectual and visceral level. "I realized right away that what is really clear to me is not clear to everyone," he told me. Reflecting on another line that Buck didn't understand in the song "World Leader Pretend" on the 1988 *Green* album, its first for major label Warner Bros. Records, Stipe spoke about its meaning in terms of Jungian psychology, the reptile brain, masculine/feminine dichotomy — it was a typical R.E.M. song.

Oblique as the lyrics sometimes were, R.E.M. had no trouble engaging with the daily politics of the 1980s. They opposed the U.S. support of the rebel, right-wing Contras against the democratically elected socialist government of Nicaragua throughout the decade. They have been avid supporters of environmental group Greenpeace and the human-rights group Amnesty International. They got involved with local zoning issues in Athens, and backed candidates going back to 1988, when they voted for Michael Dukakis, the Democratic victim of George H. W. Bush, Reagan's two-term vice president.

Stipe also seemed to be more comfortable onstage, as a front man, and as a vocalist, singing more clearly and directly engaging the audience. "I'm coming to grips right now with the idea that what we do is essentially entertainment," he told me.

As with every other band in the eighties, intriguing videos helped R.E.M. develop a wide audience. But they built their success slowly. In the early days, they would simply get in a van, drive to concerts within a weekend drive of Athens, and sleep on the floor in fans' houses or apartments. The little airplay they got was from college-radio stations, the prime outlet in most areas for independent-label rock during that decade. College radio lived in its own low-budget, noncommercial reality, with its own trade magazine, *College Media Journal* (which evolved into CMJ's *New Music Report*), and charts. The playlists and charts published by CMJ unified these usually low-wattage stations throughout the country.

The most creative bands of the 1980s — R.E.M., the Replacements, the Police, and U2 — all established themselves on the college radio circuit.

But while R.E.M. simmered, and Minneapolis's Replacements self-destructed through alcohol, the Police rose more explosively — but not by design.

The Police

Though the Police — singer/bass player Sting, guitarist Andy Summers, drummer Stewart Copeland (the band's sole American) —

formed in 1977 at the height of punk rock in England, they never got stuck in that rut — artistically or philosophically. They were each excellent musicians, and their absorption of a reggae beat created a fresh, distinctive sound. More important, they began with and stuck to a successful business strategy.

It helped that the Police were managed by Miles Copeland, who also ran the I.R.S. label, and booked by Ian Copeland of Frontier Booking International, or FBI. The choice of acronyms was no accident: the Copeland brothers grew up in hotspots around the globe, where their father, an agent of the CIA, was posted.

The Police strategy was the template for what became successful with R.E.M.: hit the road in a van, play small clubs, sleep in the van or on the floor somewhere, and create a foundation with a small but passionate following.

They did not work as opening acts for larger groups, but headlined wherever they went, even if they weren't known. "Instead of the widest possible exposure, we were interested in the quality of the exposure," Copeland told me in a 1982 interview.[30] "If we played a club that was only half full, we'd turn on 60 people intensely. Our goal was an intense response, rather than a wide response."

Indeed. Their first single, "Roxanne," was not an instant hit, but it was instantly loved by anyone who heard it. Their concentrated blend of streamlined rock and loud, propulsive reggae rhythm and bouncy pop (their first big hit was "De Doo Doo Doo, De Da Da Da" in 1980) brought them from club dates to the arena circuit in about a year. Between 1979 and 1983, they made five increasingly successful albums culminating in 1983's *Synchronicity,* which was No. 1 for seventeen weeks. Their success divided critics at the time: some felt Sting's aloof posturing to be irritating, as well as the sentiments in hits like "King of Pain." They must have bothered each other as well, since *Synchronicity* was their final studio recording together. (Sting has since become one of the world's most popular pop singer-songwriters.) They gave were what supposedly their final performances in 1986 at some benefit concerts for Amnesty International's "Conspiracy of Hope" tour, which did much to heighten awareness in the United States of the organization's efforts on behalf of political prisoners. Unexpectedly, the Police performed live on the Grammy Awards TV show in February 2007. It was the prelude to a world tour.

U2

U2 also started at the height of the punk era, in Dublin in 1976. Thirty years later, they're the biggest rock band in the world. Their debut album, *Boy*, was released in 1980. Songs like the anthemic "I Will Follow," the group — guitarist The Edge, drummer Larry Mullen, bassist Adam Clayton, and the singer known as Bono — already expansive, sounding like they're performing to the people in the last row of a huge stadium. "The shocking thing is that well before we had a right to, we had this belief that we would become a very successful band," The Edge said in 1998.[31]

Boy was the perfect name for an album that *Rolling Stone* called "the inside story from children at the brink of manhood … sparked by the tension between The Edge's world-beating guitar playing and Bono's fearful pride," wrote Jon Pareles.[32]

What gave U2 its longevity is its transparency. They haven't been afraid to fall on their faces, to express grandiose concepts, picking themselves back up after every experiment gone awry to reach a new level of excellence. After the "incoherence"[33] of *October* (1982), they bounced back with the aggressive, focused *War*, with amped-up in-your-face songs like "Sunday Bloody Sunday."

The song is about the events of January 30, 1972, in Derry, Northern Ireland. (The independent nation of Ireland is predominately Catholic; the United Kingdom state of Northern Ireland is predominately Protestant. Mutual hatred ran deep.) At a Catholic protest march, British soldiers opened fire on the crowd, killing thirtteen and hardening the rift between the two sides. An official British inquiry exonerated the troops, further fueling anti-British fervor among Catholics in the north.

"Sunday Bloody Sunday" set the tone for U2's social activism that has evolved with its success. And the ferocity of its sound and message stood apart from the more polished popular music of the year. "More than any other record, 'War' is right for its time," Bono said of the 1983 album.

It is a slap in the face against the snap, crackle and pop. Everyone else is getting more and more style-orientated, more and more slick. John Lennon was right about that kind of music; he called it "wallpaper music." Very pretty, very well designed, music to eat your breakfast to. Music can be more. Its possibilities are great. Music has changed me. It has the ability to change a generation. Look at what happened with Vietnam. Music changed a whole generation's attitude towards war.[34]

The Unforgettable Fire (1984) was the first of a series of albums produced by audio visionaries Brian Eno and Daniel Lanois, a change of pace after the direct, hard-hitting earlier albums recorded by Steve Lillywhite. Songs like "4th of July," and two tributes to Martin Luther King — "MLK" and "Pride (In the Name of Love)," underlined the band's increasing fascination with the history and pop culture of the United States. Despite its volatile subject matter ("early morning, April 4, shot rings out in the Memphis sky"), "Pride" was U2's first top-forty U.S. hit, though a minor one. (It reached No. 33.)

U2's performance at the final show of the 1986 "Conspiracy of Hope" tour signaled the band's readiness to conquer America. The passion of their performance turned the massive Giants Stadium in East Rutherford, New Jersey, into a small club. On a bill of superstars (the Police, Bryan Adams, Lou Reed, Peter Gabriel, and others) on a show broadcast by MTV and nationally syndicated radio, U2 was the most dynamic, and memorable. "At almost every concert the fans belonged to U2, as Bono and The Edge ripped out 'New Year's Day' and 'Sunday, Bloody Sunday.' The girls threw lingerie, the guys waved Irish flags, and everybody screamed wildly when Bono lifted girls onstage, hugged them and left them in puddles of tears."[35]

That set the stage for *The Joshua Tree*, in 1987, firmly establishing U2 as the best and most popular band of the era, selling more than 10 million copies. Its two No. 1 singles, "I Still Haven't Found What I'm Looking For" and "With or Without You," both exuded a spiritual yearning that touched listeners in ways that other blockbusters of the time, by Bon Jovi or Def Leppard, for example, never could.

Success didn't spoil U2: it freed them to indulge in making a not-very-interesting movie (*Rattle and Hum*) based on their only incrementally better two-LP set of recordings, some live, some recorded at rock's most sacred studio shrine in Memphis.

> "We thought people would actually love a record on which we were loose enough to actually screw about Sun Studios and put it out," Bono told me. "We thought, let's show the side of America we love, which is the music that we don't know shit about ... We were completely taken aback when people thought it was egomania. But I understand it now. It was size. Bands can get too big. We were just in people's faces. I understand. 'Get outta my face.' It was just that."[36]

The 1991 masterpiece *Achtung Baby* was an attempt at deflating the sound, and image, of the band. But there were other miscues (*Zooropa* and *Pop*, 1993 and 1997, respectively). But that relentless drive to reinvent themselves that came so naturally to the Beatles, Bob Dylan, the Rolling Stones, the Who, and rock's other great artists also came, with a good deal of apparent thought and planning — to U2.

"I still can't get over how some people don't give rock 'n' roll artists the latitude they give book writers," Bono said. "You do the work, and you move on to something else. You get into new subject matter, and you lose yourself in that."

And that comes with a kind of unflinching refusal to romanticize the world, but to live in it, address it. "From the beginning we were excited when music met the real world,"[37] Bono has said, speaking of 2000's *All That You Can't Leave Behind*. And with the release of *How to Dismantle an Atomic Bomb* (2004), they showed the ability to maintain an older audience while appealing to a younger generation, merging their own image with the most iconic youth culture product of the twenty-first century, the Apple iPod digital music player. U2's hit "Vertigo" launched both the album and a major iPod campaign. While earlier generations might have accused the band of "selling out," U2 members have been hailed as marketing geniuses for its ability to take as much as $20 million[38] in Apple money (for tour support and the like) without losing a shred of credibility.

The more U2 changes, the more durable it seems. This is important, because it explains why too many rock bands can have big hits, but can't sustain long careers. Those are the bands that give the audience what it wants, until the audience gets tired of it and moves on to something else.

Not U2. Something Bono told me in 1992 still holds true for the band. "You think about where you'd want to go, and you might wonder if they'd come with you," Bono said of his band's ideas and their relationship to the audience. "You'd be stupid if you didn't. But if you're smart, you can take your audience with you. I think they're smart, and have followed us down some roads, maybe some of them more interesting than others. But ... they seem to want us to challenge them, and take them on a ride. Some of them aren't interested and get off; others get on. But you can't have the tail [the audience] wag the dog [the band's creativity]."[39]

Bono was knighted by Queen Elizabeth in 2007 for his charitable work and musical contributions.

U.K. Music in the 1980s

New Romantics

The London scene in the 1980s was very much driven by fashion. There was the riot of color and sexual ambiguity of Culture Club's Boy George; the slick video style of handsome Robert Palmer; and the babe-magnet masculine beauty of Duran Duran. There were the pirate costumes of Adam Ant. And there were the synthesizer driven tunes of the famous-forever-for-their-bad-haircuts A Flock of Seagulls.

Except for Palmer, a bit more mature than the others and more of a blue-eyed soul singer than rock star, most of these London-based bands were included in what was called the New Romantic movement. A reaction to punk's austere, down-market sound and style, New Romantics liked to dress up dandily —no wonder these acts were immediate MTV favorites.

Adam and the Ants made one appealing album, *Kings of the Wild Frontier*, full of buzzwords and marketing hooks: there was "antmusic" and "sexmusic," not that there was any difference. (The group had formed in 1976, but three original members left to form the dim Bow Wow Wow in 1980.)

Adam (Stewart Goddard) wore pirate clothes on his body and American Indian makeup on his face. The solid if undistinctive music featured tribal drumming and some musical intelligence provided by guitarist Marco Pironi. The Ant music frenzy spread through Britain for a few minutes in the early 1980s, and one song, "Goody Two Shoes" peaked at No. 12 on the *Billboard* U.S. chart.

Adam and the Ants typified the gimmickiness of the New Romantics. And for the most part, their moments in the spotlight were the length of rock videos.

Culture Club

One exception, Culture Club, were propelled to near-immediate stardom by videos and an endless tabloid obsession over Boy George's sexuality. Though gay, and hardly embarrassed at appearing flamboyantly so, Boy George fanned the flames of publicity by being not quite closeted, but coy.

Of course, coming to great fame as the AIDS epidemic killed off the culture and fashion world's greatest talents and ordinary men alike perhaps made discretion sensible. The public backlash against AIDS was palpable; it was ghettoized as a gay disease, and the intolerant and moralistic fringe thought it was God's punishment for engaging in sodomy. Though Elton John and Madonna were early crusaders for an AIDS cure, the rock world would not widely recognize AIDS until the news that Freddie Mercury, the beloved lead singer of the band Queen, had died of the malady November 24, 1991.

It helped Culture Club's case that Boy George (née George O'Dowd) had a fine if limited voice, and that their first two albums, *Kissing to be Clever* and *Colour By Numbers,* had no fewer than six consecutive top-ten singles in little more than a year between the beginning of 1983 and spring 1984. MTV latched on to the visually arresting group; endlessly repeated videos and skillfully executed melodies gave the band a vast, if temporary mainstream audience. Culture Club won the Best New Artist Grammy Award in 1983.

But the camera soon tired of Boy George in his colorful dresses and odd-looking hats. They were arguably the biggest band in pop in 1983. But in the fall of 1984, just weeks before Ronald Reagan's landslide reelection, they released a single called "The War Song" that was totally at odds with the spirit of the time. (It was also a dull record.) Culture Club's third album, *Waking Up with the House on Fire,* lacked the easy appeal of its predecessors, and shortly after the release of another single, the all-too-appropriately titled "Mistake No. 3," Culture Club faded quickly.

The '80s Manchester Scene and Goth

But the superficial London scene was not all that the United Kingdom had to offer in the 1980s. A grass-roots music scene sprang up around the northern city of Manchester, featuring an array of good and interesting bands way out of proportion to the city's size. Like many industrial cities, Manchester had fallen on hard times, and the incipient music community leaned more to the grit of punk music than New Romantic fashion.

The scene was built around Factory Records, a local independent label started by entrepreneur Tony Wilson. The event that launched dozens of bands had been a Sex Pistols concert attended by perhaps eighty people in the cafeteria of a local college. The scene is fictionalized in the Michael Winterbottom film *24 Hour Party People,* a pseudo-documentary about the Manchester scene in the late 1970s and 1980s, from postpunk through rave culture.[40]

Joy Division's brief career was a too-perfect compression of the life cycle of a legendary rock band, from concept to amateurism to local stardom to competence to excellence, dissolution, death, and immortality. Starting in the late 1970s as a punk/metal band Warsaw, this most famous of Manchester's Factory bands, in the words of Simon Reynolds, made their originality clear when they slowed down the tempo. "Shedding punk's fast, distortion thickened sound, the music grew stark and sparse. Peter Hook's bass carried the melody, Bernard Sumner's guitar left gaps rather than filling up the group's sound with dense riffage, and Steve Morris' drums seemed to circle the rim of a crater." And the body and voice of tormented and doomed singer Ian Curtis "intoned from a 'a lonely place' at the center of this empty expanse."

Reynolds's description sounds like an apt description for Manchester in the 1970s, not just another industrial city gone to seed but the iconic city of the industrial revolution cast in a relentless, ghostly gloom. High-minded attempts at razing poor neighborhoods and locating its denizens in high-rise housing projects had the same effect that such "urban renewal" had in American cities: the loss of community, of roots, of anchor and mooring, replaced with bland blocks of high-rise projects that became "unintended laboratories for social atomization." The U.K. government had a very different approach than the U.S., however. In the United States, illegal drugs like heroin and cocaine flooded these projects, with drug pushers as capitalists making investments, taking risks, and protecting their trade with semi-automatic weapons. In the United Kingdom, the government gave out prescription medication in Manchester, tranquilizers that were "massively overprescribed to help ordinary people ... not so much manage their lives than be manageable." And anti-depressants "were prescribed so freely (a quarter million tablets in 1977 alone) they verged on a form of social control."[41]

Joy Division presented a vision of doom you could dance to. Fascinated with World War II and totalitarian imagery, the band took its name from a section of the Auschwitz concentration camp where women were maintained in sexual slavery for German soldiers. They claimed their dalliance with Nazi iconography reflected their contrariness rather than their political views. Drummer Morris told Simon Reynolds it showed an identification with "the oppressed, rather than the oppressor."[42] Reynolds also notes that Curtis and Joy Division were inspired by the "Berlin chic" of their heroes David Bowie, Iggy Pop, and Lou Reed. (Bowie and Pop lived and recorded in Berlin in the later 1970s; Iggy, in fact, recorded two of his best albums produced by Bowie in Berlin, *The Idiot* and *Lust for Life*, both released in 1977. Reed's 1972 alienated *Berlin* album was among the darkest of a career noted for its solemnity.)

One reason they were so effective at communicating mental anguish was that it was being experienced first-hand by singer Curtis. The singer may or may not have been epileptic at first; his provocative, spasmodic onstage behavior preceded his diagnosis with epilepsy after an attack in 1978. Curtis also worked in a rehabilitation center where he helped care for an epileptic girl who died during a fit, and was, Reynolds believes, the inspiration for one of Joy Division's essential songs, "She's Lost Control," from their debut album, *Unknown Pleasures*.

The heavy antiseizure medications prescribed for Curtis made an already troubled personality even more depressed. Before the release of *Closer* in 1980, Curtis committed suicide by hanging himself on May 18. The posthumous single, "Love Will Tear Us Apart" is considered one of the most powerful and lasting recordings in modern British rock.

After Curtis's death, Sumner, Hook, and Morris carried on as a trio called New Order. Moving to New York — or at least spending considerable time there — New Order was attracted to the postdisco club scene, bringing drum machines and computerized keyboards into the mix. They became one of the prominent electronic dance bands of the 1908s with albums such as *Substance* (1987) and *Technique* (1989).

The gloomy vision projected by Joy Division helped spawn a related movement of English bands that became popular on both sides of the Atlantic known as goth, for gothic. While most teens and twentysomethings experience alienation and depression to some degree, goths wore it on their sleeves, not to mention their torsos, their legs, their faces and hair. In goth world, everything was black: black hair, black eye-shadow, black clothes, black moods.

A goth timeline might begin with gloomy late 1970s postpunk bands like Siouxsie and the Banshees and move into such introverted 1980s bands as the Sisters of Mercy, Bauhaus, Joy Division, and New Order, and continues into the 1990s and current day with Nick Cave, Marilyn Manson, and Nine Inch Nails. A particularly good definition comes from a Web site called Music Moz:

"[Goth] took the synthesizers and processed guitars of post-punk and used them to construct foreboding, sorrowful, and gloom-ridden opuses. Its lyrics were usually introspective and personal, but also included a taste for literary romanticism, morbidity, religious symbolism, and/or supernatural mysticism." [43]

Goth has many offshoots, from industrial to darkwave to death rock, but those who were just passing through in the 1980s identified with the Smiths and the Cure, two of the Britain's best depressing rock bands. With his spiky hair and cadaverous makeup, the Cure's Robert Smith was a style setter. But it was Morrissey who carried on his sagging shoulders the aesthetic of sadness, both with the Smiths in the 1980s and as a solo artist in the 1990s.

In fact, with guitarist Johnny Marr's jagged solos and the singer known as Morrissey's vulnerable yet sturdy vocals, the Smiths earned their place as one of the United Kingdom's best bands, with U.K. hits like "This Charming Man," "Last Night I Dreamt That Somebody Loved Me" and "Heaven Knows I'm Miserable Now." Their master-piece is considered *The Queen is Dead*, which, on the album's twentieth anniversary, *Uncut* magazine described as "a howl of near-Swiftian disgust at Thatcher's decaying Britain."[44]

In the *Uncut* interview, Marr puts his fingers on the underlying melancholy aesthetic of the songs he and Morrissey wrote. "We both recognized the beauty in melancholia," Marr said. "We talked about it, often. About the difference between depression and melancholia. About how depression was just useless, but melancholia was a real emotion and a real place, a creative place that dealt in images and music and creative aspects of the self."

For some the sound of these bands, with keyboards, drum machines, and self-conscious obsession with depression seemed the antithesis of rock 'n' roll's original liberating spirit. But though too dour for some, they conveyed an emotional honesty that was refreshingly real in an era of MTV's shallow mock-rock hair bands. And the reflectiveness of these bands would inspire a rebirth of guitar-driven rock'n'roll early in the 1990s, under the perennially cloudy skies of Seattle.

THE 1990S AND BEYOND

At least once in every decade, rock 'n' roll has been declared dead. When Elvis Presley went into the army in 1958; before the Beatles, in 1963; during disco fever in the 1970s; during a country music boomlet known as the moment of the *Urban Cowboy* in the 1980s. In 1990, rock was declared dead again. But this time, there was "proof."

During the 1990 calendar year, no rock album hit No. 1 on the *Billboard* 200 Album chart. The year was owned by female vocalists (Madonna, Mariah Carey), crossover rap albums (by Vanilla Ice and M. C. Hammer), pop acts (Wilson Phillips, Phil Collins), and teen sensations New Kids On the Block. The erosion of rock's popularity could be attributed to a number of causes. One was the fragmentation of radio formats. There were three main rock formats: classic rock played older groups from the 1960s and 1970s — such as the Beatles, the Doors, the Rolling Stones, Led Zeppelin, the Who — exclusively. Album rock stations also played music from the 1960s and 1970s, including new records by a handful of "core" artists; and alternative rock, which at that time had come to be defined as mostly synthesizer-driven postpunk dance music.

The dependence on a pantheon of proven superstars meant that there was no room to develop the new artists who might become the new Rolling Stones or David Bowie, Paul McCartney, Elton John. And these older artists stayed active on the arena and stadium touring circuit, but their current music had little appeal and no impact. They seemed to be suffering from creative burnout. And the contemporary rock musicians who could have galvanized a mass audience in 1990 — Bruce Springsteen, U2, R.E.M., Van Halen, or Guns N' Roses — did not release new albums that year. The rock bands that were successful, from Australia's AC/DC to Texas's ZZ Top, were not breaking any new ground artistically, and even the new traditionalists like the Black Crowes simply appropriated the riffs of 1970s bands like the Faces and the Rolling Stones. And the "hair bands" made popular by MTV in the late 1980s such as Winger, Warrant, Cinderella, and Slaughter followed contrived formulas that had diminishing appeal.

Most seriously, rock had lost its distinction as the line separating teens and their parents, who themselves had been raised on the more vital rock of the 1960s. "Rock and roll was music to kill your parents with," Mercury Records co-president Mike Bone told me in a 1991 interview.

> The most outrageous thing I could bring home to my [white] parents in Macon, Ga., was Jimi Hendrix, a black man playing guitar, singing 'let me stand next to your fire.' It drove them crazy. Now, if a kid were to bring home the new Bruce Hornsby or the Black Crowes' record, their parents, who are now my age (I'm 41), can say, 'I like that.' Teenagers don't want to have music their parents can say, 'that's cool, let me borrow that.' So what's the most outlandish thing a 16-year-old suburban kid can bring home? [Hardcore rap music like] Ice-T. Or Public Enemy. That's why rap has made the big crossover.

Facilitating that crossover, *Yo! MTV Raps* started in 1989. Hosted by rap pioneer Fab 5 Freddy, it was the first nationwide outlet for rap videos and commentary and bringing the style, sound, and element of voyeuristic danger into the TV dens of suburban America.

Rap, though constantly mutating — perhaps *because* it is constantly mutating — has dominated much of the teenage music agenda ever since.

But rock was not finished. In the United Kingdom the situation was slightly different. As it had been in the early 1980s, Manchester was setting the scene with bands playing music for "raves": all-night warehouse-sized parties with frenzied dancing and inhibitions-reduced by widespread use of the hallucinogenic drug Ecstasy. The bands, such as the Stone Roses, Happy Mondays, Charlatans U.K., and Inspiral Carpets all gave guitar-based rock a boost in Britain, but their impact in the United States was minor.

So was the phenomenon known as "Britpop," which peaked in the mid to late-1990s. Oasis, Blur, and Pulp were the big three; Elastica, Supergrass, Menswear, and Suede were other notable bands. Britpop was a rebellion against grunge, in the United States. For the first time in memory, Britain had broken off with the mother country of rock 'n' roll. An early nineties, forty-four-city U.S. tour by Blur was said to be the spark that inspired the reaction. Disdained by apathetic audiences, Blur came back to the United Kingdom with a mission: "'Get rid of grunge,' 'declare war on America' and make music that was identifiably English."[1]

Pulp, led by the charismatic Jarvis Cocker, followed in the tradition of the Kinks and the Jam, performing "wry songs about everyday life" like their biggest hit, "Common People," and only-in-England gems like "Last Days of the Miner's Strike."

Blur, featuring Damon Albarn (now also half of the popular genre-bending cartoon act Gorillaz and a member of the Good, the Bad and the Queen), made its breakthrough with its 1994 album *Parklife*, which was successful in its effort to depict British life at that time. "Coffee and TV," "Country House," "Girls and Boys," and "Parklife" were some of the Blur songs to have a major impact in the United Kingdom. The pride in British youth culture coincided with the selection of youthful rock fan Tony Blair as leader of the Labour Party in 1994. The culturally stifling Conservative rule seemed to be coming to an end, and the rise of both Blur and Blair signaled a moment of "possibility and expectation."

The only group to challenge, and indeed surpass, Blur's dominance of Britpop was Oasis. Led by brothers Liam and Noel Gallagher, Oasis had simple ambitions: they wanted to be the biggest group in the world, the biggest since the Beatles. Their arrogance was almost refreshing: rock 'n' roll needed a shot of preening hauteur. In the United Kingdom, people responded: *Definitely Maybe* (1994) made Oasis immediate stars with hits like "Supersonic," "Cigarettes & Alcohol," and "Live Forever." And in an interview with *Spin* magazine, singer Chris Martin of Coldplay declared Oasis's debut, "The greatest rock 'n' roll album ever made — bar none. The only thing that comes close is [AC/DC's] 'Back in Black.'"[2]

Though *Definitely Maybe* had some U.S. success, it peaked at No. 58 on the *Billboard* album chart. Oasis's only U.S. top-ten single was "Wonderwall" from *(What's the Story), Morning Glory. Champagne Supernova*, another track from that 1996 album, was an anthemic self-portrait of a band intent on stardom. But they never broke big in the United States. Their conquest of their homeland was easy and instantaneous, thanks to its compact geography and a small handful of national radio stations, newspapers, and magazines to spread the word. But many British acts hailed as stars at home are unwilling or unable to put in the overwhelming effort required to gain attention on the American continent. The drunken brawling and egomaniacal outbursts by the Gallagher brothers were welcomed by Britain's celebrity-hungry tabloid newspapers. In the United States, they never attained the level of celebrity to make the gossip columns, much less the front pages. So Oasis, even with appealing but Beatles-imitative albums *Heathen Chemistry* (2002) and *Don't Believe the Truth* (2005), remain a UK phenomenon.

Sonic Youth Finds Nirvana

During the 1980s, many edgier rock bands went underground, recording for newly empowered independent labels that could market new music quickly and credibly to the rock fans who disdained the superficial glitz of MTV. Bands such as Black Flag, Dinosaur Jr., Hüsker Dü, Jane's Addiction, Soul Asylum, and the Mekons catalyzed a postpunk, guitar-rock community. But by far the most important rock band in 1990 was New York's Sonic Youth.

The most influential band of the 1990s had already been together for nine years and recorded nearly a dozen albums before being recognized by what might be called the public. But since its beginnings in 1981, Sonic Youth had a huge influence on other musicians.

The band was founded by guitarists Thurston Moore and Lee Ranaldo and bass player Kim Gordon. (Steve Shelley joined on drums in 1984; that quartet has continued without turnover, though occasionally an extra musician, like producer/guitarist Jim O'Rourke [*Murray Street*, 2002], has joined the band for a limited time.) Though their raw sounds antagonized some, the band itself has established a reputation for professionalism and even "family values": Moore and Gordon have been married since 1983 and have a daughter, Coco, born in 1994.

Sonic Youth emerged from the late 1970s to early 1980s "no wave" scene of downtown Manhattan, when struggling artists and musicians could still afford the rents. The pun on "new wave" is obvious. No wave represented a wide variety of styles, from punk to funk to avant-garde jazz and conceptual art, embraced nihilism and rejected the commercialism of new wave. Besides Sonic Youth, other no wave acts included Glenn Branca, the Contortions, Teenage Jesus & the Jerks and its singer Lydia Lunch, the Lounge Lizards, and DNA. The commonplace, as Renaldo described it, was "harsh, challenging, abrasive music informed by rock, noise, jazz and modern composition/experimentation."

What Sonic Youth did, however, was to use this atonal, nihilistic music as the jumping-off point for the next era of rock. No wave "destroyed all the aspects of rock and roll the Sex Pistols said they were destroying, when actually they were just sort of speeding up Chuck Berry chords and playing them a little louder,"[3] Thurston Moore told me during a 1990 interview.

Their first record, a self-titled extended play disc, was released on Neutral Records, a label started by experimental composer/guitarist Branca, whose unconventional strategies of guitar tunings and symphonic compositions using massive numbers of guitars had a major impact on Sonic Youth.

Through the 1980s, Sonic Youth was synonymous with underground rock guitar music, and their following spread to England, where they toured to wide acclaim in 1984. "Their sound had developed into a mature pop/noise hybrid with a genuine experimental flair for structure."[4]

Sonic Youth recorded for a number of independent labels in the 1980s: Blast First, Homestead, SST, Enigma, continuing to develop parallel lines of wildness and structure. Rare among rock bands in their intellectual curiosity and literacy, they released in an album in 1987, *Sisters,* that reflected literary influences from futurist fiction writers like Phillip K. Dick and William Gibson. "They are such incredible consumers of fringe culture and have achieved a unique awareness about what they are doing," said longtime observer, critic Byron Coley.[5] Under the name Ciccone Youth, they released the *The Whitey Album* in 1988, which included deconstructed versions of Madonna hits "Burning Up" and "Into the Groove" (as "Into the Groove-y") as well as a rock-out rendition of the one of the 1980s quintessential video hits, Robert Palmer's suave "Addicted to Love."

Their indie masterpiece was the 1989 *Daydream Nation,* a two-record set Moore described in 2006 as "a celebration of the sprawling wilderness that is musical America and beyond. No limits, no boundaries. The feeling of mystery. Made us famous whether we liked it or not." [6]

Alternative/underground rock bands with guitars began to walk a little taller thanks to *Daydream Nation*. Seeing the diminishing interest young rock fans had with the more routine rock that was being released, major labels began to get interested. Sonic Youth signed with Geffen Records' DGC label later in 1989, and in 1990 released their major label debut, *Goo*. Peaking at No. 96 on the *Billboard* Top Albums chart, Sonic Youth obviously didn't sacrifice their principles, mixing what was now a lush, fierce, driving sound with plenty of irreducible noise. Broadening their range a bit, rapper Chuck D of Public Enemy appears on the track (and single) "Kool Thing."

Now on the mainstream radar, Neil Young invited them to join his 1991 "Ragged Glory" tour with Crazy Horse, a loud electric thrash-fest that resulted in the live albums *Weld* and *Arc*, the latter a withering blast of feedback and noise that seemed to have been influenced by Sonic Youth's earliest experimental sounds.

Sonic Youth was not universally embraced by Young's fans; in fact, the tour was marred by tension between Young's road crew and the band. They were not permitted to play as loud as the headliner; Kim Gordon seemed particularly taken aback by the condescending and sexist way she was treated. "The Neil Young tour was actually the first time I encountered so-called sexism," Gordon said. "Every time it was somebody's birthday, there'd be strippers hanging around."

But Young himself was a fan. "It's obvious that I like Sonic Youth," he told a magazine in 1992. "In my book, they really do modern rock. They make magnificent music. You know that one, 'Expressway to Your Skull'? It's incredibly good, so beautiful. It's a classic. Superb melody, and even better live. They have quite a few that are that good. So that's one great group."

Young was aware that many of his own fans, especially the older ones who had never heard of Sonic Youth nor been exposed to their in-your-face fury, might not share his fondness for the band. "I didn't want acts that people were going to say 'Oh, I can take them or leave them,'" Young said in 1991. "I wanted to get somebody that people were going to love or hate. And I think we did a good job there. Sonic Youth are way out there on the cutting edge with what they're doing. And it's also extremely similar to what we've been doing for a long time."[7]

After the Young tour, in summer 1991, Sonic Youth went on their own headlining tour. In an opening slot was a group called Nirvana.

Nirvana's musical development was fueled both by punk rock, Sonic Youth's dense noise, and that friend of every teen, alienated or well adjusted, Led Zeppelin. Nirvana made their first album, *Bleach,* for Seattle's small but important SubPop label. It was Nirvana that Sonic Youth chose for their own 1990 tour, and when all the big-time labels came calling to sign Nirvana, the band went with DGC as well, largely based on the comfortable feeling that if it was OK for Sonic Youth, it was OK for them.

Soon Nirvana had not just surpassed Sonic Youth as the most popular cult band — they became a mass phenomenon that, like the great rock insurrections, no one could have planned.

"Nirvana emerged in the U.S. towards the end of the Reagan era — a conservative period for rock music remembered for big hair, spandex and stadium bombast," Chris Heard of *BBC News Online* wrote in 2004, ten years after leader Kurt Cobain's 1994 suicide by shotgun blast. "Cobain stripped away the excess, combining the raw simplicity and DIY ethics of punk with powerful yet melodic metal to craft a sound that appealed to millions."[8]

The 1991 album *Nevermind* was a phenomenon, staying on the *Billboard* chart for nearly a year and spawning the strangest anthem in all of rock, "Smells Like Teen Spirit." The title is a play on words about a female deodorant brand. But it also suggests something that the Rolling Stones' "Street Fighting Man" hinted at: that group consciousness was no more than shallow consumerism, the notion of generational unity as false as the teen spirit at a high school pep rally. The song turns the tables on the audience. In the bridge of the song, Cobain repeats the word "hello" sixteen times before demanding, "Here we are now, entertain us! I feel stupid and contagious/Here we are now, entertain us."

It wasn't contempt for the audience; it was contempt for the outsize expectations that had been established between artist and audience in rock since the 1960s.

In Nirvana's formative years, teenage angst had become a commodity: hair bands may as well have been toupee bands for all the originality and authenticity they represented at the end of the 1980s. It had become entirely too easy to have a hit record by fashioning an image that would be appealing to MTV, which had developed such an insatiable appetite for superficiality and trends that even the channel was evolving from screening rock videos twenty-four hours a day and broadcasting more "lifestyle" programming. Youth culture, said Sonic Youth guitarist Thurston Moore, had become monopolized by big business.[9]

It seemed that in Seattle, they didn't really want their MTV. In that politically liberal, environmentally aware, caffeine-fueled corner of the Pacific Northwest, a new generation of bands was emerging. In addition to Nirvana, Pearl Jam, Soundgarden, Alice in Chains, and a few dozen other bands (and they were all bands) developed an organic mutation of rock. These guitar-based bands had the intensity and independent spirit of punk, but slowed it down and matched it with the massive, roiling power of heavy metal. Add some improvisation, an element of social awareness, and lyrical intelligence, and you had an interesting direction for American rock in the 1990s.

"Initially, it was an isolated subculture,"[10] Soundgarden bass player Kin Thayil said in a 1992 interview. "It was a handful of people interested in similar kinds of music, [in bands that were] more cooperative than competitive."

The media called it "grunge."

Of course, none of the acts called themselves "grunge" bands, any more than a member of the Grateful Dead or Jefferson Airplane would describe themselves as "acid-rock" musicians. But every phenomenon required a handle, and "grunge" seemed to fit. (Mark Arm, the vocalist for the Seattle band Green River and later Mudhoney, is widely credited as being the first person to use the term "grunge" to describe the style. However, Arm meant the term in a negative connotation; he called the band's style "pure grunge, pure shit.")[11]

Among the indicators of grunge, the bands generally had long hair whose care did not require depleting the ozone layer with hairspray, as their more corporate kin, the hair bands, did. The uniform was flannel shirts and jeans, and it didn't matter whether they came from thrift shops, Army-Navy stores, or mass marketers such as Sears, JC Penney, or Kmart.

Flannel, though, was a good symbol for the music, which didn't pander to fashion, avoiding the worst musical excesses of punk and metal. It tended to shy from the nihilism of punk's extreme and the machismo thrust of metal. Pearl Jam's singer Eddie Vedder had some of the husky, grainy poetic delivery of the Doors' Jim Morrison, but as with most Seattle singers, it was his spirit and soul, not his loins, that were on fire.

Nirvana's tragic lead singer Kurt Cobain conveyed a tortured presence, so trapped inside his own skin that if he wasn't onstage, he seemed to be suffering a kind of autism, although it could have been the drugs: Cobain, like too many others in the Seattle scene, isolated himself even further from the world with heroin.

Many were open about their troubles with addiction. Heroin paraphernalia was found next to the decomposing body of Layne Staley when the Alice in Chains singer was found dead in April 2002 at age thirty-four in his Seattle apartment. A obituary on the BBC Web site noted that Alice in Chains stopped touring in the mid-1990s when Staley sought treatment for his heroin addiction, and quoted him telling *Rolling Stone* magazine about the drugs in 1996, "They worked for me for years, and now they're turning against me — and now I'm walking through hell, and this sucks." [12]

Among other heroin grunge deaths were Andrew Wood (Mother Love Bone, 1990) and Kristin Pfaff (Hole, 1994). Heroin was found in Cobain's system after his shotgun suicide.[13]

Cobain's tragedy wasn't just personal: it changed the direction of musical history in the way that it hastened authentic rock's loss of influence in pop culture. "In September of 1991, when 'Smells Like Teen Spirit' first hit MTV, I was a 14-year-old high school freshman, already a voracious music fan, but mostly enamored of artists that had been passed down to me by my parents, artists who predated my birth by more than a decade — the Beatles, Dylan, the Doors," Susan Visakowitz wrote in Billboard.com. "I didn't know it until I first saw Kurt Cobain alternately mumbling and howling in front of those black-clad cheerleaders, but I was desperately in need of a band for my cultural moment. Nirvana was it."

Thanks to Nirvana, alternative rock had entered the mainstream. Yes, Cobain, drummer Dave Grohl (now of the popular hard-rock band Foo Fighters) and bassist Kris Novoselic had become darlings of MTV: MTV was about stars, and Nirvana were stars.

But young people identified with Nirvana in a very deep and personal way. "His lyrics were often bleak and uncompromising — whether detailing his personal trials or ranting against corporate America — and delivered in a strained vocal style that could seem like a howl of rage. The songs articulated an anger, sometimes a despair, that struck a chord with disaffected young listeners ... His music offered refuge for the dispossessed and the marginalized — but also for the everyday angst-ridden adolescent."[14]

Cobain's sometimes painful identification with victims of prejudice was most clearly displayed in the notes he wrote to the album *Incesticide,* a collection of their early recordings for the SubPop label, released after *Nevermind:*

"I have a request for our fans. If any of you in any way hate homosexuals, people of a different color, or women, please do this one favor for us — leave us the fuck alone! Don't come to our shows, and don't buy our records."[15]

Pearl Jam

Among the other Seattle bands, only Pearl Jam approached Nirvana's influence. In commercial terms, in fact, Pearl Jam even surpassed it. The albums *Ten* (1992), *Vs.* (1993), and *Vitalogy* (1994) sold more than 17 million copies combined at the time. Pearl Jam owns the RIAA record for most copies of a debut album sold: *Ten* topped 12 million.

Pearl Jam's success allowed band members to apply their principles to their careers. In 1994 the band canceled a tour and appealed to Congress to investigate concert-ticket giant Ticketmaster, which it accused monopolistic behavior and of tacking on excessive fees.

It also played numerous benefits for liberal causes. In September 1998 it did a concert for Voters for Choice, which raised funds to support candidates favoring a woman's right to choose an abortion. "If we lived in a world where men got pregnant but still had the same drive and mindset, this would not be an issue ... men would not allow this kind of oppression... .," Vedder said at the show. Shortly after the September 11, 2001, terrorist attacks, they performed at "America: A

Concert for Heroes" to raise funds for families of those killed in the attacks. And in 2004, they joined Bruce Springsteen, R.E.M., the Dave Matthews Band, and many other acts in the "Vote for Change" tour, urging people to register and support Democratic candidate John Kerry in his race to deny President George W. Bush a second term.

The "Vote for Change" tour did not succeed in preventing Bush's reelection. Yet occurrences during their 2003 tour showed just how far the rock audience had become estranged from the progressive politics that Pearl Jam and their predecessors had purveyed going back to the 1960s. At the opening concert in Denver, hundreds of fans walked out during the encore after Vedder impaled a mask of Bush on a microphone stand in protest of his policies. "Several concertgoers booed and shouted Vedder to shut up as he told the crowd he was against the war and Bush."[16] Though Pearl Jam noted that several dozen out of 12,000 was not a large amount (and that many concertgoers traditionally leave during an encore to get a head start on traffic), it was clear from the war of words on the Internet that a number of fans found Vedder's expression of free speech to be offensive. Many of the comments echoed the "America: Love It or Leave It" rhetoric spewed by hawks during the Vietnam protests, and made one lament that the country had not learned anything since.

The nineties punk movement didn't die with Nirvana. Band survivors Kris Novoselic and Dave Grohl formed the successful band Foo Fighters. Smashing Pumpkins, from Chicago, shared a number of fateful intersections with Nirvana. Their 1993 album *Siamese Dream* was produced by Butch Vig, who had recorded both *Nevermind* and Sonic Youth's *Goo*.

Smashing Pumpkins' guitarist, singer, and songwriter Billy Corgan was less reticent about fame than many of his alternative-rock counterparts. He wanted it, badly. He went for big, heavy-guitar grandeur that owed less to punk and grunge than it did to the aural majesty of 1970s prog-rock. Those ambitions were signaled most clearly on the 1993 album *Siamese Dream* and on the 1995 album *Mellon Collie and the Infinite Sadness*, a twenty-eight-track, two-CD set that was a career pinnacle, commercially and artistically. Despite its pretensions (disc one was called "Dawn to Dusk"; disc two, "Twilight to Starlight") it has been certified for sale of more than nine million copies. The success of

Siamese Dream allowed Smashing Pumpkins to be named headliners at 1994's Lollapalooza festival (after Nirvana decided to withdraw from the tour), a summer-long musical carnival that toured North America with multiple stages and local crafts- and issues-oriented booths.

Lollapalooza ran from 1991 to 1997 before being revived as a two-day event in Chicago in 2003. It was the creation of Perry Farrell, a Los Angeles scenester originally from Queens, New York, who created the band Jane's Addiction in the late 1980s. The group's two albums, *Nothing's Shocking* (1988) and *Ritual de lo Habitual* (1990) treated metal and funk as a kind of ambient sound. At best, they were as heady as a hipster Van Halen; at worst, they were as pretentious as a hipster Van Halen. Lollapalooza's distinction was the diversity of its acts, a definitive menage of nineties rock, punk, and rap. In 1994, for example, the year Smashing Pumpkins headlined, the main stage also included the Beastie Boys, George Clinton & the P-Funk All-Stars, and Green Day. The second stage featured the Flaming Lips, Guided by Voices, Lambchop, and rappers/marijuana advocates Cypress Hill. In 1995, Sonic Youth, Hole, Cypress Hill, and alt-rock pioneers Pavement played main stage, with pop-rapper Coolio, electronica star Moby, and the newly popular L.A. singer-songwriter and experimental studio visionary Beck on the side stage.

To properly understand what a cultural watershed this was, one should know that Sonic Youth, Smashing Pumpkins, and Cypress Hill each appeared as cartoon characters based on themselves in the "Homerpalooza" episode of the animated TV series *The Simpsons*. Considered one of the great moments in *The Simpsons* canon, the 1996 episode features Homer Simpson seeing those bands at a rock festival and finding himself onstage performing his specialty freak-show act: catching cannonballs with his stomach.[17]

Though Lollapalooza packed it in after 1997, the idea of large multi-act summer touring festivals was established as an annual rite. Coincidentally, 1997 was the year Canadian singer-songwriter Sarah McLachlan launched Lilith Fair, a touring aggregation of all-female musicians. It ran through 1999. Focusing on such acts as Sheryl Crow, Indigo Girls, Fiona Apple, Dar Williams, and Suzanne Vega the first two years, Lilith took a more varied approach in 1999, featuring country stars the Dixie Chicks, rapper Queen Latifah, and the reunited rock band the Pretenders.

McLachlan only planned Lilith for three years. Her purpose was to defy the conventional wisdom of the concert-booking industry, which was that people would not pay to see two women artists on the same bill. (The same absurd formula applied to radio, where most commercial music stations would not program two songs in a row by women.) McLachlan made her point. It was the top-grossing festival tour in 1997 and 1998, and more than 100 performers rotated through the Lilith roster during its three years.

The two major summer tours are Ozzfest and the Vans Warped Tour. The Ozzfest, created in 1996 and run by heavy-metal guru Ozzy Osbourne and his manager wife, Sharon, not surprisingly leans heavily towards metal. The Vans Warped Tour began in 1994. Its founder, Kevin Lyman, had worked on skateboard tours. (Sponsor Vans manufactures skateboard apparel) and features hard rock that leans towards punk and the subgenre known as emo: Senses Fail, the Academy Is ..., From First to Last, Motion City Soundtrack. The 2006 Warped tour also featured veteran metal/punk band Helmet and rockers Joan Jett & the Blackhearts. Interestingly, Lilith Fair excepted, the Vans Warped tour is the rare rock event that attracts large amounts, perhaps a majority in some cities, of female teens.

In addition, rural Manchester, Tennessee, is the site of the annual Bonnaroo Music & Arts Festival one weekend every June. When it started in 2002, Bonnaroo featured jam bands, which tend to be groups who can trace their spiritual ancestry to the Grateful Dead and the Allman Bros. Band — improvisational, blues/country/roots-inspired acts. Bonnaroo can be considered a descendent of the H.O.R.D.E. tour, founded by jam band Blues Traveler, which took kindred bands across the country from 1992 to 1997.

The 2002 Bonnaroo featured such dominant jam names as Widespread Panic, Galactic, Robert Randolph & the Family Band (one of the few black rock bands on the circuit), String Cheese Incident, Gov't Mule, and Trey Anastasio; the latter is the former guitarist of one of the most revered post-Dead jam band, the Vermont quartet known as Phish. Another immensely popular group associated with jam bands is the Dave Matthews Band. Founded in 1991 in Charlottesville,

Virginia, the Matthews Band adds two ingredients that put them at the head of their class: accomplished songwriting and inclusion of first-rate jazz musicians, giving their improvisations both substance and texture. The DMB, like many others, were quick to use the Internet to create and communicate with a community of fans. Their 2006 album compilation *The Best of What's Around,* consists of two discs: one of previously unreleased live tracks, the other studio recordings selected by fans via the davematthewsband.com Web site.

Sensing a lull in the appeal of a jam band-focused event, Bonnaroo's promoters successfully expanded their palette in 2006, bringing in such mainstream rock bands as Radiohead, Tom Petty & the Heartbreakers, Sonic Youth, blues rocker Bonnie Raitt, Elvis Costello & the Imposters, and British cult favorites Gomez in addition to venerable jam acts like the Grateful Dead's Phil Lesh & Friends, and new heroes of the scene, My Morning Jacket.

Yet another annual festival, the Coachella Valley Music Festival, near Indio, California, specializes in "edgy" alternative rock and dance music. Its setting, at the end of April in the Mojave Desert, wouldn't seem conducive to dance music, but 2006 headliners included the resurrected eighties dance-rock band Depeche Mode, and contemporary danceable rock bands like Franz Ferdinand, the Scissor Sisters, Daft Punk, and Bloc Party. But the Coachella community takes its edgy vibe seriously, and the inclusion of superstar Madonna in the dance tent was greeted with disfavor by some.

What we can see from this multitude of somewhat exclusive festivals (there is inevitably some overlap) is just how fragment the rock audience became in the 1990s, and remains so. In a 2006 interview with the online culture magazine *PopMatters,* critic Robert Christgau bemoaned the Balkanization of musical styles. "Right now there are so many divisions in music, I wouldn't try to list them now." Christgau lamented the passing of what he called a "monoculture," a time when "everyone listened to the same music on the radio."[18]

The lack of a cultural consensus as to even who the top stars are in rock makes it difficult to establish an overarching theme, or even genre definitions to rock from the early 1990s on. As Christgau puts it, "go to a New York record store and there are 20 different kinds of alternative music."

So there are probably a few dozen rock acts that deserve attention here, and leaving some important ones out is almost unavoidable. (Recently, an entire biography chronicling the undeniably modest achievements of the band Modest Mouse was published.) And the career trajectories have also become unpredictable. A few noteworthy anomalies follow.

The Pixies: The Boston quartet's debut album, *Surfer Rosa* was released in 1988 and became an influential cult favorite. Critic Douglas Wolk called it "a shocking new idea: noise rock your little sister could sing along to."[19] The Pixies released three other albums: *Doolittle, Bossanova,* and *Trompe Le Monde,* none of which reached higher than No. 70 (*Bossanova*) on the *Billboard* Top Albums chart. Bassist Kim Deal also had a band called the Breeders with her twin sister Kelley. Singer/songwriter Black Francis began a career as Frank Black after the Pixies broke up in 1993. The breakup was acrimonious, and the band was supposedly history until a reunion tour in 2004 that sold out every show throughout the world. Neither band nor promoters nor fans can really explain why Pixies-mania broke out on a level that never existed before. But reviewing the tour DVD, one reviewer said, "The fury, anguish and melodies sound so fresh it's as though they've been vacuum-sealed."[20]

Green Day: Just a boyish poppy punk trio from Berkeley, California, Green Day exploded in 1994 with its album *Dookie,* which sold more than 9 million copies, and was thought to be a fluke. The next album, *Insomniac,* sold respectably, but Green Day didn't show any signs of lasting. Half a dozen albums followed, sustaining a relatively low level of awareness for the band. Ten years after *Dookie,* the band released *American Idiot,* a punk "rock opera." Some songs ran longer than nine minutes; titles included "Boulevard of Broken Dreams" and "Jesus of Suburbia." This reinvigorated Green Day's career and had people looking at them in a completely different way. "In its musical muscle and sweeping, politically charged narrative, it's something of a masterpiece, and one of the few — if not the only — records of 2004 to convey what it feels like to live in the strange, bewildering America of the early 2000s." [21] The awards seemed like they'd never stop: Grammy Award for Best Rock Album; "Favorite Album" from the American Music Awards; and winner of seven of eight MTV Video Awards, including Video of the Year (for "Boulevard").

Red Hot Chili Peppers: Founded as a rap/funk/punk/rock band in Los Angeles in the late 1980s, the Chili Peppers have had their ups and downs. Cofounding guitarist Hillel Slovak died of a heroin overdose in 1988 just as the band's star was ascending. With Anthony Kiedis (vocals) and a bass player known as Flea, the band went through a number of guitarists over the years, with Dave Navarro, formerly of Jane's Addiction, stabilizing the lineup in 1993. When Navarro left in 1998, Slovak's original replacement, John Frusciante rejoined the group. Their 1991 album *Blood Sugar Sex Magik* established them as stars, and the melodic paean to a homeless man, "Under the Bridge," made them fixtures on MTV and radio. Though albums like *Californication* (2000) sold well, they seemed to have been overshadowed by any of a dozen alternative or modern rock groups in the increasingly fragmented marketplace. In 2004, a three-night series at London's Hyde Park in June stunned the concert world by selling out nearly a quarter-million tickets. The unexpected triumph inspired the band's creative resurgence, and their 2006 double-album *Stadium Arcadium* debuted at No. 1 in the United States and as many as twenty-five other countries; the single "Dani California" was one of the rare tracks that transcended radio's format divisions, and was a hit on *Billboard*'s modern rock, mainstream rock, and pop (Hot 100) charts. The video has been described as a "quasi-chronology" of the history of rock. Flea told a U.K. music magazine, "We mainly did eras, not actual people: rockabilly, British Invasion, psychedelia, funk, glam, punk, goth, hair metal, grunge, and ourselves being the sum of all those parts."[22]

Hip-Hop Ascendant

By the mid-1990s, hip-hop had supplanted rock as music of protest and teen rebellion. Since the breakthroughs of Run-DMC, LL Cool J, Kurtis Blow, and others in the 1980s, rap spread from urban areas to completely penetrate suburban and even rural America.

"Grunge had restored rock music as the voice of American youth rebellion,"[23] writes Bakari Kitwana. "Unfortunately, for a generation in need of a cultural movement to call its own, by 1995 ... grunge had reached its peak." After Kurt Cobain's death, as grunge declined in popularity and influence, "countless white kids, joining their

African-American and Latino counterparts, began to identify more strongly with hip-hop's cadence."

By 1997, one-time Harlem entrepreneur Sean Combs (known since as Puff Daddy. P. Diddy, and currently Diddy) and his Bad Boy label had or was featured on three No. 1 records, as his protégé the Notorious B.I.G. had or shared two No. 1's, including "No Money No Problems" with Puff Daddy & Mase. At the same time on the West Coast, entrepreneur Suge Knight, a mammoth man with gang connections, had put his Death Row label on the map, beginning in 1992 with acts like Snoop Doggy Dogg, Dr. Dre, and 2Pac (Tupac Shakur).

By conventional measures, it seemed as if the hip-hop world was bent on mutually assured destruction. In 1995, Shakur was shot in a supposed robbery outside a recording studio in New York; he publicly blamed former friends Combs and "Biggie" for the shooting. The competitiveness fueled by publicly displays of disrespect kept tensions spiraling between Knight's Death Row on the West Coast and Combs's Bad Boy on the East Coast. Members of Tha Dogg Pound, a Death Row group, were shot at in 1996 while filming a video called "New York, New York;" Tupac released a track called "Hit 'Em Up" which attacked Biggie and aimed sexual innuendo at Bad Boy's female rapper (and Biggie's estranged wife) Faith Evans.

Finally, after a heavyweight championship fight in Las Vegas, a car carrying Knight and Shakur came under a fusillade of bullets. Knight's wounds were minor; Shakur's were fatal. A few months later, in early 1997, the Notorious B.I.G. was assassinated in a drive-by shooting after the "Soul Train" awards in Los Angeles. Biggie had just completed an album called *Life and Death;* released a few days after his death, it was a multimillion seller. No one has ever been arrested or tried in either murder.

Though a great deal of soul-searching took place in the rap community after the murders, business was too good to stop. In 1998, hip-hop artist Lauryn Hill, formerly of the Fugees, and her album, *The Miseducation of Lauryn Hill,* won five Grammy Awards, sealing hip-hop's legitimacy at the top level of the music industry. Soon there were primarily white rock bands — Rage Against the Machine, Korn, Linkin Park, Kid Rock among them — integrating rap into their presentation and creating a new hybrid sometimes called nu metal.

The popularity of a white rapper from Detroit named Eminem (for the initials of his given name, Marshall Mathers) raised some eyebrows. This was the pattern that had been seen whenever any black form of music became popular, the inevitable white "interpreter," generally came along, draining the music's authenticity while outselling the originators. But Eminem was no Pat Boone to, say Tupac's Little Richard. If anything, it was as vulgar, raw — and engaging — as any black hip-hop. With the black Dr. Dre, formerly of Death Row, as his producer and with a knack for controversy, Eminem became a huge star. That he is as dexterous, sharp, and rhythmic as any of the greatest rappers does not undermine his case at all.

A brilliant provocateur, Eminem understands the potent payoff he represents as a white rapper. In "White America," the lead song of his 2002 album *The Eminem Show*, he boasts, "Look at these eyes, baby blue … if they were brown Shady lose." Well, maybe not lose, but not do as well: "Look at my sales, let's do the math, If I was black, I would've sold half."

Another white rapper, known as The Streets (Mike Skinner), became one of England's first successful rappers. Working the mic in with an emphatic local accent (he is from Birmingham) over relaxed beats, the Streets' breakthrough was 2002's *Original Pirate Material*, a critical and commercial tour de force in the United Kingdom. Tracks like "Stay Positive," "Let's Push Things Forward," and "Don't Mug Yourself" established him as the philosophical voice of Britain's young white working class. Of course, his quick stardom created a distance between himself and that working class. After *A Grand Don't Come for Free* (2004) Skinner found himself living the celebrity life he could not have imagined three years earlier. On his MySpace page, The Streets describes his third album, *The Hardest Way to Make an Easy Living* (2006): "The album starts and ends with a drug and alcohol inspired panic attack. So what else happens? Lets see … Losing hundreds of thousands of pounds spread-betting … Watching the unnamed female pop star he'd been taking crack cocaine and having sex with the night before looking surprisingly presentable on CD-UK the next morning." Whatever you make of The Street's music or lifestyle, he did allow a spotlight to shine on other U.K. rappers, most notably Dizzee Rascal.

The Streets seemed to be going in the direction of Pete Doherty of The Libertines. One of the United Kingdom's most promising rock bands in the early-twenty-first century, the Libertines stalled as Doherty's arrests and overdoses from substance abuse threatened both his career and his life.

Meanwhile, the U.K. rock scene seemed as lively and progressive in the best sense. The sharply dressed Franz Ferdinand, from Glasgow, added some much needed style and celebration on their 2004 self-titled debut album. Recorded for the independent Domino label, the album sold 1.2 million copies in the United Kingdom and eventually 1 million in the United States. Their second album, *You Could Have It So Much Better*, released in 2005, was solid, but sold only a fraction (300,000 in the United Kingdom, 500,000 in the U.S.) of what its predecessor sold. This illuminated a reality of the twenty-first-century rock music business: the difficulty of developing artists with career longevity in an era when single-track Internet downloads and competition from other entertainment options (video games, cell phones, instant messaging, and social networking sites such as MySpace and Friendster) make rock music just another commodity.

Some bands seemed to have an instinct for using the Internet to create excitement before an album was even released. The Arctic Monkeys had given away free song downloads on its Web site. Word –of mouth, spread virally on the Web, led to an unprecedented level of anticipation. Unlike record industry "hyping" of the past, however, enthusiasm for the Arctic Monkeys came from a spontaneously developed fan base. When their 2006 debut album, *Whatever I Say I Am, That's What I'm Not*, was released in January 2006 it sold well over 100,000 copies in the United Kingdom the first day, and 400,000 its first week, including online sales. Featuring the singing and lyrics of nineteen-year-old Alex Turner, the tunes featured irresistible guitar-and-dance groove of the hit "I Bet You Look Good On the Dancefloor" and witty, prodigiously mature insights into youth-culture mating habits, best exemplified by the ironic song title, "You Probably Couldn't See for the Lights But You Were Looking Straight at Me."

But the United States has not responded to the Arctic Monkeys. Its 34,000 first-week sales when the album was released in March 2006 was good for a debut album by an act on an independent label. But reviews of their concert performers were lukewarm. And sales peaked at about 258,000, just a fraction of the over 1 million sales in the much smaller United Kingdom.

American bands had similar problems attracting buyers attention. Two of the most heralded bands, the Strokes from New York City, and the White Stripes, from Detroit, have received endless press coverage, critical respect (more for the White Stripes than the Strokes), but have never developed more than a cult following. (These bands sell better in the United Kingdom, where the competition from hip-hop artists for the youthful dollar is not as keen.) The Strokes revived a kind of New York fashion consciousness, and have made three albums that show surface similarities to the seventies rock of Lou Reed without any accompanying musical depth. The White Stripes, the duo, have considerably more depth. Jack White plays guitar and sings; Meg White is the drummer. Writing compelling original tunes and variations on classic blues and hard-country themes, the White Stripes play with volcanic power. White's accomplishments include producing *Van Lear Rose,* a 2004 album by country legend Loretta Lynn that stands with the most interesting work of her forty-year career.

So many bands, so little time: the Flaming Lips, from Oklahoma City, had been around since the early 1990s but released their classic, *Yoshimi Battles the Pink Robots,* in 2002, a beautiful blend of song craft and dreamy, psychedelic sounds. Wilco, the showcase for ambitious singer-songwriter Jeff Tweedy, was formed after the 1994 split of the seminal alt-country band Uncle Tupelo. (Tupelo's Jay Farrar left to form Son Volt.) Wilco has evolved from that urban-twang style to the wildly creative *Yankee Hotel Foxtrot* (2002) and *A Ghost Is Born* (2004). The long-delayed *Foxtrot* was considered lacking in commercial appeal by Wilco's longtime label, Reprise Records. Instead, it was released by Nonesuch Records (which, like Reprise, is part of the Warner Bros. Records group). Summing up the critical consensus, it was "A carefully layered, multifaceted album in terms of its sound, music, lyrics, and thematic cohesion — in short, a great musical achievement."[24]

The experimental, genre-defying sound of these two albums place Wilco on the cutting edge of rock creativity in the twenty-first century.

You'd have to go all the way back to 1997 to the Radiohead album *OK Computer* to find mainstream music that is as daring and successful.

Spin magazine chose *OK Computer* as the No. 1 album of the 100 it selected for the magazine's twentieth anniversary issue in 2005. "It's not an effortless collection of obvious melodies, nor is it a barricade of esoteric noise — it's somewhere in between," Chuck Klosterman wrote in that issue. Songs like "Airbag," "Paranoid Android," and "Karma Police" conjure a future controlled by technology; what makes *OK Computer* so special is that the studio technology used to create that audio imagery sounds so warm and human. For those who found the effort of leader Thom Yorke and his bandmates to be "pretentious," Klosterman smartly says, "Pretentious implies that the album is something that it is not, and this is not the case; 'OK Computer' is supposed to be artful and exploratory and accessible, and that's what it is … It's more like [it] extended far beyond their wildest expectations."

iTunes & Downloads

In the eyes of the record business, if it weren't for illegal downloads, Eminem would've sold twice as much. Or three times as much. For by 2002, illegal file-sharing — the download of compressed audio files, or MP3s — traded freely on the Internet, had become epidemic as legitimate CD sales plummeted. The appearance of Apple Computer's iTunes Music Store at the end of 2003 gave hope that paid downloads could become a source of revenue while the RIAA cracked down on file-sharing abusers and sued them in civil court. The record industry has been especially tough on colleges. In 2003, the RIAA sued the operators of private computer networks on the campuses of Rensselear Polytechnic Institute, Michigan Technical University, and Princeton University. According to *Wired News*, "the association described the file-sharing systems, which are open only to students on the universities' internal networks, as miniature versions of Napster" — the software and network that led to the explosion of music file swapping.

The four networks were offering nearly 2.5 million files, it said, including more than 1 million files on the largest network alone.[25]

The complaints ask for the legal limit on damages in such cases, $150,000 per each copyright infringed. It's a controversial tactic that even some musicians object to — it's a desperate business that sues its own customers.

In February 2006, iTunes sold its one-billionth download, but at 99 cents apiece and with many hands splitting the pot, it has not been enough to turn around the blockbuster-deprived record business. Hip-hop and pop continue to dominate. Trendy rock bands come and go, but even good ones, like Scotland's Franz Ferdinand, have trouble selling the huge numbers and building the solid, loyal fan base that the R.E.M.s, and U2s spent so much time developing. In the rush for immediate gratification, the music industry has skimped on talent development, going for the quick hits with young R&B acts and proven crossover pop stars like Mariah Carey.

This is also the cultural moment of *American Idol,* where the pop stars of tomorrow are selected through a process of elimination, and sometimes humiliation. Stars like the pop singer Kelly Clarkson and country hit-maker Carrie Underwood got their start on *Idol.* The first rock 'n' roller with an authentic style appears to be Bo Bice, who has thus far been unable to create his own musical footprint outside the efficient but creatively limited *Idol* machinery. Since then, Daughtry has become the first hit rock band to be led by an *American Idol* contestant, Chris Daughtry.

There is another arena in which fans vote for their favorite artists, albeit more directly. The rise of immensely popular social networking sites like MySpace and video networking site YouTube has allowed literally tens of thousands of musical acts to avoid the music industry and take their music and videos directly to fans. Copyright-ownership issues still remain to be worked out, and the major labels are trying to establish some sort of foothold in these new viral outlets before the corporate world is reduced to the sidelines entirely.

In that marketplace, rock 'n' roll is still a vital niche, but a niche it is. In an era of quick technological change, of downloads to cell phones and instant messaging and video games, ownership of music is no longer a priority for teens. Rock 'n' roll is here to stay, though whether it will ever permeate as much of the culture as it did in the previous fifty years is doubtful. But as Chuck Berry once sang, "You Never Can Tell."

Bibliography

Alderman, John. *Sonic Boom: Napster, MP3, and the New Pioneers of Music*. Cambridge, MA: Perseus Publishing, 2001.

Austen, Jake. *TV a-Go-Go: Rock on TV from "American Bandstand" to American Idol*. Chicago: Chicago Review Press, 2005.

Azerrad, Michael. *Come As You Are: The Story of Nirvana*. New York: Main Street Books/Doubleday, 1993.

———. *Our Band Could Be Your Life: Scenes from the American Indie Underground 1981–1991*. New York: Little, Brown & Co., 2003.

Bangs, Lester. *Psychotic Reactions and Carburetor Dung*. New York: Anchor Books, 1988.

Baughman, James L. *The Republic of Mass Culture*. Baltimore: Johns Hopkins Press, 1992.

Black, Jeremy. *Altered States: America Since the Sixties*. London: Reaktion Books, 2006.

Bronson, Fred. *The Billboard Book of Number One Hits*. New York: Billboard Books, 1985.

Bryant, Clora, et al. *Central Avenue Sounds: Jazz in Los Angeles*. Berkeley, CA: University of California Press, 1999.

Carlin, Peter Ames. *Catch a Wave: The Rise, Fall and Redemption of the Beach Boys' Brian Wilson*. New York: Rodale Books, 2006.

Christgau, Robert. *Any Old Way You Choose It*. Baltimore: Penguin, 1973.

———. *Christgau's Record Guide. Rock Albums of the '70s*. New Haven, CT. Ticknor & Fields, 1981.

———. *Christgau's Record Guide: The '80s*. New York: Pantheon Books, 1990.

———. *Christgau's Consumer Guide, Albums of the '90s*. New York: St. Martin's, 2000.

Coleman, Rick. *Fats Domino and the Lost Dawn of Rock 'n' Roll*. Boston: Da Capo Press, 2006.

Crenshaw, Marshall. *Hollywood Rock: A Guide to Rock 'n' Roll in the Movies*. New York: Agincourt Press, 1994.

Dalton, David. *The Rolling Stones: The First Twenty-Five Years*. New York: Alfred A. Knopf, 1981.

Davies, Hunter. *The Beatles*. New York: Dell, 1968

Davis, Clive. With James Willwerth. *Clive: Inside the Music Business*. New York: William Morrow & Co., 1974.

Dettmar, Kevin. *Is Rock Dead?* New York: Routledge Books, 2006.

DiMartino, Dave. *Singer-Songwriters*. New York: Billboard Books, 1994.

Didion, Joan. *The White Album*. New York: Simon & Schuster, 1979.

Edelstein, Andrew J., *The Pop Sixties*. New York: World Almanac, 1985.

Emerick, Geoff, and Howard Massey. *Here, There and Everywhere: My Life Recording the Music of the Beatles*. New York: Gotham Books, 2006.

Emerson, Ken. *Always Magic in the Air.* New York: Viking, 2005.

Fonarow, Wendy. *Empire of Dirt: The Aesthetics and Rituals of British Indies Music.* Middletown, CT: Wesleyan University Press, 2005.

Fong-Torres, Ben, ed. *What's That Sound: The Contemporary Scene from the Pages of Rolling Stone.* New York: Anchor Books, 1976.

Fornatale, Peter, and Joshua Mills. *Radio in the Television Age.* Woodstock, NY: The Overlook Press, 1980.

Frith, Simon. *Sound Effects.* New York: Pantheon, 1982.

Gaines, Donna. *Teenage Wasteland: Suburbia's Dead End Kids.* New York: Harper Perennial, 1991.

George, Nelson. *The Death of Rhythm & Blues.* New York: E.P. Dutton, 1989.

George-Warren, Holly, intro. *Neil Young: The Rolling Stones Files.* New York: Hyperion, 1994.

Goldberg, Danny. *Dispatches from the Culture Wars: How the Left Lost Teen Spirit.* New York: Miramax Books, 2003.

Guralnick, Peter. *Sweet Soul Music.* New York: Harper & Row, 1986.

———. *Dream Boogie: The Triumph of Sam Cooke.* New York: Little, Brown & Co., 2005.

Henderson, David. *'Scuse Me While I Kiss the Sky: The Life of Jimi Hendrix.* New York: Bantam, 1978.

Heslam, David, ed. *The Rock 'n' Roll Years: The Chronicle of the Lives and Times of the Rock 'n' Roll Generation from 1955 to the Present Day.* New York: Crescent Books, 1990.

Heylin, Clinton. *Bob Dylan Behind the Shades.* New York: Summit Books, 1991.

———, ed. *The Penguin Book of Rock & Roll Writing.* London: Viking, 1992.

———, ed. *All Yesterday's Parties: The Velvet Underground in Print 1966–1970.* Cambridge, MA: The Da Capo Press, 2005.

———. *From the Velvets to the Voidoids: A Pre-Punk History for a Post-Punk World.* New York: Penguin Books, 1993.

Hirshey, Dave. *Air Guitar.* Los Angeles: Art Issues Press, 1997.

Hoskyns, Barney. *Hotel California.* Hoboken, NJ: John Wiley & Sons, 2006.

Howard, Gerald, ed. *The Sixties: The Art, Attitudes, Politics and Media of Our Most Explosive Decade.* New York: Marlowe & Co., 1995.

Jancik, Wayne. *The Billboard Book of One-Hit Wonders.* New York: Billboard Books, 1990.

Jenkins, Phillip. *Decade of Nightmares: The End of the Sixties and the Making of Eighties America.* New York: Oxford University Press, 2006.

Johnson, Haynes. *The Age of Anxiety.* New York: Harcourt, 2005.

Kaiser, Charles. *1968 in America.* New York: Grove Press, 1988.

Killen, Andreas. *1973 Nervous Breakdown: Watergate, Warhol and the Birth of Post-Sixties America.* New York: Bloomsbury U.S.A., 2006.

Kitwana, Bakari. *Why White Kids Love Hip-Hop.* New York: Basic Books, 2005.

Klosterman, Chuck. *Fargo Rock City: Heavy Metal Odyssey in Rural North Dakota.* New York: Scribner, 2001.

Luftig, Stacy, ed. *The Paul Simon Companion.* London: Omnibus Press, 1997.

Lydon, Michael. *Rock Folk: Portraits from the Rock 'n' Roll Pantheon.* New York: Citadel Press, 1990.

———. *Flashbacks: Eyewitness Accounts of the Rock Revolution,* 1964–1974. New York: Routledge, 2003.

Lytle, Mark. *America's Uncivil Wars: The Sixties Era from Elvis to the Fall of Richard Nixon.* New York: Oxford University Press, 2005.

MacDonald, Ian. *Revolution in the Head: The Beatles' Records and the Sixties.* New York: Henry Holt, 1994.

Marcus, Greil. *Ranters & Crowd Pleasers: Punk in Pop Music, 1977–1992.* New York: Doubleday, 1993.

———. *Mystery Train: Images of America in Rock 'n' Roll Music.* New York: E.P. Dutton, 1975.

———, ed. *Stranded.* New York: Alfred A. Knopf, 1979.

———. *Like a Rolling Stone: Bob Dylan at the Crossroads.* New York: Public Affairs Press, 2005.

———. *Invisible Republic: Bob Dylan's Basement Tapes.* New York: Henry Holt, 1997.

———, ed. *Rock and Roll Will Stand.* Boston: Beacon Press, 1969.

Marsh, Dave. *Born to Run: The Bruce Springsteen Story.* New York: Doubleday, 1979.

———. *Glory Days: Bruce Springsteen in the 1980s.* New York: Pantheon Books, 1987.

———. *Louie Louie.* New York: Hyperion, 1993.

———. *Trapped: Michael Jackson and the Crossover Dream.* New York: Bantam, 1985.

———. *The Heart of Rock & Soul: The 1001 Greatest Singles Ever Made.* New York: Da Capo Press, 1999.

McDonnell, Evelyn, and Ann Powers, eds. *Rock She Wrote.* New York, Delta, 1995.

Melly, George. *Revolt into Style: The Pop Arts.* Garden City, NY: Doubleday Anchor, 1971.

Miller, James. *Flowers in the Dustbin: The Rise of Rock and Roll, 1947–1977.* New York: Simon & Schuster, 1999.

Moorhead, Virgil. *The Producer as Composer.* Cambridge, MA: The MIT Press, 2005.

Neely, Tim. *Standard Catalog of American Records, 1950–1975.* Iola, WI: Krause Publishing, 2004.

Norman, Philip. *Sympathy for the Devil: The Rolling Stones Story.* New York: Linden Press, 1984.

Nuttall, Jeff. *Bomb Culture.* New York: Dell, 1968.

Otis, Johnny. *Listen to the Lambs.* New York: W.W. Norton Co., 1968.

Pareles, Jon, and Patricia Romanowski. *The Rolling Stone Encyclopedia of Rock & Roll.* New York: Summit Books, 1983.

Pollock, Bruce, and John Wagman. *The Face of Rock & Roll: Images of a Generation.* New York: Holt, Rinehart and Winston, 1978.

Reid, Jan. *Layla and Other Assorted Love Songs by Derek and the Dominos.* New York: Rodale Books, 2006.

Reynolds, Simon. *Rip It Up and Start Again: Postpunk 1978–1984.* New York: Penguin, 2006.

Ro, Ronin. *Gangsta: Merchandising the Rhymes of Violence.* St. Martin's Press, NY, 1996.

Robbins, Ira, ed. *The Trouser Press Record Guide, Fourth Edition.* New York: Collier, 1991.

Robbins, Ira, ed., and David Sprague, deputy ed. *The Trouser Press Guide to '90s Rock.* New York: Fireside, 1997.

Robbins, Tom. *Wild Ducks Flying Backwards: The Short Writings of Tom Robbins.* New York: Bantam Dell, 2005.

Savage, John. *England's Dreaming.* New York: St. Martin's Press, 1992.

Sinclair, John. *Guitar Army: Street Writings/Prison Writings.* New York: Douglas Book Corp., 1972.

Stambler, Irwin. *The Encyclopedia of Pop, Rock and Soul.* New York: St. Martin's Press, 1989.

Terkel, Studs. *And They All Sang: Adventures of an Eclectic Disc Jockey.* New York: The New Press, 2005.

Time-Life Books. *Rock & Roll Generation: Teen Life in the 50s.* Alexandria, Va: Time-Life Books, 1998.

Troy, Gil. *Morning in America: How Ronald Reagan Invented the 1980s.* Princeton, NJ: Princeton University Press, 2005.

Wexler, Jerry, and David Ritz. *Rhythm and the Blues.* New York: Alfred A. Knopf, 1993.

Whitburn, Joel. *Billboard Top Pop Albums 1955–2001.* Menomonee Falls, WI: Record Research, 2001.

———. *Billboard Top Pop Singles 1955–2002.* Menomonee Falls, WI: Record Research, 2003.

White, Charles. *The Life and Times of Little Richard.* New York: Harmony, 1984.

White, Edmund M., ed. *The Pop Culture Tradition: Readings with Writings for Analysis.* New York: W.W. Norton Co., 1972.

Willis, Ellen. *Beginning to See the Light: Pieces of a Decade.* New York: Wideview Books, 1982.

Williams, Paul. *The 20th Century's Greatest Hits: A Top 40 List.* New York: Tom Doherty Associates, 2000.

Williams, Paul. *Outlaw Blues: A Book of Rock Music.* New York: Pocket Books, 1970.

Wolk, Douglas. *James Brown's Live at the Apollo.* New York: Continuum Books, 2004.

Discography: Recommended Listening

The purpose of this list is to reinforce the importance of some essential rock recordings, as well as to compensate somewhat for the absence, neglect, or short-shrift that some important recording artists may have received in the main text because of narrative strategy, space limitation, forgetfulness, or any other rationalization one could give for their omission.

Because so many historic rock recordings, especially ones by major artists, have been reissued numerous times in various CD packages or configurations, I have given preference to those readily available. The label (record company) may be different from the one on which it was originally issued: current companies that excel in such reissues are Rhino, Shout Factory, and Sony BMG's Legacy series. Although my preference might be for individual albums as distinct artistic works, there is something to be said for accessibility and inclusiveness of many "best-of" or "greatest hits" compilation. I've tried to avoid expensive multi-disc box sets where those boxes are aimed at the passionate collector or completist, but some, especially label anthologies, can be recommended to the reader. In many instances, I'll also recommend individual tracks deemed either great or important or meaningful or representative, which with few exceptions can be purchased for download from online stores such as iTunes.

AC/DC. *Back In Black*. 1980.
>Testosterone and alcohol fueled hard rock from Australia, no subtlety, but undeniable in its power.

Aerosmith. *Toys in the Attic*. 1975.
>Swaggering and substantial, the foundation on which their thirty-plus-year career is based.

Allman Brothers Band. *At the Fillmore East*. 1971.

———. *Brothers and Sisters* (1973). The band that defined southern rock.

Band, The. *Music from Big Pink*. 1968.

———. *The Band*. 1969.
>Evocations of a less angry America resonated at the end of the'60s courtesy of Bob Dylan's former backup band, now standing firmly on their own.

Beach Boys. *20 Good Vibrations, The Greatest Hits, Vol. 1.* 1999.
    Good anthology, strong on the band's early '60s surf music and hot rod roots.
———. *Pet Sounds.* 1966. Their masterpiece as a group that challenged the Beatles for artistic supremacy.
    See also Brian Wilson.
Beastie Boys. *Licensed To Ill.* 1986.
    White rap trio pulls off its bad-ass ambition. thanks to producer Rick Rubin's sampling of heavy metal guitar riffs.
Beatles, The. *Meet The Beatles.* 1964.
———. *Rubber Soul.* 1965.
———. *Revolver.* 1966.
———. *Sgt. Pepper's Lonely Hearts Club Band.* 1967.
———. *The Beatles* (aka "The White Album"). 1968.
———. *Abbey Road.* 1969.
———. *1962-1966.* 1973.
———. *1967-1970.* 1973.
    The quartet from Liverpool that reinvigorated, then reinvented rock, pop music, and changed the way a generation thought about themselves and the world around them. These albums provide a timeline for their era.
Berry, Chuck. *His Best, Vol 1.* 1997.
    The foundation of any rock 'n' roll collection.
Black Flag. *Damaged.* 1981.
    Suburban alienation from the flag bearers for hardcore punk rock..
James Brown. *Star Time.* 1991. Four CD set, and not a slack or unnecessary moment on any one of them.
Buffalo Springfield. *Buffalo Springfield.* 1973.
    Collection from their three albums. Neil Young, Stephen Stills and Richie Furay led a group combining rock, r&b and country in a very original way, full of interesting peccadilloes.
Byrds, The. *Mr. Tambourine Man.* 1965. Folk-rock starts here.
———. *Sweetheart Of The Rodeo.* 1968. Country-rock starts here.
Cameo Parkway, 1957-1967. CD box, 2005.
    The Philadelphia label that had America twisting (Chubby Checker) and dancing to teen idols (Bobby Rydell), but also introduced Bob Seger and Question Mark & the Mysterians.
Captain Beefheart. *Trout Mask Replica.* 1969.
    A surreal noisefest from avant-garde rock's big dada.
The Cars. *The Cars.* 1978.
    Catchy singles that sounded great on the radio ("Let's Go"), with avant-garde undercurrents that made them a quintessential new wave band.
Cooke, Sam. *Portrait of A Legend 1951-1964.* 2003.
    From gospel to r&b to soul to rock, from one of the era's most charismatic and influential performers.

Costello, Elvis. *My Aim Is True.* 1977.

———. *This Year's Model.* 1978.

———. *Armed Forces.* 1979.

New-wave rock's angry young man eventually revealed himself to be a musician of great range and sophistication, but the bitter diatribes of his early records with the Attractions are still his best.

Cream. *Disraeli Gears.* 1967.

On this second album, the right blues-rock balance for a super trio that could also go too far.

Creedence Clearwater Revival. *Chronicle, the 20 Greatest Hits.* 1991.

Hippie? Frat boy? Soldier? One thing everyone in the '60s could agree on: That CCR was a roots rock band that could party with a message. "Proud Mary," "Bad Moon Rising," "Fortunate Son."

Diddley, Bo. *His Best: The Chess Anniversary Collection.* 1997.

Creator of rock's most important rhythms and a brilliant primitive guitar sound. Essential.

Doors, The. *The Doors.* 1967.

———. *L.A. Woman.* 1971.

One of the most important West Coast bands of the 1960s, the only ones to look deeply into L.A.s dark underbelly. "Light My Fire."

Dion & the Belmonts. *Dion & the Belmonts Greatest Hits.* 2001. Twenty tracks by the great Bronx doo-wop group, plus standouts from Dion's solo career ("The Wanderer," "Runaround Sue").

Dylan, Bob: *Bringing It All Back Home.* 1965.

———. *Highway 61 Revisited.* 1965.

———. *Blonde on Blonde.* 1966.

———. *Blood on the Tracks.* 1975.

———. *The Bootleg Series, Volumes 1–3.* 1991

The most important singer-songwriter of the rock era changed the way people wrote songs, and the way they heard songs.

Eminem. *The Marshall Mathers Album.* 2000.

Offensive to some for its violence, misogyny and other politically incorrect attitudes, established Eminem as one of rap's most dexterous, effective and musical practitioners.

Eno, Brian. *Here Come the Warm Jets.* 1974.

Experimental sound treatments and wry lyrics within conventional song structures provided a winning combination.

Fall, The. *458489 A Sides.* 1990.

Mark E. Smith, the leader and embodiment of the Fall, has made dozens of idiosyncratic albums since 1979. Controlled ranting never sounded as good as it does in this collection of singles, which were of course never hits and hardly heard in the United States.

Franklin, Aretha. *I Never Loved a Man the Way I Love You.* 1967.

———. *Lady Soul.* 1968.

All royal titles in rock, pop and soul are open to debate, except for Aretha, who has been Queen of Soul since these records were released.

Funkadelic. *One Nation Under a Groove*. 1978.

> At the height of the disco era, a dance record with real, deep grooves, guitar jams and a jumping, freewheeling feel..

Gaye, Marvin. *Anthology: The Best of Marvin Gaye*. 1974.

———. *What's Going On*. 1971.

Geils, J., Band. *The J. Geils Band*. 1970.

> Boston's blues-rock champs, one of the most underrated bands of the early 1970s.

Grateful Dead. *Grateful Dead*. 1967.

———. *Workingman's Dead*. 1970.

———. *American Beauty*. 1970.

———. *Terrapin Station*.1977.

———. *Live at the Cow Palace, New Year's Eve. 1976*. (2007.)

> The debut album in 1967 packed a bluesy wallop with the late Pigpen as focus. The band that supposedly lost itself in the studio made some memorable studio albums, especially the two from 1970, expanding their mellow mythology of trippers and truckers united.

Guns N' Roses. *Appetite for Destruction*. 1987.

———. *Use Your Illusion I* (1991).

> L.A. eighties glamorously degenerate hard rock; GNR walked the walk. Inspiring, formidable. "Welcome to the Jungle."

The Jimi Hendrix Experience. *Are You Experienced*. 1967. ("Purple Haze," "Foxy Lady," "The Wind Cries Mary," "Hey Joe.")

———. *Axis, Bold as Love*. 1968. ("Up from the Skies," "Little Wing," "Spanish Castle Magic.")

———. *Electric Ladyland*. 1968. ("Voodoo Chile," "All Along the Watchtower.")

> The three Hendrix Experience albums prove that magic can be bottled, or at least, recorded — they sound as daring and original today as they did in 1967 and 1968. All three were originally released by Reprise, more recently via MCA/Experience Hendrix.

Holly, Buddy. *50 Classic Recordings*. 1993. ("Not Fade Away," "Peggy Sue," "That'll Be the Day," and forty-seven more.)

> A very complete musical portrait of Holly, the most promising rock artist after Elvis and certainly the most musically influential.

Hüsker Dü, *Zen Arcade*. 1984.

> Minneapolis band whose collision of speed punk and melody made it the hardcore band that came closest to a commercial breakthrough.

Jefferson Airplane. *The Worst of Jefferson Airplane*. 1970.

> Later reissued on CD as *The Best of Jefferson Airplane* by a record company that was not amused by the band's original title for a fairly good selection of strong songs and performances.

Joan Jett & the Blackhearts. *I Love Rock & Roll*.1981.

———. *Sinner*. 2006.

> Every record label passed, so Jett and manager/producer Kenny Laguna started their own Blackheart label. The title song hit No. 1, and throughout the 1980s and early '90s (with a timely 2006 return),

guitarist/singer Jett presented no frills rock 'n' roll with a message of independent, self-reliant womanhood that hugely influenced the riot grrrls and mainstream indie rock, then till now.

John, Elton. *Greatest Hits*. 1974. ("Rocket Man," "Bennie and the Jets," and more.)

———. *Captain Fantastic and the Brown Dirt Cowboy*. 1975.

Deluxe two-CD edition (2005) includes previously unreleased live 2005 performance of John's best album, along with plenty of bonus tracks and the all-important "Philadelphia Freedom."

Kinks, The. *Something Else*. 1967.

———. *Muswell Hillbillies*. 1971.

———. *One More for the Road*. 1980. A live album that really captures the band's energy and occasional loveable sloppiness.

Love. *Forever Changes*. 1967.

The most neglected, influential masterpiece of the sixties, Arthur Lee's multiracial folk-rock-psychedelia alternated fierce potency and cloudlike gentleness, sometimes within the same song.

Lynyrd Skynyrd. *Pronounced Leh-Nerd Skin-Nerd*. 1973.

———. *Second Helping*. 1974.

———. *Nuthin' Fancy*. 1975.

More than a southern rock band, their reputation unfairly sullied by radio's overplay of "Free Bird," they were the outlaw band always one step ahead of the law. "Sweet Home Alabama," "Gimme Three Steps."

Marley, Bob and the Wailers. *Legend*. 1984.

———. *Africa Unite: The Singles Collection*. Either of the above is a suitable introduction to the music of reggae's superstar.

Dave Matthews Band. *The Best of What's Around, Vol. 1*. 2006.

With a selection of tracks from studio albums on one disc, and favorite live performances chosen by fans on the second, this is a fine introduction to one of the most modest, skillful and successful of the '90s-00s jam bands.

Mayfield, Curtis. *Superfly*. 1972.

The great blaxploitation movie soundtrack is also Mayfield's great black rock album.

Moby Grape. *Moby Grape*. 1967.

They were hailed as San Francisco's best group in the year prior to the album's release but hit an immediate backlash as Columbia Records released five debut singles simultaneously. But the songs were that good, though drug and personality clashes resulted in quick oblivion.

Mothers of Invention. *Freak-Out!* 1965.

Debut album by composer-guitarist-bandleader Frank Zappa. Possibly rock's first two-record set, it showcased Zappa's vast musical range of passions, from doo-wop to avant-garde pastiche. This savage anti-authoritarian satire ("Help I'm a Rock," "Trouble Every Day," "Who Are the Brain Police") helped draw the lines in the culture war that would begin raging in the next few years.

Morrissette, Alanis. *Jagged Little Pill*. 1995.

Young woman with guitar, a stark, angry voice and specific grievances; the polished production, rocking band and channeled fury helped it sell 16 million copies, a high-water mark for confessional hard rock by women in the 1990s.

Motorhead. *No Sleep 'til Hammersmith*. 1988.

British speed-metal loud enough to make the neighbor's lawn turn brown, as leader Lemmy once said.

Mott the Hoople. *All the Young Dudes*. 1972 (Legacy edition 2006.)

An album that had everything: Lou Reed's "Sweet Jane," a title song written and produced by David Bowie. Not a big hit, but a compelling snapshot of its era.

New York Dolls. *New York Dolls*. (1973)

———. *Too Much, Too Soon*. (1974)

———. *One Day It Will Please Us To Remember Even This*. (2006)

Rambunctious street swagger on the'70's albums; rambunctious street swagger refined and grown up on the 2006 release..

Nirvana. *Nevermind*. 1991.

Made grunge a household word, whether they liked it or not. Kurt Cobain's unexpected emergence as voice of his generation, whether he liked it or not.

Parliament. *Mothership Connection*. 1976.

Funk-rock masterpiece.

Pearl Jam. *Ten*. 1991.

The Rolling Stones to Nirvana's Beatles, a good place to begin exploring a rich catalog. "Alive," "Jeremy."

Liz Phair. *Exile in Guyville*. 1993.

Using the Rolling Stones' *Exile On Main St.* as a blueprint, Phair's sexually bold songs were a kind of musical precursor to *Sex in the City*.

Pickett, Wilson. *A Man and a Half*. 1992.

Two discs of gritty uptown soul covering the lengthy career of "the wicked Pickett."

Presley, Elvis. *The Sun Sessions*, 1987. ("That's All Right, Mama," "Mystery Train.")

———. *Elvis: 30 #1 Hits*, 2002.

The Sun Sessions is where Elvis, and the story of rock, begin in 1954. The 30 #1 Hits show his expanse as a rock star and show business phenomenon.

Pretenders, The. *The Pretenders*. 1979.

CD reissue (2006) of flawless debut album, one of new wave's peak moments, led by singer/guitarist Chrissie Hynde.

Prince. *Purple Rain*. 1984.

Rock/funk sexuality unleashed.

Public Enemy. *It Takes a Nation of Millions to Hold Us Back*. 1988.

———. *Fear of a Black Planet*. 1990.

With the stentorian delivery of Chuck D., leavened by the outrageous humor of Flava Flav (now an unlikely reality-show celeb) and a sound that lived up to the name of producer Hank Shocklee's "Bomb Squad," this black consciousness group from Long Island helped hip-hop's hardest message reach the suburbs.

Rascals. *Time Peace/The Rascals Greatest Hits.* 1968.

The New York area's best "blue eyed soul" band. ("Groovin'," "Good Lovin.'")

Ramones. *The Ramones.* 1976.

———. *Rocket to Russia.* 1977.

Punk rock: No more, no less, the best.

Redding, Otis. *The Otis Redding Story.* 1987.

Three-CD set that captures the essence of the '60s great male soul singer.

R.E.M. *And I Feel Fine: Best of the I.R.S. Years 1982-1987.* 2006.

Long-awaited, well-chosen anthology of the groundbreaking early work of the alternative rock pioneers.

Replacements, The. *Pleased To Meet Me.* 1987.

Pinnacle of a band with a great songwriter (Paul Westerberg) and a destructive penchant for alcohol that often got in the way of great work.

Robinson, Smokey, and the Miracles. *Anthology.* 1986.

Motown's great tunesmith, producer and distinctive voice, consistent over the years.

Rolling Stones. *Big Hits, High Tide, Green Grass.* 1966. The early hits.

———. *Aftermath.* 1966.

———. *Beggar's Banquet.* 1968.

———. *Let It Bleed.* 1968.

———. *Sticky Fingers.* 1971.

———. *Exile on Main St.* 1972.

———. *Some Girls.* 1978.

———. *Tattoo You.* 1981.

Rock'n'roll, as we know it today, defined.

Run-D.M.C. *Raising Hell.* 1986.

A lean, tough, eloquent rap album took on added significance by the collaboration with Aerosmith on their "Walk This Way," which helped take hip-hop mainstream.

Ryder, Mitch, and the Detroit Wheels. *Rev up: The Best of...*" 1989.

Seminal American hard-rock band.

Santana. *Santana.* 1968.

Debut album by guitarist Carlos Santana's popular and long-lasting (in name only) Latin rock outfit; still his best.

Sex Pistols. *Never Mind the Bollocks, Here's the Sex Pistols.* 1977.

The orneriest band in rock actually walked the walk as well as they ranted the rant on their one studio recording.

Simon, Paul. *Graceland*. 1987.

> The vibrant South African/rock fusion, guided by a master storyteller and composer.

Smith, Patti. *Horses*.1975.

> The 2005 special edition includes remastering of the original, essential spiritual/punk masterpiece and a London concert performance on a second disc, thirty years later.

The Smiths. *Singles*. 1995.

> The best of introverted British rock in the 1980s, loveable where it could have been laughable.

Specials, The. *The Specials*. 1980.

> Multiracial U.K. group mixing rock with ska, a Jamaican rhythm similar to reggae propelled by horns.

Springsteen, Bruce. *Greetings from Asbury Park, N.J.* 1973.

———. *Born to Run*.1975.

———. *Born in the U.S.A.* 1984.

———. *The Rising*. 2002.

> The first three document the rise and triumph of the most original and passionate rocker of his time. *The Rising* showcases the introspective Springsteen, in tales of spiritual rebirth in the wake of the September 11, 2001, terrorist attacks.

Steely Dan. *Can't Buy A Thrill*. 1972.

———. *Countdown To Ecstasy*. 1973.

———. *Pretzel Logic*. 1974.

> History seems to be defining the duo of Walter Becker and Donald Fagen by their later, smoother jazz-rock albums like *Aja*. But their first three made history, as oblique, cynical lyricism subverted the top 40. ("My Old School," "Rikki Don't Lose That Number.")

Talking Heads. *Talking Heads: Talking Heads 77*. 1977.

———. *More Songs about Buildings and Food*. 1978.

———. *Remain in Light*. 1980.

———. *Speaking in Tongues*. 1983.

> Art school eccentrics discovered a new musical language on their early records, then showed surprising elastisity as they evolved from trio to quartet to tribe.

Temptations, The. *Anthology*. 1995.

> Perhaps the most versatile of the Motown singing groups, from "My Girl" to "Cloud Nine."

Van Halen. *Van Halen*.1978.

———. *1984 MCMLXXXIV*. 1984.

> Southern California's most virtuosic party rockers-turned stadium rockers, featuring the inventive guitar work of Eddie Van Halen and the enjoyable brash boasting of singer David Lee Roth. Roth was replaced by Sammy Hagar in 1985, and the band remained popular but fell from musical excellence.

Velvet Underground. *The Velvet Underground and Nico*. 1967.

———. *Loaded*. 1970.

Andy Warhol wasn't a great record producer, but the 1967 album is a still compelling introduction to the New York band that fused art and the gutter. The 1970 swan song really shows Lou Reed's emergence as one of rock's most brilliant songwriters. ("Sweet Jane," "Rock & Roll.")

Williams, Lucinda. *Car Wheels on a Gravel Road*.

Literate, passionate, desperate, and real country/folk-rock that embodies the subgenre known as "Americana."

Brian Wilson. *Smile*. 2004

Finished and released thirty-seven years after this planned follow-up to "Pet Sounds" was abandoned — worth the wait.

X. *X: Los Angeles*. 1980.

———. *Wild Gift*. 1981.

Los Angeles punk, shot through with a heavy dose of roadhouse roots rock.

Warren Zevon. *Excitable Boy*. 1978. ("Werewolves of London.")

A Southern California songwriter (this album was produced by Jackson Browne), Zevon out-rocked and out-wrote most of the L.A. crew with his sardonic worldview.

The Who. *Sing My Generation*. 1965.

———. *A Quick One*. 1966.

———. *The Who Sell Out*. 1967.

———. *Tommy*. 1969.

———. *Who's Next*. 1971

———. *Meaty, Beaty, Big and Bouncy*. 1971

———. *Odds & Sods*. 1974

Among rock bands, only the Beatles and Rolling Stones have been as influential as the Who. Eschewing the psychedelic musical indulgences of their contemporaries, the Who were as ear-bleedingly loud as they were intellectually curious, thanks to the songwriting talents of guitarist Pete Townshend. They have done good work since, but their stature is based on their body of work during the first 10 years.

ZZ Top. *Eliminator*. 1983. ("Legs," "Sharp Dressed Man.")

Rocking Texas boogie finally explodes nationwide after years of regional fame.

Notes

Chapter One: Introduction: What Is Rock 'n' Roll?

1. http://www.empire.k12.ca.us/capistrano/Mike/capmusic/glossary
2. Definition from *America and Its Peoples Online,* a companion Web site/study guide for the book of that title Addison Wesley Longman division of Pearson Education. occawlonline.pearsoned. com/bookbind/pubbooks/martin_awl/medialib/glossary/gloss_27.html
3. http://www.dictionary.net/rock+and+roll
4. Jonathan Yardley, "J. D. Salinger's Holden Caulfield, Aging Gracelessly," *Washington Post,* Oct. 9, 2004, http://www.washingtonpost.com/wp-dyn/articles/A43680-2004Oct18.html
5. Jon Pareles, preface to *The Rolling Stone Encyclopedia of Rock & Roll.* Page vii. Rolling Stone Press, N.Y. 1983.

Chapter Two: 1950s: Rock Begins

Author Note

Unless otherwise indicated, quotes and information from Jerry Leiber and Mike Stoller are from lengthy individual interviews with the author. I interviewed Leiber Nov. 13, 1992, in an apartment in Manhattan. Stoller was interviewed shortly after, at breakfast in a Manhattan hotel restaurant. The two had traveled to New York to publicize the Leiber & Stoller ASCAP Music Scholarship, which also coincided with the 40th anniversary of their partnership. I was the pop music critic for Newsday/New York Newsday, and it was in that role that the interviews were arranged. For reasons long forgotten, a story never ran, but I kept the tapes and transcripts for a time when they might be useful in the future. The future is now, and I'm grateful to Randall Poe of Leiber-Stoller Music for setting up the interviews.

Similarly, I was the staff pop music writer for *Newsday,* based in Melville, N.Y. (1975-2005) and the now defunct *New York Newsday* (1985-1995). Over that span I interviewed many of the artists, writers and music industry figures referred to in this book. Some quotes and information is from unpublished interview transcripts. Where noted, quotes and information is gleaned from articles written by me for *Newsday/New York Newsday* that were published during this period.

1. http://music.aol.com/artist/johnny-otis/484/biography. From the All-Music Guide, written by Bill Dahl.

2. John Grooms, "Keeping Down the King," essay on Pop Politics.com, http://www.poppolitics.com/articles/2002-08-14-elvis.shtml

3. "The Pentecostal family of denominations form one branch within conservative Christianity. A major defining feature of Pentecostalism is their belief in Glossolalia, or the ability to speak 'in tongues.' Another is the unusual freedom and spontaneity exhibited during their religious services. Otherwise, their beliefs, practices and social policies are similar to those of other conservative Christians. (As defined by Web site of Ontario Consultants on Religious Tolerance http://www.religioustolerance.org/chr_pent.htm.)

4. Grooms.

5. As quoted by Grooms from an early interview with Kays Gary of the *Charlotte, N.C. Observer.*

6. *Brown v. Board of Education*, Case #347 U.S. 483 (1954), Supreme Court of the United States.

7. James M. Salem, "'Sh-Boom' and the Bomb: A Postwar Call and Response," http://www.columbia.edu/cu/cjas/print/shboom.pdf

8. Peter Potter hosted a U.S. TV show called *Juke Box Jury* and was known as an anti-rock crusader. He is quoted in the *New Musical Express*, London, May 1955, in "The Rock 'n' Roll Years," a history taken from the pages of *NME* (New York, Crescent Books, p. 14.)

9. All Georgia Gibbs quotes from an interview with the author at the Four Seasons Hotel, ca. 1998. The interview was for the unpublished book, *50 Years of Mercury Records.*

10. Pat Boone bio on Senior Site Web site http://seniorsite.com/patunderlinespaceboone/index.asp

11. Ambassador Luce's intercession to prevent the showing of *Blackboard Jungle* at the Venice Film Festival was defended by *Time* magazine, which her husband, Henry Luce, was founder and publisher. *Time's* article in the issue dated Sept. 12, 19955 is online at http://www.time.com/time/magazine/article/0,9171,893106,00.html?iid=chix-sphere

12. Marshall Crenshaw *Hollywood Rock: A Guide to Rock 'n' Roll in the Movies* (New York: Harper Perennial, 1993), 155.

13. Michael Bertrand, *Race, Rock, and Elvis*, University of Illinois Press, 2000.

14. Pete Thamel, "Breaking the Sugar Bowl Color Line," *The New York Times*, Sunday, January 1, 2006.

15. Ibid.

16. Little Richard interviewed by the author for *Newsday* story, June 18, 1992. most likely in advance of a performance at the Westbury Music Fair, Long Island, N.Y.

17. Dan Bern, in his song "Tiger Woods."

18. Greil Marcus, *Mystery Train,* New York: E.P. Dutton, 1975.

19. Charles White, *The Life and Times of Little Richard, the Quasar of Rock* (New York: Harmony Books), 1984.

20. Ibid.

21. Ibid.

22. Little Richard, interview with the author, 1984, in a New York coffee shop every passerby stopped to shake hands with Little Richard. Mr. Penniman was doing interviews on behalf of the White biography.

23. Elvis Costello quoted in interview with the author, 1993, New York City. Costello spoke about Little Richard in the context of rock as "art" as opposed to the self-conscious art of the project he was promoting, his collaboration with the Brodsky Quartet, *The Juliet Letters*.

24. Steve Garber, "Sputnik and the Dawn of the Space Age," NASA History Web Curator, updated 2/21/2003. Contact histinfo@hq.nasa.gov

25. Mark Carreau, *Houston Chronicle,* October 4, 1987.

26. Allen Ginsberg, *"Howl" and Other Poems* (San Francisco: City Lights Books, 1956).

27. Ginsberg biography by Michael Schumacher, http://www.poetryconnection. net/poets

28. Ferlinghetti quoted by Iorio, Paul Iorio, "A Howl That Still Echoes: Ginsberg Poem Recalled," *San Francisco Chronicle*, October 28, 2000.

29. psychcentral.com/psypsych/Howl#The_1957_Obscenity_Trial. Psychcentral.com is an online mental-health Web site published by Dr. John Grohol. 30. http://www.enotalone.com/books/0140042598.html. Anonymous, from a book discussion social networking site eNotAlone. com. Accessed Sept. 1, 2005. No longer available.

31. http://www.litkicks.com/BeatPages/page.jsp?what=AllenGinsberg

32. From various sources, including Holly profile on Famous Texans Web site.

33. "From Eros to Agape; Reconsidering the Chain Gang's Song in McCuller's *Ballad of the Sad Café*" by Margaret Whitt, *Studies in Short Fiction*, winter, 1996.

Chapter Three: The 1960s

1. In a review of director Ron Mann's 1993 documentary about the dance and its moment, *Twist*.

2. Fred Bronson, *Billboard Book of No. 1 Hits* (New York: Billboard Books, 1985).

3. United States State Department International Information program http://usinfo.state.gov/usa/infousa/facts/democrac/66.htm

4. Widely published, various sources.

5. *Watchtower* magazine, February 15, 1969, as cited by http://www.escape-fromwatchtower.com/chubby.html

6. http://www.history-of-rock.com/brill_building.htm

7. From Spectropop, the Web site about Phil Spector, Girl Groups, Brill Building et al http://www.spectropop.com

8. Virgil Moorhead, "*The Producer as Composer*," MIT Press.

9. Ibid.

10. Interview with Wilson by Andy Battaglia, published August 30, 2005, in *The Onion,* online at http://avclub.com/content/node/40133/4.

11. Wilson writes about the Beach Boys rivalry with the Four Seasons in the liner notes to CD reissue of Capitol Records "two-fer," with *Shutdown, Vol. 2.* (1990).

12. The Four Seasons under the pseudonym the Wonder Who singing a Bob Dylan song was a hit, too, peaking at No. 12 on the Billboard Hot 100 in late 1965

13. From a Civil Rights timeline online at http://www.infoplease.com/spot/civilrightstimeline1.html

14. *Billboard Book of No. 1 Records*, p. 143.

15. 15. Cliff Richard's single "Living Doll" reached No. 30 in the United States in 1959, his only stateside hit until the Top 10 "Devil Woman" for Elton John's Rocket label in 1976.

16. As recounted by John T. Marck, "I Am the Beatles" web site, (http://www.iamthebeatles.com).

17. Bruce Spizer, author of *The Beatles Are Coming*, interviewed on NPR, Feb. 6, 2004.

18. Paar audio recording from same NPR show as above.

19. Lewis' news reports about the Beatles are reprinted in "Forever Fab: Original News Coverage from the *New York Times*," available for purchase at nytimes.com.

20. Ibid.

21. Skiffle described in Steve Turner's *Too Late to Stop Now*, a biography of Van Morrison, who like the Beatles was inspired to play music by the U.K.'s d.i.y. folk-blues phenomenon.

22. From *Imagine*, a film about John Lennon.

23. Among many reports and interpretations of the infamous urinating against the garage wall incident is one from About.com http://classi-crock.about.com/od/rollingstonesfaq/f/stonesarrest.htm. Accessed in 2005; link is now to About.com classic rock page.

24. This video interview of the Stones at their most youthfully sullen was found on the *Canadian Broadcasting Corp.* web site. http://archives.cbc.ca/IDC-1-68-832-4888/arts_entertainment/rolling_stones

25. Bosley Crowther review is in the "Forever Fab" *New York Times* package and originally appeared in the newspaper August 12, 1964.

26. Even a panel of "experts" was unable to articulate the Fabness of the Beatles in the article in the "Forever Fab" package. "Beatles Stump Music Experts Looking for Key to Beatlemania," by Richard D. Freed, *The New York Times*, Aug. 13, 1965.

27. Ibid.

28. Irma Thomas in a telephone interview with the author for *Newsday*, in advance of a performance in New York. Circa 1992.

29. Lyrics from "Eve of Destruction" by P.F. Sloan and Steve Barri, Trousdale Music/Dunhill Records.

30. Dylan got to play "Song for Woody" for the dying Guthrie in February 1961.

31. Lyric from "Song to Woody" by Bob Dylan, copyright 1962, renewed 1990, MCA Music publishing.

32. Bob Dylan writing in his autobiographical *Chronicles, Vol. 1*, New York: Simon & Schuster, 2004, p. 61.

33. Davis, Clive, with James Willwerth, *Clive: Inside the Record Business*, William Morrow & Co., New York, 1975 p 49.

34. Interview with Ed Bradley on CBS-TV's "60 Minutes." Transcript at http://www.cbsnews.com/stories/2004/12/02/60minutes/main658799. shtml

35. Ian Macdonald, "Revolution in the Head," p. 99.

36. Greil Marcus, *Like A Rolling Stone: Bob Dylan at the Crossroads*. p. 26.

37. Ibid., p. 149.

38. Keith Richards has told this story many times, to many people, including the author. In this case, credit goes to *The Early Stones: Legendary Photographs of a Band in the Making. 1963-1973*. New York: Hyperion, 1992. page 5. Text by Terry Southern, photographs by Michael Cooper, with foreward and commentary by Richards.

39. Ibid.

40. MacDonald, p. 130.

41. "My Generation," by Pete Townshend, copyright TRO-Devon Music, Inc. (BMI). All rights reserved.

42. Interview segment from the CD *The Who Live: BBC Sessions*.

43. Michael Lydon speaks to McCartney in his book *Flashbacks: Eyewitness Accounts of the Rock Revolution*, (New York: Routledge, 2003). P. 12.

44. Marcus discusses *Rubber Soul* in the appendix he called "Treasure Island" from *Stranded*, a collection of essays by assorted rock critics on "desert island" albums which he edited. (Alfred A. Knopf, 1979) p 257.

45. Brian Wilson looks back in the liner notes to the 1990 Capitol Records reissue of *Pet Sounds*.

46. From the Answers.com Web site, which also channels wikipedia.

47. Ibid.

48. Ibid.

49. Berry Gordy's days at the Ford Motor Co.at its effect on the Motown sound from Virgil Moorefield, *The Producer as Composer*, p. 22-23.

50. Rob Bowman, essay booklet included with the none-CD boxed set, *The Complete Stax/Volt Singles: 1959-1968*. (Atlantic Records, 1991.)

51. Ibid.

52. Sources for Study of the 1965 Watts Riots, University of Southern California. http://www.usc.edu/isd/archives/la/watts.html

53. James Graham, "Why Non-Violence Waned," at Historyorb Web site, http://www.historyorb.com/america/civilrights2.html

54. From *Africana: The Encyclopedia of the African and African American Experience*, edited by Henry Louis Gates and Kwame Anthony Appiah. P. 1202. quote accessed through Amazon.com search engine

55. Wilmer quoted by Cliff White in liner notes to the 1973 Polydor Records album, *The James Brown Story: Doin' It To Death, 1970-1973.*

56. Frank Kogan, "Death Rock 2000," http://www.villagevoice.com/music/0002,kogan,11707,22.html. Village Voice, Jan. 12-18, 2000 issue.

57. Paul Grushkin, The Art of Rock (New York: Abbeville, 1987).

58. Swiss scientist Albert Hofmann's notes about his experiences discovering LSD in 1943 are widely available. For further research see http://www.hofmann.org.

59. The famous quote (which also gave the rock band the Doors their name), is from William Blake's "The Marriage of Heaven and Hell": "If the doors of perception were cleansed every thing would appear to man as it is: infinite."

60. Tom Robbins.

61. Adler's comments printed in the booklet accompanying the Rhino Records four-CD set, *The Monterey International Pop Festival.*

62. Joplin's words, from Janis, a 1974 documentary directed by Howard Alk.

63. The Hollywood film *The Rose*, starring Bette Midler, was based loosely on Joplin's life.

64. Langdon Winner, The Rolling Stone Illustrated History of Rock 'n' Roll, p, 183

65. Sheila Whiteley, The Space Between Notes: Rock and the Counter-Culture (New York: Routledge, 1992. p. 61.

66. *The New York Times*, Sunday, June 18, 1967.

67. These quotes from Mick Jagger are from David Dalton's The Rolling Stones: The First Twenty-Five Years, pp. 105-106.

68. Ibid.

69. Jeff Turrentine's article, "Holy Pop Relic," in online magazine *Slate.* Slate.com/id/2095025.

70. -71. Clinton Heylin, *Bob Dylan: Beneath the Shades* (Summit Books, 1991) 174-175.

72. Heylin quoting something Dylan said in 1978.

73. Heylin found this in an interview Dylan once did with *TV Guide.*

74. Some of the information about Clapton during this period came from the book by Jan Reid, *Layla and Other Assorted Love Songs*. Rodale Books, 2006.

75. Carmichael black power quote from Infoplease.com

76. Rutgers University study of the Newark riots, at http://www.67riots.rutgers.edu/n_index.htm.

77. Rutgers study on Detroit riots, http://www.67riots.rutgers.edu/d_index.htm

78. Information for 1968 came partly from transcripts of interviews made available to the author for the book *VH-1's Behind the Music 1968*, written by the author and published by Pocket Books, 2000.

79. Broadway "Hair" review by John Wingate on New York's WOR-TV, April 30, 1968

80. Buckley in his *National Review*, May 21, 1968.

81. Beatles' recording engineer Emerick with Massey in Here,There and Everywhere, p. 140.

82. "The Influence of the Beatles on Charles Manson," from a paper at the University of Missouri Kansas City law school, online at http://www.law.umkc.edu/faculty/projects/ftrials/mansonbeatles.html. Much of the analysis credits prosecutor Bugliosi's book, *Helter Skelter*, as mentioned in text.

83. Mitchell appeared the morning after Woodstock on *The Dick Cavett Show*, as did members of Crosby, Stills and Nash and Jefferson Airplane. Now available on the Shout Factory DVD set The Dick Cavett Show: Rock Icons.

84. Mitchell interviewed by the BBC, http://www.bbc.co.uk/music/profiles/mitchelljoni.shtml

85. *The Village Voice*, "The 10th Largest City in the United States," by Steve Lerner, August 21, 1969.

86. Victor Bockris, *Transformer, the Lou Reed Story*, (New York: Simon & Schuster, 1995) pp 90-91 of uncorrected proofs attained by the author in 1995.

87. Kurt Loder, liner notes to Polygram Records reissue of *White Light, White Heat*, 1984/1985.

88. Glam and glitter definitions from the Merriam-Webster online dictionary. http://www.m-w.com/dictionary.

89. The author attended this Detroit concert and was bewildered at the time how a band that could be so good on most nights in New York could be so messed up elsewhere.

90. Lenny Kaye, liner notes to 1994 compilation, *New York Dolls Rock 'N Roll*, released by Mercury Chronicles.

91. Ira A. Robbins, ed. Trouser Press Record Guide, 4th edition, published by Collier.

92. -93. Pareles and Romanowski, Rolling Stone Encyclopedia of Rock & Roll, 561-562.

Chapter Four: The 1970s

1. "Doors' singer Jim Morrison found dead." BBC.co.uk On This Day, July 3, 1970. http://news.bbc.co.uk/onthisday/hi/dates/stories/july/3/newsid_3776000/3776701.stm

2. Tom Robbins, *Wild Ducks Flying Backwards: The Short Writings of Tom Robbins* (Bantam, 2005), 94. This quote, from the section called "The Sixties," is taken from remarks delivered at the Northwest Bookfest in 1996.

3. Phillip Caputo, *13 Seconds* book about Kent State. From Chapter 1, as published on NPR Web site, http://www.npr.org/templates/story/story.php?storyId=4630596

4. Fred Bronson, *Billboard Book of Number One Hits*, 296.

5. Barney Hoykins, e-mail interview with the author, October 2005.

6. Barney Hoskyns, *Hotel California*, (Hoboken, NJ: John Wiley, 2006).

7. Ibid.

8. Ibid.

9. Ibid.

10. Ibid.

11. From liner notes to compilation *Citizen Steely Dan*, http://www.steely-dan.com/citizenliners.html

12. From interview CD from the boxed set *Led Zeppelin Remasters* (Atlantic Records, 1990).

13. Robert Plant at a lunch interview with the author, SoHo, New York City, 1993.

14. From Atlantic Remasters interview disc, 1990.

15. Amazon.com, by Billy Altman.

16. Author of *Stairway to Hell: The 500 Best Heavy Metal Albums in the Universe.*

17. *Running with the Devil: Power, Gender, and Madness in Heavy Metal Music* (Wesleyan University Press, 1993). Excerpt from *Esquire* magazine, Nov. 1991.

18. Liner notes by Don Kaye, *Black Sabbath: Greatest Hits 1970–1978* (Warner Bros. Records/Rhino Records, 2006).

19. Christgau's *Record Guide, Rock Albums of the '70s* (New Haven: Ticknor & Fields, 1981) 156. He gave the album a grade of "C."

20. Robert Plant interview with author, same as note No. 13, above.

21. Robert Moog obituary, August 22, 2005. BBC online archive.   http://news.bbc.co.uk/1/hi/entertainment/music/4696651.stm

22. Interview with the author for "The Hardest Rock Among the Stones," *Newsday*, January 25, 1983.

23. Jagger interview with the author, ca. 1976.

24. Joey Ramone interview with the author in Ramone's East Village, N.Y. apartment for *Newsday* 10th anniversary of Ramones story. 1986.

25. From Kaye's liner notes.

26. Interview with the author for release of her *Rockbird* solo album, New York City.

27. As reported at the time by *NME* in the collection, *The Rock'n'Roll Years*, New York, Crescent Books, no year given.

28. *Rolling Stone* review by Paul Gambaccini, March 14, 1974. Now archived at http://www.rollingstone.com/artists/genesis/albums/album/143564/review/5943327/selling_england_by_the_pound

29. David Sinclair, *Q* magazine, reprinted at http://www.superseventies.com/pinkfloyd2.html

30. Geddy Lee, interview with Wayne Robins, *Newsday,* March 13, 1992.

31. Hal Crowther, *Gather at the River: Notes from the Post-millennial South* (Baton Rouge: Louisiana State University Press, 2005), 4–5. Advance uncorrected proof.

32. These are the author's recollections of working at (Columbia/Epic) CBS Records as writer/ editor of the promotional magazine *Playback,* from October 1972 to July 1974, when the magazine was discontinued as part of a corporate restructuring.

33. The author is the interviewer and writer of the Columbia Records press bio and *Playback* magazine article about Springsteen.

34. (c) Bruce Springsteen (ASCAP).

35. Jon Landau, *The Real Paper,* May 22, 1974, from an online archive.

36. Springsteen, quoted in *The Making of "Born to Run"* DVD.

37. Marsh, 28.

38. http://www.imdb.com/title/tt0081242/usercomments

Chapter Five: The 1980s

1. Speech at Cow Palace, San Francisco, 1966, http://sfgate.com/.

2. Dave Marsh, *Glory Days: Bruce Springsteen in the 1980s* (New York: Pantheon, 1987), 28.

3. Ibid.

4. Ted Leopold, "President Loomed over the 80s, an Era at Odds with Itself," CNN.com, June 16, 2004.

5. Ibid.

6. Mellencamp interviewed by Wayne Robins, "John of the Thickened Skin," *Newsday,* November 24, 1987.

7. Ibid.

8. In an interview with *Billboard* magazine for Petty & Heartbreakers thirtieth-anniversary special, March 18, 2006.

9. (c) 1991, Gone Gator Music/EMI April Music Inc. (ASCAP).

10. Chicago Museum of Broadcast Communications, http://www.museum.tv/archives/etv/M/htmlM/musictelevis/musictelevis.htm.

11. Interview with the author for "Rock Video: The Audience Wants to See the Music It Hears," *Newsday,* January 30, 1983.

12. Author interview with Ken Walz video director, for *Newsday* story, January 30, 1983.

13. Interview with Len Epand, VP Press and Promotion, Polygram Records, for *Newsday* story, January 30, 1983.

14. http://www.defleppard.com

15. Interview with the author for *Newsday* "Rock Video" story, January 30, 1983.

16. The Nashville Network was about to launch. It later became CMT, the dominant country-music video channel.

17. Interview by the author with Walter Yetnkikoff for *Newsday* story, ca. 1984.

18. Source: Fred Bronson, Billboard Book of Number One Hits" (New York: Billboard Books, 1985), 600.

19. Madonna performance attended by the author. Details provided by Songfacts.com. http://www.songfacts.com/detail.lasso?id=1116

20. Ibid.

21. Wayne Heisler Jr., for UCLA academic journal *Echo* (online at http://www.echo.ucla.edu/volume6-issue1/heisler/heisler1.html). Heisler is referencing *Gender Politics and MTV* by Lisa A. Lewis (Temple University Press, 1990).

22. http://www.temple.edu/tempress/titles/687_reg.html

23. All Chuck Klosterman, *Fargo Rock City: A Heavy Metal Odyssey in Rural North Dakota* (New York: Scribner, 2001).

24. Klosterman, 18.

25. *Fargo Rock City,* 28

26. Midge Ure quote about LiveAid from Web site Pure 80s Pop, http://www.pure80spop.co.uk/liveaidquotes.htm

27. Danny Goldberg, *Dispatches from the Culture Wars: How the Left Lost Teen Spirit* (New York: Miramax Books, 2003, 115.

28. Ibid.

29. All REM quotes from an interview with the author for "Rock's Brainy Bunch," *Newsday,* December 18, 1988, at REM offices in Athens, Georgia.

30. Interview with the author. Quotes from Wayne Robins, "The Police's World View," *Newsday,* January 22, 1982.

31. From discography on U2.com, quote from *Q* magazine, December 1998.

32. Jon Pareles, *Rolling Stone* review of *October,* October 31, 1981.

33. Pareles, *Rolling Stone.*

34. Bono, June 1983, on the U2.com Web site.

35. Cathy Booth, *Time* magazine, June 23, 1986.

36. Interview with the author during dinner break at a U2 rehearsal in Hershey, Pennsylvania, for Wayne Robins, "Practicing their scales: At rehearsal with U2 as they inflate the Zoo TV tour to Stadium size," *Newsday,* August 12, 1992.

37. From commentary on u2.com Web site.

38. *Billboard* magazine estimates.

39. Interview with the author for *Newsday* article.

40. Thanks to Internet Movie Database (imdb.com) as reference.

41. Simon Reynolds, *Rip It Up and Start Again: Postpunk 1978–1984* (New York: Penguin, 2006), 105–7.

42. Ibid., 111.
43. "Goth Defined," at Web site Music Moz, a volunteer-edited compendium of musical information. http://musicmoz. org/Styles/Rock/Alternative/Goth/.
44. Johnny Marr interview, *Uncut,* January 2006, page 48.

Chapter Six: The 1990s Begin

1. Ian Youngs, "Looking back at the birth of Britpop," *BBC News,* August 15, 2005. BBC.com, http://newsvote.bbc.co.uk/mpapps/pagetools/ print/news.bbc.co.uk/2/hi/entertainment/4144458.stm
2. "The 100 Greatest Albums, 1985–Now," *Spin,* July 2005, p. 80. Oasis was No. 28.
3. Thurston Moore interview by the author for *Newsday* appeared Aug. 5, 1990.
4. From Sonicyouth.com Web site. No author attributed, but may be Lee Ranaldo, writing in the third person.
5. "Sonic Youth/25 Years of Cool," summer 2006, p. 59.
6. Ibid., p. 63.
7. One of the best fan sites on the Internet is the Neil Young source, Thrashers Wheat. http://www.thrasherswheat.org/jammin/sonic_youth.htm
8. April 6, 2004, http://news.bbc.co.uk/1/hi/entertainment/ music/3568909.stm.
9. Paraphrased from the movie *1991: The Year Punk Broke.*
10. Interview with the author for Wayne Robins, "Muscular Metal With a Brain, Soundgarden Grows..." *Newsday,* May 8, 1992.
11. http://news.bbc.co.uk/1/hi/entertainment/music/1943410.stm
12. http://news.bbc.co.uk/1/hi/entertainment/music/1943410.stm
13. http://news.bbc.co.uk/1/hi/entertainment/music/1943410.stm
14. Ibid.
15. Notes to *Incesticide* (David Geffen Company, 1992).
16. From wire services, as reported by St. Petersburg Times, April 4, 2003.
17. *Homerpalooza,* written by Brent Forrester, directed by Wesley Archer. Production Code: 3F21 Original Airdate in U.S.: May 19, 1996.
18. Interview with Robert Christgau, popmatters.com, October 17, 2006.
19. Spin, July 2005, p. 68.
20. Betty Clarke, "Pixies Sell Out: The Reunion Tour 2004" (DVD review), *The Guardian* (U.K.), September 30, 2005. http://arts.guardian.co.uk/ filmandmusic/story/0,,1581076,00.html
21. Metacritic, quoting All-Music Guide. http://www.metacritic. com/music/artists/greenday/americanidiot/
22. http://en.wikipedia.org/wiki/Dani_California. Quoting June 2006 issue of *UK Classic Rock* magazine.
23. Bakari Kitwana, *Why White Kids Love Hip-Hop* (New York: Basic Books, 2005), 25.

24. Wilco CD review from http://www.popmatters.com, 2002.
25. http://www.wired.com/news/technology/0,1282,58340,00.html

Index